Facing The Fold

Essays on scenario planning

James A. Ogilvy

Published by:
Triarchy Press
Station Offices
Axminster
Devon. EX13 5PF
United Kingdom

+44 (0)1297 631456
info@triarchypress.com
www.triarchypress.com

James Ogilvy 2011

Cover design and image by Heather Fallows -
www.whitespacegallery.org.uk

ISBN: 978-1-908009-22-7

Contents

Contents

For Peter Schwartz

Acknowledgements

Since my very first introduction to scenario planning over thirty years ago, so many people have taught me so much. I learned most, I am sure, from Peter Schwartz, to whom this book is dedicated. Peter has been a marvelous guide, an inspiring teacher, and a very good friend. I cannot thank him enough.

But of course there have been others, not least the great guru of scenario planning, Pierre Wack. On one of my first visits to California in 1978, I had the great pleasure of taking a 3-day road trip to northern California in the company of Peter and Pierre. We stayed at a little cabin owned by Paul Hawken, with whom Peter and I were then writing the book, *Seven Tomorrows*. I'm grateful to Paul for more than his cabin.

The team I joined that Peter led at SRI contained other inspiring colleagues and teachers: Arnold Mitchell, Willis Harman, Don Michael, Ian Wilson, Vic Walling, O. W. Markley, Dick Carlson, Marie Spengler, and Tom Mandel. When, in 1981, Peter left SRI to head up the scenario team at Shell, I then had an opportunity to work with some of their best: Ted Newland, Arie de Geus, Napier Collyns, and Ged Davis.

After Peter left Shell and I left SRI, Peter and I reached out to Napier Collyns, Stewart Brand, and Lawrence Wilkinson to create Global Business Network. What a marvelous set of partners with whom to build a company, and a network! Over the years since 1987, when the five of us sorted through our rolodexes to come up with candidates for the network, it has been such a pleasure to work with and become friends with many of our network members. I call out particularly and alphabetically: John Perry Barlow, Mary Catherine Bateson, Raimondo Boggia, Albert Bressand, Denise Caruso, Esther Dyson, Bo Ekman, Brian Eno, Betty Sue Flowers, Francis Fukuyama, Robert Fuller, John Gage, Joel Garreau, Charles Hampden-Turner, David Harris, Danny Hillis, Robert Horn, Chuck House, Adam Kahane, John Kao, Kevin Kelly, Art Kleiner, Jaron Lanier, Amory Lovins, John McIntire, Michael Maccoby, Irving Mintzer, Ian Mitroff, Michael Murphy, Maureen O'Hara, John Petersen, Nancy Ramsey, Howard Rheingold, Chris Riley, Richard Rodriguez, Paul Saffo, Orville Schell, Lee Schipper, Michael Schrage, Rusty Schweickart, David Sibbet, Alex Singer, Gary Snyder, Bruce Sterling, Hirotaka Takeuchi, Hardin Tibbs, Sherry Turkle, Kees van der Heijden, Heinrich Vogel, Steven Weber, and Michael Zielenziger.

Then there's the amazing group of colleagues at GBN—such a pleasure to work with. Erik Smith co-authored one of the papers in this volume. I've enjoyed project work and co-teaching scenario planning with Eamonn Kelly, Gerald Harris,

Susan Stickley, Chris Ertel, Jonathan Star, Matt Ranen, Stewart Henshall, and Don Derosby. I want also to thank Lynn Carruthers, our talented graphic recorder, for the help she's provided on a number of projects. Thanks also to Katherine Fulton, Jenny Collins and Nancy Murphy, all long-standing and strong pillars of GBN. For sheer fun, though, a tip'o'the hat to The Green Team: Eric Best and Ben Fuller. Remember Rio?

In recent years I've had the good fortune to get help on scenario planning projects from several independent consultants, Bram Briggance and Tom Portante. I also want to thank my colleague at Presidio Graduate School, Teddy Zmrhal, with whom I've enjoyed co-teaching for the past several years.

It's been my good fortune to have good clients who became good friends: Peter Arum of the National Education Association, Jack Huber at BellSouth, Tom Davis at Motorola, Carl Lehmann at American Express, Jeremy Seligman at Ford, Matt Bencke at Microsoft, and my colleagues in Japan, Noboru Konno and Jiro Nonaka.

Thanks to those with whom I've had the opportunity to tilt at the windmills of health care reform: Will Straub, David Reynolds, Ann Monroe, Laura Likely, Elliott Fisher, Don Berwick, John Sterman, Peter Senge, and the rest of the team at Re>Think Health.

I want to thank Tim Mack, editor of *Futures Research Quarterly* and Riel Miller of the OECD for soliciting several of the following papers. And special thanks to Alfonso Montouri for encouraging me to pull these several papers together to create this volume.

Finally I want to thank the good people at Triarchy Press. My editor, Alison Melvin, has been a pleasure to work with. Thanks also to Matthew Fairtlough, who is the son of the late Gerard Fairtlough, founder of Triarchy Press, former GBN Network Member, good friend, and much missed.

Facing the Fold

From the Eclipse of Utopia To the Restoration of Hope

Been down so long it looks like up? Does the prospect of a double dip cloud your future? Just as many of us could see nothing but boundless growth during the go-go years of the late 1990s, so have many fallen into a pessimistic slough following the last two years of economic woe.

Some might like to reach for good old cyclicality as a rationale for recovery. "What goes up must come down; what goes down must come back up." But I'd like to reach even higher: toward those good old utopias.

We lost something when we hurled utopian thinking into the dustbin of history. And hurled it we have. Too bad! For utopian thinking had its moments. To the extent that various utopias, from Plato's *Republic* to the works of Thomas More and Samuel Butler, allowed their readers to lift their sights from a miserable present toward a better future, to just that extent those utopian fantasies provided hope.

When Ernst Bloch wrote the three volumes of *The Principle of Hope* he was opening an imaginative space for fantasy, clearing the ground for imagination and creativity. His *Spirit of Utopia* wasn't handing down a recipe for perfecting humanity in perfect dwellings in perfect cities. When Barack Obama advertises the *Audacity of Hope,* he isn't pressing for the perfection of human nature.

I want to hold on to the aspirational aspect of utopian thinking by liberating it from the debilitating stain of perfection. I want to lay out a case for optimism by linking it, paradoxically, to pessimism. Precisely by paying attention to prospects for disaster—nuclear, biological, or environmental—I want to clear a space for a *scenaric stance* that holds best case and worst case scenarios in mind at once. This is the way to face our unpredictable future responsibly. This is the way to grapple with uncertainty and act nonetheless. This is the way to deal with the passage of time.

Once upon a time, there was no truly historical time. The ancient Greeks thought that time moved in a circle, cyclically like the seasons. Call that first chapter the time of *tradition.* Then came chapter two, the time of *modernity* with its optimistic faith in progress. Then came chapter three, postmodernism with its pessimistic doubts regarding progress, and the eclipse of utopia. But this won't do. As it is written in Proverbs 29:18, "Where there is no vision, the people perish." Likewise with hope. We need it. So now it's time to move beyond postmodern time. Now it is time to take up a new stance toward time, a scenaric stance. Let's call it *facing the fold.*

Let's trace the history of utopian thinking through its first three chapters, the better to get a running jump across the chasm of pessimism that postmodernism bequeaths us. And let's *not* burden ourselves with a title so bulky as post-postmodernism. Let's look ahead, and not backwards toward a postmodernism that has run out of steam.

The Cyclical Time of Tradition: Chapter One

Once upon a time there was the time of no history, the time of the ancients and the traditionalists in which the basic features of reality were understood to be unchanging and eternal. More than two millennia before Darwin, Aristotle taught that the number of species is fixed, not evolving. For Plato, time was "the moving image of eternity." Plato's ideal Forms don't change. They are eternal.

The forms of everyday life that were consistent with this image of time followed tradition, as they still do in some, but ever fewer, parts of the world. Daughters expected to live lives very much like their mothers', and sons expected to live lives very much like their fathers'. Identities and aspirations were reflected in last names like Jackson, Johnson and Clarkson.

In Homeric times, if you wanted to know how to build a boat, you recited to yourself those lines in the *Iliad* that described the building of boats. You didn't try to design a *better* boat. The very idea of progress—as J.B. Bury's classic, *The Idea of Progress* makes clear—is a modern invention.

Yes, there was a distinction between better and worse, and there were aspirations to gain access to the idea of the good. But those aspirations were not so much toward the good yet to come. The love of wisdom, philosophy, was an upward quest toward eternal ideals, toward a kind of great blueprint in the sky that did not change.

Modernity and Progress: Chapter Two

Following the first "chapter" when time was regarded as "the moving image of eternity," there came the time of progressive history and evolution. Starting with hints in the works of Vico and Herder in the 18th Century, then gaining full articulation in the works of Hegel and Darwin in the 19th Century, this sense of progressive history came to define the very spine of modernity. From getting better every day in every way to "Better living through chemistry," the march of progress through advances in science gained a firm foothold in western culture.

During this second chapter in the history of utopia, the quest for the good no longer followed an upward path toward eternal truths. Instead a more worldly path lay in the direction of a better future. Invention flourished. People imagined better boats, and built them. In some of the earlier utopian literature you find an amazing amount of space devoted to things like drainage systems. Sewers were a big deal, as they needed to be given important discoveries relating public health to good hygiene. But just as people were inventing better boats, so they invented better utopias. The very nature of utopian thinking underwent its own form of progress.

When you look at the history of 19th century utopian thinking you see an evolution away from the physical particulars of cities and towards the more ethereal aspects of the human spirit. Utopian thinking passed through a period during which it shifted from architecture, city planning and drainage systems to psychology, philosophy and states of mind. So by the time Karl Mannheim published his *Ideology and Utopia* a century later, he wasn't concerned with city planning; he was almost entirely focused on the chains that bind men's and women's minds.

Let's call it *the sublimation of utopia.* In modern and postmodern times, the terms 'utopia' and 'utopian' have come to connote more about minds than about bricks and mortar.

Postmodernism and the eclipse of utopia: Chapter Three

The march of progress hit some speed-bumps in the 20th Century: senseless deaths in the muddy trenches of the First World War, the Holocaust, the advent of nuclear weaponry and humanity's ability to extinguish itself by our own technologically enhanced hands. Just as Hegel served as the philosopher who could render (more or less) articulate the world-historical actions of Napoleon and thereby induce a broad self-consciousness regarding *the promise of modernity,* so the French heirs of Hegel—Alexandre Kojève, Claude Lévi-Strauss, Michel Foucault and Jacques Derrida—rendered (more or less) articulate these world-historical atrocities and thereby induced a broad awareness of *the threats of postmodernity.*

Socio-political utopianism in the 20th century foundered on the shoals of failed revolutions. The improvers of mankind had their chances and each, one after the other, ended in their own respective versions of a reign of terror. The American experiment succeeded, but it was based not on some grand vision of a social order that would improve men's and women's souls. Quite the opposite: The founding fathers held a more modest belief that people left to their own devices would get on with their lives best if you let them make up their own minds about how to make a living, how to raise their children, how to relate to their immediate neighbors, and how to pray. In short, the American experiment was based on the idea of individual liberty. Unlike the French and Russian and Chinese revolutions, each of which turned oppressive, the American Revolution was fought by people who were not motivated by some shining ideal of a life very different after the revolution. They just wanted to get the Brits off their backs and get on with living life *their way.*

The founding fathers were very clear about wanting to leave everyday life pretty much as it was. Let the butcher continue to be a butcher and the baker continue to bake. Let people raise their children as they wished and worship as they pleased. There was no moving rhetoric about a new and better humanity, no strategic vision with goals and objectives very different from life in rural New England or urban Philadelphia. Just a commitment to the preservation of life, liberty, and the pursuit of happiness.

For all the faith in individual progress that the American Dream allowed, there was very little by way of collective dreaming—for the race, for the species, for the human condition. But here lies the rub: After the sublimation of utopia, the eclipse of utopia means flushing out the baby of a better humanity with the bathwater of utopian living arrangements.

God knows the bathwater of utopian politics was dirty. "The final solution," seventy years of Soviet communism, China's cultural revolution—these were political, ideological fantasies that caused so much misery that most rational survivors of the 20th century look back and say, *never again.* We now know better than to listen to tyrants and philosopher kings with their bright ideas about classless society or a thousand year *Reich.*

But what about the baby? Can't we hope for a better humanity? Haven't we seen progress with respect to slavery, racism and sexism? Granted, a partial eclipse of utopia might save us from crackpot schemes for the radical reform of human nature by Jacobin revolutionaries. But the total eclipse of utopia shuts out the light of hope for even a fairly gradual, evolutionary rather than revolutionary, improvement.

Call this third chapter the time of decline, the time of postmodernism. Every day in every way we're getting worse and worse, from the pollution of the atmosphere to the extinction of species to the threat of terrorism, and on, and on… Reading Sir Martin Rees and his doomsday scenarios in Our Final Hour, we're told that the human species has no better than a 50/50 chance of surviving the 21st century. The so-called march of progress is by no means assured by advances in science. To the contrary, advances in science may be our undoing. Even though less apocalyptic than nuclear holocaust, we are made increasingly aware of several more insidious threats: CFCs and the ozone hole, CO_2 and global warming, the relentless withering of biodiversity…

This declinism is tired, tiresome, and tiring. Such pessimism gets us nowhere, but it enjoys a certain intellectual respectability just because it is so dark. The lowered brow of the pessimist cannot possibly be taken as naïve. The pessimist has looked into the abyss and, by god, he has not flinched. Such courage! No sugar coatings for him! No rose-tinted glasses!

The fourth turning: A Tragi-comic Future

Now time itself is taking yet another turn, a fourth turning. We no longer live in the ahistorical or circular time of the ancients. Nor do we enjoy the optimistic, progressive time of the moderns. Nor, hopefully, the apocalyptic closing time of the postmodernists. Now we live in the tragi-comic time of multiple scenarios. Now the future is flying at us both faster and less predictably than ever. Surprise is its middle name. There's promise to be sure, but risk just as surely. Our research labs are churning out discoveries at an unprecedented rate. The life expectancy of individuals is increasing even as the life-expectancy of the species, according to Sir Martin Rees, is not.

Neither as optimistic as modernity nor as pessimistic as postmodernity, the sensibility appropriate to multiple scenarios is one of wide-eyed wonder at the nearness of Heaven and Hell both to us and to one another. The sheer proximity of best case and worst case scenarios induces a psychic shear factor between updrafts of hope and downdrafts of despair. Should one laugh or cry? Or master a capacity for both each and every day?

This fourth form of lived time—the first being the traditional, the second progressive, the third apocalyptic, and the fourth tragic-comic—has about it a certain intensity. The stakes are high. Choices matter. It would be half-right but also half-wrong to call it *existential*: Half-right in its sense of urgency and its call upon our sense of freedom and responsibility; but half-wrong to the extent that the existentialists themselves were poised between the moderns and the postmoderns, and for the most part pretty gloomy about it—all that gazing into the abyss, Being-towards-Death, and European brooding.

The fourth attitude toward time peeks through the gloom with Woody Allen's wry humor asking, "What Ate Zarathustra?" Or Ken Kesey's question, "Whose movie is this?" Or Hunter Thompson's gonzo sensibility; or R. Crumb's Zippy the Pinhead asking, "Are we having fun yet?"

Martin Amis caught a piece of this new attitude toward time and history in his *London Fields*. "We're all coterminous," he writes, referring to the imminent ecological apocalypse that looms over his novel. "We used to live and die without any sense of the planet getting older, of mother earth getting older, living and dying. We used to live outside history. But now we're all coterminous. We're inside history now all right, on its leading edge, with the wind ripping past our ears. Hard to love, when you're bracing yourself for impact."

Facing the Fold

Adopting a perspective toward our tragi-comic future is like facing a landscape described by mathematician Rene Thom. Thom developed a series of mathematical models he called "catastrophes," not because they are bad or disastrous, but rather because he wanted to call attention to their mapping of *discontinuities*. Thom's "catastrophe theory" has a lot in common with what Nobel Prize winner, Ilya Prigogine, called "bifurcation theory." Both were interested in the ways that nature *branches* from time to time, and often in ways that a calculus of continuity has difficulty describing.

Thom theorized seven different types of catastrophe. But the force and power of his analysis can be grasped from a brief description of just one of his seven different types, the "fold" catastrophe, and its application to modeling the "bifurcation" between fight and flight in the behavior of dogs.

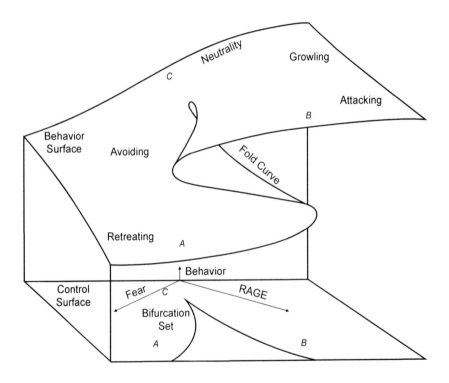

Figure 1: Model of Aggresssion in Dogs

Imagine the behavior of a dog as following a path on the upper behavior surface beginning at point C and moving, on a path of increasing rage, toward B. While launching an attack, the dog sees a man with a large stick. The dog's behavior then moves from point B towards point A. The beauty of this mathematical model, the beauty of Thom's catastrophe theory, lies in the way it models, on a continuous surface, the discontinuity in behavior we observe when we see the dog rapidly shift from fight to flight. Moving on the behavior surface from B to A, the dog will enter the intrinsically unstable area between the dark lines on the lower "control surface" labeled "bifurcation set." Mapping this shift on the behavior surface, it's easy to see where the path from B to A will "fall" discontinuously from the "attacking" plane of the behavior surface to the "retreating" plane.[1]

Life in the fourth era of time is like standing at point C looking at a utopian point B even as one sees the distinct possibility of disaster at point A. Our hopes hide fears of disaster. Our fears eclipse the optimism of our hopes. The oscillation we experience as we toggle back and forth between brave optimism and knowing pessimism is enough to induce a sense of irony. Or at least a call for alternative scenarios if we need help in handling multiple futures at once.

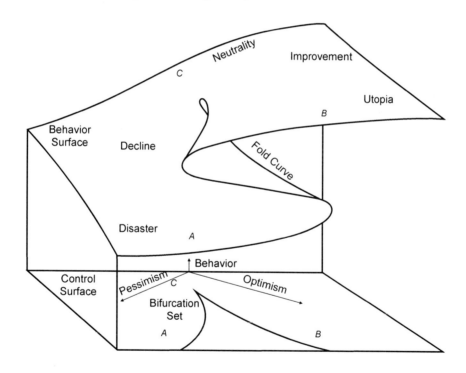

Figure 2: The High Road and the Low Road

---

1   This application of Thom's catastrophe theory is drawn from E.C. Zeeman's article, "Catastrophe Theory," *Scientific American,* April 1976.

Scenario Planning and the Scenaric Stance

When considering this line sequence—from the eclipse of utopia to the restoration of hope by way of the four eras of time—one can do a lot worse than pick up the tools and mental habits of scenario planning. Facing both positive and negative scenarios at once can be disconcerting in its complexity. Both optimism and pessimism share the advantage of simplicity. We need some tools to handle the uncertainty and complexity of an unpredictable future.

The optimism of the entrepreneur goes a long way toward providing clarity of vision. Nothing can stand in the way of a single-minded focus on success. But the optimist is easily dismissed as a simpleton, or as naïve, or as insensitive to the ills of the world and therefore shallow. Pessimism is somehow deeper, more knowing. But pessimism, too, is too simple. The pessimist gets dismissed as a Cassandra.

However correct the optimist or the pessimist proves to be over time, his or her optimism or pessimism by itself was too simple when it was originally held. Still, one can hold on to the content of both the optimistic and pessimistic visions, while avoiding the sting of their critics' comments, by holding on to both the optimistic scenarios and the pessimistic scenarios at the same time in the capacious space of scenario thinking.

Despite its disconcerting complexity, there are advantages to facing the fold. First, one acquires an acute sense of freedom. Quite the opposite of living in a fatalistic rut, facing the fold heightens the sharpness of Kierkegaard's existential imperative: Either/Or. You cannot do both. It is yours to choose. But at least you have a choice. As opposed to this sense of freedom, both optimism and pessimism appear as two sides of the same coin of fatalism.

Second, when one faces the fold, one is relieved of the intellectual dishonesty involved in holding either branch of the fold as a single-point forecast. One is relieved of the naiveté of callow optimism, even as one is spared the amoral defeatism of the all-knowing cynic. You've looked at the dark side; you've seen the very real risk; and still you're able to move ahead constructively.

Third, having made a choice in full knowledge of the alternatives and the risks involved, you'll act deliberately and resolutely, but not rashly or foolishly. You choose the high road, but you are always well aware of the off-ramps to the low road. You don't kid yourself that success is guaranteed, as the Bush administration did so foolishly as they marched into Iraq. And scenarios had been written and shared. A team in the State Department under the direction of Thomas Warrick had created scenarios that detailed the prospect of an insurgency and the dangers of looting in the aftermath of a purely military "victory". But Warrick was known as a prickly if brilliant fellow; second, he was at State, traditionally at odds with both the Bush White House and the hawks under Rumsfeld at the Pentagon; and third, those scenarios had been composed during Clinton's tenure in the White House. So Bush, Cheney, Wolfowitz and Rumsfeld were not about to let such lily-livered cautionary tales inhibit their march to Baghdad. They simply swept those negative scenarios into the waste basket.

The attitudinal aspect of facing the fold—retaining the ability to act resolutely even as you maintain an acute awareness of how things could go wrong—is hard to over-value. It's the kind of thing that venture capitalists look for in lending money to people who have already suffered one or two failures. Hardly gun shy, they are nonetheless all too aware of the ways things could go wrong.

The tragi-comic aspect of the scenaric stance can turn abstract thoughts toward profound emotions. We're talking about hopes and fears here. It could get scary. Or it could get hokey if only hopes and no fears are in play. Laughter and tears—are these not direct physiological responses to rapid reinterpretations? Do we not see a mixing of mind and body in laughter and tears? The fairly violent physiology of laughter and its absolute irrepressibility under certain circumstances—good jokes—is a function of a nervous system that has somewhere within it a toggle-switch twitching between the planes on a fold. Your nervous system is interpreting and re-interpreting the same signals first in one way and then another, back and forth, very rapidly. Likewise alternative scenarios give you a kind of stereoscopic vision that lends emotional depth to your experience.

In adopting the scenaric stance, facing the fold in which multiple futures are held simultaneously and constantly in view, one achieves a kind of emotional and intellectual maturity that is not available to either the simple optimist or the simple pessimist. Yes, things could turn out badly. But, no, that is not in itself reason for inaction. Yes, things could turn out very well, but, no, that is not in itself reason for foolish bravado. By holding in mind several different futures at once, one is able to proceed deliberately yet flexibly; resolutely yet cautiously.

The scenaric stance isn't simply a tool to solve a problem, like a calculator, or double-entry bookkeeping. It's a frame of mind. Its framework can be measured in three dimensions: First, you find a relentless curiosity, a willingness to learn, an eagerness to experience new frames of reference. The scenaric stance is curious not just for facts, though certainly you want plenty of those. A good scenario shows you a way of looking at the world that you hadn't seen before. Call this the outside-in dimension. Second, you gain a capacity for commitment, a resoluteness toward action, and once having acted, a clarity of follow-through. Call this the inside-out dimension. Third, you achieve a capacity to balance these in-coming and out-going flows.

The scenaric stance is subtle. If you emphasize the either/or of decisiveness too much, you risk cutting off the branches that constitute alternative scenarios once you have opted for one course of action. Likewise if you emphasize too much the both/and of maintaining multiple scenarios before the mind's eye, you risk the indecisiveness of a wavering Hamlet: To be, or not to be, etc. So you have to climb up a level of abstraction and maintain both the both/and and the either/or even as you learn how to assume either the capaciousness of the both/and or the decisiveness of the either/or.

But, hey, welcome to the ways of the world and the inevitability of surprise. Further, the times demand it. He or she who sees no opportunities is blind. He or she who senses no threats is foolish. But he or she who sees both threats and opportunities shining forth in rich and vivid scenarios may just be able to make the choices and implement the plans that will take us to the high road and beyond.

Overview of the following chapters

Assuming that you want to adopt the scenaric stance, the following essays can help. Section I is about the nuts and bolts. Chapter 1, co-authored with Peter Schwartz, gives a succinct summary of the steps involved in the practice of developing scenarios. Chapters 2 and 3 offer further reflections on method.

Section II situates scenario planning in the larger context of the human sciences. The long essays in Chapters 4 and 5 originally appeared in *Futures Research Quarterly*. Parts of those essays formed the spine of my book, *Creating Better Futures*, but they appear here in their more fully developed original form. Chapter 6, "What Business Strategists Can Learn from Sartre," originally appeared as a cover story in *Strategy+Business*. Much less available to English and American readers, Chapter 7 appeared as a chapter in a book published in Singapore.

Section III offers a set of case studies—actual scenarios created for real projects. So often we are unable to provide examples of the genre because so many of our projects are proprietary. But here you can find examples of the kinds of narratives developed and used in the course of several projects.

Section I:

Scenario Planning: What, Why, and How

1. Plotting Your Scenarios

by James Ogilvy and Peter Schwartz

From Learning from the Future, editors Liam Fahey and Robert M Randall; Copyright 1996, Liam Fahey and Robert M Randall . Reprinted with permission of John Wiley & Sons, Inc.

Scenarios are narratives of alternative environments in which today's decisions may be played out. They are not predictions. Nor are they strategies. Instead they are more like hypotheses of different futures specifically designed to highlight the risks and opportunities involved in specific strategic issues.

To be an effective planning tool, scenarios should be written in the form of absorbing, convincing stories that describe a broad range of alternative futures relevant to an organization's success. Thoughtfully constructed, believable plots help managers to become deeply involved in the scenarios and perhaps gain new understanding of how their organization can manage change as a result of this experience. The more involved managers get with scenarios, the more likely it becomes that they will recognize their important but less obvious implications. Moreover, scenarios with engrossing plots can be swiftly communicated throughout the organization and will be more easily remembered by decision makers at all levels of management.

This essay offers an approach to developing alternative scenarios with engrossing plots. Part One describes two different methods for answering a fundamental challenge: how to whittle the virtually infinite number of possible futures that could be described down to a finitely manageable three or four plots that will shed the most light on a specific organization's future. Part Two then addresses the inverse question: Once you have determined the skeletal premises of just three or four scenarios, how do you put flesh on the skeletons? How do you elaborate the basic logics of skeletal scenarios into compelling stories? If Part One is about whittling an infinite number of possible futures down to a finite number of skeletal scenarios, Part Two is then about beefing up those skeletal outlines to discover the insights managers need. Part Three then adds ten tips based on our twenty years of experience developing and using scenarios.

1 Finding a Few Plots

Scenario plots—we call them scenario "logics"—can be effectively developed during a two-day workshop, which preferably takes place at an off-site location. When all goes well, a highly interactive, imaginative team process can occur at these sessions.

1.1 Composition of the team.

Participants should be carefully recruited to include people with a thorough knowledge of the company and the critical issue or issues to be addressed. The team should be as diverse as possible, encompassing a wide range of levels of management, perspectives, and roles. Ideally, the people on the scenario team will be acquainted with a variety of intellectual disciplines—social sciences, economics, political sciences, and history. If possible, a variety of cultures—Asian, European, American, Latin, and African—should be represented. The full spectrum of organizational functions should also be present—finance, R&D, manufacturing, marketing, and different executive levels. Internal diversity is critical to the success of the project. The key to failure, on the other hand, is the exclusion of people who are unorthodox, challenging thinkers from inside and outside the organization. For example, at a workshop attended only by the intimidating head of a business unit and his malleable direct reports, little divergent thinking occurred. In contrast, at an AT&T scenario workshop for executives, it was an outsider who jump-started a provocative discussion about the future of telecommunications.

1.2 Decision Focus.

On the first morning the team begins the first hour by identifying the key decision facing the organization, discussing it, and developing a clear understanding of useful questions to ask about the decision. For scenarios to be truly useful learning and planning tools, they must teach lessons that are highly relevant to the company's decision makers. In other words, they must speak to decisions or direct concerns. When the team is developing such decision-focused scenarios it is critically important to ask the right focal question: Should we build a new coal-fired power plant? Should we acquire, (or divest or expand) certain businesses (or product lines)? Should we build a manufacturing facility in China? Should we invest a substantial fraction of the firm's resources in a new interactive media venture?

When determining the focal issue, it is important to first remember the time frame of the scenario. This is important because it will affect the range of movement and creativity within the scenario. In medical scenarios, for example, biotechnology, genetic medicine and non-invasive surgical procedures should be mature technologies someday, but they may not be relevant to a scenario with a five-year time horizon.

Sometimes the question the team starts with changes after the initial discussion. For example, in a project to examine the future of white collar work the team began by thinking that the principal question was, "How should white collar work be physically and organizationally designed?" But the pressing issue facing the company that emerged from a discussion with senior management was: Employees no longer saw white collar work as prestigious, so white collar skills were not highly valued. Many of the employment pressures and discontents previously experienced in the blue collar work force were now souring the white collar work force. The project shifted from an effort to look simply at the future of the design and organization of white collar work to one that asked, "Will it be possible to reestablish white collar prestige and its work ethic?"

Not all scenarios must be decision-focused, however; scenarios are also a powerful tool for exploring more general areas of risk and opportunity (e.g. What is the Office of the Future? What are the possible futures of China or Brazil ?). Such scenaric thinking can serve as the basis for subsequently developing more focused scenarios and for initiating a broader strategic conversation throughout the organization[2]. But even exploratory scenarios must be built around a relevant question or the scenarios will lack focus and internal consistency.

1.3   Brainstorming a list of key factors.

After the decision focus of the session is selected, the brainstorming begins. From our experience, it pays to have this part of the workshop led by a person experienced at facilitating brain storming sessions—usually someone from outside the business. One of the keys to successful creativity group sessions is making it a practice that no idea is immediately disparaged or discarded—a difficult rule to enforce when brainstorming sessions are headed by the CEO or led by the chief of a business unit for his or her direct reports.

When working with clients we use flip charts to write down all the ideas—often as many as 60 to 100 key factors. Then we tape the loose sheets to the walls so participants can refer to them as the meeting progresses. Much of the brainstorming revolves around identifying driving forces and key trends. These are the most significant elements in the external environment. They drive the plots and determine their outcome.

Be sure to consider five general categories of forces and trends: social, technological, economic, environmental, and political forces that interact with one another to create complex and interesting plots. Suppose Wal-Mart was looking at the future of shopping malls. A social force for consideration is crime: A rising crime rate would keep shoppers off the streets. Would malls that invested heavily

---

2   (Cf. Kees van der Heijden, *Scenarios: The Art of Strategic Conversation*, John Wiley, 1996)

in security be perceived as a safer place to shop, and thus gain market share? A technological force that will affect malls is electronic shopping. An economic force that drives mall revenues is rising or falling disposable income. An environmental problem—increasing pollution—could lead to higher gas taxes and reduced personal automobile travel, and the result could be fewer mall trips for recreational shopping. A political force—the desire to revive local real estate assets—could lead to an effort to find creative new uses for shopping mall property.

Examples of other key factors include: the impact of more women in the workplace; ever cheaper, yet more powerful computers; the emergence of China as an economic power; or the changing values of teenagers. Each organization must compile its own set of driving forces and key trends. However, the list for firms in the same industry will probably be quite similar.

1.4   Distinguish the pre-determined elements from uncertainties.

Once the team has openly brainstormed a number of issues it is time to look at the various forces and related environmental factors more closely:

- *Which key forces seem inevitable or pre-determined?* These are trends already in the pipeline that are unlikely to vary significantly in any of the scenarios. These might be slow-changing phenomena (the development of new oil resources), constrained situations (the U. S. social security crisis), trends already in the pipeline (the aging of the baby boomers), or seemingly inevitable collisions (branch banking vs. banking through personal computers). These forces should be reflected, implicitly or explicitly, in each of the scenario plots. For example, any set of scenarios about banking would include the globalization and integration of financial services although these might assume a different shape or priority depending on political, regulatory, and technological factors.

- *Which forces are most likely to define or significantly change the nature or direction of the scenarios?* This assessment should be measured by two criteria—how uncertain are you of its outcome and how important is it to your organization? Organizations should develop the plots of their different scenarios by assuming their organization has to contend with the logical consequences of new forces that are both very important and very uncertain. One large professional services company, for example, found that the degree to which young college graduates—prospective employees—would be driven by individual versus collective values was a major uncertainty that would significantly affect their ability to attract top-notch recruits and therefore the growth of their business.

1.5   Identify a few scenario logics.

A fair amount of discussion may be required before a group reaches consensus on which forces to choose as the main drivers of a small set of scenarios. Here we distinguish two fundamentally different approaches to determining the basic premises of a small number of scenarios. One method is inductive, the other deductive. The inductive method is less structured and relies largely on the patience of a group to talk and talk until consensus is reached. The other, deductive approach uses simple techniques of prioritization to construct a 2 x 2 scenario matrix based on the two most critical uncertainties. We'll describe the inductive method first, then the deductive.

1.5.1   The Inductive Approach

The inductive approach has two variants. In one, the group brainstorms different events that are typical of different scenarios. In the other, the group agrees on what we call "the official future" and then looks for ways that the future could deviate from that path.

1.5.1.1 Emblematic Events

The first variant of the inductive approach starts with individual events or plot elements, and spins larger stories around these seeds. For a hospital that specializes in cardiology, for example, it might be worth asking: What if researchers at Johns Hopkins announce the successful testing of a roto-rooter pill that can clear plaque from arteries? If 45 percent of the hospital's revenues come from bypass surgery, such an event would have a serious impact. What might lead up to such an event? What would be a plausible chain of consequences leading from such an event? By starting from such episodic plot elements, a group can build a scenario that will have future consequences that call for some strategic decisions in the present. Building up scenarios from singular plot elements like this can yield powerful results in many cases, but the process is unsystematic and calls for a degree of creativity and imagination that may be lacking in some organizational cultures.

1.5.1.2 The Official Future.

A slightly more systematic variant of the inductive approach begins with what we call "the official future:" the future that the decision makers really believe, either explicitly or implicitly, will occur. This is usually a plausible and relatively nonthreatening scenario, featuring no surprising changes to the current environment and continued stable growth. But the "Official Future" can also reflect the manager's fears that the company is in serious trouble. We did one scenario exercise for a utility whose Official Future, contained in the chief economist's annual forecast, anticipated a serious and deep economic recession with very negative implications for the company's revenues and work force. Clearly, this had a number of serious implications ranging from possible layoffs and downsizing to the reduction or elimination of innovative service and R&D programs. We started by describing radically different and more optimistic futures and then explored the forces and factors which would enable such futures to unfold, driven by such things as the evolution of new industries, higher levels of investment and venture capital, and increasing entrepreneurial activity within the firm. In fact, these more optimistic scenarios did gradually unfold.

Identifying the important components of the Official Future—its key drivers—is best done through interviews with the scenario team and other key decision makers prior to any scenario exercise. We often conduct ten to fifteen interviews, including the CEO and top managers in different parts of the company who are likely to have different perspectives and concerns, as well as individuals who are known to be provocative or unorthodox thinkers. In addition to asking such questions as "What will the future look like in 10 years," and "Where will you be sitting ten years from now (and how did you get there)?" we also use the interviews to elicit concerns and fears ("What keeps you up at night?"). Annual reports, forecasts, and the analysis done on individual business units are also valuable information sources.

The failure of the Clintons' attempt at health care reform was a prime example of the dangers of planning for the Official Future without seriously examining other scenarios. Insurance industry and consumer pressure, government budget crises, the spread of managed care, technological change, and myriad other factors all pointed to a restructuring of the industry. Yet, many, many health care organizations simply assumed that this restructuring would be defined by the Clintons' proposals and scrambled to position themselves accordingly. When these reforms were derailed, many industry players were surprised, disadvantaged, and unprepared to act— sometimes missing the chance to seize new and unexpected opportunities.

After identifying the key driving forces and uncertainties, it is usually easy to discover which ones are most important and influential in the Official Future. Next, have your team brainstorm variations to the Official Future that are based on possible but quite surprising changes to the key driving forces of the official story. Consensus on a few scenarios that vary from the Official Future can sometimes be reached more quickly by grouping similar driving forces together. Explore how different interactions between key forces might produce unexpected outcomes and build several new scenario logics along several different dimensions. In the health care industry, for example, different scenarios might have suggested an increasingly fragmented health care system differentiated entirely by ability to pay or a privatized system with minimal government regulation or influence.

Whether beginning from emblematic events, or from the Official Future, gaining consensus on which driving forces are truly of paramount importance can be a difficult group exercise. In cultures that lack the patience for the open-ended debate that these two inductive approaches require, beginning with the deductive approach can sometimes be more effective.

1.5.2 The Deductive Approach: Building a Scenario Matrix

Here the idea is to prioritize the long list of key factors and driving trends in order to find the two most critical uncertainties. One method—quick and dirty, but effective nonetheless—is to award every participant 25 poker chips (real or virtual) and ask each person to assign all 25 chips to different forces on the list—more chips for forces of greater importance and uncertainty and fewer or no chips for forces of lesser importance and uncertainty. This exercise in prioritization accelerates the discussion by narrowing the group's focus to the two most critical forces, which then become the axes of a 2 x 2 scenario matrix.

If you prioritize driving forces using the poker chips or a similar narrowing exercise, your team will pick forces that are highly unpredictable as well as highly relevant to the focal issue. For example in a 1984 Detroit study of the design criteria for an entry level automobile, the price of fuel—high or low—was an important and uncertain key factor; and so were the values of consumers. Would the consumers of the 90's prefer more conventional family sedans, or would they want a less conventional assortment of light trucks, hybrid vehicles, and small cars of the sort that Japan and Germany were manufacturing? When the study was conducted in the early 1980s, very few could imagine that Americans might want smaller, more versatile, and individualized cars. Hybrid vehicles like car/vans were also off the radar screen. What most imagined was a continuation of the status quo: Detroit producing similar cars using similar production techniques. Using the scenario matrix helped the participants to see that this was only one of several possible scenarios.

The axes of the matrix were very different for another project on the future of higher education in Hawaii. In this case the price of fuel was not important; much more important and uncertain was the health of the overall economy of the Pacific Basin, and the attitude of Hawaiians toward the usefulness of a college education: would graduates enter the workforce of Hawaii's traditional tourist economy, or would they look outward to the rest of the world's economy and want to join other industries? By mixing the attitude of the Hawaiians and the health of the economy, four very different scenarios were created.

Yet another example of a scenario matrix comes from a set of scenarios done on the future of the California wine industry. In this case the regulatory environment around the wine industry and the image of wine to consumers were deemed as most important and uncertain. If studies came out saying that a glass of wine every day was good for your health and there was a protectionist regulatory environment for wine, you could get the Safe at Home scenario where there would be a high demand for wine and higher prices for wine. Conversely, if zealous citizens launched a new prohibitionism, and there was an open trade environment, the World Awash scenario might result, characterized by weak demand for wine, excess supply, and falling prices.

There are a number of advantages to building scenarios on a matrix. First, using a matrix assures that scenarios are qualitatively different in a logical, deductive, non-random way. Second, it assures that the top scoring key factors will be drivers in all scenarios. Arriving at the axes is an interactive group process, driven as much by challenge as consensus. Once these axes of your model have been identified, the team can then determine which different scenario plots can be constructed and their details filled in.

In a project on the future of public education for the National Education Association, for example, we looked at the interaction between different community orientations and the provision of education. The axes were defined as hierarchical vs. participatory approaches to education and exclusive vs. inclusive community and educational orientations (see diagram below). This matrix created four quadrants which described very different worlds:

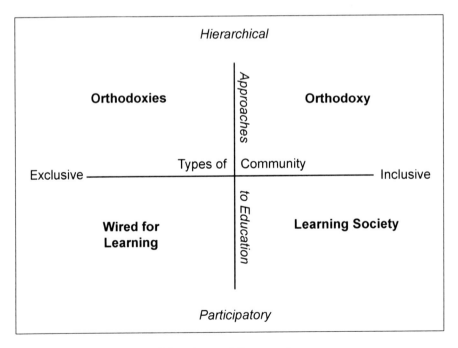

Education and Community

One dimension of uncertainty surrounding the nature of community was labeled hierarchical versus participatory, capturing a contrast between various kinds of more traditional down-from-the-top, authoritarian approaches to education on the one hand (teacher lectures from front of class, curriculum defined and controlled) and an up-from-the-bottom, grassroots, more radical approach on the other emphasizing site-based control, more Socratic methods, etc. Another dimension describing different types of community contrasts inclusive (ideologies that claim to include everyone under the umbrella of their guiding principles) versus exclusive (that separate people—the pure from the impure, believers from the heathen, tenured teachers from part-time paraprofessionals). These two axes—hierarchical (traditional) vs. participatory (radical), and inclusive vs. exclusive—yielded a scenario matrix on which the scenario team built four scenarios.

Orthodoxy (Hierarchical and Inclusive) assumes a turn toward traditional values, and the effort to enlist educators to impose those values on any and all who might resist them; in Orthodoxies (Hierarchical and Exclusive) values are also central to education, but different values guide different schools: Wired for Learning (Participatory and Exclusive) assumes the rapid evolution and transformative power of new applications of information technologies, in education over the next decade. The result would be a highly interactive, participatory education for some, but might exclude those who don't have access to the new technology. In The Learning Society (Participatory and Inclusive) technology also propogates rapidly, but serves the ideals of inclusive community by facilitating a more participatory process, serving the interests of play as well as work, and enhancing community.

In most cases it is best to keep the number of dimensions in the matrix down to two for the sake of simplicity and ease of representation. Sometimes, the scenario logics can be represented by a spectrum (along one axis) or you may need a model with three axes. But beware of three dimensions: they may satisfy a scenario team that is unwilling to squeeze a complex industry down to just two main dimensions of uncertainty, but when it comes to communicating the scenario logics to others who were not part of the process, three-dimensional, eight-celled frameworks sometimes prove to be too complex to communicate easily. Sometimes a group has trouble getting from a long list of key factors down to just two most critical uncertainties. They would like instead to settle on three. Those who fear that they've done violence to the complexity by over-simplifying 60-100 factors down to just two driving forces can be reminded that they will get back all the complexity they want during the next step of the exercise: fleshing out the scenarios into rich, compelling plots.

2   Fleshing Out the Scenario Plots

There is no one right way to develop scenarios. Different cultures, different facilitation styles, and different industries may dictate the use of one or another of the approaches for settling on the basic logics of a few skeletal scenarios. The inductive approach works well in the oil industry, for example, because everyone knows going into the exercise that at the end of the day there is just one key variable that has to drive the difference between just two or three scenarios: the price of a barrel of oil at some future date. In other industries where there are several, or many key variables, the deductive approach will help to cut through the complexity.

While the interplay between the most important and uncertain forces ultimately shapes the logics that distinguish and drive these scenarios, the other significant environmental factors identified in the brainstorming phase must be used to compose the scenario plots. Here's where you get back all of the complexity squeezed out in whittling an infinite number of possible futures down to just four skeletal scenarios. If a 2 x 2 scenario matrix has been developed, the group can then go back to the lists of other key factors and ask, "What is the value of this variable in each of the four quadrants of the matrix?"

These other factors might include such things as political changes or events resulting in more or less restrictive trade policies or regulations; incremental or volatile economic growth; indicators of increasing environmental degradation; the emergence of new technologies, products, or processes; changing consumer values, etc. Each of the key factors and trends should be given some attention in at least one scenario; some (including the predetermined elements) are likely to show up in all the plots. Demographic trends, for example, are likely to be implicit in all the plots, although they may have different implications depending upon how political, social, and economic factors affect such things as education, employment, immigration, and consumption. Sometimes it is obvious how an uncertainty should be accounted for in a given scenario, sometimes not. For example, if two scenarios differ over protectionist or non-protectionist trade policies, then it probably makes sense to put a higher inflation rate in the protectionist scenario and a lower inflation rate in the non-protectionist scenario. It is just such connections and mutual implications that scenario logics are designed to reveal.

2.1   Tools for Fleshing Out Scenarios

Several tools are available for fleshing out scenarios. Systems thinking is good for deepening the scenario plots; narrative development is good for lengthening the basic premises into stories with beginnings, middles and ends; characters are good for populating the scenarios with significant or illustrative individuals who personalize the plots.

2.1.1 Systems and Patterns: Systems thinking

Studying the way the parts of a system interact can be a powerful tool for exploring the logic of a scenario. Most of the time, we focus on individual events—for example, a sudden and dramatic decline in stock prices, a war between two countries, the election of a new president or prime minister. But sometimes we need to explore the underlying patterns of events so we can understand the appropriate plot for a scenario. In helping the scenario team to think more systematically, we often use the metaphor of the iceberg, adapted from Peter Senge. At the tip lie events—those things we see happening around us like the election of certain politicians or the rise and fall of companies. Next we can delve deeper to examine the patterns that these events suggest—increasing priority given to social issues, for example, or industry consolidation. Beneath these patterns lie important structural changes which can define meaningful scenario logics, for example, fundamental shifts in values or industry restructuring.

An application within the current information technology arena might focus on the behavior of an industry leader at the "Events" level: the creation of the MSNBC network, Microsoft's announcement that it is helping Apple to build Internet software, and the integration of Internet-style tools into Microsoft Office. The pattern signaled by these events is a move on the part of Microsoft to strengthen its competitive position. The structural implications might suggest a shift from a desk-top oriented environment to an Internet-worked environment.

If the scenario team is having a difficult time understanding the interactions between different forces, it is often useful to have them map out the events, patterns and structure individually and then together create systems diagrams of how different forces interact. We often do this using post-its to describe and then cluster (and recluster) events, recognize and link patterns, and then identify the underlying structural issues.

2.1.2 Building Narratives

When the basic logics of the different worlds have been determined, then it is time for the group to weave those pieces together to form a narrative with a beginning, a middle, and an end. How could the world get from the present to the reality proposed by the new scenario? What events might be necessary to make the end point of the scenario possible? One of the most frequent mistakes made by fledgling scenario teams is falling into the temptation of settling for a single state description of, say, the year 2020. A static description sacrifices the opportunity to see how the "moving parts" in an industry can interact, and then interact again, sometimes producing counter-intuitive consequences well on down the road.

Narratives are also important to capture issues of timing and path dependency. We may all agree that twenty years from now the twisted pair telephone line and the cable TV will be largely replaced by optical fiber. But billions will be won and lost depending on whether the Regional Bell Operating Companies or the cable companies are the gate-keepers. Shorter term issues of regulation, technology, economic competition, and industry consolidation will have a lot to do with which path we take toward the final rationalization of broadband communications.

A productive exercise at this stage of the workshop is to ask the scenario team to write newspaper headlines describing key events or trends that take place during the course of the scenario. "Philip Morris divests cigarette business," "Dow Jones Falls to 4000," "Moore's Law Disproved" "Eighth Hurricane in 20 Days Ravages Florida Coast." The headlines are a quick way of defining successive stages of a narrative that includes repetitions of the phrase, "and then... and then... and then." Good headlines might mark a surprising beginning, perhaps a turbulent middle period, and a satisfying resolution, for example. Imagine that you are looking out to the year 2025. What would the headlines for your scenario read in 2015? In 2020? What social, technological, economic, environmental, and political events or trends would be reported in the paper? For example, a scenario for an educational products company might include such headlines as: Seattle, WA, 2015 "Bill Gates Appointed Internet Czar," Phoenix, AZ 2020: "Chamber of Commerce Takes Over School District;" Princeton, New Jersey, 2025 "ETS Reports Dramatic Rise in SAT Scores for 2 year olds." This exercise not only hones the scenario logics but provides an intriguing source of ideas for the narratives.

2.1.3 Characters

Are there known individuals or institutions that espouse specific changes, for example, the successful promotion of conservatism by Ronald Reagan and Margaret Thatcher? Would a scenario that calls for a radical change in values benefit from the invention of a charismatic leader gaining a following? In most scenarios the "characters" are driving forces and institutions, nations, or companies as opposed to individuals. But sometimes a known or an invented character can crystalize the logic of the scenario.

Beware of building the entire plot around an individual's personality or power, however. A case in point: When we were developing scenarios for the future of Mexico, political issues, as embodied in the impending election, emerged as a major uncertainty. One of the scenarios was built around a victory by Colosio, the dominant PRI party's presidential candidate; in another scenario Colosio lost. We put the scenarios in the mail on Friday; Saturday morning the headlines proclaimed Colosio's assassination. On the other hand, an individual (real or imaginary) can personify the intersection of key structural or driving forces. A plot about Cuba, for example, could begin with the death of Fidel Castro, and the battle for succession, not because the individual who assumes power is important, but because this can illuminate the political, economic, and cultural struggles that Cuba may face.

Creating characters who live in the scenarios is also a way to convey the magnitude and direction of change. In the Education and Community scenarios described earlier, students, parents, and their teachers populated each of the scenarios to personify the differences; former Secretary of Education and conservative, Bill Bennett is elected President in 2000 in the Orthodoxy scenario. Even though much history is written from the perspective of individual leaders, some of the best historians are scenaric in their way of thinking. Ferdinand Braudel, for example, looks beneath the "great man" theory of history to find the economic and cultural forces and their interactions in an underlying belief system. Mancur Olson's economic history of the U.S. also illuminates deep, structural forces and their interplay. Writing the "history" of the future—and creating vivid characters who live in it—has always been the domain of science fiction—scenario thinking can also be found in the works of Bill Gibson, Neal Stephenson, and Bruce Sterling.

2.2 Typical Plots

Each scenario plot or logic should be different, yet relevant to the focal question. Nonetheless, there are a few archetypical plot lines that seem to arise over and over. These plots are derived from observing the twists and turns of our economic and political systems, the rise and fall of technologies, and pendulum swings in social perceptions.

To be effective, scenario plots must make people rethink their assumptions about the future. For example, many people assume that Asia's continued economic growth is inevitable with little, if any, downside. In fact, this is a dangerous assumption that could be derailed by a whole host of political and environmental factors. On the other hand, plots that are too frightening or implausible tend to be easily discounted and thus weaken the value of the scenario process overall: a study on the future of paper for a forest products company that suggests that technological advances will result in the disappearance of paper and paper products such as books, for example, or a doom and gloom scenario that portrays a complete economic, political, and social breakdown that no company can survive.

Please do not assume from reading the following set of common scenario plots that scenarios can be prepared according to a formula, nor that these are the only plots that work or matter. Instead, use these examples in your group's discussion of how driving forces may interact to create plausible plots.

2.2.1 Winners and Losers.

This is a familiar plot, not only in scenarios but in life. It is based on the concept of a zero sum game: if one company, country, or institution wins, then others will lose. Some examples of winners and losers:

- An ascendant Asia Pacific bloc vs. Europe in decline

- Government regulation of the Internet vs. free expression and entrepreneurial opportunities.

- Microsoft vs. Apple and IBM.

In these plots conflict is often inevitable. But sometimes, after an initial flareup of contention, the conflict quickly burns down to an uneasy detente or balance of power (covert or overt). Sometimes the potential conflict escalates to outright war, military or economic. The "cola war" in the soft drink market is an example of a contemporary U.S. corporate battle. In this hypercompetitive global battleground, every move Coca-Cola makes is met by Pepsi Cola, and every initiative by Pepsi is quickly countered by Coke.

Another example of hypercompetitive rivalry is the battle for market share between long distance telephone carriers. Any effective advertisement by MCI immediately stimulates a response by AT&T and vice versa. The result is an advertising war in which collective annual spending has topped $1 billion.

2.2.2 Crisis and Response

In the early 1980s at Shell, we constructed several scenarios for the future of Soviet Union around a crisis. The defining question: What would be the logical route out of the crisis—the new Stalinism or, alternatively, a loosening of the system? We called one scenario, "Clamp Down" and another, "The Greening of Russia." The plot of both these scenarios was crisis/response, and each posed a logical, but totally different future.

This is a typical adventure story plot. First, one or more challenges arise and then adaptation occurs (or fails to occur). If the adaptation is effective it may create new winners and losers, and may ultimately change the rules of the game altogether. A good example of a crisis and response plot is the scenario that attempts to answer the question' "How much development is sustainable?" First comes the scenario's crisis: initial signs of environmental degradation lead reputable scientists to conclude that an environmental disaster is fast approaching. A few leading governments and companies change the way they do business. Disasters begin to occur in countries that could not, or chose not to adapt, and there is public outcry. The playing field—the organizational operating environment—is suddenly dramatically altered. The innovative firms that learned to make difficult changes in their business practices to avoid environmental degradation are now positioned to become market leaders.

2.2.3   Good News/Bad News

It's important to incorporate elements of both desirable and undesirable futures. For example, a scenario prepared for a global telecommunications company provided the firm with a valuable look at a world shaped by conflict, violence, and corruption—a scenario in which their high ethical standards would become a distinct disadvantage. When writing scenarios for Mexico in late 1994, our team failed to anticipate the devaluation of the peso, in part because there was an unwillingness (possibly culturally induced) to look down the cellar stairs at a bad news scenario.

2.2.4   Evolutionary Change

The logic of this plot—that over time, growth or decline occurs in all systems—is based on studies of biology. Man-made systems tend to plow ahead, at least during the growth period without giving much thought to their inevitable decline. And even if change is anticipated, its nature and magnitude are seldom comprehended and therefore rarely managed appropriately. A classic example from the '80s is when IBM turned a great opportunity into a catastrophe by missing the significance of the personal computer. IBM saw the death knell of the computer industry instead of its transformation.

A variation on this plot is co-evolution. Change in one system interacts with and causes change in other systems. Technology often spurs co-evolutionary change— new innovations appear and flourish (or die) giving rise to other innovations, while at the same time interacting with the political and economic systems.

2.2.5   Other typical plot lines include:

- Revolution: Abrupt discontinuities, either natural or man-made. Examples: an earthquake, a breakthrough invention.

- Tectonic Change: Structural alterations which produce dramatic flareups, like a volcano, which cause major (but certainly foreseeable) discontinuities. Examples: a breakup of China; the end of apartheid in South Africa.

- Cycles: Economics and politics often move in cycles; their timing is important and unpredictable. Examples: health care reform; real estate booms; gentrification.

- Infinite Possibility: The seductive idea that continued growth is possible, often enabling sights to be set higher than before, e.g. the computer industry in the 1980's; global connectivity via the Internet today.

- The Lone Ranger: This plot pits an organization or a main character against the established practices of politics, trade, or technology. Often the protagonist group sees itself as battling a perceived evil, a corrupt system or an antediluvian competitor. This plot frequently matches up a startup firm and a market leader—a David and Goliath scenario. Some examples: Apple Computer vs. IBM, MCI vs. AT&T, Ted Turner vs. the networks.

- Generations: This plot revolves around the emergence of new cultures—groups with different values and expectations. Examples: the Baby Boomers, Generation X, or the overseas Chinese network.

- Perpetual transition: This plot is a variation on the evolutionary and infinite possibility themes. It expects change to be continuous and predicts that adaptation will be anything but uniform. There will be no New World Order or rules of the game; the Internet—enabled by new products which continually push the boundaries of speed and connectivity—will become a vast, ever-evolving marketplace with no regulation, control, or limits.

When constructing scenario plots, remember that expecting change is not enough. Scenario developers must also anticipate a response to the change. Most forecasters make the mistake of assuming that a powerful, highly successful organization can control its destiny to a large extent. For example, Japanese car makers assumed they could sell more and more cars in America by making their products better and better. But every system has the capacity for response and self-correction. Continued, fast economic growth leads to resistance. The threat of war results in demands for peace. High oil prices promote exploration, new discoveries, more oil, and an eventual lowering of the price as happened in the mid-eighties.

2.2.6 Wild Cards

Whereas scenarios are something you plan for, wild cards are things that you plan against. Wild cards are surprises that have the power to completely change your hand—and the outcome of the entire game. Wild cards might be:

- Wholly discontinuous events like natural disasters or assassinations.

- Discontinuities that might be anticipated but which have significant unintended consequences, like ERISA which was developed to insure pensions for the elderly and created institutional investing.

- Catalytic developments, so different in degree or scale that they are different in kind. Mosaic/Netscape, for example, transformed the World Wide Web into a global meeting and marketplace.

In scenario exercises built around a matrix of four logically contrasted scenarios, we will sometimes include a fifth "wild card" scenario that takes into account a dramatic yet relevant surprise that doesn't fit neatly on the matrix. After constructing four logically related scenarios for Oregon's Department of Public Health, for example, we added a fifth Wild Card: What if Mt. Hood Blows? Other examples: that cold fusion works; a breakthrough in nanotechnology accelerating its commercialization by a decade or more; the discovery (as we recently witnessed) of possible life forms on another planet. Wild cards can reinforce the importance of continually "thinking out of the box."

3   Ten Tips for Successful Scenarios

Having had time and experience enough to make all the mistakes there are to make, we offer these ten tips to keep others from stepping into various familiar pot-holes:

3.1   Stay Focused

Your scenarios should be developed within the context of the focal question: a specific decision to be made or a critical issue or uncertainty of great importance facing the organization. Keep your sights on addressing the raison d'etre for the exercise.

3.2   Keep It Simple

Although clever and creative plots that illuminate the interaction of key forces can help to make scenarios memorable, don't get the idea that this is primarily a creative writing project. Simple plots and a short list of characters help managers to understand, use, and communicate the scenarios.

3.3   Keep It Interactive

Scenario plots should be the unique product of your organization's interactive team-based effort. If they are off-the-shelf stories, reflect the prejudices of only the most powerful people in your organization, or do not take into account the insights of all levels of your organization's management, they will likely fail to be relevant and they will certainly fail to capture the imagination of your organization's future leaders.

3.4   Plan to Plan and Allow Enough Time

3.4.1   Prep time:

Before the first scenario workshop, you will need about a month to select the scenario team, conduct a series of interviews, round up relevant literature, and book a site for the workshop.

3.4.2 Day One:

The initial scenario workshop should be at least two days long. It takes time to think of everything that could affect the focal issue. It takes time to pry people loose of the present. As described earlier, a typical scenario workshop will begin with about an hour devoted to articulating the focal issue, about three to four hours of listing key factors and environmental forces, and two or three hours to prioritize forces and settle on an official future or a scenario matrix.

3.4.3 Time to "sleep on it":

After a day of brainstorming, we suggest leaving the evening relatively unstructured to give participants in the workshop a chance to socialize and informally compare impressions. We find that after the participants sleep on their ideas, debates, and conversations of the first day, they often awaken with fresh insights that contribute to generating the scenario logics.

3.4.4 The second day…

…will begin with second thoughts about the skeletal scenario logics, then the group will spend one to two hours fleshing out one scenario in plenary—tracing a narrative line from a beginning, through a middle, to an end—before breaking up into smaller groups to flesh out the other scenarios. By the end of the second day, the group will be able to see several different scenarios in sufficient detail so that it's possible to draw out preliminary implications of each scenario, and, if you're lucky, some strategic implications of the set of scenarios taken as a whole. But this work of asking, So What?, often takes more time and reflection than a single workshop can provide.

3.4.5 Interim Research:

After developing the scenario logics and outlines of their plots, allow for at least four to six weeks of interim research and reflection while writing the final scenarios and exploring their implications. As soon as possible, circulate draft scenario logics or plots to other managers whose opinions you value. To speed up the process of drafting narrative scenarios based on the first workshop, we often recruit an experienced note taker to record the workshop so that the ideas of the participants can be captured and quickly organized. There is brainstorming software that can also facilitate this work.

A key purpose of this interim phase is to research more extensively—both qualitatively (through interviews) and quantitatively—the important forces, trends, and uncertainties. Ask the team what the things are that we really don't know but need to know—geographic economic growth trends; industry structure; the financial performance and strength of new or potential competitors; consumer trends; emerging technologies; regulations in different countries.

For a recent project in the aerospace industry, for example, substantial research was conducted on the restructuring and convergence of several industries—and what the industry structure might look like under each scenario. The better your scenario team understands the nature, magnitude and possible interactions of these key forces, the more likely it is that your scenarios will be plausible. On the other hand, if you fail to do good research and your underlying assumptions don't hold water, then your scenarios are likely to be quickly discounted. In practice, some scenarios are abandoned after more research and others may be substantially redirected based on new research findings.

3.4.6 A Second Workshop:

After the interim research has been conducted and preliminary scenario narratives drafted and circulated, reassemble the original scenario team for at least a day, perhaps two. At this second workshop there are three main objectives:

- Correct, revise, amend the draft scenarios

- Explore the implications of each scenario individually

- Answer the strategic *So What?* based on all of the scenarios taken collectively

This last point calls for a separate essay—or book—about the very nature of strategic planning. Is the objective to develop a long-range plan or blueprint that aims the company in one direction for five years and then lashes down the wheel? Such five-year plans may be necessary in some industries with long lead times or slow cycle times. Detroit cannot retool for quarterly changes in automotive fashions. In other industries, however, the objective may be to use scenarios to enhance a strategic conversation that enables many managers to steer through quarterly, or monthly, shifts in the business environment. Depending on the nature of the industry and the nature of the focal issue, the relevant So What may be a single decision with a "long tail" that managers will have to live with for many years; or it may be to enhance the learning of many managers so that they can revise their mental maps of their business environment in a way that changes the way they make daily decisions.

3.5 Don't settle for a simple high, medium and low.

Although the scenarios being developed will share the same organizing question, each scenario should be based on a fundamentally different logic. Simply focusing on high or low interest rates, for example, is less illuminating than painting worlds in which interest rates change for very different reasons; rising interest rates due to strong economic growth have very different origins and implications than higher interest rates caused by rampaging inflation. The team's goal should be to develop a few scenarios that are all plausible, but don't share the same assumptions about the environment, such as an economy which varies only by rates of growth: flat, 3 percent, 6 percent.

3.6   Avoid Probabilities or "Most Likely" Plots.

Remember that some of the most surprising scenario plots may be the ones your organization learns the most from. Though all must be plausible, don't just select ones that appear to be the most likely to unfold. Do not assign probabilities to the scenarios. Do not categorize them as either the most or least likely. Keep your mind open to all possibilities. Don't fixate on just one scenario that you want to achieve. Scenarios are meant to illuminate different futures, complete with negative and positive dimensions. Choosing one scenario as a goal may blind you to other developments and possibilities. A classic case occurred in the 1970s when oil companies focused exclusively on high oil prices — in their best interest—while remaining in denial about the possibility of an oil price bust.

3.7   Avoid drafting too many scenarios, many of which are merely variations on a theme or "contingency plans."

A number of years ago, we were involved in a project for the U.S. Environmental Protection Agency which was using scenarios to look at alternative futures for pesticide policy. The team developed ten scenarios but their distinctions were so blurred that they were neither meaningful nor useful. We finally reduced the number to three scenarios whose differences really did make a difference.

In our experience, four scenarios are usually all you need. Groups have great difficulty discussing or even remembering more than four scenarios. In particular, beware of the "middle of the road" approach trap—that is, selecting three scenarios that offer "large, medium, and small" versions of the future. Too often, managers will be tempted to identify one of the three—usually the one with a "middle of the road" approach to the future—as the "most likely" scenario. These single forecasts do not portray truly divergent futures which challenge the mental maps of the decision makers and suggest very different strategic options and implications. Moreover, there is a tendency to treat the "most likely scenario" as a prediction, thus failing to explore the other scenarios fully and wasting the whole multiple scenario exercise. In truth, some people simply can't think about scenarios. They always want to find the "right" answer which can be derived mathematically. When one or more participants in a scenario exercise feel that they know "the Right Scenario" and aren't willing or able to entertain others, the process becomes very frustrating. It is important to continually emphasize that there are no right or wrong, good or bad scenarios, but a set of distinct and plausible futures that could unfold.

3.8   Invent Catchy Names for the Scenarios.

Apply a generous amount of creativity to come up with evocative scenario names that quickly convey the crucial changes in the business environment that will affect your organization. When your managers feel the hot breath of crisis they should be able to recall the appropriate scenario by name. "Wasn't sudden volatility in currencies we're now experiencing a key force in our 'Interest Rate Hell' scenario? What were the other warning signs that it might be unfolding now?" Culturally referential names—popular songs, movies, TV shows, even countries—are often memorable. One set of our scenarios was named for recordings by the Beatles: A Hard Days Night, Help, Magical Mystery Tour, and Imagine. We have also used regional and country images like Siberia (an isolation scenario) and Bosnia (a fragmented, divisive world).

3.9   Make the Decision Makers Own the Scenarios.

One of the most powerful contributions to a good scenario process is the direct and ongoing involvement of key decision makers. These are the people who will be responsible for using and communicating the scenarios throughout the organization. If at all possible, these are the people who should actually write the scenarios. We have had success with several different strategies:

- Assign the job to one author. This works if the organization has an important member who both enjoys writing and is a collaborative thinker (a person who is willing to solicit and incorporate comments from the rest of the team).

- Assign a pair of authors—one who writes well and another who is a veteran team leader—to work together to draft the scenarios.

- Assign a different author for each draft narrative with "technical assistance" available from an experienced editor/scenario writer. This may result in wildly uneven efforts but it is a way to engage the most senior executives.

No matter which participant drafts the scenarios, he or she must thoughtfully and fairly solicit and welcome comments and suggestions from the rest of the team.

3.10   Budget sufficient resources for communicating the scenarios.

Communicating the scenarios and their operational implications is a critical part of the scenario planning process. Scenario planning will fail if its product is merely a handsome report, read once by only a few executives, and then allowed to gather dust on the shelf. Instead scenarios must become drivers of an organization's ongoing strategic conversation and learning. Once the scenarios have been successfully tested on a small group, plans should be made to expose larger groups to the learning experience.

We like to tell our scenario stories from the perspective of a person living in the future (the end point of the scenarios), for example, 2020. This provides for smoother and more interesting narratives. While written scenarios should eventually be produced, think of other ways to communicate them to the organization, to help people live in the scenarios. We have used various techniques for doing this—including dramatization, computer simulations, role playing, and multimedia presentations.

For one organization's annual Board of Directors retreat, we made audiotapes of the scenarios for the members to listen to before arriving. During the retreat, they watched videotaped "newscasts" of the scenarios and then engaged in a role playing exercise that involved interacting as very different characters in the future worlds. Finally, a team of improvisotory actors took premises from the group and acted out mini-dramas consistent with the different scenario logics. This made the scenarios come alive and served as the basis for ongoing conversations.

For a major computer manufacturer and systems integrator we facilitated a scenario exercise involving 15 of their key customers in one industry. Scripts were written for scenarios set in different locations around the world looking back from the year 2020. Five-minute films using professional actors were produced to show various industry events unfolding.

The show-biz component that can enhance the communication of scenarios suggests one final axiom: If you're not having fun, you're not doing it right. Be creative and have a good time. Remember, scenarios are a tool for unexpected learning, learning about the unexpected, and thinking outside of the box.

While several decades of experience have allowed us to come up with what might seem to be hard and fast rules or a tried and true technique, the fact is that scenario planning is more of an art than a science. While it should be fun, it can be very un-fun if the process breaks down into a muddle of unordered uncertainties. As one of our favorite clients likes to put it, "Don't do this at home. Proceed only under adult supervision!" The various approaches, steps, and tips we have outlined should be enough to give you a clear idea of what is involved in scenario planning. But if the process is to be as fun and creative as it should be, you will also need skilled facilitators of the group process, talented writers, creative thinkers, and quite a lot of hard work.

2. Scenario Planning: Art or Science?

Permission granted to reprint from World Futures: The Journal of General Evolution, Vol. 61, Number 5, July-August, 2005, pp. 331-346

Is scenario planning an art or a science? We know that Peter Schwartz's book is titled The Art of the Long View. But if scenario planning is only an art but not a science, then only artists can practice it, not the rest of us ordinary mortals. If art alone, then scenario planning depends more on talent than on training. If art alone, then scenario planning becomes difficult to judge by shared, inter-subjective, repeatable means.

But if it's a science, then what kind of science? Certainly not a predict-and-control positivism. Scenario planners do not try to engineer the future.

This article will argue that there is a science of scenario planning; or at least a *logos,* a logic, a *scenarology.* Will scenarios foretell certain things about the future as astronomy will allow you to foretell the positions of the planets on some distant future evening? Absolutely not. But a good set of scenarios, scientifically developed, can reliably and predictably *change minds.* And that, after all, is what planning is really about. As Arie de Geus notes, "Planning is about changing minds, not making plans."[3]

In this essay I'll argue that scenario planning is both art and science, but that in joining the club of the sciences, scenario planning calls for a change in the policies used by the membership committee. What does it take to get into the club of the sciences? What counts as science? This is the question that launches the discourse known as the philosophy of science. There are those who think that it's possible to articulate a set of very clear criteria for what is and what is not science. There are others like P. K. Feyerabend who are more inclined to say , "I know one when I see one," and leave it up to the members of the membership committee to use their noses.

While I am sympathetic to Feyerabend's critique of positivistic philosophy of science, I think that recent developments in complexity theory allow for a philosophy of science that is neither as restrictive as the kind of positivistic philosophy of science to which Feyerabend objects, nor as loose as his methodological anarchism. Just as we can ask of scenario planning, *Is it an art or is it a science?* So we can ask of science, *Is it positivistic, or is it enriched by complexity theory?*

---

3   Arie de Geus, *The Living Company,* John Wiley, Boston, 1997.

Faced with these two binary choices, the best way to set the course of this essay will be to construct a 2X2 matrix constructed from these two binary oppositions, then chart a course through its quadrants.

	Science is Deterministic	Science is enriched by Complexity Theory
Scenario Planning related to art	**Part One:** Scenario Planning is *only* an art	**Part Four:** Aesthetics contribute to judgments regarding better futures
Scenario Planning related to science	**Part Two:** Scenario Planning tries to be a science	**Part Three:** Scenario Planning adds narrative to a new kind of science

The question, Is scenario planning an art or a science gains a different significance in each of the quadrants of this matrix. My guess is that when most planners first hear this question, they hear it in the context of the northwest quadrant. In Part One I'll argue that scenario planning risks being demeaned as a *mere* art when held up against the standards of positivistic science.

Part Two will move down to the southwest quadrant. Here you find attempts to raise scenario planning to the status of a science where 'science' is understood according to a monological paradigm, according to which explanations are reductionistic and the world is understood as in principle predictable.

Let the phrase, 'monological science,' stand for that kind of scientific reasoning that is not so much wrong as incomplete. The term 'monological' has been chosen to suggest a scientific rationality that over-emphasizes singleness, unity or unification in three different respects:

> **Formal unity:** the view that to understand or explain something is to subsume it under some singular, Platonic ideal; the subsumption of many

particulars under one universal; the subsumption of several different explanatory systems under one covering law, e.g. the explanation of rusting, respiration and combustion by their subsumption under the single concept of oxidation; the further extrapolation from such limited unifications toward the demand for a unified field theory for the explanation of everything, as if, for the universe to be rational, there must be some single peak to the hierarchical pyramid of monological abstractions; a Platonic Form of forms as deserving of rational respect as the Lord of lords is deserving of monotheistic reverence.

Substantive unity: a metaphysics that privileges things over structures, differences, or relationships; the long tradition since Aristotle who affirmed that to be is to be an individual; atomistic materialism; the preference for interpreting Bohr's complementarity principle in terms of particles rather than waves.

Explanatory monism: the view that to explain something is to find a single cause, e.g. the mosquito as the cause of the spread of malaria; the plot structure of the whodunit with one villain; the germ theory of disease; an understanding of causality that takes the combination shot on the pool table as a model for monolinear sequences of causes and effects—cue stick strikes cue ball which then drives the 3-ball into the 7-ball in order to nudge the 9-ball into the side pocket. Explanatory monism imagines that every effect can be explained by such a monolinear sequence of causes and effects.

While I'm eager to find as much method and rationality in scenario planning as possible, I'm equally sure that the future remains unpredictable, and that the predict-and-control school of planning based on monological science, decision analysis and rigorous quantification is an ill-conceived waste of time and resources. But how to make that case without falling back into the northwest quadrant where scenario planning is demeaned as a *mere* art?

The strategy of this essay will be to move to the right side of the above matrix using complexity theory to expand our sense of what counts as a science. Part Three will draw mainly on the work of Stuart Kauffman of the Santa Fe Institute in order to show what is wrong with the predict-and-control approach of monological science. Kauffman argues, "Our inability to prestate the configuration space of a biosphere foretells a deepening of science, a search for story and historical contingency, yet a place for natural laws."[4] Kauffman's "search for story and historical contingency" will be interpreted as a call for something very like scenarios as the means for "a deepening of science." This is where scenario planning exerts a pressure on the

---

4   Stuart Kauffman, *Investigations,* Oxford University Press, 2000, p. 135.

philosophers of science on the membership committee to change their rules for entry into the science club.

Part Four will summarize the argument by moving into the Northeast quadrant to show why scenario planning need not be demeaned as *mere* art, even as parts of its practice remain irreducibly artistic, namely, the role of the beautiful in reaching evaluative judgments regarding what counts as a better future.

Part I: What's wrong with regarding scenario planning as only an art?

There was a time when scenario planning lacked a method. Prior to the 1980s, scenario planning was essentially a guru-led practice. If you wanted to do scenario planning, you couldn't find a textbook or a set of guidelines for how to do it. If you wanted to do scenario planning, you pretty much had to hire one of the gurus like Herman Kahn or Pierre Wack or Peter Schwartz. These men practiced the art somewhat like magicians. Pierre Wack was fond of using the image of "pulling the rabbit out of the hat."

The genius of these men is not to be underestimated but respected. They were pioneers and creators and we are profoundly in their debt. Yet none of them was at all interested in rationalizing their practice in a way that could be transferred or taught or practiced by others. They led their workshops without pre-planned agendas. Like genuine artists, they made it up as they went along. At the Hudson Institute, at Royal Dutch/Shell, and at SRI, these men commanded immense respect, and rightly so. By sheer dint of genius and intuition, they always seemed to know where to go next, and they brought great learning to their art.

I had the pleasure and the privilege of working just a bit with Pierre Wack, and a great deal with Peter Schwartz. I often marveled at their erudition, and at their sense of the right question to pose next. Very like Socrates, their practice relied more on questions than on learned lectures. Yet their questions often derived from deep knowledge of many subjects, and an intuitive sense for where some hidden rabbit might be found.

During the 1980s, after Peter Schwartz accepted Napier Collyns and Pierre Wack's invitation to replace Pierre in his role of directing scenario planning at Shell, I found myself at SRI sitting in scenario workshops led by others, people who had worked with Peter and Pierre more than I had and who, presumably, had apprenticed sufficiently to be able to practice the art. Yet I found that, in the absence of the gurus, the apprentices often seemed to be floundering. What question to ask next? Once a long list of key factors and environmental forces had been arrayed and discussed, how to proceed toward just a few scenario logics?

That was when Ian Wilson and I hammered out a step by step process for developing scenarios, the same one that I wrote up for inclusion in the Appendix to Peter Schwartz's book, *The Art of the Long View,*[5] and the same one we teach in the courses on scenario planning offered by Global Business Network. Since then, there's been a long-running lovers' quarrel among various practitioners, some of whom insist that there is no step by step method for generating good scenarios, and others who believe that the practice can be rationalized, taught, and learned by still others, at least to an extent. I count myself among the latter, but I retain a healthy respect for the views of the former. Why?

It is important to appreciate the degree to which scenario planning neither can be nor should be reduced to some paint-by-the-numbers, fill-in-the-blanks routine. One thing we've seen again and again in the practice of scenario planning is the importance of unconventional insight: The ability that some people have to connect the same old dots in new ways. At GBN we retain a practice begun by Pierre Wack at Shell, namely, drawing on the insights of "remarkable people." This may sound very much like a reliance on artistic talent or magical ability—something that some people have but others do not—and as such it may sound very unscientific.

Prior to the development of modern scientific method, Paracelsus was known as a great scientist because there were experiments that he could do that no one else could perform with the same success. From the perspective of contemporary science and its demand for replicability, Paracelsus' claim to greatness should evoke a chuckle. If it's science, it has to be repeatable by others. Think of the flurry of excitement over cold fusion… until it was discovered that others could not produce the same results when following what were ostensibly the same procedures.

Replicability is an important criterion for science. And scenario planning, as rationalized into a step by step method, passes the test. At GBN we have been able to build a business because the method we use is describable and replicable—even though it includes as one of its components a reliance on remarkable people who are not replicable or replaceable. But is this so different from other kinds of science? While laboratory science may follow rigorous guidelines for practices of measurement and the use of controls, the construction of novel hypotheses calls for a degree of creativity that some people have in greater measure than others. You can think of our "remarkable people" as our hypothesis generators. While their interventions may not be replicable, the overall method that includes their interventions is eminently replicable. Unlike the early scenario workshops run by the gurus, our workshops today follow fairly fixed agendas. We know what we have to do first and what we have to do second and what we have to do third, and

---

5   A longer version can be found in Peter Schwartz and James Ogilvy, "Plotting Your
     Scenarios," in *Learning From the Future,* ed. Liam Fahey and Robert Randall, John Wiley,
     1996., reproduced as Chapter 2 above.

we know approximately how long each step will take. Workshop after workshop, we find ourselves saying to one another, "It works! The method is amazingly reliable and replicable!" Without floundering, or making it up as we go along, we arrive at a set of different scenarios that lead to actionable insights and useful strategic options.

Granted there are lots of ways of going wrong. Some facilitators are more skillful than others. But it is not magic, or pure art cloaked in mystery.

Part II: How does scenario planning differ from predict-and-control, monological science?

If the membership committee for the science club raises the bar to the level of a positivistic, deterministic, predictive science, then there is no way that scenario planning can make the grade. If it were possible to raise the bar that high, however, then it wouldn't make sense to engage in scenario planning in the first place. There is a paradox at best, or a contradiction at worst, in even trying to raise scenario planning to the level of a deterministic, predictive science: If prediction is possible, then who needs alternative scenarios? If it were possible to marshal enough data and enough laws to achieve certainty for a single-point forecast of the future, then why waste time on other forecasts of what certainly *won't* happen?

Given the obvious unavoidability of risk and uncertainty in the world we live in, it might seem absurd to entertain the prospect of scientific predictability. Indeed, it is absurd. Nonetheless it's worth following out the thought experiment of a scientifically predictable future for several reasons: First, the ideal of predictability lies just below the surface assumptions of many who see science through the lens of positivism. Second, the thought experiment has in fact been seriously entertained. It is not just some fictional straw man. The mathematician, Henri LaPlace once wrote to the effect that a sufficiently large intellect, given the positions and momenta of every particle in the universe at a given moment of time, could then calculate state descriptions of the universe for every subsequent moment in time. Think of the universe as a perfect, frictionless billiards table with flawless bumpers. The LaPlacian demon can figure all the angles. Given sufficient precision in managing his cue stick, he would never miss a shot.

Absurd as this fantasy might seem to anyone steeped in the messiness and indeterminacy of the real world, the fact is that this fantasy *has occurred,* not only to LaPlace but to many others. This fantasy of perfect predictability also gains support from some of science's remarkable successes. We *are* able to achieve amazing accuracy in ballistics. We *have* put a man on the moon. We *can* predict eclipses with precision. So why can't we achieve similar successes in the social sciences, in politics, in business?

In Asimov's *Foundation* trilogy, "the donkey" stands in for the positivistic dream of reducing the social sciences and history to the determinism of Newtonian mechanics. Likewise Nietzsche's notion of eternal recurrence also presupposes the kind of determinism necessary to ensure that, when the train of possibilities on the cosmic billiards table has run its course once, it is bound by iron necessity to repeat itself endlessly—like Bill Murray's replays in the movie, *Groundhog Day.*

This fantasy of a pre-determined future *has occurred*—to LaPlace, to Nietzsche, to Asimov. I'm not just making it up. A third reason for thinking through this fantasy of predictability lies in the fact that it lurks among the assumptions of those who imagine that business strategies can be based on reliable single-point forecasts of the future. But see how fundamentally paradoxical this fantasy becomes when you think through the thought experiment. If you can predict the future, then you can't change it. If you, or more to the point, someone else can change the future, then you can't predict it. Aristotle articulated this paradox over 2,000 years ago,[6] but many a strategy based on a single-point forecast falls into this paradox.

How many telecom companies based their strategies and aggressive investments in the late 1990s on predictions of market demand that failed to greet them, in part because so many other telecom companies planned on capturing the same market? They predicted their success based on a future in which they captured large market share. But other companies changed that future by pursuing the same market share.

We *can* influence the future, and therefore we cannot predict it. If we could predict the future, we couldn't change it. We'd have to give up planning in favor of reading tea leaves or Tarot sticks to find our (pre-)destiny. If you believe in fate, there's not much point in planning or acting on behalf of your shareholders' interests. If you believe in fate, you might as well just lie back and let in unfold.

This is the paradox implicit in the fantasy of predictability. It renders intentional action superfluous. No wonder fatalists tend toward quietism. Like Pascal, they will aver that we would all be a lot better off if more of us learned to sit quietly in our rooms. Convinced of the power of destiny, they become reconciled to the vanity of human action. With Zen equanimity or Heideggerian *Gelassenheit*, they let be what is.

---

6   Aristotle, *Nichomachean Ethics,* Book VI, especially chapters 2, 5, 9, and 12. Cf. esp. "For what is known scientifically is demonstrable, whereas art and practical wisdom are concerned with things that can be other than they are." (Ch 6, 1140 b 35 -1141 a 1) "Practical wisdom, on the other hand, is concerned with human affairs and with matters about which deliberation is possible. As we have said, the most characteristic function of a man of practical wisdom is to deliberate well: no one deliberates about things that cannot be other than they are, nor about things that are not directed to some end, an end that is a good attainable by action." (Ch 7, 1141b 8-12)

But the rest of us don't run our lives this way. We engage in intentional action, both as individuals and as planners for our companies. We do our best to mold our futures to our liking. We carve the near edge of the future so that its farther edges will conform to our dreams and our desires. In doing so, as this thought experiment shows, we presuppose the unpredictability of the future. But if that is so, then we can't expect scenario planning, or any other kind of planning for that matter, to leap over the bar of deterministic prediction. We cannot expect scenario planning to mimic astrophysics with precise calculations of converging trajectories.

Let me be clear about the several different arguments that are parts of the preceding thought experiment:

1. The future is not predictable. This claim can be supported by a range of arguments, from the evidence of common sense to a combination of Heisenberg's Uncertainty Principle and chaos theory's emphasis on the importance of minor fluctuations in initial conditions (the famous "butterfly effect").

2. If the future *were* predictable, then planners would be out of business. They would be replaced by seers or pre-cogs[7] who could see the shape of our inevitable destiny, our ineluctable fate.

3. If the future were predictable, then alternative scenarios are unnecessary. Only one so-called scenario could correspond to the predicted future. Its probability would equal 1.0. All others have zero probability and are therefore useless.

4. The high bar of deterministic predictability is more than implicit; it has been rendered explicit by positivists from LaPlace to the philosophers of the Vienna Circle—figures like Rudolph Carnap, Hans Reichenbach, and A. J. Ayer.

5. The fantasy of deterministic predictability lives on and lurks among the assumptions of those who regard scenario planning as insufficiently scientific.

Connect these points together in any of several combinations and you will see that judging scenario planning against the standard of deterministic science is non-sensical, paradoxical, and ultimately absurd.

7　See the pre-cognition experts in Steven Spielberg's *Minority Report,* based on an imaginative story by Philip Dick.

Part III: Scenario Planning and A New Kind of Science

But what if we measure scenario planning against the standards of a different kind of science? What kind? Consider complexity theory and the ideas of Stuart Kauffman.

In his *Investigations,* Kauffman reflects on the fact that in an evolving universe where new forms of order emerge from complex concatenations of already complex molecules, it is not only impossible to predict the future; we cannot even anticipate the parameters of the configuration space. Not only can we not calculate the measure of the future; we cannot even anticipate the correct measuring rods to use.

Kauffman is not shy about drawing appropriately radical conclusions about the nature of science itself. Once again: "Our inability to prestate the configuration space of a biosphere foretells a deepening of science, a search for story and historical contingency, yet a place for natural laws."[8]

I think Kauffman is right to deduce the need for story from our inability to prestate the configuration space of the biosphere, but there are some premises missing from his deduction. What is it about story that makes it essential to his new kind of science? What is it about narrative that makes it so important to complexity theory?

In order to answer this question, we need to look elsewhere. But before we do so, it's worth recalling that scenarios are stories—narratives of alternative futures. If stories are essential to Kauffman's new kind of science, and scenarios are stories, then scenario planning might be far more compatible with this new kind of science than with the science of LaPlace and the positivists. We seem to be getting closer to an understanding of scenario planning as not just art, but also part of science. But before we get there, we still need to know just what it is about story or narrative that makes it essential to this new kind of science.

Despite the rash of recent interest in narrative and the growing fascination with story-telling in organizations,[9] I find it necessary to go all the way back to Hegel to find an account of narrative sufficiently profound to serve Kauffman's needs.

---

8   Kauffman, *Investigations, op. cit.,* p. 135.

9   See Roger Shank, *Tell Me a Story,* Northwestern University Press, Evanston, 1990;
     Steven Denning, *The Springboard: How Storytelling Ignites Action in Knowledge-Era
     Organizations,* Butterworth-Heinemann, Boston, 2001; Julie Allan, Gerard Fairtlough and
     Barbara Heinzen, *The Power of the Tale: Using Narratives for Organizational Success,* John
     Wiley & Sons, New York, 2002; Robert Fulford, *The Triumph of Narrative: Story telling in
     the Age of Mass Culture,* Broadway Books, New York, 1999; Annette Simmons, *The Story
     Factor: Inspiration, Influence, and Persuasion through the Art of Storytelling,* Perseus,
     Cambridge, 2001; Gianluca Bocchi, Mauro Ceruti, *The Narrative Universe,* Hampton Press,
     Cresskill, New Jersey, 2002.

Since Hegel's prose is obscure to the point of being unintelligible to those not steeped in the language of German philosophy, it will be helpful to borrow from one of his modern interpreters, Hayden White, a formulation of his insights more lucid than Hegel's own. White interprets Hegel as saying, "The reality that lends itself to narrative representation is the conflict between desire and the law."[10] I think Hayden White and Hegel are on to something very important here, something that completes Stuart Kauffman's argument in ways that not even he may have anticipated.

Put Hegel and Kauffman together (with Hayden White's help), and you get a science that not only covers the force of necessity; you get a science that also accommodates the power of desire—not only what *must* be, but also what we *want* to be; not only a degree of determinism, but also some room for freedom. We get the kind of science we need for shaping the future as well as we can without falling into the paradox of a scientifically predictable fate defeating the efficacy of good intentions. In short, there is reason for hope.

The law that Hegel and Hayden White are talking about is the law of the State, but if Kauffman is right about the need for story to comprehend what is otherwise incalculable under monological causality, then the principle may hold true for the conflict between desire and natural law as well. Synthesizing the insights of Kauffman and Hegel (as interpreted by White) we arrive at a systemic set of mutual implications among four concepts: (1) law, representing the realm of *necessity;* (2) desire, which wants what it wants in the face of what supposedly *must be;* (3) narrative, or story, which tells the tale of the conflict between desire and law; between freedom and necessity; between spontaneous variation and ruthless selection; and, finally, (4) the emergence of subjectivity as constituted by desire's struggle with necessity, as told in the form of biography or history, and self-referentially re-told as the self-constituting autobiography of an emergent subject, whether an individual, or a community. In the latter case, the scenario workshop turns out to be an ideal context in which to work out and crystallize the shared hopes of the community, and thereby bring into being the subjectivity of that community as a collective, autonomous entity.

Because the struggle between law and desire is not just the playing out of necessity under the covering law model—a description using equations stating generalities about what *must be*—but a struggle between necessity and desire, monological science must be supplemented by narrative or history. The only way to make sense of this struggle is to see it as the struggle of an individual or collective subject who *cares about what happens* against an indifferent realm of law that doesn't. White

---

10   Hayden White, *The Content of the Form,* The Johns Hopkins University Press, Baltimore, 1987, p. 12.

continues his rendering of Hegel in a way that links back to both agency and law. "Where there is no rule of law, there can be neither a subject nor the kind of event that lends itself to narrative representation."

Monological science is not simply wrong; it is a necessary condition for the emergence of subjectivity from the conflict between desire and that law. Rather than staking out a romantic opposition to the force of law; rather than restating New Age complaints about the failure of "Western science" (whatever that might mean); rather than giving in to Feyerabend's methodological anarchism, it seems wiser to define as precisely as possible what I've called monological science, grant it its due under laboratory conditions, but then declare its limitations in applications outside the laboratory, especially where intentional agents have their say. The point is to appreciate the tension between the force of law and the force of desire. Wishing something doesn't make it so. But there is reason for hope, even in the face of harsh necessity.

Once we grant the force of law, together with its limitations somewhere short of the pre-determined, billiards table universe of the positivists, then there's room for entertaining the role of hope, desire and care without falling into overly wishful thinking or belief in some benign teleology. This is precisely where *normative scenarios* come into play. As I've argued elsewhere,[11] investing our scenarios with our values is not a mistake. It is not an error to recognize one scenario as aspirational, another as an evil to be avoided at all costs.

The effort to create scenarios that are simply *different* without being recognized as *good* or *bad* derives from the mistaken belief that pure objectivity is possible. It is not. Of course it is worth every effort to explore and identify our biases. But it is a mistake to maintain that we can root out all of our biases, all of our predispositions, all of our assumptions and pre-judgments,[12] to achieve some sort of context-free objectivity.

Once we grant that evaluation is not only an unavoidable but a legitimate aspect of the way we read our environment, then we are plunged headlong into grappling with ethics. If values are not just a set of subjective preferences added on top of a solid world of facts, but are instead ingredient in the way we see "the facts," then it is incumbent upon us to come to terms with the role of values and evaluation in the way we come to know our environment.

---

11 See James Ogilvy, "Scenario Planning and the Human Sciences: The Case for Normative Scenarios," *Futures Research Quarterly,* Vol. 8, No. 2, 1992, pp. 5-65; "Normative Scenarios as the Fulfillment of Critical Theory," *FRQ,* Vol. 12, No.2, Summer, 1996, pp. 5-33; and *Creating Better Futures,* Oxford University Press, New York, 2002.

12 Cf. Hans Georg Gadamer, *Wahrheit und Methode,* (Truth and Method), the classic text of the discipline known as hermeneutics, where Gadamer uses the term *Vorurteilungen* for what translates better as pre-judgments rather than prejudices.

What are values? Whose values? Must values be universal in order to be values at all? Or are values merely subjective preferences—I like what I like, you what you like, whatever?

In appropriating ethics and values into the methodology for futures research, the challenge consists in steering a path between subjective relativism and nihilism on the one hand, and overly universalistic ethical systems on the other, e.g. Platonism; monotheism of whatever hue, Christian or Muslim; even de-ontological ethics from Kant to Habermas; even utilitarianism if practiced in an authoritarian, totalistic way.

Finding this path is no easy thing. On the one hand you have people saying that postmodernism is inherently relativistic and therefore, ultimately, nihilistic. You do your thing, I'll do mine, a kind of easy going, Californian permissiveness. On the other hand you have people trying to turn postmodernism into its own very complex, very complicated master theory: Derrida with a conscience. Neither is correct. Postmodernism is not a theory; it is a condition—one in which the problem is not no values at all, but too many values, too many competing perspectives, too many rival contexts.

This situation, this condition, then creates a problem for "world futures": How do we generate some sort of global ethics if we have forsworn universalistic ethics? And if we cannot defend a genuinely global ethics, aren't we then reduced to contests of power rather than knowledge? (Here the skepticism of Michel Foucault is the dead end we want to avoid.)

It is at precisely this point that scenario planning has a contribution to make in solving puzzles that political scientists and philosophers have never properly solved. A set of alternative scenarios that play out various world futures, each presupposing a different set of ethical principles, can demonstrate to one and all the various consequences of different ethical principles. We can have our "good intentions" and our consequences, too. (In the technical language of philosophers, we can balance de-ontological *and* consequentialist ethics; Kant *and* Mill; the ethics of good intentions *and* utilitarianism.) Different sets of intentions drive different scenarios, and then the texts of the different scenarios can illustrate the utilitarian consequences, after which we can choose those consequences that are most appealing.

Most appealing. What does this mean? On one interpretation it could sound extremely subjectivistic, like a matter of taste. On another interpretation, what is most appealing is the kind of beauty that appeals to almost everyone, e.g. famous art that lasts the ages: Shakespeare, Bach, Renoir. This nexus between ethics and beauty in the concept of the *most appealing* takes us from Part Three of this essay, where we have been considering scenario planning in its relationship to a new kind of science of complexity, to Part Four, where we consider the role of art and beauty as guiding lights for the inevitably evaluative dimension of normative scenarios.

Part IV: Art and Ethics—the Aesthetics of Normative Scenarios

What we've seen in Part One is that scenario planning should not be dismissed as *merely* art; nor, as shown in Part Two, can it be admitted to the club of the sciences if the membership committee raises the bar so high that only deterministic, predictive sciences can join. In Part Three we saw how a new kind of science, influenced by complexity theory and enriched with story, can benefit by being supplemented with stories called scenarios. But a question remains: By what criteria should one scenario be regarded as *more appealing* than another? Is it just a matter of individual taste? Is it simply a question of subjective preferences? Or are there inter-subjective and shared criteria for judging one future as more appealing, and therefore better, than another? If we can find *objective* criteria, would they therefore be operative for all people everywhere, universal?

When confronted with these thorny questions at the heart of ethics, aesthetics—the theory of art and beauty—has a contribution to make. Beauty is not *just* in the eye of the beholder. It is not completely subjective. Nor is it so objective as to be universal. Different cultures have different standards of beauty. The history of art shows that, even in the traditions of one culture, ideas about beauty are subject to gradual change. In western European culture, Rubenesque plumpness was more prized in previous centuries than in today's Slim-fast America.

If we try to model our ethics on mathematics, if we require our standards for The Good to exhibit the universality and eternity of Platonic Ideas, then we are bound to be disappointed by the discoveries of anthropologists who rub our noses in the *differences* among value systems. Different cultures really do have different values. It's a fact. Read the evidence of values surveys that span different cultures.[13] But the cultural relativity of preferences for individualism or collectivism, to take just one example, should not blind us to commonalities where they exist. Amnesty International will have little difficulty in finding broad acceptance for its opposition to torture, so long as it does not frame its opposition in the distinctly Anglo-European tradition of human rights.

There are both differences and commonalities among values—differences sufficient to arouse a postmodern skepticism regarding standards that are true and objective for everyone everywhere, and commonalities sufficient to refute the nihilism of

---

13   See, for example, Geert Hofstede, *Culture's Consequences: International Differences in Work-Related Values,* Sage Publications, London, 1984; Charles Hampden-Turner and Alfons Trompenaars, *Seven Cultures of Capitalism,* Doubleday Currency, New York, 1993.

subjective relativism. Dostoyevsky's Smerdyakov was wrong. Even if God is dead, it is *not* true that all is permitted.

Where do we see standards like this—standards that transcend individual whim, even as they lack universal objectivity or eternal fixity? In art, that's where. Our sense of beauty is neither utterly subjective nor totally objective; neither fleeting nor eternal. In taking art and beauty as a guide for ethics, I do not mean to maintain the Epicureanism of the aesthete or dandy. I'm not trying to *reduce* ethics to aesthetics, but I am claiming that the cultural relativity, context dependency, and historicity of our sense of beauty provide a guide or a likeness for the way ethics work.[14]

The point worth making within the pages of *World Futures*, is that future studies in general, and scenario planning in particular, can supply a crucial missing link in an argument that Richard Rorty, in his resuscitation of John Dewey, almost makes, but not quite. Let me quote Rorty, who quotes Whitman:

> The best way to grasp the attitude towards America which James and Dewey took for granted, and shared with the audiences who heard their lectures, is to reread Whitman's *Democratic Vistas*, written in 1867. That book opens by saying:
>
> *As the greatest lessons of Nature through the universe are perhaps the lessons of variety and freedom, the same present the greatest lessons also in New World politics and progress…*
>
> *America, filling the present with greatest deeds and problems, cheerfully accepting the past, including feudalism (as indeed, the present is but the legitimate birth of the past, including feudalism) counts, as I reckon, for her justification and success, (for who, as yet, dare claim success?) almost entirely on the future… For our New World I consider far less important for what it has done, or what it is, than for results to come.* *
>
> In this essay I shall focus on Whitman's phrase 'counts… for her justification and success… almost entirely upon the future'. As I see it, the link between Whitmanesque Americanism and pragmatist philosophy — both classical and 'neo-' — is a willingness to refer all questions of ultimate justification to the future, to the substance of things hoped for. If there is anything distinctive about pragmatism it is that it substitutes the notion of a better human future for the notions of 'reality', 'reason', and 'nature'. One may say of pragmatism what Novalis said of Romanticism, that it is 'the apotheosis of the future'.[15]

---

14 For a longer and more careful articulation of the relationship between ethics and aesthetics, see my essay, "Art and Ethics," in *The Journal of Value Inquiry,* Vol. X, No. 1, 1976, pp. 1-6.

15 Richard Rorty, *Philosophy and Social Hope*, Penguin, 1999, pp. 26f.; * Walt Whitman, *Complete Poetry and Selected Prose*, New York: The Library of America, 1982, p. 929.

If I can summarize Rorty's and Whitman's point as succinctly as Hayden White summarized Hegel, it seems to me that, if what they are saying is right, then *the future has replaced objectivity as the horizon of justification.*

If that is so, then postmodern critiques of "the myth of objectivism" need not lead to a nihilistic, relativistic morass. We can have our hopes, and the discipline of justification too.

And if *that* is so, then scenario planning becomes the arena in which global ethics can be legitimately practiced, with a rational basis for binding obligation even in the multiple contexts of irreducible cultural pluralism. A set of scenarios can provide a very broad tent under which different traditions and cultures can gain a hearing. But once we spin out the scenarios that follow from their stories thus far, then we are in a better position to judge which consequences are preferable, which are *most appealing.*

Judgments based on appeal amount to interpretations of value. As opposed to a utilitarianism that thinks it can *calculate* the greatest good for the greatest number, an appreciation for the irreducibility of interpretation knows that some people will see the facts one way, others another. Hermeneutics is the discipline or philosophy of interpretation. In a world filled with symbols and a plethora of different cultural contexts, we cannot escape the need for hermeneutics. But Hermes was known as a trickster. Hermeneutics is tricky.

Philosopher Paul Ricouer distinguished between what he called "a hermeneutics of suspicion," and "a hermeneutics of belief."[16] The former is reductionistic; the latter amounts to a more hopeful interpretation of the symbolic products of sublimation. The former will say that art (to put it very crudely) is *nothing but* a sublimation of the smearing of feces; the latter will say that art can create something new under the sun whose meaning and beauty cannot be reduced to rearrangements of the same old stuff. The symbols may be the same—a painting, a piece of music, a play—but the interpretations will be quite different depending on whether one approaches those symbols with a hermeneutics of suspicion or a hermeneutics of belief.

Ricouer's distinction can serve as a bridge toward higher levels on a hierarchy of desire, a hierarchy that includes Maslow's hierarchy of need, but extends even lower to animal hunger, and even higher than individual self-realization toward the shared hopes of a community. Scenario planning provides *alternative interpretations* of the present as the first chapter to several different futures, some good, some bad, some beautiful, some ugly.

A normative scenario of a better future can act like a *telos* luring a community toward a better state of being. A better future is a beautiful future. A better future can

---

16   Paul Ricouer, *Freud and Philosophy: An Essay on Interpretation,* trans. Denis Savage, New Haven, Yale University Press, 1970.

motivate a community to action much in the way that the object of love motivates a lover. To the extent that the articulation of a normative scenario motivates a community toward the action required to realize that future, the articulation of a normative scenario then acts like a *telos.*

Teleological behavior is no mystery where the articulation of a normative scenario has efficacy in the present. Causality isn't running backwards from the future to the present. But it does make sense to speak of a "downward causality" where the emergence of symbolic consciousness exercises an influence on the manipulation of matter in the present—say, the building of a dam to create a water supply and electric energy in the future.

Here's the significance of the argument built on Rorty and Whitman, that the future has replaced objectivity as the horizon of justification: The future will tell us *which interpretation* of the present was correct. *We'll see* whether the hermeneutics of suspicion or the hermeneutics of belief turns out to have made more sense. *Time will tell,* not the time of monological science, but the time of history.

The time of human history, the time of the evolution of increasing complexity, is different from the time of monological science. The little t in all those equations containing ds/dt, or even its differential, $\delta s/\delta t$, is not the time of lived human existence. This was Heidegger's main point in *Being and Time.* The time of monological physics is a flattened out, Cartesian time, well symbolized by graph paper whose every square is the same size as every other. It is *chronic* time—the time of *Chronos* not *Kairos.*

In kairotic time, the time of genuine history where something new under the sun can occur, epiphanies are possible. In chronic time, on the other hand, the future is *nothing but* a series of rearrangements of the same old stuff. As LaPlace quite rightly understood, events in chronic time *are* in principle predictable once you have sufficient data about the stuff, together with a table of laws covering the dynamics of its rearrangement. Chronic time can be calculated forwards as well as backwards. Chronic time lacks an arrow. The inability to explain lived time's arrow stands as the great embarrassment of monological physics. Nor will entropy do the trick of explaining time's arrow.[17] But kairotic time, the time of history and lived human existence, points inexorably from the actual toward the possible.

Uncertainty regarding the interpretation of the present is justified because the future of kairotic time is not predictable. Kairotic time is not just "the moving image of eternity," as in Plato's *Timaeus,* or the unrolling of a predestined plan, as in Christian eschatology. Our blessedness does not consist in salvation guaranteed by forgiveness. Forget the rapture of the chosen people. Our blessedness consists

---

17   Cf. Kauffman, *Investigations, op. cit.,* p. 151.

in the genuine possibility of both heaven and hell here on earth. This is why our choices matter, and why freedom is so important.

To the extent that communities can frame more beautiful futures in the form of normative scenarios, then their shared hopes can act like a shared desire that constitutes a *telos*. Such *teloi* then exercise downward causality. They inform present action toward the ends of better futures.

Nothing, of course, is guaranteed. Teleological explanations of the form, *x happened for the sake of y*, where no consciousness was at work in making *y* happen are, as Spinoza showed us, otiose. Our blessedness consists precisely in the fact that happy endings are in suspense, that no amount of monological science is sufficient to make beauty predictable. It is not the case that everything happens for a reason. Some things are just caused. Contingency is real. Feces occur. Just as it can all come together in instances of emergence where the whole is greater than the sum of the parts and irreducible to the properties of prior components, so can it all come apart. The center may not hold.

With episodic exceptions like the imminent arrival of my ravishingly beautiful wife, or yet another performance of the Goldberg variations, beauty is never predictable. At a level of abstraction above the episodic repetition of known beauty, there will never be another Tricia Mulligan Ogilvy; there will never be another Johan Sebastian Bach. This is how history and life *are*, and it explains why contemporary art can never just repeat yesterday's genius (with the shocking exception of Warhol's repetitions that artfully challenge, at yet a higher meta-level, this very principle of unrepeatability).

Part of the preciousness of each particular instance of beauty lies in its almost infinite unlikelihood. This is why Georges Bataille went to the trouble of calculating the probability of his genetic inheritance as one out of 225 trillion.[18] And this is why Kauffman is so right to observe that:

> ...if the biosphere is getting on with it, muddling along, exapting, creating, and destroying ways of making a living, then there is a central need to tell stories. If we cannot have all the categories that may be of relevance finitely prestated ahead of time, how else should we talk about the emergence in the biosphere or in our history—a piece of the biosphere—of new relevant categories, new functionalities, new ways of making a living? These are the doings of autonomous agents. Stories not only are relevant, they are how we tell ourselves what happened and

---

18   George Bataille, *Œuvres complètes*, Paris, Gallimard, Vol. VI, p. 445.

> its significance—its semantic import. In short, we do not deduce our
> lives; we live them.[19]

Since the interpretation of current events, and the very categories we use to interpret them, are contingent on their outcome, what *will* come true; and since the outcome of current events is genuinely in doubt—uncertain, subject to the unpredictability of the future—we are therefore pressed nose to the glass against the *sublime*, which the romantic poets and philosophers found to consist not in some high plateau, but in the contrast between the heights and the depths. That's why the romantic poets, particularly Wordsworth in the Simplon Pass passage of the *Prelude*, rely so heavily on the imagery of the Swiss Alps as a favorite medium in which to express their sense of the romantic sublime. It's not just the heights that impressed them, but the cliffs, the steep descents from lofty peaks down into the abyss. High mountain waterfalls do it. You could watch them for hours. Big surf does it, with rhythm. The collapse of the World Trade Center towers did it as tragedy. Orgasm does it as ecstasy.

You need multiple scenarios to appreciate the sublimity of the present. False confidence and insipid affirmations of inevitable progress point only to the heights. Cynical contempt for hope and all-knowing declarations of imminent doom point only to the depths. Just as Fitzgerald declared genius to lie in the ability to hold two contrary ideas in mind at the same time,[20] so it seems that access to the sublime requires a healthy respect for both the tragic and transcendent potentials of the human condition.

My colleague and co-founder of Global Business Network, Stewart Brand, is fond of quoting Bernal's pithy line, "Desire always misreads fate." For reasons stated above (about the folly of believing in fate) I find this saying insightful but one-sided. It contains a kernal of wisdom shrouded in a cloak of pessimism. I would rather revise it to read, *Desire often misreads facts.* Our values, our biases, our hopes and desires often lead us to misread the evidence in front of our faces. But sometimes desire, in the form of shared hopes articulated in normative scenarios, can lead us to create what we end up calling fate in retrospect: *So it had to be, because we cared enough to make it so.*

What was and is does not reach the limits of what could be or should be. This is the gift of time and futurity—the reality and importance of possibility, the potential for new beauty and greater good. We should not limit ourselves to the best of the past. Better futures await us if we take the trouble to design them and make them so.

---

19   Kauffman, *Investigations, op. cit.*, pp. 134f.

20   In the opening pages of *The Jazz Age.*

In Tony Blair's powerful speech to the Labor Party Congress at Blackpool on October 1, 2002, he made the point that politics is all about the conflict between hope and pessimism. Without hope, the people perish. With hope alone, devoid of a respect for truth or science, the people will perish just as surely. Narratives—stories with suspense, alternative scenarios—contain this perpetual conflict between the creative art of articulating what we want on the one hand, and the science of what must be on the other. Scenario planning is the medium through which we mediate this age-old dialectic. Both the science of what is and the art of what might be come together in sets of scenarios. These stories about the future pit our desire for the good and the beautiful against our obedience to what is and must be.

3. Equity and Equality: Education in the Information Age[21]

Originally published by OECD under the title: Ogilvy,J.(2006), "Education in the Information Age: Scenarios, Equity and Equality", in OECD, Think Scenarios, Rethink Education, OECD Publishing, http://dx.doi.org/10.1787/9789264023642-3-en

In this paper I'd like to address the application of scenario planning to the future of education. The first part of the paper is about method. The longer second part of the paper fills in some content. The third part reflects on the combination of method and content. The brief first part talks about different uses of scenarios, while the second illustrates some of the methodological points by offering an example of scenaric thinking specifically directed to one of the main preoccupations of 21st century education scenarios: The promise of the information age and the tools we'll need to make good on that promise. The third part then points toward the integration of that promise into scenarios for the future of education.

Part I: Implementing Scenario Planning

When different teams from different school districts meet to discuss a common set of scenarios, there's a danger that they find the scenarios irrelevant to their own particular locale. "These are not *our* scenarios. This is not *our* reality." This is a common problem. At Global Business Network we have a saying: *Scenarios are a little like sex—talking about other people's is never as interesting as your own.*

In propagating the use of scenarios we face a dilemma: If you supply ready-made scenarios, buy in and ownership can pose a problem. But if you expect each nation, each district, each school site to create its own customized scenarios, you may lack the resources to provide skilled facilitation, research, and the time necessary to do the job right.

There is a way through this dilemma. Very briefly, the solution is to provide a scenario starter kit, a toolbox. The question is just how much or how little to put in the toolbox. To answer this question, I would like to frame my remarks in terms of three different uses of scenarios:

---

21   This paper has been modified from a speech presented to a conference sponsored by the Organization for Economic Cooperation and Development (OECD), The 2nd *Schooling for Tomorrow* Forum, "Learning from Schooling for Tomorrow—Advancing the International Toolbox," June 6 - 8th, 2004, in Toronto, Ontario. Part of the work leading up to that speech was supported by the Annenberg Institute for School Reform.

1. To provoke strategic conversation

2. To stimulate genuinely new, visionary thinking

3. As a motivator for getting unstuck

1. Scenarios as tools to provoke strategic conversation

One of the main benefits of scenarios is their capacity to engage participants in a process of civil conversation about the future of education. A set of alternative scenarios provides a very broad tent under which people with widely differing, and often passionately held, views can speak with one another about their children's future. Because scenarios are "just stories," and not yet plans cast in concrete, they can be entertained and discussed in a realm well short of dedicated commitment. Because scenarios are divergent, because they do not, at first, force convergence on consensus, they allow widely different views go gain a respectful hearing. For this reason, they are good tools for engaging an entire community or an entire nation. Scenario planning is a safe game for consenting adults where you don't get blood on the walls.

This positive feature of scenario planning has its downside for educators, however. Where business people tend to be action oriented, educators tend to be talk oriented. When conducting scenario planning in a business context, it is often difficult to get entrepreneurial managers to have the patience needed to develop a set of scenarios about different possible environments without leaping ahead toward actions to be taken this coming Monday. Business people don't want to talk about what their world may do to them; they want to talk about what they can do to their world. They don't want to take the kind of "outside-in" perspective characteristic of scenario planning; they want to take an "inside-out" perspective—an activist perspective characteristic of entrepreneurs.

Having worked both sides of the street—in education policy and in business—I'm here to suggest that scenario planners in education need to be cognizant of these tendencies. It's important to be aware of educators' preference for talk over action. Faced with strategic choices, educators are inclined to ask for further research and more deliberation where business people will opt for immediate action. As business consultant, Tom Peters, put it: "Ready, fire, aim!" Educators want to aim, and aim carefully, before they fire. They want to think first—for good reason—and act later, sometimes so much later that action never quite happens.

Knowing this, scenario planners in education need to make sure that scenarios do not become a pretext for endless conversation. They need to make sure that scenarios *get used to make decisions*. To that end, they need to make sure that those who are capable of making and implementing decisions take ownership of whatever ready-made scenarios are placed in front of them. And for that purpose, one of the best methods is to engage participants in a participatory exercise that *uses and enhances* the scenarios without necessarily disassembling and reassembling them.

In our experience, one of the best such exercises is the development of lists of *early indicators*. This exercise has a dual function: first, the process of brainstorming early indicators for each scenario requires an immersion in the content and logic of each scenario. As people try to imagine the first signs of a given scenario, they inevitably find themselves imaginatively occupying the world described by that scenario. Once so engaged, and once they find themselves contributing early indicators, they are more likely to take ownership of the scenarios. Where this first function may be a covert result of the *process* of engagement, the second function is providing the overt product—the lists of early indicators. As the second part of this paper will argue in greater detail, early indicators—of scenarios, and of the success or failure of schools or individual students—are much more to be desired than trailing indicators when remediation is inevitably too late.

So to summarize this first methodological point about the uses of scenarios: the good news—their divergence allows different views a respectful hearing; the bad news—educators may listen and talk forever without acting. So make sure that people *engage* with the scenarios and use them to make and implement decisions. And to that end, engage them in the process of developing lists of early indicators.

2. Scenarios can stimulate new, visionary thinking

Just as we tend to parent the way we were parented, so we tend to educate the way we were educated. It's not easy to imagine genuinely new ways to do something so utterly familiar to all of us. So fundamental a feature of the human experience is about as subject to innovation as eating or sleeping. But we *have* changed our eating habits. Improved nutrition has extended life expectancy. Surely we should be able to imagine better ways to educate.

Part of the challenge lies not only in the inertia of fixed habits but in the systematic interconnections among the many parts of our educational systems. As systems theorists are wont to say, *you can't change just one thing.* Try to change one aspect of the curriculum—e.g. class size—and you upset other parts of the system. In California, Governor Pete Wilson surprised both the citizens and the teachers' union with a reduced class size initiative. What a wonderful idea! We all knew that young children were not getting enough individualized attention in large classes. But what seemed like a good idea at the time had not been thought through. Had there been detailed scenarios, the Governor might have seen the consequences of the consequences, namely, that smaller classes would require more teachers and more classrooms. As it happened, the initiative resulted in a sharp increase in the number of inner-city children learning in makeshift trailers from hastily recruited and uncredentialed "teachers." What seemed like a good idea at the time ran the danger of increasing, not decreasing, the inequality between poor inner-city schools and rich suburban schools.

Scenarios, just because they are whole stories and not analytic theories, can provide a format for entertaining systemic change. Well short of pie-in-the-sky utopian thinking, positive scenarios can depict the interactions among the many, many parts of the education *system:* teachers, students, buildings, parents, the local community, new technology, the school-to-work transition, economics, etc. There is no single silver bullet for educational reform, and no one reform is likely to survive unless it is synched up with other parts of a *new* system that will support it. Change just one thing, and the rest of the system will pull that reform back into the old equilibrium, as many reformers have discovered. But in order to change everything at once, you need the kind of holistic, comprehensive vision that a positive scenario can provide.

Just because systemic reform is so challenging, positive scenarios are very difficult to invent. Negative scenarios are much easier—you just describe the demise and destruction of what you already know. But positive scenarios must paint something new under the sun, a reality as yet unseen. For this reason, positive scenarios run the risk of rejection for being too Pollyannaish, too optimistic, too utopian. Just as it's difficult to anticipate technological breakthroughs—who knew they needed a Xerox machine before it was invented—so it is difficult to anticipate what a better school would look like. But unless we are prepared to believe that the schools we have are the best we *could* have, we have to believe that the breakthroughs are out there, just beyond the horizon of habit and familiarity. And scenarios are the tools for stimulating us to imagine those holistic, comprehensive, systemic reforms that go beyond simplistic, silver bullet solutions.

In keeping with the methodological hint about using early indicators to engage audiences in scenarios they did not invent themselves, here is a hard won hint for shaping positive scenarios in a way that will enhance their acceptability: Let them be short, not long; sketchy, not detailed. In a book entitled *The Springboard: How Storytelling Ignites Action in Knowledge-Era Organizations,* author Stephen Denning advocates what he calls a "minimalist" style of story-telling—brief vignettes that purposely leave a lot to the hearer's own imagination. Precisely by leaving a lot of space for the reader or hearer to fill in for him or herself, minimalist stories enhance the likelihood that the reader or hearer will take ownership of a story to which he or she has contributed.

Minimalist storytelling also manages a marriage of convenience with the main challenge of positive scenarios: Smarter minds than ours have tried to invent a better education, and they haven't succeeded yet. This is a *hard* problem. If we had solved it already, we'd already be in that more positive scenario. The fact that we *need* school reform is itself evidence that we lack the solutions we need to give a detailed description to a more positive scenario. So for that reason as well, best to leave the positive scenarios somewhat sketchy. Paint the allure, but leave a veil of unknowing. Precisely in order to seduce, don't try to show it all.

3. Scenarios as motivators for getting unstuck

The methodological advice is precisely opposite in the case of negative scenarios. Muster all the production values at your disposal to paint worst case scenarios that are so ugly they function like morality plays: There but for the grace of good planning go we, and we don't want to go there!

The movie, *The Day After Tomorrow,* does not claim to be great science... but the special effects people in Hollywood and their portrait of New York under ice may have done more to stimulate broad concern about carbon-dioxide and rapid climate change than any number of scholarly discourses on the subject. Doom and gloom scenarios are psychologically difficult—we don't like worst case scenarios, even in our imagination—but they are intellectually easy to draw. You don't have to invent a *better* way; you just have to destroy the existing way. By rehearsing the disaster in imagination, you may avoid it in reality. Negative scenarios drawn in all their gory detail can deliver a kind of *anticipatory disaster relief.* They can motivate lethargic masses by inspiring the fear of God—or the hell of the worst case scenario.

It's not hard to imagine bad scenarios for education. In his book, *Savage Inequalities,* Jonathan Kozol describes schools so decrepit and classrooms so hopeless you want to weep. We've already seen how bad it can get in some places. It could get that bad in other places, too... unless we attend to those savage inequalities. The second part of this paper is therefore devoted to the issue of educational inequality, and what it might take to reduce it. While not cast in the form of a scenario—it is not a story with a beginning, a middle, and an end—it nonetheless illustrates some of the methodological points made in this first part. Though far short of a systemic solution to educational reform, it provides a minimal sketch for improvement by way of an extended analogy between what I'll call "precision schooling," and the already existing practice of precision farming. It's just a sketch, but it highlights the importance of early indicators, and the promise of new information technologies.

Part II: A Declaration of Educational Equity

Over two centuries ago, America's *Declaration of Independence* stated, "All men are created equal." Women, unfortunately, had to wait over a century before they received the vote, and some women are waiting still for full respect of their humanity. And people of color continue to fight racism and the legacies of disadvantage.

Over a century ago The United States fought its only civil war to put an end to slavery. During the 1960s the civil rights movement, led by the likes of Martin Luther King Jr., sacrificed more lives to bring an end to segregation in our schools. The idea of "separate but equal" education did not deliver on the promise of equal rights to "life, liberty, and the pursuit of happiness."

The noble quest to honor the dignity of all citizens is being tested once again. For many reasons—from the invention of the automobile and the advent of the suburbs to the information revolution and the globalization of the job market—we now find ourselves in a situation where people of color are not receiving the equal rights granted to them under the laws of most OECD countries. Nor are the poor in developing nations around the globe receiving the kind of schooling that would help lift them out of poverty.

Call the problem the crisis of urban education in the advanced nations, or— following Manuel Castells' description of pockets of poverty in both advanced and developing worlds in the new, globalized information economy—call it the crisis of the "black holes of informational capitalism."[22] In fact it is most sorely felt as a crisis for people of color. During the last half of the 20th century, white flight from the centers of many major cities left minorities in old and run down schools while many of the mostly white children attended newer and better staffed schools in the suburbs.

According to the law, or *de jure,* the U.S. ended segregation with the Civil Rights Act of 1964 and Supreme Court decisions like *Brown vs. the Board of Education.* But *de facto*— in fact—segregation is still with us. The facts are overwhelming and irrefutable. When you compare the educational performance of inner city children with suburban children, you find an intolerable gap in achievement.

This gap is morally intolerable. We are all worse off if some of us are denied the tools they need to pursue life, liberty and happiness. This gap is also economically intolerable. In the information age, in what some call the knowledge economy, we are all worse off if some of us cannot read. We are all worse off if some of us

---

22 Manuel Castells, *The Information Age, Vol. III: End of Millennium,* Blackwell Publishers, Cambridge University Press, Cambridge, 1998, esp. Chapter Two, "The Rise of the Fourth World: Informational Capitalism, Poverty, and Social Exclusion," pp. 70-165.

cannot write. We are all worse off if some of us cannot solve the simple tasks of reading a bus schedule or writing a check. We are all worse off if some of us can't cope with more complex tasks like filling out the forms to manage our own health or the health of our loved ones.

The benefits of the information revolution and the knowledge economy extend mainly to those who have the knowledge to use information to their own and others' benefit. As long as we fail to close the education gap between people of color in our inner cities and the rest of our children, we will be denying those minority children their hard won rights to life, liberty, and the pursuit of happiness. And we will be denying our economies a crucial resource: a skilled labor force capable of competing in today's global economy.

Educational inequity is everybody's problem. We all have much to gain—or much to lose—depending on how well we address what Kozol calls *Savage Inequalities*. You cannot blame parents, black or white, for moving to the suburbs to find better schools for their children. And you cannot blame minorities for poor academic achievement in schools that their classmates abandoned for good reason. But you can and should expect citizens to tackle a problem which, left unsolved, will hurt all of us.

We must come to grips with educational inequity—boldly, intelligently, and with the courage of our convictions. If the great mission of the 20th Century was to extend the vote to many people worldwide, regardless of race, religion, or gender, then the great mission of the 21st Century may well be the extension of educational equity to all people, regardless of race, religion, or gender.

Over 40 years ago President Lyndon Johnson declared a "War on Poverty." Institutions like The World Bank, the IMF and the OECD have been fighting this war around the world. We have not won this war, in part because we mistook the real enemy. In a knowledge economy, the only way you can win the war on poverty is to wage war on ignorance. We can finally win the war on poverty if, first, we win the war on ignorance. But in order to win the war on ignorance, we need to address the black holes of informational capitalism in developing nations and in the urban ghettoes. How will we go about solving the problems of educational inequity and *de facto* segregation? And what should the role of federal governments be in providing a solution?

The first step consists in recognizing the seriousness of the problem. The second consists in gaining clarity about its origins and causes. Our public schools bear the scars of their birth in the agricultural and industrial eras. Unlike other professionals, teachers get long summer vacations because, when our public school system was first founded, students were expected to spend their summers tending animals and harvesting crops.

The industrial revolution also left its marks on our schools. During the first half of the 20th century there was a major change in the way we educated our children. Educators were deeply influenced by the lessons of scientific management that allowed the industrial revolution to lift so many out of poverty. Henry Ford introduced methods of mass manufacturing for the mass market of America's increasing middle class. Where craftsmen in the 19th Century hand-crafted carriages one by one for an elite clientele, Henry Ford invented the assembly line to mass-manufacture identical Model-Ts at a price his workers could afford. The cars were cheap because they were produced by the tens of thousands. Mass manufacturing produced economies of scale.

Scientific management and the industrial revolution were great achievements that helped to build economies. No wonder our educators wanted to model schools after factories. The scientific progressives of the early 20th century achieved economies of scale in education by creating large schools to replace the one room school houses. Students were seated in rows as rational and orderly as the factory floor. In the name of equity, they were given identical lessons in lock-step sequences modeled on the assembly line [23] Industrial age education worked after a fashion. High school graduation rates increased many-fold between 1900 and 1960.

But that was then, and this is now. That was the industrial era improving on the one room school houses of the agricultural era. Now we are heirs to an information revolution every bit as important as the industrial revolution. But we haven't yet updated our schools according to the lessons of the information revolution.

Industry now uses the fruits of the information revolution to achieve efficiencies without resorting to economies of scale. Rather than relying on mass markets that want more and more of the same, same, same, new methods of manufacturing use computers to customize different products for different customers.

From Precision Farming to Precision Schooling

Not just industrialists but farmers as well are using the fruits of the information revolution to improve their yields. In the past ten years, information technology has come to agriculture under the name Precision Farming. Farmers now track last year's yields foot by foot as their combines cross their fields. They use satellite imagery to spot patterns on their fields, sensors on the ground to test for moisture, and global positioning satellites and onboard computers to customize the distribution of seeds, water, herbicides and fertilizers foot by foot as their combines cross their fields.

---

23   For a much fuller description of the influence of the industrial age on education, see Peter Senge, "The Industrial Age System of Education," in *Schools That Learn,"* Doubleday, New York, pp. 27-58.

Some information is gathered at harvest time. Equipped with GPS, a combine can pick and weigh a crop and record the information as it crosses a field. (Think of outcomes, standards, and accountability as analogues.) GPS, plus data storage in an onboard computer, can record the yield from every square foot of field. This information is then used when the field is next tilled, planted, treated and fertilized.

Sensors on the ground and satellite imagery also gather information on soil quality and moisture. That information, too, can be factored into the application of seeds, herbicides and fertilizer, foot by foot across a field, all automatically as an onboard computer adjusts the settings for sowing, tillage, fertilization, or spraying.

By knowing what each square foot of field needs, then using that knowledge to administer what is wanted, precision farming moves beyond an industrial paradigm.

In the past, the fertilizer plant mixed the ingredients in known proportions, and the farmer distributed them from one tank in the field. However, today's most advanced equipment carries the fertilizer elements in separate tanks, both to and in the field, and mixes them on-the-fly just before dispersal. To accomplish this, the farmer must mount a GPS receiver on the fertilizer truck so that the equipment knows its location in the field. An in-vehicle computer must contain the fertilizer-needs maps, which it compares to the field position data arriving from the GPS receiver. It also controls the distribution valves and gates to provide an appropriate fertilizer mix.

> As the truck moves about the field, thus changing the GPS-derived address, the fertilizer mix will change as directed by the fertilizer-needs maps. When everything is working right, the equipment applies the appropriate amount of each fertilizer element to every area (site) in the field. This is where the words 'site-specific-farming' were derived. [Think 'site-based management' as the educational analogue.] Each site in a field is treated uniquely according to its needs. Not only does this process have the potential to reduce the amount of fertilizer used, and thereby lower cost, it also has the potential to protect the environment by minimizing the quantity of chemicals released.[24]

The old industrial paradigm would "mass manufacture" plants using a standardized, uniform distribution of elements. The new paradigm treats each plant site individually, optimizing the mix of elements—what is wanted and what is provided—foot by foot.

---

24   Rex L. Clark, "Practices and Potential: Assessing an Agricultural Revolution in Progress," University of Georgia, available at http://www.precisionfarming.com/features /0497Clark. html

We used to ask, "If we can put a man on the moon, why can't we [and we would fill in the blank with phrases like 'end poverty,' or 'cure cancer?']" Let us now ask, "If we can apply technology to optimize our farming, individual plant by individual plant, then why can't we apply technology to optimizing our schooling, individual student by individual student?"

Once upon a time we farmed and we schooled individual by individual. A farmer walking his fields could treat different plants differently depending on an up close appraisal of what each plant needed. The teacher in the one room school house could treat each student individually because she knew them each as individuals. Then the industrial paradigm took over, both in agriculture and in education. Individual-by-individual craftsmanship was inefficient. We started mass manufacturing both plants and students. Industrial agribusiness worked pretty well at increasing crop yields. Mass manufacturing students according to an industrial paradigm was less successful. It seems that students are less responsive to standardized procedures than plants. One size/dose does not fit all, whether we're talking about fertilizer or arithmetic. But plants don't talk back, at least not so as most of us can hear them.

The industrial paradigm works with economies of scale: The more widgets you produce using the very same elements and procedures, the lower the cost per widget. Impressed by the economies of scale achieved by industry, both our schools and our farms fell under the influence of the industrial paradigm. But now industry itself, in our new information era, is yielding to what some call "a post-Fordist paradigm." Using computers and programmable robotics, our manufacturing facilities are achieving economies of scale with much shorter runs. They call it "adjustable manufacturing." Levi's can be cut to order using information gathered about individual bodies. Benetton can adjust the mix of dyes and colors upstream at its manufacturing facilities depending on the colors that consumers pulled off the shelf on any given day. By retrieving that information from every Benetton shop in the world every day, Benetton can optimize its supply chain to meet customer needs and desires for the immediately following days. And now even agriculture is yielding to this post-industrial, information-driven, post-Fordist paradigm. Can education be far behind?

For many decades, education was managed according to inputs: How many teachers? How much seniority did each teacher have? How many hours of in-service training? These were the criteria used to allocate resources and adjust rewards. Now, as in other industries like health care, the attention is shifting from inputs to outputs. In health care we hear talk of "outcomes research." In education we hear talk of standards and accountability.

What precision farming adds to the picture is a portrait of the way the measurement of outputs can be used in real time: "on-the-fly just before dispersal," as the quotation above puts it. It's important to know that one hospital has a better record of results than another in its cardiology unit when your mate needs bypass surgery. It's important to know that one school does better than another at getting its graduates into their first-choice colleges. But how much better it would be if the measurement of outputs could be combined with the measurement of conditions "foot by foot" and "on-the-fly" so that inputs could be adjusted in real time to treat each student "uniquely according to its needs."

School district turnaround consultant, Karen Hawley-Miles writes:

> We already know that most urban schools do not meet state or district performance standards. Student performance is a lagging, not immediate measure of whether schools are providing the kind of instruction that is likely to improve student performance. Estimates of how long it takes to improve test scores range from three to seven years... Reviews of efforts to intervene once schools have failed show that such rescue attempts are unpredictable and expensive. By the time a school has dramatically failed, the cost to turn it around can be high and the time it takes to do so even longer.[25]

Efforts at farming once fields have failed—once the nutrients have been stripped, or erosion has taken its toll leaving dust or hard-pan—are likewise unfruitful. So farmers don't wait for fields to fail. They close the cybernetic feedback loop from assessment to intervention in real time, minute by minute, as combines cross fields, foot by foot.

Hawley-Miles suggests the need for *leading* indicators of performance rather than lagging indicators of failure. If we can find leading indicators analogous to the evidence of on-the-ground sensors and satellite imagery, then we'll gain the "Ability to act *quickly* to *support* and make necessary *changes* in failing schools."

How far can we push this analogy? Clearly there are limits to both its accuracy and its usefulness. One thinks of the character, Chauncey Gardner in Jerzy Kozinski's novel (and the movie starring Peter Sellars), *Being There*. Gardening images seemed to provide profound and refreshing insights compared to the stale rhetoric of Washington politics: "A time to plant... a time to harvest..." Let's beware of pushing this analogy too far.

Children are not vegetables. There are important differences between plants and higher vertebrates, most especially those that can talk. Vegetables may be more

---

25   Karen Hawley-Miles, "What 'Equity' Means for Urban District Design," Annenberg Task Force on the Future of Urban Districts, The Annenberg Institute for School Reform, 2001.

complex than the inorganic materials that are baked and bent by industrial processes, but children are even more complex than vegetables. Hence Hawley-Miles cautions: "The idea of measuring leading indicators of instructional improvement does not suggest mandating a particular curriculum, instructional approach or way of organizing schools."

Even if we had better measures of success or failure, school by school or student by student, it's not clear that we know what to do with that data. We probably know more about what it takes to grow asparagus under different conditions than we know about what it takes to grow young minds under different condition.

We lack the educational equivalent of a precisely articulated formula for balancing the mix of nutrients needed for maximum plant growth because human beings are far more complex than artichokes. And so much the better! Let's hear it for human freedom and creativity, even if we pay a price in complexity!

To be more specific about the *differences* between children and vegetables, it's worth pausing on what we are learning about the differences between children. As we made the transition from the agricultural era to the industrial era, one of the main missions of the public education system—in the United States at least—was to *socialize* children from many different backgrounds. As rural families came down off the farms to find jobs in cities, and as immigrant families came to America from different lands, there was a need to offer a common curriculum that would socialize children toward a common experience of shared citizenry.

In the information era, the job of socialization is largely accomplished by the media. The first signs of this functionality of the media came when families huddled around their radios to hear the first national broadcasts of shows like Milton Berle's Comedy Hour, or Edward R. Murrow's newscasts. Today, much to the chagrin of the French, American media beam American culture worldwide. The job of shared socialization is being accomplished all-too-well for those who would like to protect indigenous cultures. But this means that the mission of public education can shift: from industrial era standardization to information era customization. Like information era farmers, information era educators can afford to treat each student differently, and the differences that make a difference are not only differences in age, income, and ability—analogous to plant heights and irrigation needs—*but also differences in learning style.*

As a result of the pioneering work of Harvard psychologist, Howard Gardner, we now have a cogent theory, and an increasing body of evidence, to support the idea that simple measures like IQ (Intelligence Quotient as measured by Alfred Binet) need to be supplemented by subtler diagnostics on at least seven different types of intelligence—linguistic, musical, logical-mathematical, spatial, bodilykinaesthetic, inter-personal, and intra-personal intelligence.[26] Skilled teachers have always recognized that some students learn better by listening, others by reading, still others by acting out new ideas with their whole bodies. Now we have a theory that allows us to diagnose and systematize these different aptitudes and learning styles.

In the future, there is every reason to believe that we will have learning tools that will allow us to diagnose each individual student in ways that will permit us to treat each student, individually, every hour of every day, "on the fly," with just those educational tools and lesson plans best suited to his or her needs and aptitudes. We will have interactive educational computer games that will automatically diagnose each player's learning style. Such software will accommodate itself not only to so-called "self-paced learning;" it will also permit self-styled learning.

With due respect to the differences between growing minds and growing plants, the force of the precision farming analogy is to underline the fact that we are currently acting as if we do have the formula for raising minds, and it's *one size fits all.* Much of the rhetoric of the standards movement pushes toward industrial era standardization. The power of the precision farming analogy is to stress the need for more accurate early indicators and assessment tools in order to make nonstandard adjustments "on the fly"—granting the fact that we still lack a precisely articulated formula for adjusting our "nutrients" once we have better assessments.

Another aspect of precision farming might also suggest limits on how far we can push the analogy to precision schooling.

> When yield-mapping technology first emerged, many thought the goal would be to produce a uniformly high yield. However, the cost of such an approach (both in real dollars and in environmental impact) may lead toward a system that attempts to optimize yield in relation to profit. We may find that some areas should not be farmed. In fact, precision farming may cause farmers to adopt practices that produce even more yield variability than they initially found in the fields.[27]

Because farmers needn't value the dignity of every plant, it makes sense to *optimize* rather than maximize or equalize. But educators committed to equity should not be willing to write off a single school or a single student.

---

26   Howard Gardner, *Frames of Mind: The Theory of Multiple Intelligences,* Basic Books, New York, 1985; and by the same author, *Intelligence Reframed: Multiple Intelligences for the 21st Century,* Basic Books, New York, 1999, where Gardner entertains the addition of three additional types of intelligence: naturalist, spiritual, and existential.

27   Clark, *op. cit.*

Granting such limitations to the analogy, however, it is precisely the distinction between equity and equality that calls for careful assessment of leading indicators and quick interventions. 'Equality' can be legislated, and equal dollars per student may flow to different schools. But a closer look at the differing needs of different students—special education, bilingual education, students at risk, and different learning styles for different types of intelligence—shows that the industrial standardization of 'equality' is not adequate.

In place of industrial standardization, we need a more organic understanding of different needs and how to satisfy them. And for that understanding, we could do worse than take a few lessons from the analogy with precision farming. There we find the application of information technology to the task of identifying different needs, and real-time interventions applying different "solutions" to make a difference "on the fly." If farmers can grow cornstalks one by one using information to customize their nutrients one stalk at a time, isn't it high time that we educate our children one by one, one student at a time?

According to the old industrial model, equity meant equality: masses and masses of the same, same, same. When someone suggested to Henry Ford that he produce Model-Ts in different colors, he replied, "They can have any color they want so long as it's black." Given the manufacturing methods of his time, to introduce other colors would have been too expensive. But with computer-aided manufacturing, different colors, even different color combinations, are less costly. Information technology makes custom coloring affordable, just as it makes custom fertilizing affordable. A farmer tries to grow equally tall corn by adding different amounts of nutrients as needed by each different plant.

Likewise with education, equity is not achieved by pumping the same inputs into every school. An information age approach to schooling can close the gap by treating each school, each student, differently as needs require. You use information technology to identify particular needs, and then you meet those needs by using information technology to administer different "nutrients" affordably.

Skilled teachers have always known that each child is unique, and they've done their best to teach one student at a time. But skilled teachers have been fighting uphill against over-crowded, factory-like classrooms and assembly-line lesson plans. In order to achieve educational equity in the information era, we need to make a break from the old industrial-era model of mass-manufacturing well-socialized, identical students. We need to gather information about each district, each school, each student, and use that information to adjust the levels of "nutrients"—whether dollars, or teachers, or text books, or computers—as each school, each student requires. As the example of precision farming shows, this is an affordable, attainable dream in the information age.

We've already begun to gather some of the information we need. This is what the educational standards movement is all about—finding out who is doing well and who is not. But the standards movement, at least as it is currently being practiced in the United States, is out of step with the information revolution. It is entirely too focused on standardization—as if the federal government were trying to tell each and every state and school district how to run its schools. Educational standards could be used to gather information to treat different schools differently in order to achieve educational equity. But in most States and most school districts, the standards movement has become a club to punish under-performing schools, not a diagnostic tool to enhance the education of individual students. Just as the farmers need those geographic positioning satellites looking over everybody, so we need some national standards as tools of measurement. But we must use that information to differentiate: to customize the spread of nutrients, not to impose some uniform solution.

Differences that Make a Difference

If our first principle for reform is educational equity, then our second principle, derived from the difference between the industrial era and the information era, is that equity calls for differences that make a difference, not just a uniform spread of the same standardized inputs.

Consider a third principle that should guide our retooling of education for the information era. That third principle is the role of market forces when it comes to spreading valuable resources. Government still has a job to do. But government's job has more to do with assuring that markets operate fairly and properly.

How might market mechanisms apply to public education? Our public education system has been described as the last bastion of socialist bureaucracy. School boards and district central offices operate like state monopolies. Parents and students have no other choice of provider, as they would in a free market. In most businesses a manager can make changes to accommodate the different needs of different customers. But after decades of tough negotiations between school boards and teachers' unions, the public education system, in the U.S. at least, has become hog-tied by hundreds of agreements that forbid teachers and principals from making the changes needed by students. The American public education system is not so much broken as it is locked—frozen into immobility by miles of print in volumes of code sitting on yards of shelves in every state capitol. We must unlock this System if we are to unleash the innovation we need to educate our children for the information age.

Let's not blame the unions for defending the interests of underpaid teachers. Let's not blame the school boards or superintendents or their staffs in those much maligned central offices. These are for the most part good people trying to do the best job they can. But the game has been rigged in such a way that the harder you play, the more you lose. Teachers lose when the rules won't allow them to be rewarded for jobs well done. School administrators lose when the rules won't allow them the flexibility they need to make improvements. And worst of all, students lose when locked into obsolete, industrial assembly lines that give them no choice among schools or teachers. We must cut through this educational gridlock and create the rules for a better game, one where students win and teachers and administrators win as well.

Here's how.

First, we will use the information we are gathering from standard tests and other more subtle diagnostic tools to identify the needs of each student, each school, and each district.

Second, we will allow each school to purchase the supplies, the skills, the personnel it needs to satisfy the needs of its students. Because the information we gather will show that some students have special needs, schools will be allocated special funds to meet those special needs.

Third, students and their parents will be given the opportunity to shop around for the schools and teachers that best meet their needs. Funding will follow the flow of student choices. Schools will be allocated funds based on the needs of the students in their care. Schools that are chosen by unusually high numbers of students with special needs will be given correspondingly larger budgets. Those budgets can be spent on increased salaries for those unusually gifted and heroic teachers who can succeed with students at risk.

A system like this will allow market mechanisms to allocate valuable resources far more equitably than the system now in place. Market forces will reward results—outcomes rather than inputs. Our current system rewards inputs—years of service, courses taken, credentials—rather than proven effectiveness of teachers or schools. The genius of the market is precisely to process information: information about needs and preferences that a monopoly can afford to neglect. Part of the reason for the fall of Communism lay in the fact that centrally planned economies were literally *stupid:* They ignored information about individual needs and preferences because they had no way to register the results of preferential choices. Centrally planned economies were all push, no pull, all efferent nerves, no afferent nerves. Resources were allocated by central planners, not by the millions and millions of choices made everyday in the marketplace.

Clearly, markets have their limits. We now know better than to push for the privatization of everything. Market mechanisms tend to produce winners and losers. Wherever there is a social mandate for universal service—e.g. for communications systems, national security, health care, *and education*—there is a role for governments to play in compensating for market imperfections. But an abiding role for government should not fool us into thinking that centrally planned education monopolies are superior to a combination of market mechanisms and governmental oversight.

We should be prepared to pay much more for good teachers than we pay them today. Good teachers deserve to be compensated like other skilled professionals. But we will not be able to free up the funds to reward those good teachers until we break the rule-bound bureaucratic gridlock of most current systems.

If we're going to pay more to those teachers who step in to close the gap between inner-city students and others, where are we going to get the money? A fourth principle says that *urban education is a national crisis that federal governments must address.* Our largest cities are national cities, not just the prides of different states or provinces. Some have even called them global cities.[28] New York and London are the financial capitols of the world. Paris and Milan are the fashion capitols of the world. Los Angeles is the entertainment capitol of the world. The San Francisco Bay Area is the global capitol of the internet. Miami has been called the capitol of Latin America, just as Sidney and Brisbane serve many needs throughout Southeast Asia. It would be wrong to expect local districts to shoulder by themselves the costs of closing the gaps in their urban schools. This is a job for federal governments.

Still, education is a local responsibility because young children need to sleep in their own beds at night, close to their parents and their local jobs. Unlike manufactured goods that can travel from low cost producers to consumers around the world, schools are as geographically rooted as corn stalks. Children should go to schools in their own neighborhoods. Like good managers of successful businesses, local school boards should have the ability to make decisions about the allocation of precious resources. The reforms we need will not take the form of some single cookie-cutter plan imposed on all states, all provinces, and all school districts. Quite to the contrary, by introducing market forces into the system, we can allow different districts to purchase the resources they need to meet the different needs of the students they know best.

But you can't send someone to market with no money and then expect market mechanisms to work fairly. The way the system is now operating, urban districts are at a disadvantage. In the U.S., 18 different States have declared their current educational funding systems unconstitutional because they fail to deliver on the constitutional promise to educational equity. We must right this wrong, but not by taking money away from some to compensate others. Left to their own devices,

---

28   Cf. Saskia Sassen, *The Global City,* Princeton University Press, 1991.

different States could achieve equity only by redistribution—leveling to the middle, taking from the privileged to compensate the under-privileged. Because educational equity is a national if not a global problem, federal governments need to get involved to level the playing field by "leveling up"—by giving extra funds to urban districts so that they can come to market with the funds they need.

To summarize the principles that will guide us going forward:

First, equity as the equal right to life, liberty, and the pursuit of happiness which, in the information age, demands an end to ignorance.

Second, in this information era, equity calls for *differences that make a difference*, not just a uniform spread of the same standardized inputs.

Third, market mechanisms must supplement down-from-the top bureaucracy when it comes to allocating different resources to different local needs. This is how we get different inputs to make a difference in outcomes.

Fourth, while education is a local responsibility, federal governments have a job to do to make sure that urban districts have the funds they need to level up.

Putting these principles into practice is a big job. It calls for leadership and local support. We all have a lot to gain—students, teachers, school administrators, parents, and employers—if we can break the gridlock we've inherited from our agricultural and industrial models of education. We now live in an information era with a knowledge economy. We must wage a war on ignorance, a war we all can win.

Part III: Putting Information Era Content into Scenario Form

In Part One I suggested that positive scenarios are best presented with a suggestive minimalism, while negative scenarios should be painted in gory detail with all the production values that Hollywood can muster. Part Two suggests an analogy: from precision farming to precision schooling. Precisely because it is *only* an analogy, the argument of Part Two leaves plenty of room for readers and hearers to fill in the analogy *for themselves*, and thereby to take ownership for the corresponding scenarios and the reforms they suggest.

If there is one thing we have learned about educational reform it is surely this: *Educational reforms do not travel well.* Inspired teachers create inspiring classrooms. Dedicated principals create high performing schools. Great leaders can even create superior school districts. But rarely have reforms invented and applied in one place taken root in others. It is as if education is condemned to act out the not-invented-here (NIH) syndrome: If *we* didn't invent it, *we* won't use it!

Perhaps there is a good reason for the NIH syndrome. Rather than fighting it by attempting to find ways to "scale up" or "scale out" various local reforms, perhaps we should join with our neighbors to acknowledge our need to perpetually re-invent the wheel of customized, individualized education. After all, different locales, different communities, and different schools are every bit as unique as different students. Why should we expect one size to fit all? The aspiration to discover reforms that can be scaled up to fit everyone everywhere is an aspiration that bears the obsolete mark of the industrial age. Educational reform cannot be mass produced for a mass market. Educational reform, if it is to be true to what we now know about individual human beings in the information era, *must* be customized—to the district, to the school, to the individual student. This is a large part of what we mean by "precision schooling."

Does this discovery mean that no one in one country or community has anything useful to say about education to anyone in any other country or community? No. For there are useful tools that can be applied to produce customized results in many communities, e.g. scenario planning.

In this concluding section, I would like to suggest two reasons why scenario planning works especially well for effecting educational reform in widely different contexts. The first has to do with simply motivating the effort; the second speaks to the beauty of the fit between what is needed—customized solutions—and what scenario planning provides.

A large part of the challenge of improving education consists in generating the *political will* to address the problem. In all too many countries and communities, people simply don't care enough about education to devote the resources required. But experience has shown that if you gather together a few dozen members of a community and ask them to engage in scenario planning to improve the future of their community—without stating in advance that the agenda is education—by the end of a single scenario workshop lasting 10-15 hours, they are almost bound to conclude that one of the best things they can do is to improve their schools.

The train of logic is almost ineluctable: Who will occupy the future? Their children. How can they create a better future for their children? By making sure that their children are sufficiently well educated to create that better future for themselves.

Once a community has built the political will to allocate resources to education, then comes the question: How best to allocate those resources? The answer will depend in part on local conditions: What sorts of jobs are locally most plentiful? What languages and customs are locally prevalent? What sorts of values predominate? Individualist or collectivist, sacred or secular? Answers to these questions are not the same the world over, so the educational philosophies that guide curricula should not be expected to be the same the world over, no matter how much it may be true that $2 + 2 = 4$ everywhere and always.

Negative scenarios painted in gory detail can motivate a community to devote sufficient resources to improving education. Positive scenarios that only suggest by analogy certain directions for improvement can seduce local ingenuity. That local ingenuity will then fill in the gaps left by minimalist scenarios. Local ingenuity will create specifics that are appropriate to local conditions. Finally, the reforms invented by local ingenuity will be proudly owned by local reformers. Local ingenuity is required because countries, communities, and individuals really are different. This is part of the gift of freedom: that we make up the human game as we go along, and that we do so differently according to the local lights of human creativity. Scenarios are tools for social creativity—tools for creating better futures, not one best future.

Section II:

Scenario Planning in Context

4. Future Studies and the Human Sciences:

The Case for Normative Scenarios

Originally published in Futures Research Quarterly "Future Studies and the Human Sciences: The Case for Normative Scenarios," Vol. 8, No. 2, Summer 1992, pp. 5-65. Reprinted with permission.

Introduction

Simply to be a human being is to be a futurist of sorts. For human freedom is largely a matter of imagining alternative futures and then choosing among them. Conversely, to be a good futurist, I will argue, one must at least aspire to being a good human being. One must care about the welfare of others. One's visions of the future must be informed by more than the science of what *is* or an imagination for what *might be*; one's visions of the future must also be informed by a sense of what *ought* to be.

In order to achieve a convincing justification for better futures, we need to rethink the very nature of future studies in the larger context of disciplined inquiry. If there is such a thing as futurology—a disciplined *logos* or discourse about the future—is it an art or a science or, as many suspect, nothing more than hopes and fears dressed up as science?

Put the question in a very concrete way: if futures research is indeed a legitimate field of disciplined inquiry, then why are there so few courses or departments of future studies in our major universities? Why is futures research not recognized by academics as one among the many *disciplines?*

Let's face it: those of us who call ourselves futurists are not likely to wear this badge proudly when we are surrounded by academics. We are thought to be intellectual charlatans, soothsayers in business suits, tea-leaf readers and crystal ball gazers with little more credibility than astrologers. Where is our body of evidence? What is our methodology? How can we possibly claim a place at the academic high table when we have so little in the name of legitimate scholarship that we can offer? Go to the library today to do research on the future and you will not find one book copyrighted in the year 2020.

Faced with the slimness of our academic portfolio, we find ourselves on the defensive. We turn to our computers and our databases; we develop models; we debate methodology as if we were building the foundations for a science. We refine our polling procedures, twiddle our statistical techniques, and do our very best to make our trend analyses and technology forecasts look as thoroughly engineered as the technologies we are forecasting.

In our anxiety about our academic credentials we are tempted to become holier than the Pope, more scientific than the scientists, more rigorous than mathematicians. And in such a mood, the last thing we want to hear about is normative scenarios. We want *facts*, not values. We want well-founded theory, not well-meaning morality.

There is, consequently, a constant danger of bad faith in the work of most futurists. Eager to escape the charge of subjective bias, of claiming that what we want to happen will in fact happen, we do everything we can to make sure that our scenarios of what *will* happen have been scourged of every relic of what we ourselves might *want* to happen.

I call this bad faith, not because I think we are unsuccessful in scourging our hopes. I call it bad faith just to the extent that we *are* successful. To the extent that we mimic scientists in claiming value-free objectivity in our view of the future, we deny the very thing that makes us good human beings and good futurists. We deny that we *care*. But we must care. If we do not, we are doomed to a dreadful future.

All very well and good, you say. But so far we have only the makings of a windy commencement address. Where's the beef?

One approach to establishing the legitimacy of future studies would be to argue, from accepted ideas about what constitutes a science, that future studies is indeed a science, but that, because we are good, caring people, we will use this science for the betterment of humankind by developing better futures. We might place future studies on the firm foundations of accepted science and then, on the strength of that foundational manoeuver, make the further argument that a good science must be an ethical science. This is precisely *not* the strategy I will follow.

Rather than defensively placing future studies on the firm foundations of science, I want to pursue an offensive strategy. I want to show how very infirm the so-called foundations of science have become. Rather than dragging future studies over into the camp of the sciences, I want to show how the so-called human sciences are moving in the direction of future studies.

In short, *we futurists* (including all human beings trying to shape their own futures) don't have to learn how to play *their* game of objective, value-free science; *they* are learning to play ours. The human sciences are moving through a paradigm shift that makes them much more amenable to the work of the futurist and far less pretentious about their place at the academic high table with the hard sciences.

The burden of Part One is to *show* this movement among the human sciences. It is not enough simply to *say* that the paradigm shift is here. And there is no brief way to demonstrate in detail the very real movement taking place in the fields of anthropology, psychology, literary criticism, philosophy and sociology. All it takes is a passing glance at recent trends in these disciplines to show that the human sciences are moving toward a widespread recognition of the need for value-laden better futures. These disciplines are adopting normative scenarios as an essential feature of their own new ways of seeing the facts.

What a sad irony it would be if, just as these reinforcements from the human sciences arrived to support futures research, futurists themselves had decamped in the direction of the hard sciences!

Given the range of subjects to be discussed, and the conclusions yet to be reached, it may be worth a few more words about how I came to the views I am expressing. While teaching philosophy at Yale, I found myself under the imperative to specialize. I found myself being backed into the corner of becoming an expert on Hegel—the pre-eminent generalist. But my real interest lay in accomplishing today something akin to what Hegel achieved in 1807: a holistic view showing how the different parts of human endeavor relate to one another in the dance of history.

Then I moved to California, and, at the invitation of Peter Schwartz and Arnold Mitchell, spent seven years working at SRI International (formerly known as Stanford Research Institute) where it seemed easier to Hegelize than at Yale. An academic environment riven with departmental barriers that are maintained by an imperative of specialization does not provide a congenial environment in which to Hegelize, which is quite different from specializing in Hegel.

One of the first tasks I undertook at SRI International was a collaboration with Peter Schwartz on a monograph entitled, The Emergent Paradigm: Changing Patterns of Thought and Belief. In that 1979 report we reviewed thirteen different disciplines to trace the features of a new paradigm. To our surprise that report, which was not easy going for most readers, generated quite a bit of interest. This book is an attempt to push further some of the ideas contained in that 1979 report.

At GBN, our main method for fostering strategic conversation is the generation and use of alternative scenarios. We build those scenarios around specific decisions being made by policy makers and strategists. We do not make predictions. Instead we think through several possible sets of consequences that today's decisions might have. By developing alternative scenarios that are explicitly linked to decisions facing executives, we guarantee that the differences that divide our scenarios from one another are differences that will make a difference to the decisions in question. We design our scenarios in such a way as to highlight the most important uncertainties surrounding the outcome of today's decision.

Sometimes the most important uncertainties are technological: will battery technology move ahead fast enough to permit a light enough electric car? Sometimes the most important uncertainties are economic: will the growth of the economy in general be strong enough to sustain demand in a specific market? More often than many futurists may care to admit, the most important uncertainties are social and cultural: the differences between the sixties and the eighties are best described in socio-cultural language rather than in technological or economic terms. The new values of the sixties and seventies, the anti-authoritarianism that drew strength from the resistance to the Vietnam war, the experiments with consciousness with drugs and mysticism, the rise of feminism, the awakening of awareness of the environment, and the preoccupation with self-realization that ranged from the quest for spiritual enlightenment to the narcissism of what Tom Wolfe called the Me-decade—each of these waves of social change that began in the sixties are still rippling through the nineties. But as these waves break on the shore of the next millennium, how will they give shape to the future?

Rather than trying to predict the future of American values on the basis of some theory of social change, the best we can do is develop alternative scenarios. But these scenarios need not be completely neutral. A case can be made for constructing scenarios that range from normative portraits of what *ought to be* to negative portrayals of the punishments in store for us if we do not clean up our act. The case for normative scenarios needs to be made these days because the worship of science over the past century or so has led us toward a kind of methodological embarrassment over our values.

I have seen big science at SRI, I have plowed the fields of the humanities at Yale, and I have experienced their uneasy union in the practice of contract research and corporate consulting. It is just the uneasiness of this union that provokes me to publish this monograph. The union of the sciences and the humanities is uneasy precisely where human beings with values try to be scientific about the values of human beings. This is a situation that is ripe for self-deception when the analyst and the analysand are one and the same.

We cannot lift ourselves by the bootstraps up and out of the practice of the revaluation of values we are purportedly studying. We are both the experimenter and the experiment. We are both the laboratory technician and the laboratory itself. But it is just this sort of self-referential, foundationless reflection that distinguishes philosophy from other well-founded disciplines. Just this sort of high wire act differentiates philosophy from the ever so much safer piling of fact upon fact—the humble masonry of historians or the simple carpentry of botanists, or the complex but well-founded explanations of physicists. Philosophy has no such solid foundations.

In the following pages I hope to tease out some relationships between future studies and philosophy, but this endeavor should not be confused with an attempt to give a philosophical *foundation* to future studies. It is precisely the quest for firm foundations—whether philosophical or scientific—that current philosophy tells us is impossible. Rather than borrowing firm foundations from philosophy, it is just the recognition of foundationlessness in philosophy that I would take as a guide for learning how to do without the pretensions of scientific foundations for future studies.

In our work with alternative scenarios, we constantly come up against several interrelated questions having to do with human values. It is clear that one of the most important drivers of energy demand is people's willingness to conserve energy. Will people be willing to drive a "green" car that is slow off the mark at stop lights? How much air pollution are they willing to breathe? How many homeless will they allow on their doorsteps?

These questions are all questions about values. They do not turn on questions of technological feasibility but on the very human question of what people will want in their lives in ten to twenty years' time. What part of a full human life will be most scarce and therefore of the highest value? Time? Meaning? Money? And if we could know that a sense of meaning will be more important than money, how would that skewing of the ecology of value tend to revalue other parts of life? For anticipating fundamental shifts in the economics of *value,* anticipating changes in *values* is essential.

But very difficult. Possibly impossible. Because if anything is a function of human freedom, you would think that the revaluation of human values would be a prime candidate. If our values are like a hard-wired, read-only program, then we are pretty mechanical creatures, hardly free at all. Only if we can write over at will, only if we can reprogram the human biocomputer can we be said to be free.

The primacy of freedom as defining the human means that the prediction of human values is in principle impossible. As Aristotle formulated the paradox over two millennia ago, if you can know the future, then you can't do anything about it; if you can do something about the future, then you cannot know it in advance.

You can no more predict human values than you can predict movements in contemporary art. It is the artists that will do something about the future of art, and it is human beings who will revalue their values. If either one is predictable, then she is not an artist, he is not a human being. Both beauty and humanity share an inherent unpredictability.

Likewise neither humanity nor art can invent their futures by the force of novelty alone. New for the sake of new won't do. There must be some sense of continuity, some connection with eternal depths, even as there is a clear articulation of just why some break with tradition is so urgently required. The battle of the young against the old will always be at play in the playfulness of creativity. Does it require strong elders for the struggle to be intense? Is intensity what one most wants out of this struggle? What about clarity of identity, which is, after all, what this struggle is all about. *Who will we want to be* ten or twenty years hence? What passions will most motivate us? *What is the future of desire?*

So one objective of this study is to deal with the question: What will the values of Americans look like in the year 2020? I say 'deal with' rather than 'answer' the question because my response is oblique. Rather than trying to forecast American values over the coming decades, I will tell you, as one among several possible scenarios, what I want and hope American values will become. And I will add to this normative scenario an account showing why such *advocacy is the only epistemologically authentic stance where values are concerned.*

I cannot predict American values in the year 2020, not only because we lack a covering law to serve as the engine of prediction, but also because the very nature of valuation is to transgress all attempts at prediction. It would be nice to imagine that advances in sociology and anthropology would allow us to take some reading from our distant past, our recent past and our present and plot them on some theoretically grounded metric where we could apply some elegant covering law to project a series of readings for the near and distant future—with increasing plus or minus estimates of uncertainty for increasingly distant futures. It would be nice to imagine that futures research could aspire to reducing these plus-or-minus error factors, refining skill in prediction, minimizing risk. But this is not what our discipline is about. It is instead the articulation of risk so that we have some sense of *what is at stake* in our daily decisions.

To summarize the major point of this introductory section, the line of argument I am pursuing—away from a foundation on fact or scientific theory and towards a more creative and willful endeavor—drives future studies toward becoming a kind of collectively practiced existentialism. The existentialist philosophers—Heidegger, Camus, Sartre—had a great deal to say about the importance of entertaining the various possibilities that open before an individual entertaining his or her future. While I am eager to acknowledge the importance of the existentialists' emphasis on temporality and the future, I want to part company with their emphasis on the individual. Camus' stranger is the quintessential solitary misfit. Heidegger's authentic *Dasein* may die alone, but is this any reason to believe that we must live alone? In his *Being and Nothingness* Sartre struggles to cross what can only be regarded as a self-imposed "reef of solipsism." All of this philosophical individualism is, I would argue, an artifact of the very limited, parochial perspective of two centuries of West European philosophy. Sartre saw as much late in his life but he had to lurch into Marxism to find a congenial medium for a social perspective to balance his early emphasis on the solitary individual. But Marxism is not the only medium for acknowledging the sociality of human existence. In steering future studies toward becoming a *social existentialism,* I hope to be able to avoid both the individualistic extremes of existentialism as well as the socialistic extremes of Marxism.

All these -isms—individualism, socialism, existentialism, Marxism—are just so many ways of talking about that same uneasy union between the sciences and the humanities, the uneasiness I experienced moving from academic philosophy departments into contract consulting at SRI, the uneasiness C. P. Snow addressed in his famous essay on the two cultures; the uneasiness that comes from the fact that science wants to be value-free but the future is very much shaped by values. This uneasiness is captured in the phrase 'the human sciences,' which some regard as an oxymoron. The human sciences seem to straddle the gap between the hard sciences and the humanities.

What I hope to show by the following review of recent developments in the human sciences is this: rather than trying to found their own legitimacy on mimicking the hard sciences with their solid methodologies and confident access to objectivity, the human sciences are accepting their irreducibly symbolic and therefore inevitably ambiguous status. They are acknowledging their foundationlessness and accepting the finality of interpretations in place of facts. They are therefore waking up to the ineluctable *interestedness* of the human sciences, to the absurdity of claiming that sociology or social philosophy can conduct their inquiries in a wholly disinterested manner. We must *care.* If we don't, then all is lost. But if we do, then we are hardly disinterested.

Thus do these several strategies and objectives come together: the first, a justification for normative scenarios; the second, the placement of future studies in the context of the human sciences; the third, coming to terms with the risk of bad faith by ignoring our own values in shaping our visions of the future. These three strategies support one another. Having justified normative scenarios, it is easier to stop ignoring one's own values in the name of objectivity. And the claim to objectivity turns out to be empty in any case, if reports from the other human sciences are to be believed.

We begin with these reports from the human sciences, for it is there that the criteria for scientific objectivity are tested. The basic criteria that define the difference between science and mere opinion can be said to make up a paradigm. While future studies could not sit easily in the context of the scientific paradigm inherited from the Enlightenment, it can play a central role among the human sciences following a paradigm shift away from the old paradigm toward something new, something that lacks a name, something that might clumsily be described as a post-modern paradigm.

I will begin by saying more about the concept of a paradigm in general, the nature of paradigm shifts, and the outline of the Enlightenment paradigm. The rest of of this essay takes a tour through recent paradigm-bursting developments in anthropology, literary criticism, philosophy, psychology and sociology.

1. The Emergent Paradigm in the Human Sciences

During recent decades, a good deal of attention has been given to some fundamental shifts in assumptions about science and scientific method. T.S. Kuhn's *The Structure of Scientific Revolutions* is usually invoked as the source of talk about paradigm shifts. But earlier sources arguing the perspectival and historical nature of science can be traced back to the philosophies of Kant and Hegel, and later sources are necessary to argue for a contemporary paradigm shift where Kuhn describes only past paradigm shifts.

For our present purposes, the point at issue is not so much the fundamental assumptions underlying any one discipline; rather, the point at issue is the nature of scientific explanation or inquiry in general. What counts as good science?

Scientists and philosophers of science have been working at cross purposes. While philosophers of science have been trying to codify the methods of scientists in earlier centuries as a way of arriving at a precise method for what counts as good science, physicists, chemists, biologists and many researchers in the human sciences have been merrily forging ahead using methods quite different from their predecessors.

Philosophy of science flourished under the banner of logical positivism, a school of thought founded by the Vienna Circle which included the young Ludwig Wittgenstein, Moritz Schlick and Rudolf Carnap. Their insights were anglicized by Bertrand Russell and A.J. Ayer. The essence of this worldview, and its implications for science, can be captured in a few propositions.

1. The world is the totality of empirically measurable atomic elements moving in space and time.

2. Motion in space and time takes place according to universal, deterministic, causal laws that cover all situations.

3. In order to explain complex phenomena like biological growth or human thought, it is necessary and sufficient to reduce those phenomena to their physical, constituent, simple parts and then plug state descriptions of those parts into equations representing well confirmed general laws.

4. One way to confirm general laws is to test their predictive power. Thus, if laws L1, L2, ..., Lr enable one to predict events of type E from antecedent conditions C1, C2, ... , Ck, then those laws are confirmed, and event E can be scientifically explained. In a classic statement by Carl Hempel and Paul Oppenheim:

> If E describes a particular event, then the antecedent circumstances described in the sentences C1, C2, ... , Ck may be said jointly to "cause" that event, in the sense that there are certain empirical regularities, expressed by the laws L1, L2, ... , Lr, which imply that whenever conditions of the kind indicated by C1, C2, ... , Ck occur, an event of the kind in E will take place.[29]

The import of logical empiricism for future studies is as follows. If everything under the sun really can be described according to deterministic, predictive, causal laws, then the agenda for futurists is plain: take the past and present as antecedent circumstances C1, C2, ... , Ck, discover general laws L1, L2, ... , Lr, and set about predicting future events E1, E2 *ad infinitum.*

No one, of course, thinks this sort of cranking out of predictions is really possible. But debates over methodology in future studies hinge on the precise reasons *why* the positivist program is not possible. Is it simply that we have not yet discovered the relevant laws of social change and technological diffusion? Or is it that we have not yet clarified the correspondence rules that would relate complex epiphenomena like thoughts or social change to their atomic, material constituents?

Any number of reasons could be given for the current failure of the positivist program. As long as the reasons given are of the type suggested, then the debate over methodology in future studies will gravitate toward better measurement techniques, improved polling procedures, or statistical techniques and modelling tools that might uncover lawlike regularities amidst masses of data.

I would like to suggest that such efforts, however useful for particular purposes, are fundamentally misguided as putative answers to current questions about futures methodology. As an alternative to the covering law model of scientific explanation, I would like to suggest a new paradigm of scientific explanation. In short, futurists should borrow a few leaves from their colleagues in some other human sciences.

In the following sections, I want to take a brief tour through some new developments in the human sciences. The purpose of these brief explorations is not to glean new discoveries or general laws that can be exploited by futurists in their efforts

---

29   Carl G. Hempel and Paul Oppenheim, "The Logic of Explanation," *Philosophy of Science,* 15, 1948; reprinted in *Readings in the Philosophy of Science,* ed. Feigl and Brodbeck, New York, 1953, p. 324.

to make predictions. To the contrary, the purpose is to see how researchers in several disciplines that may be regarded as more mature than future studies have already abandoned their pretensions to the kind of predictive science to which some futurists still aspire.

Each of these sections will begin (*a*) with a discussion of recent paradigm shattering developments in the field under review, then conclude (*b*) with a brief discussion of some direct implications for future studies. Section 7 will then abstract from the human sciences taken as a group a set of features of an emergent paradigm.

2a. Anthropology: From Explanation by Law to a Semiotic Discipline

Once upon a time, the practice of anthropology was a pursuit of the origins of mankind. Grubbing about among the bones and broken crockery of ancient civilizations, anthropologists sought clues from which to reconstruct the social habits of prehistoric human beings. Among more than a few students of anthropology, this quest after origins was also a quest after *essence*: if we knew more about the advent of civilization, then perhaps we would better understand the deepest mysteries in the contemporary human heart. Perhaps the riddle of human nature, and the endless debate between nature and nurture, could be unlocked if we just knew more about the first humans. Were they noble savages? Were they social beings or loners? Loving or aggressive? Matriarchal or patriarchal? These questions were pursued as if their answers could tell us something important about contemporary society, e.g. the fate of feminism or the plausibility of a political ideology based on the perfectibility of the human heart. From Marx to Margaret Mead, arguments based on anthropology made claims about human nature that were based on anthropology's access to the first terms in the "language" of human culture. Call it the Adam and Eve school of anthropology.

The achievement of structural anthropology was a breakthrough from a preoccupation with individual terms—first or last—to an articulation of structures and relations. And not just relations among terms, but relations among relations among relations.

Levi-Strauss asserts that, "The kinship system is a language,"[30] but denies that the "meanings" of its terms can be derived from some anthropological analogue to etymology. "A kinship system does not consist in the objective ties of descent or consanguinity between individuals. It exists only in human consciousness; it is an arbitrary system of representations, not the spontaneous development of a real situation."[31]

---

30   Claude Levi-Strauss, *Structural Anthropology,* trans. Jacobson and Schoepf, New York, 1963, p. 47.

31   *Ibid.,* p. 50.

Also like languages, kinship systems reveal structures of relations so abstract as to defy any attempts at foundational analysis seeking an origin in some first term. In studying societies of the Cherkiss and Trobriand types, one finds, "the relation between maternal uncle and nephew is to the relation between brother and sister as the relation between father and son is to that between husband and wife."[32] Not originary or natural terms, but relations among relations determine the meanings of the resultant relata.

Structural anthropology, as developed by Claude Levi-Strauss, made the move from atomic terms to "molecular" relationships. But Levi-Strauss tended to think of some relationships as fundamental, even universal. However varied and arbitrary the vocabularies of different myth systems, for example, "The vocabulary matters less than the structure." Further:

> If we add that these structures are not only the same for everyone and for all areas to which the function applies, but that they are few in number, we shall understand why the world of symbolism is infinitely varied in content, but always limited in its laws. There are many languages, but very few structural laws which are valid for all languages. A compilation of known tales and myths would fill an imposing number of volumes. But they can be reduced to a small number of simple types if we abstract from among the diversity of characters, a few elementary functions.[33]

Levi-Strauss moved anthropology away from the atomism of an original, essential human nature that could biologically dictate the structure of human society. But the structures of relations he put in place of elementary atoms came to play a role in anthropological theory that was not so very different from the role of Adam and Eve terms. To reach these unchanging essences—relational though they may be—all we have to do is, "abstract from among the diversity of characters, a few elementary functions."

More recently, anthropology has moved beyond the quest for universals of the sort that might be evident in first terms or first relationships. The problem is simply that the quest for universals leads toward insights that tell us less and less about more and more until we learn nothing about everything. It is always possible to say *something* that will be true of everything and everyone. But as the rich variety and distinctnesses of different cultures become evident with ever more research, the question arises: are the samenesses more essential to human nature than the differences? As Clifford Geertz puts the question:

> Is the fact that "marriage" is universal (if it is) as penetrating a comment on what we are as the facts concerning Himalayan polyandry, or those

---

32   *Ibid.,* p. 42.

33   *Ibid.,* p. 203f.

> fantastic Australian marriage rules, or the elaborate bride-price systems
> of Bantu Africa?... it may be in the cultural particularities of people—
> in their oddities—that some of the most instructive revelations of what
> it is to be generically human, are to be found.[34]

Geertz's contributions to anthropology manifest several aspects of a paradigm shift. Not only does he accept the move from primary terms to structures of relationships—"In short, we need to look for systematic relationships among diverse phenomena, not for substantive identities among similar ones"[35]—but further, he argues that these systematic relationships, once revealed, have a different status from that of the laws of human nature anthropologists once sought. Geertz regards anthropology as, "not an experimental science in search of law, but an interpretive one in search of meaning."[36] The difference is immense.

The difference between the quest for law and the quest for meaning has implications that extend far beyond anthropology. The distinction extends throughout the human sciences to psychology, sociology, and history. At stake in this distinction is nothing less than the nature and reality of human freedom.

Geertz calls his concept of culture "essentially semiotic." Semiotics is the theory of signs, of how they signify and mean what they mean. In regarding culture as semiotic, Geertz is treating the artifacts of culture like a language. The advantages of this approach are several. For one thing the old debate between subjectivism (culture is in people's heads) and objectivism (culture is patterned behavior) seems simply irrelevant since language is so clearly both. Another advantage lies in the quick end-run around the closely related issue: is culture public or private? "Culture is public because meaning is."[37]

The greatest advantage of the semiotic approach to culture, however, is the light it sheds on the role of symbols in constituting the human condition. According to an older view, symbols, sign systems, language and literature come only very late in the human story. First, it was thought, we had to deal with nature. Only later could we afford to dabble in culture. It is mankind, after all, that manufactures symbols.

But symbols manufacture man as well. We *are* our marriages, our wars fought beneath flying banners, our oaths cast in blood and language. We *are* the results of our dedications to our symbols. Human beings are unique among animals for this self-making evolutionary creativity that takes place alongside of strictly biological

---

34   Clifford Geertz, *The Interpretation of Cultures,* New York, 1973, p. 43.

35   *Ibid.,* p. 44.

36   *Ibid.,* p. 5.

37   *Ibid.,* p. 12.

evolution. "What this means is that culture, rather than being added on, so to speak, to a finished or virtually finished animals, was ingredient, and centrally ingredient, in the production of that animal himself."[38] Our physical and cultural evolution is thus a kind of mutual bootstrapping operation in which nature and culture are interwoven into the web of meaning.

One hope of social science, to know the nature of man so well that optimal living arrangements could be computed, is a naive hope if Geertz is right. If cultures are objects for interpretation rather than calculation under laws, then the study of culture is endless. There is no hope of a definitive answer to the nature of human culture. It is always and forever up for grabs, ever subject to new creation through reinterpretation of what has become old.

Geertz tells a story, heard elsewhere in connection with William James. It is an old story that reappears here in the form of an Indian tale told to an Englishman who is asked to believe that the world rests on a platform which rests on the back of an elephant which rests in turn on the back of a turtle. When the English gentleman persists with the question as to what the turtle rests on, he is told, *another turtle*. And after that? "Ah, Sahib, after that it is turtles all the way down."[39]

So it now appears for the human sciences, with anthropology among them: *interpretations all the way down.* "The fact is that to commit oneself to a semiotic concept of culture and an interpretive approach to the study of it is to commit oneself to a view of ethnographic assertion, as, to borrow W.B. Gallie's by now famous phrase, 'essentially contestable.'"[40]

Will we discover that collectivism as opposed to individualism is the most natural, and therefore essentially correct ideology for the optimal arrangement of human cultures? No. Nor will we discover that individualism is *the right answer*. To say that these interpretations are essentially contestable is just to say that there is no foundational essence or human culture that is incontestable. On this and other issues, rival interpretations will continue to contest the proper reading of whatever evidence is brought to bear.

Where meaning is concerned, it is not a matter of converging on closer and closer measurements. Where meaning is involved, alternative contexts can determine widely divergent significances for the same physical entity, whether it be a bone or a pun. And what finally stymies the positivist is the fact that the divergent contexts are determined in turn *not* by some secure and single basis, but by other interpretations

---

38   *Ibid.*, p. 47.

39   *Ibid.*, p. 29.

40   *Idem.*

which are the symbolic products of an unpredictable human creativity. Turtles and interpretations, all the way down.

In his work since *Interpreting Cultures*, from which all the previous quotations are taken, Geertz has become far more explicit about the semiotic, sign-interpreting nature of anthropology, and about the contagious spread of semiotic methods across the whole range of social sciences. Further, he has become more self-conscious about the significance of this movement *as a movement*, as a change of approach (or paradigm shift) reflecting a broadly recognized failure of earlier, more mechanical approaches that tried to mimic the hard sciences.

> Ten years ago, the proposal that cultural phenomena should be treated as significative systems posing expositive questions was a much more alarming one for social scientists—allergic, as they tend to be, to anything literary or inexact—than it is now. In part, it is a result of the growing recognition that the established approach to treating such phenomena, laws-and-causes social physics, was not producing the triumphs of prediction, control, and testability that had for so long been promised in its name.[41]

While the shift of method in anthropology is in part a function of the failure of the older laws-and-causes approach, it is in part also a function of a new blurring of disciplinary boundaries. Once upon a time, the articulation of different academic disciplines—mathematics, English, anthropology, sociology, and so on—was thought to represent much more than arbitrary conveniences erected for purposes of university administrators. The different disciplines were thought to represent the different branches of a naturalistic tree of knowledge. The differences between the disciplines rested, it seemed, on real differences in the world, like the differences between sheep and goats, or the organic and the inorganic, or the human and historical as opposed to the eternal laws of nature and mathematics.

In recent years, these lines between the disciplines have come to seem increasingly arbitrary, and it is this phenomenon within the working lives of researchers that is the subject of Geertz's opening essay in *Local Knowledge*. "Blurred Genres: The Refiguration of Social Thought."

> It is a phenomenon general enough and distinctive enough to suggest that what we are seeing is not just another redrawing of the cultural map—the moving of a few disputed borders, the marking of some more picturesque mountain lakes—but an alteration of the principles of mapping. Something is happening to the way we think about the way we think.[42]

---

41   Clifford Geertz, *Local Knowledge*, New York, 1983, p. 3.

42   *Ibid.*, p. 20.

In place of the laws-and-causes approach, three different metaphors now vie with one another in the methods and imaginations of anthropologists. The first is part of the legacy of recent discoveries in the physical sciences: the game. Just as Manfred Eigen finds games with rules a fruitful way to organize the play of determination and chance in a whole range of phenomena from genetics and evolution to economics and the arts, so some anthropologists use the game metaphor to describe cultures and the structure of everyday life. Erving Goffman is one of the chief proponents of the game metaphor. His analyses of institutions' social practices are peppered with references to implicit rules, strategies and "moves," as if all of life were an elaborate Parker & Brothers creation. But, of course, we make up and maintain the rules, rarely consciously, but always conscientiously in our efforts to "do the right thing" in whatever circumstances present themselves.

The second dominant metaphor, one which Goffman also exploits, is the metaphor of life as a stage, society as theater, history as drama. The dramaturgical metaphor has the merit of being particularly apt for the handling or rituals—weddings, funerals, coronations, and all sorts of pomp and circumstance whose stagings give clues to what matters to a society. Consider, for example, the Super Bowl as the indicator of what counts in American society, not only the nature of the competition, the players and their coaches, but also the details of the staging or frame: the role of television, the ads, the half-time show, and the fact that more than 70 million Americans simultaneously participate in this event, a larger number than those joining in any other ritual with the possible exception of Christmas and New Year's Eve, whose celebrations tend to be more localized and customized in any case. Geertz's own studies tend to the dramaturgical, partly as a result of the fact that one of his targets, Bali culture, is a society where politics is very clearly enacted through theatrical rituals in which to perform a role is to play a part.

The third analogy following *game* and *drama* as model objects for the anthropologists is the *text*. This third analogy is the one that draws Geertz's attention most, and it is the one that most clearly opens up the boundaries between anthropology and literary criticism.

When looking at a culture as if it were an interpretable text, one is hardly limited to looking at literal texts. Geertz is hardly interested in a 'textual anthropology' on the model of a 'textual history' based on the readings of important written documents. The point is to look at all the pieces of a culture—not only its texts, if there are any, but its rituals, its ways of life—as elements in a larger 'text' that the anthropologist interprets much as a literary critic reads a poem or a novel. "To see social institutions, social customs, social changes as in some sense 'readable' is to alter our whole sense of what such interpretation is and shift it toward modes of thought rather more familiar to the translator, the exegete, or the iconographer than to the test giver, the factor analyst, or the pollster."[43]

In his conclusion to another essay, "Art as a Cultural System," Geertz further refines his description of the interpretive anthropologist in terms that emphasize the reading of living texts:

> It is not a new cryptography that we need, especially when it consists of replacing one cipher by another less intelligible, but a new diagnostics, a science that can determine the meaning of things for the life that surrounds them. It will have, of course, to be trained on signification, not pathology, and treat with ideas, not with symptoms. But by connecting incised statues, pigmented sago palms, frescoed walls, and chanted verse to jungle clearing, totem rites, commercial inference, or street argument, it can perhaps begin at last to locate in the tenor of their setting the sources of their spell.[44]

Text and context; the event or sign gains meaning through its setting in its social or literary surroundings. And because it is *meanings* that are sought, not measurements, the physical particulars, whether the type font or the details of the headdresses, may not be as important as the patterns of relationships linking particulars and their contexts. These patterns are read as the literary critic reads a text.

2b. Implications of New Anthropology for Future Studies

These movements in modern and postmodern anthropology—Levi-Strauss's structuralist turn, Geertz's interpretive turn—suggest similar moves on the part of futurists. Forget about the laws-and-causes approach toward a predictive science. Focus instead on multiple interpretations of the present. This, after all, is what a set of scenarios amount to: alternative interpretations of the present as the first chapter of several very different narratives. Today's decisions and events take on different *meanings* depending on the different tomorrows that are their possible consequences. Contemporary anthropology has made this shift from a positivistic emulation of the hard sciences toward a more literary, narrative approach—what Geertz calls *thick description:* a story-telling approach that stresses the narrative relationships among specific details more than general laws or universal principles. Again, this is just what good scenarios accomplish: a narrative synthesis of many details into a story about the future that makes sense of the present. And there are always several such stories for any given present.

As anthropologists and futurists alike make the move from a laws-and-causes positivism toward a more literary interpretive approach, both would do well to

---

43   *Ibid.,* p. 31.

44   *Ibid.,* p. 120.

turn their attention from the methods of the hard sciences toward the methods—or is it madness—of literary critics. For it is the literary critics who are the experts at reading and interpreting texts.

But how do literary critics read texts these days? In reaching from the physical sciences to literary criticism to find a better model for the anthropologist's (and, by turns, the futurist's) task, Geertz can only find more turtles, for the foundations of literary theory are no firmer today than the foundations of anthropology.

3a. Literary Criticism and the Legacy of Existentialism

If it weren't for the fact that Geertz's inquiries steered us in this direction, literary criticism would qualify on its own for inclusion among contemporary disciplines reflecting a paradigm shift. In recent years, a paradigm war has been raging in the upper stories of that vast academic mansion known on lower floors simply as "The English Department." Some of the generals in this titanic battle of paradigms are actually from departments of French or Comparative Literature. The labels over the door don't much matter, though careers may be made or lost depending on whether the main heat of the battle moves from one flank to another. The major point of importance, whether your battalion talks French or English, is that the rules of the contest are changing. The reading of texts isn't what it used to be.

Surely there have always been fashionable -isms to complicate the un-self-conscious act of reading a good novel. From Russian formalism to the New Criticism (now quite old) professors have earned their keep by telling us how the text was *really* working in ways far removed from our naive following of the yarn. But in recent years, particularly since the late seventies, the cries from the attic have become particularly intense. From the floors below the esoteric squabbles often sound like the unintelligible babble of people who have read too much European philosophy. But one ignores these squabbles at one's peril, especially when words drift down with ominous connotations like "deconstruction". The literary critics have ganged up in an intellectual wrecking crew.

Deconstructive criticism works like a corrosive against all pretences at systematic explanation. The corrosion process works at both the foundational level and at the upper stories of theoretical abstraction. At the foundational level, deconstructive criticism shows that the simple elements that make up a text are not very simple after all, that each sentence, each phrase, each word is packed with complexities introduced by the several different contexts at play: social, economic, political, psychological, to say nothing of literary and historical contexts. And if the reader should want to take a foothold in any one of those contexts, say, by taking the political context as primary, then the deconstruction operation moves to the upper stories where the status of, say, Marxism as a theory will come under attack. Deconstruction challenges the very idea of seeing the world as neatly displayed beneath the gabled eaves of theoretical hierarchies with their unifying abstractions at the peak of the roof.

Though the project might sound anti-intellectual, the principal workers make up a very literate wrecking crew. If they travelled to work in a panel truck, its sides might bear legends with names like Nietzsche, Heidegger, and the current foreman, Jacques Derrida. The program is derived in part from Heidegger's project, teased out of Nietzsche, for the destruction of the tradition of western metaphysics. What might such a program involve? And is it really necessary just for the purpose of reading a text, or a culture, or a decade of social change?

Just as Geertz proclaimed in his essay on "Blurred Genres," the story starts to get very confused when anthropology reaches toward literary criticism for help only to find literary critics reaching toward philosophy. More turtles. "The penetration of the social sciences by the views of such philosophers as Heidegger, Wittgenstein, Gadamer, or Ricoeur, such critics as Burke, Frye, Jameson, or Fish, and such all-purpose subversives as Foucault, Habermas, Barthes, or Kuhn makes any simple return to a technological conception of those sciences highly improbable."[45] Kuhn, of course, is the great promoter of the concept of paradigm shifts. But how have some of the others taken part in the destruction of the Western tradition of metaphysics?

Heidegger's contribution was, among other things, to challenge the idea of philosophy as a quest after timeless truths. Existentialism, a mid-twentieth century intellectual fashion that owes much to Heidegger, proceeds from the destruction of the Aristotelian view that essence precedes existence. An acorn's essence is to become an oak. The essence precedes the eventual existence of the oak tree. But people aren't like that. Their existence precedes their essence. What they actually do, the way they exist, determines their essence, who they really are. (Existentialism is, socially speaking, an anti-aristocratic, very American philosophy.)

This textbook description of Heidegger's existentialism misses the more radical implications of this writings, however. By hurling man into time, Heidegger also hurls man's categories, his truths, his whole world into time. Even the inquiry into Being—metaphysics—no longer appears under the guise of a precious glimpse into eternity, but becomes an historically bound activity in which the questioner must ever question his own situation, the power of the past, future possibilities, the aim of the questioning itself. Philosophizing *a la* Heidegger is an enterprise fraught with uncertainty and anxiety. Any attempt to escape that anxiety prematurely by hanging the enterprise on the skyhook of some lofty absolute, or by basing it on the firm foundations of objective "facts", will not bring the inquirer closer to "the truth," for truth, according to Heidegger, is not to be found by building a stable picture to correspond to a stable reality.

---

45   Geertz, *Local Knowledge, op. cit.,* pp. 3f.

'Being,' 'Truth'—each of the super-tools that theoreticians use to construct grand models of reality ultimately faces the corrosive power of deconstruction. Being has been bent by the tradition of western metaphysics into the distorted image of mere presence, filling space here and now. The Cartesian view of the world through the cross-hatched lens of the Cartesian coordinate system turns time into just another dimension of a space whose every volume is the same as every other. The map for representing reality within the Cartesian coordinate system—graph paper—was supposed to assist in the picturing of reality; instead it became the model of the reality to be pictured. Time is levelled out onto the endless, meaningless moments whose tedium is captured by T.S. Eliot in *The Love Song of J. Alfred Prufrock:* '"I have measured out my life with coffee spoons." One square block of Cartesian time is pretty much like another, and Being, reduced to presence in that time, is a dull business. Its model is matter, a bare, characterless substratum in which attributes coalesce to form things with shapes and boundaries.

The austere Cartesian metaphysics of matter and space and a spatialized time has very little in it of what Heidegger recognized in the writings of the Greek philosophers. There he saw a dynamic swarming of process and possibility, and an immersion of man in his environment quite different from the spectral distance assumed by later theoreticians. The separation of form from matter was all of a piece with the separation of observing subject from observed object. Descartes' separation of mind from matter has its roots in both an epistemology that separates knower from known, and in an ontology that separates Being from beings. For Heidegger, and for the pre-Socratic philosophers in which he claimed to find intimations of a livelier reality, these separations were less than tidy.

Being is not settled and measurable for Heidegger. The words we would use to describe Being are bound to reduce it to a mere presence that can be delimited on all sides. How to reveal the truth of Being when the usual tools of truth telling— words—are each matched with an attribute or property? If Being is that in which properties and attributes reside, but is not a property or attribute in itself, then words for properties and attributes will inevitably miss the mark.

Heidegger reflects on language, as does Wittgenstein. For both of these pre-eminent twentieth-century philosophers, the central drama of their philosophical careers consists in a constant struggle against the limitations of the tools of their trade: words. The early Wittgenstein thought through the old picture of language to its end. He hypothesized an ideal language, one for which true propositions would picture the facts. The later Wittgenstein deconstructs each part of that simple correspondence theory of truth: the form of the proposition, the relationship of perfect correspondence, and the givenness of so-called facts. Propositions need linguistic contexts in order to mean anything at all. Correspondence is often ambiguous: what geometric laws would prove the correspondence between "Old Faithful," and "the Stars and Stripes?" Finally, "the facts" don't come in the tidy bundles assumed by Wittgenstein's early *Tractatus*. Instead, our presuppositions and expectations always bend our selection of what is to count as "the facts."

Like Wittgenstein, Heidegger, too, challenged the simple correspondence theory of truth. Both tried to liberate themselves and their readers from the objectivist illusion that metaphor is a second-best way to represent reality. The very idea of a reality simply present behind our metaphors and linguistic attempts to picture, the very idea of an essence beneath existence, begins to crumble.

This mighty triumvirate of Nietzsche, Heidegger and Wittgenstein confronts the twentieth century with the disturbing news that the whole rationalist enlightenment, with its scientific triumphs and its philosophical systems, may rest on some drastic misunderstandings about the relationships between human inquirers, language, and the reality that inquiry would describe and explain with language and mathematics. These philosophers see their domain not as an inner sanctum of eternal truths to be sought by Promethean scientists and borne back to mortal men in pictures made with words and numbers. Instead, they see philosophy as, in large part, a matter of undoing the damage done by mistaking linguistic pictures for the reality they would represent—including those linguistic pictures that picture the relationships between speakers, language, and whatever is to be represented.

The later Wittgenstein rejects the whole picture theory of truth. The later Heidegger trades in the relatively professorial tone of his earlier tracts for an increasingly rhapsodic prose that evokes more than it pictures or describes. Poetry becomes the paradigm for a language that remains true to itself only by creating itself ever anew with neologism and unexpected combinations. For the expected is always false to the unfolding of novelty that is non-Cartesian time.

The critique of static pictures of a static presence that follows from these reflections on being, time and truth has been extended from philosophy into literary criticism, where the mighty triumvirate are read more eagerly than in Anglo-American philosophy departments, where the news was too bad to be taken seriously. Most academic philosophers simply chose finer, harder pencils to draw their pictures with greater, if more specious, precision. Literary critics, less interested in precise truth to begin with, were more open to a frontal attack on aspirations to literal portraiture. After all, modern art had already shown the way to break free of literal representation. Perhaps the truth was to be found in fiction!

The corrosive force of deconstruction came into play against the calmly assumed categories of earlier critics. Categories like 'author,' 'reader,' 'text', might not be quite as grand as 'Being,' but they were grand enough to assume a reified solidity in need of deconstruction.

In what seems at first more a pun than an argument, Edward Said deconstructs the *authority* of the *author*: "authority is nomadic: it is never in the same place, it is never always at the center..."[46] Therefore, an author like Michel Foucault (among those genre blurrers mentioned by Geertz) is necessarily concerned with relationships of "adjacency, complementarity, and correlation, which are not the same as the linear relationships of succession and integrity,"[47] the simplicities of before and after or inside and outside.

Foucault's analysis of intellectual history amounts to a kind of cultural existentialism: the course of a culture is no more driven by some logical essence than is the course of a free individual's life. Instead Foucault sees worldview following upon worldview without any particular rhyme or reason. He calls each successive worldview an *episteme*. He could as well use the word, *paradigm*. Whatever the name, the theme is the same: a preoccupation with the influence of knowers on the known, not the other way around as various materialisms or scientific determinisms would have it.

Earlier philosophers like Kant and Hegel cut through the objectivist illusion to appreciate the role of consciousness in crafting experience. But for Kant the structure of consciousness was fixed: only one paradigm for all conscious beings. And for Hegel the successive order of the forms of consciousness followed a rational dialectic, a process of unfolding that, at least retrospectively, made some kind of essentialist sense. Foucault, however, sees sharp discontinuities between the several forms of consciousness that he finds in the last several centuries of European history. There is no clear foundation, and no clear rules by which successive stories have been added to that foundation.

Under the influence—one might say intoxicated by the genres—of philosophy and intellectual history, literary critics like Said see a similar exile from secure origins in the literary tradition. Said opposes the situation of the contemporary critic to that of a critic like Leo Spitzer, who was among the last of those to draw on an orally received training in a canonical tradition of world literature and languages studied in the original. The "dynastic tradition" of interpretation could tell you where and how to begin; but the dynastic tradition has ended. So the contemporary critic is set loose in a sea of competing schools where none lays claim to the legitimacy enjoyed by received learning in the old dynasty. The foundations are lost along with essences, origins and simple presences.

Said distinguishes between *origin*, as a kind of passive foundation, and *beginning*, as both more ambiguous and more active, much like the free choice of the existential individual. There is a sense in which we do not know where to begin, but must

---

46   Edward Said, *Beginnings*, Baltimore and London, 1975, p. 12.

47   *Ibid.*, p. 290.

instead find out what we meant to say by seeing, later down the line, what we have already said. As Roland Barthes describes his process of creation, "I begin producing by reproducing the person I want to be."[48] So, for Said, "Beginnings, therefore, are for me opposed to originalities, or to those ideal Presences whose ideal originality Yeats called 'self-born mockers of man's enterprise.'"[49] Lacking a clear sense of origin, whether in a dynastic tradition or in a sense of personal essence, we must be enterprising

3b. The Import of Recent Literary Criticism for Future Studies

What Said and others have done to literary criticism has direct import for the field of future studies in several respects, one of which is as follows. Once upon a time literary criticism sought to ground the 'correct' reading of a text by tying it to the originary intentions of the author, who was considered as a kind of all-knowing and all-powerful God in relationship to the text. A second phase, the New Criticism, placed more emphasis on the creation, the text. Part of the force of deconstructionism has been to demonstrate that the text is no less ambiguous in its meaning than the intentions of an originary author. Consequently, contemporary criticism now finds itself stressing neither the author, nor the text, but the reader. As the fog of French deconstructionism begins to clear, the healthiest survivor on the literary critical horizon appears to be Reception Theory, a school of criticism that reframes the goal of criticism by emphasizing neither the author nor the text, but the role of the reader.

An instructive parallel to these stages in the history of literary criticism can be found in three analogical stages in the history of future studies. Once upon a time the study of the future was literally an attempt to uncover God's intentions. With the advent of secular science, teleological accounts of God's design gave way to scientific attempts to trace causal chains in the manifest text of physical reality. If the plot of the present could not be told by reference to God-given purpose, then the plot of the present could be completed by predictions of the future; e.g. today's struggle could be justified by dialectical materialism's "scientific proof" of what life would be like after the revolution.

But predictability in the social sciences now lies in the same dustbin alongside aspirations to unambiguous validity of interpretation via text-based New Criticism. In place of prediction, future studies might borrow a leaf from literary criticism and develop its own analogue to Reception Theory. As I shall argue at greater length in the conclusion to this essay, scenarios developed at the grassroots by those who will live one future or another may fill the bill as a close analogue to Reception theory in literary criticism.

---

48   *Roland Barthes* by Roland Barthes,Trans., Richard Howard, New York, 1977, p 99 .

49   Said, *Beginnings,* p. 380.

Just as a text finds its multiple meanings in the multiple readings of its readers, so the present has a range of possible meanings. These are not to be interpreted solely by reference to the will of a creator God, nor by reference to a single future that could be predicted by a deterministic social science. Instead, the meaning of the present is a function of the future, yet the future that in fact unfolds will be very much a function of human choices based on several different "readings" of the present. Both the interpretability of the present and the multiplicity of future goals and values introduce uncertainty and human volition into the process of history. Multiple scenarios can reflect both the descriptive and evaluative dimensions of uncertainty. Like Reception Theory in literary criticism, multiple scenarios locate the leverage for describing the future where it belongs: with the human beings who will "receive" a future they hopefully chose. So we need to know more about human beings—the human factor and its influence on the future.

4a. The Import of Psychology for the Emergent Paradigm

Evidence of an emergent paradigm can be found in other disciplines besides anthropology, philosophy and literary criticism. Contemporary psychology is in ferment. Freud's metapsychology, with its echoes of a nineteenth-century physicalism and reductionism, is regarded as an embarrassment to be set aside by practitioners and clinicians. Developmental psychologists see a dynamic unfolding of personality that is not utterly determined in the first three years of life. Jungian psychologists engage in semiotic interpretations of symbols whose meanings are always overdetermined—too rich in possible meanings to be reduced to one unambiguous interpretation of significance. Finally, the object relations school—Melanie Klein, D.W. Winnicott, Ronald Fairbairn and Harry Guntrip—sees the self as a structure of evolving relationships, not as a substance or thing with clearly defined boundaries. Their theories and their therapies treat the development of personality as a succession of relationships beginning with the primary relationship between parent and infant. Just as structural anthropology turns away from the attempt to build a kinship system out of atomic elements and locates structure in the lattice of kinship relationships, so psychology no longer begins with the assumption of a self-contained, atomic ego, but regards the self as established—successfully or unsuccessfully—through its relationships.

This shift in emphasis from *things* to *relationships* is important. Its significance extends from the abstractions of ontology to concrete decisions about everyday life. In ancient philosophy, especially in the influential writings of Aristotle, to be is to be an individual, and to be an *individual* is to be a *substance*. Relations were regarded as ontologically secondary or derivative, as added by the perceiving mind. If A is to the left of B, that relationship depends in turn on the relationship between A, B, *and an observer*. Substance, on the contrary, was defined as that which is self-sufficient.

This Aristotelian ontology of self-sufficiency was rendered even more explicit by Spinoza, who defined substance as "that which is completely self-sufficient and needs no other in order to exist." It doesn't take a card-carrying feminist to identify the *macho* presuppositions underlying the ontological priority of substance so defined. Nor does it take a degree in psychoanalysis to see the import of Spinoza's—and behaviorist psychology's—attempt to reduce human subjectivity to a set of observable behaviors and properties of physical substance. The reduction of subject to substance, and the privileging of self-sufficiency over relatedness, are part and parcel of a positivistic paradigm that puts facts before values, objects before subjects, and matter before mind. Even as his psychology opened up the symbolic dimensions of subjectivity and mind, Freud's meta-psychology—his tacit and sometimes explicit beliefs about what counted as science—constantly dragged him back toward materialistic metaphors for describing the vicissitudes of the unconscious. Especially in his earliest work—*Project for a Scientific Psychology*—he held out the hope of reducing all psychological explanation to neuro-physiological descriptions of electronic and chemical reactions—reductionism rampant. Like some futurists, he felt that he could never get a fair hearing for psychology unless he turned it into a step-child of the hard sciences.

According to nineteenth and early twentieth century criteria for what counts as scientific inquiry, psychology often comes up short. William James and Freud based many of their insights on introspection. But if observer and observed are one and the same person, claims to objectivity are likely to be tainted by the subjectivity of the observer. Where does fantasy leave off and reality begin? Is the child's experience of the primal scene of parents making love based on fantasy or actual experience? Freud vacillated on this very question. But how could one ever know if one has only verbal reports to go on?

In an effort to live up to the requirements dictated by the physical sciences, behaviorist psychology eschews the evidence of introspection. Only observable behavior counts as evidence, thus leading to the quip that one behaviorist psychologist greeted another with the remark, "You're fine. How am I?"

The behaviorist rigor with respect to observability leads to suspicions about all "inner" phenomena—not just how to describe them, but whether they even exist. The constraints of rigorous theory construction forbid hypotheses that cannot be tested by experiments in which predictions are verified or disconfirmed in laboratory conditions involving controls and repeatable observations of carefully isolated independent variables. These constraints drove academic psychologists ever further away from clinical therapy with complicated human beings, and ever closer to laboratory experiments with rats and rabbits, who are plentiful enough to allow statistical significance, and uncomplaining in their submission to repeated experiments. Meanwhile, clinical psychologists seemed to be relegated to the role of latter-day priest-confessors, or scientific charlatans.

In his review of the object-relations school, Harry Guntrip takes up the challenge of the scientific status of clinical psychology, but he does so very differently from the behaviorists. Rather than reducing human experience to an interplay of theoretical entities—instincts, drives, or the "mechanisms" of repression, displacement, sublimation, etc.—his best defense is a strong offense. He challenges the adequacy of the nineteenth century scientific paradigm.

After describing a case history "so utterly individual and unique that no possibility would exist in practice of finding an adequate parallel case to serve as a control," he observes: "Such a case points out a fact that we must never ignore, that in psychoanalysis science is for the first time challenged to understand and thereby explain the unique individual, and that this must lead to a new development in our concept of what is science."[50]

The problem of understanding unique phenomena is not unique to psychoanalysis, of course. History has a similar liability in its attempt to become a science: no era, no decade, no war is quite like any other. Nor does history yield easily to testable predictions or readily available control groups. Yet events might be predictable and still add up to a history. The subject of psychoanalysis—a person—is in principle less predictable. "In fact, the more possible it is to predict consistently exactly what a human being will do, the less a real person he has become, and the more he presents what Winnicott calls 'the false self on a conformity basis.'"[51]

It is tempting to retreat to the position that psychoanalysis is an art, not a science. A work of art is, like an individual person, unique. But the goal of psychoanalysis is neither entertainment nor edification. Psychoanalysis uses knowledge to achieve a particular purpose—mental and emotional health. Art is supposed to be devoid of external purposes, an end in itself. But in the last analysis the categorization of psychoanalysis as an art or a science is less interesting than the use of psychoanalysis as an example showing the inadequacy of our understanding of what makes any discipline an art or a science. Rather than trying to learn more about psychoanalysis by glibly categorizing it as an art or a science, Guntrip leads us to learn more about science by assuming that psychoanalysis is a science and then revising our idea of science to accommodate psychoanalysis. In dealing with unique individuals, he writes, "We are dealing with a different order of reality, which cannot be dealt with by orthodox traditional scientific methods."[52]

---

50 Harry Guntrip, *Psychoanalytic Theory, Therapy, and the Self,* New York, 1971, p. 177.

51 *Ibid.* p. 182.

52 *Ibid.* p. 193.

Part of the difference between "orthodox traditional scientific methods" and a new paradigm for science lies in the stress on (local knowledge of) the unique individual rather than the laying on of the universal and repeatable. But part of the difference lies in a closely related phenomenon: the difference between reductionism and holism. Reductionist analysis sees the individual as an assemblage of separable elements, each of which can be characterized by permanent properties. Magnesium is always magnesium, and it retains its atomic structure wherever you find it. Likewise, a carburetor is always a carburetor and can be transferred from one automobile to another of the same make and model. But Alice's paranoia is not just like John's. Despite the use of the same diagnostic label, the treatments appropriate to Alice and John may benefit more from an appreciation of how their paranoias are different rather than the same. Why are they different? Because paranoia is not a precisely repeatable, unchanging element like magnesium, but a syndrome whose nature is determined more by its relational context in a given character than by some list of intrinsic properties. This is the meaning of holism: that the whole determines the part more than the part, through its intrinsic properties, determines the nature of the whole.

Working within the "orthodox traditional" scientific paradigm, "Freud did not start with the concept of the whole person. Psychoanalysis became obsessed with distinguishable aspects functioning as parts needing to be fitted together,"[53] like so many elements or unchanging, replaceable parts of a machine.

Working within the emergent, holistic paradigm, both existential therapists and those in the object-relations school stress the importance of seeing the whole person before reducing him or her to an assemblage of syndromes, neuroses or elemental instincts.

Their holistic perspective carries over into their view of the relationship between psyche and soma, or mind and body. "It has been assumed hitherto that mind (that which enabled the scientist to create his science) as a kind of secretion, if anything, of the body. But now we have to think in terms of developing psyche as the vital stimulating factor evolving a body to meet is needs."[54]

Neither the body nor the so-called primitive instincts can be regarded as fixed elements always exerting the same pressures or constraints. Just as Geertz objects to the idea that culture is a layer of refinement that is added on top of more archaic levels of physical determinants, so the relational and existential perspectives object to the idea that archaic elements lie unchanged beneath newer layers of mental or cultural refinement. "The equation of 'mature' with 'up-to-date' and 'infantile' with 'archaic' is a misleading error perpetuated by the idea of evolutionary layers of the

---

53   *Ibid.* p. 93.

54   *Ibid.,* p.37.

psychosomatic whole. It needs to be replaced by the concept of an evolutionary whole in which every constituent is appropriately different from what it would have been in a different kind of whole." [55]

4b. Import of Object Relations Psychology for Future Studies

This last sentence could be grafted directly to a description of the way scenarios should replace predictions. Scenarios are precisely those narrative wholes whose logics cast each part into a significative context different from what it would have been in a different kind of scenario. For example, the rapid diffusion of computing technology may contribute to social decentralization in one scenario or to the spread of invasive Big-brotherism in another scenario. Ripped out of context and viewed—artificially—as an isolated element, the rapid diffusion of information technology cannot carry its meaning or significance on its own face. Only by embedding that technology in a larger text or context—a set of scenarios—can its several possible meanings be explored to meet its needs.

Neither culture, psyche nor mind is added on top of physical nature or body or technology taken as unchanging elements. From a holistic perspective, in the evolved organism of psyche and society, matter is informed and altered by mind "all the way down." There is no fixed foundation beneath holistic turtles, no unchanging elements into which organisms can be analyzed and reduced for purposes of explanation and prediction.

5a. From Critical Theory to Existential Sociology

To the extent that sociology uses the cultural and intellectual artifacts of a society—a culturally bound set of categories—to understand that very society, it is just as suspect as introspective psychology: do we trust a psychotic to offer his own best diagnosis? No, individual introspection is almost bound to be warped by the biases of self-deception. Often too much is at stake for an individual subject to see him or herself clearly. Likewise, subjective bias on the grander scale of ethnocentrism is the original sin of sociology: *thou shalt not use one's own ethnic customs as the standard for judging other societies.*

As a consequence of their suspicious origins, the claims of sociologists are often subjected to close scrutiny for tell-tale signs of self-serving biases. For this reason, sociologists have often attempted to be utterly objective and scrupulous in their methods. Knowing that they are stained by the original sin of subjectivism and ethnocentrism, they have sought to be holier (that is, more objective) than the Pope (in this case, the natural sciences).

---

55   *Ibid.*, p. 91.

For the founders, Weber and Durkheim, sociology was supposed to be "value free" (*wertfrei*). Weber's studies on the relationship between religious beliefs and economics allowed a distance between the subjectivity of the sociologist and the object under study by using evidence drawn from a safe distance. Chinese Confucianism and Indian Hinduism could be correlated with economies and societies separated by centuries and miles from his own perspective. Durkheim's landmark study of suicide attempted to base its findings on cold statistics that had nothing to do with subjective variations among individual suicides. Behavior, not subjective intention, was the object of study. Hence there was less danger that the social scientist's own intentions would cloud his understanding of the object under study. Simply by seeking correlations between actual numbers of suicides and other objective measures like economic performance and demographics, the social scientist could seek out laws that might describe the past, predict its future, and thereby explain the present. By treating society as if it were an aggregate of atomic individuals whose contrary intentions average out under the law of large numbers, sociologists might discover certain valencies, certain tendencies to aggregate and divide, certain iron laws that would unlock the secrets of social organization just as elegantly as the table of the elements unlocked the secrets of the atom. Humanity, though an aggregate of subjects, could be treated as an object after all.

A case could be made for taking Boltzmann's statistical thermodynamics as the paradigm of science to which sociology aspired. Subjective intentions, about which the sociologist could make no truly unbiased claims, could be cancelled out as so much Brownian movement. Human thought is no more than thermal noise: random perturbations at the micro-level of society. Just as the behavior of gasses at a macro-level can be predicted statistically without reference to the mechanics of forces and impacts among individual atoms, so the behavior of a society should be predictable from some of its macro-level features without reference to micro-level human intentions. Thus the paradigm of science for sociology is not exactly Newtonian, not a mechanics of individual forces and impacts. Yet the paradigm of positivistic sociology is still thoroughly objectivist. Even if society could not be treated like a clock or other complex machine, its movements might nevertheless reveal a *statistical* determinism that makes a mockery of reasoned intentions at the helm of history.

Reasonable people tend to be offended by arguments that wrest their fates from their own hands. Consequently there has been no lack of critics of positivist sociology. The romantic reaction against positivism—"Yes we *can* choose our destiny! We *do* have free will!"—unfortunately misses the point. Positivism need not deny the efficacy of intentions at the micro-level. The romantic reaction falls into a myth of subjectivism which, by its own one-sidedness, tends to keep objectivism alive—as dialectical antitheses so often do. By missing the point, by confusing statistical with mechanical determinism, the romantics offered the positivists targets for legitimate criticism. As is the case in so many paradigm wars, the parties talked past one another, neither side satisfied that it had been heard, neither side convinced that it had been justifiably criticized. In their eager attempts to find each others' dirty linen, they ended up taking in each others' wash.

As long as the romantic reaction continued to distance itself from positivism's insights as well as its failings, the world studied by sociologists remained divided by a conceptual Maginot line that separated the two camps in the ongoing paradigm war. As Richard Harvey Brown draws the lines in an essay entitled, "Symbolic realism and sociological thought: Beyond the positivist-romantic debate:"[56]

On the side of science	On the side of the subjective/ Romantic reaction
truth	beauty
reality	symbols
things and events	feelings/meanings
"out-there"	"in-here"
objective	subjective
explanation	interpretation
proof	insight
determinism	freedom

Any sociology adequate to the task of comprehending a complex society will have to integrate both columns. During the last several decades sociology has shown signs of moving beyond the old paradigm war toward a new synthesis that bears many of the marks of the emergent paradigm.

One of the crucial players is Juergen Habermas. Heir to the throne of the influential Frankfurt School of Critical Theory, Habermas has achieved a subtle synthesis of Marxism, psychology and communications theory. Complex to the point of being nearly impenetrable, his prose defies easy simplification. But as is often the case with German academics, a good deal of the obscurity owes more to pomposity than to the subject matter itself. The basic insights are not all that inaccessible.

Habermas begins from a distinction between two kinds of human interest: theoretical and practical. Theoretical interests include elements in the left-hand column above; practical, the right-hand column. Human beings are not interested

---

56   Richard Harvey Brown, in *Structure, Consciousness, and History,* ed. R. H. Brown and Stanford M. Lyman, Cambridge, 1978, p. 15.

in just one or the other column, but both. Because our knowledge serves both sets of interests, the criteria for an adequate social theory cannot exclude either set of interests.

One of the themes of his book, *Knowledge and Human Interest,* is ferreting out the "hidden objectivism" in the works of social theorists like Wilhelm Dilthey, C. S. Peirce, and John Dewey. Though firmly rooted in the Marxist tradition, Habermas does not save his criticisms for those outside that tradition. Marxist positivism—claims for an objective science revealing the iron laws of a dialectical unfolding of history—comes in for a thorough critique. After all, Marx was not a disinterested academic in search of an elegant theory. He was a revolutionary, passionately interested in the liberation of the oppressed. But what is necessary for liberation? Is the truth enough to set men free? And what *is* the truth about human potentiality? How can we know until 'after the revolution?'

Habermas grapples head-on with a basic riddle of human society: to the extent that humans are free, the object of sociology is to some extent indeterminate. If ever you pin them down under the glass of theory, what you've got is like a butterfly that cannot fly—or a humanity that isn't free. Habermas is acutely aware of the extent to which humanity makes up its nature as it goes along—and must continue to do so.

What is necessary to assure social freedom? For Habermas the answer is an unconstrained exchange of ideas: "undistorted communication," to use Habermas' often repeated phrase. Call it freedom of speech—an important if not very novel idea. But Habermas's attention to the free flowing exchange of ideas marks an important break in a Marxist tradition that had often discounted the autonomous power of ideas.

Marxism has often fallen into its own form of positivism—a belief that the objective world of economics determines everything in human experience. As Marx himself wrote in *The German Ideology,* in a passage that directly contests the significance of paradigms in general: "The production of ideas, of conceptions, of consciousness is at first directly interwoven with the material activity and the material intercourse of men, the language of real life. Conceiving, thinking, the mental intercourse of men appear at this stage as the direct efflux of their material behavior."[57] Lest there be any doubt about the reach of this proclamation, Marx goes on to add: "Morality, religion, metaphysics, all the rest of ideology and their corresponding forms of consciousness [for example, paradigms] no longer retain the semblance of independence. They have no history, no development; but men, developing their material production and their material intercourse, alter, along

---

57 Karl Marx and Friedrich Engels, *The German Ideology,* in *Marx & Engels: Basic Writings on Politics & Philosophy,* ed. Lewis Feuer, New York, 1959, p. 247.

with this their real existence, their thinking, and the products of their thinking."[58] Finally, in an oft quoted sentence that leaves no mistake about the order of causality between the objective and the subjective, "Life is not determined by consciousness, but consciousness by life."[59]

Against this solid foundation of economic determinism underlying the entire Marxist tradition, Habermas has taken pains to acknowledge two related points. First, that epistemology is important: the theory of knowledge, the dynamics of consciousness, cannot be ignored in the name of a science that could deduce consciousness from a science of objects, whether that science calls itself psychology, economics, sociology, or some combination of the above. None of these theoretical descriptions of objects can fully capture the choices of subjects. The categories and applications of these disciplines are themselves partly a function of individual and collective choices made by subjects to serve their practical as well as their theoretical interests. In other words, there is always something at stake. So-called disinterested inquiry always serves some interests. Habermas acknowledges the original sin of sociology as inescapable. Marxists have no special dispensation or claim to redemption.

Second, just as the life of the individual or the research of some limited intellectual community is always tainted by the interests and predispositions that color its consciousness, so the policies that guide nations are not purely the result of economic determinism. This, Habermas argues, is more true today than ever. Governments now play an active role in manipulating the economy: through tax policies, tariffs, monetary manipulations and interest rates. Given the extent to which ideas like Keynesian economics or supply-side economics are used to steer the economy, it seems a little backward to say that the forces and relations of production work as independent variables driving the production of ideas. The evolution of consciousness may be very much influenced by economics, but the economy is likewise directed by ideas. Hence, according to Habermas, the importance of a free and unconstrained exchange of ideas.

To put it in a polysyllabic nutshell that captures the relation between these two central points in Habermas' thinking: *social policy is the public epistemology underlying economic policy.* To unpack: liberating the oppressed is not just a matter of taking from the rich and giving to the poor. It is instead a matter of increasing the degree of truly human self-consciousness in society so that each individual and society as a whole make the kinds of choices that serve the human interests of each individual and society as a whole. An individual compelled by an obsession or compulsion to make certain "choices" is not a free individual, rich or poor.

---

58   *Idem.*

59   *Idem.*

Likewise, a society driven by economic or technological imperatives is not a free society. Both in the case of the individual and in the case of society, *deliberation among options is a characteristic of freedom.* But social deliberation is no more free than the individual deliberation of a psychotic if social deliberation is compelled by some overriding, determining force.

What the fetish is to the obsessed individual, some comparably unquestioned object of desire might be to a society. If a society forbids an exchange of ideas about some social goal—whether the MX missile, AIDS, or racial equality—then the behavior of that society turns out to be just as compulsive, just as unfree, as the obsessed individual's.

To the extent that sociologists like Habermas and Alvin Gouldner have rescued consciousness from its role as a merely dependent variable in the social equation, they have achieved a paradigm shift in sociology. Like other instances in the emergence of a broad-based paradigm shift, it is a bootstrap operation with resonances within resonances. The paradigm shift that accords more significance to consciousness is a paradigm shift that points to the importance of paradigms and their shiftings. Further, the paradigm toward which they have shifted is one that underlines the significance of thought in determining the course of the world, which in turn exercises *its* mundane and material influence on further thought (Marx was not *all* wrong).

Habermas and Gouldner have been labeled "reflexive" sociologists for their sensitivity to the feedback loops that confound all attempts to describe society as a machine obeying simple, linear, deterministic laws. This reflexivity plays an important role in their thought about society. Further, it marks their contributions with the *self-referential* feature of the emergent paradigm, and does so with all the dizzying resonances usually found when one plunges into the hall of mirrors that modern consciousness has become. Reflexive sociology has foresworn firm foundations.

The main point of distinguishing practical from theoretical interests is to acknowledge that we are (or at least can be) free to choose what we are. Objective, theoretical science does not have the last word when it comes to humanity. We are (or can be) a bootstrap phenomenon. Always within the context of very real constraints, some historical, some biological, humanity can frame its own laws. This is a liberating lesson.

Curiously, however, Habermas himself remains trapped within several other aspects of an old paradigm, both in the form and in the content of his sociological research. Its form is very much the model of scholarly, abstract, and—ironically—highly distorted communication. He's almost unreadable. Further, the content supports an unproven assumption of universal laws underlying language and communication.

Like Levi-Strauss and unlike Geertz, Habermas seems to harbor the hope that just around the corner of the the next research grant, someone is going to come up with the universal, unified field theory of language and communication, and that from that theory we are somehow going to be able to deduce the legitimacy of a universal ethical order. 'Tis a consummation devoutly to be wished. But if it turns out to be an academic's pipedream perhaps this abstract universalism will do more harm than good.

A new school called "existential sociology" fulfills the need for an alternative to the universalism implicit in Habermas's extension of critical theory. In a series of books, several published by Cambridge University Press, a group including Jack Douglas, John Johnson, Richard Brown, and Stanford Lyman are developing an approach that has all the earmarks of a new school held together and reinforced by a common paradigm.

Like Habermas, they confess their values, their interestedness in practical uses to which their researches may be put. But unlike Habermas, they will come out of the library and enter into the concrete situations they study. The paradigm case that best illustrates the impossibility of the researcher retaining his distance from the subject under study is the book by Douglas and Paul Rasmussen, *Nude Beaches*. Imagine the value-free social scientist strolling out onto the southern California sand clad in the white coat of the laboratory technician, clip-board in hand. The phenomena under study would escape him.

The existential sociologist is willing to enter into the lives he is studying. "Our emphasis on the problematic and situated nature of meaningful experience contrasts both with the structuralism of Alvin Gouldner's 'reflexive sociology' and Jürgen Habermas's 'critical theory',[60] declare Douglas and Johnson. And in their situatedness, they are not afraid to acknowledge the role of feelings. They thus distance themselves from all of the more or less parallel distinctions between the practical and theoretical; between thoughts and feelings; theory and practice; contemplation and action; form and matter; universal and particular.

Richard Harvey Brown and Stanford M. Lyman pull together many of the elements of the emergent paradigm in a virtual manifesto issued as an invitation: "Symbolic realism and cognitive aesthetics: An invitation," the essay with which they introduce a paradigm-defining anthology of essays by the school of existential sociologists. These statements deserve to be quoted at length, not only as rich *evidence* of an emergent paradigm; just as important, they are eloquent and original statements *defining* the emergent paradigm.

---

60   Jack Douglas and John Johnson, *Existential Sociology*, Cambridge, 1977., p. xiii.

In general, it might be said that the current awareness of a crisis in sociology focuses on three main issues. First, no available paradigm has achieved dominion in the discipline. Instead a plurality of approaches rooted in different and even opposed epistemologies, compete for regency. Second, none of these paradigms appears to have attained internal consistency with respect to its own... assumptions. Finally, despite sociology's lack of preparedness, a host of moral and political issues demand from it both explication and resolution. As in earlier crises, the task confronting sociology is complex...

Much of the writing in this volume is informed by what might be called a "symbolic realist" or "cognitive aesthetic" perspective. The two terms are not quite synonymous. Symbolic realism stresses ontology; cognitive aesthetics stresses epistemology. The first focuses on the possibility of our having symbolic worlds; the second provides criteria of adequacy for judging whether such worlds constitute knowledge. Cognitive aesthetics is not the romantic aesthetic of the nineteenth century, but instead a critical theory of interpretation and judgment that has much in common with dialectical hermeneutics and semiotics.[61]

What has been gained by allying cognitive aesthetics with dialectic hermeneutics and semiotics? *Dialectical hermeneutics* refers to a school of thought nourished in the tradition of Hegel, Dilthey, Heidegger and Gadamer, with or usually without a little Marx thrown in. *Hermeneutics* is the theory and practice of interpretation. To the positivist its importance is restricted to timid exercises in academic literary criticism or biblical studies. To those who grant a plurality of interpretations, each including slightly different experiences of the same (or ostensibly the same) objects, then the theory of interpretation becomes very important. Dialectics enter in with the play of *rival* interpretations—or *alternative* scenarios.

Semiotics, once again, is the theory of signs. The word came into use with the need for something broader than 'linguistics', which seems restricted to the more literal languages like 'English', 'French', 'German', or 'Swahili'. What about music, or fashions in clothes, or body language? The word *semiotics* also serves as a convenient net for containing syntax (on the relationships among the parts of a sentence), semantics (on the relationships between words in language and things in the world), and pragmatics (the uses to which words are put).

The fact that Brown and Lyman ally themselves with dialectical hermeneutics and semiotics marks their thinking as *perspectival* rather than objective. This next passage combines the exemplary with the elegant in stating and contributing

---

61   Richard Harvey Brown and Stanford M. Lyman, in *Structure, Consciousness, and History,*
      op. cit., pp. 1,2, and 5.

to the definition of the role of perspectives or frames of vision in an emergent paradigm:

> Thinkers from Giambattista Vico to Wilhelm Dilthey to George Herbert Mead have told us that man is the symbol making animal. Unlike animals that merely live, we have lived experience. The world is apprehended and organized through the mediation of our concepts, categories, and structures of thought. To say this is to say that all knowledge is perspectival. Anything we know is known *as* something; it is construed from some point of view. A library, for example, becomes a different object of experience for the accountant, the scholar, and the custodian. Likewise the rules of baseball define what will be seen as a ball or a strike, much as the rules of psychopathology or of sociology respectively define what is to be apprehended as schizophrenia or role conflict. In this view we cannot know what reality is in any absolute or objectivist fashion; instead, all we can know is our symbolic constructions, the symbolic realities that are defined by our particular paradigms or frames of vision…
>
> [A] cognitive aesthetic framework draws attention to the central role of paradigm innovation in the development of science. Both the artist and the scientist, as well as the politician or citizen who is seeking to create a new mode of public discourse, are seen as having a basic affinity: They are creating paradigms through which experience becomes intelligible.[62]

Lyman and Brown not only acknowledge the importance of paradigms and their construction; they also see the inevitability of paradigm wars—the struggles between rival paradigms over whose map provides the best guide to reality. These paradigm wars are not mere academic quibbles. To the extent that their outcomes determine the very meaning of human and social behavior, they amount to titanic struggles over the future of humanity.

The practice of sociology, anthropology, and the other human sciences ceases to be a disinterested study of distant cultures. Instead it becomes a poetizing of human purposes: whither humanity? Shall we become more like machines?

> [T]he spokesmen for cybernetic systems theory argue that society is (or is like) a great computer, with its input and output, its feedback loops, and its programs; this machine—society—is in turn guided by a servo-mechanism—the techno-administrative elite. To see this imagery as a metaphor, however, is to reject it as a literal description, to unmask it as a

---

62   *Ibid.*, p. 5.

legitimating ideology, and to provide a basis for criticizing its rhetorics. By doing a close textual analysis, it becomes clear that in the rhetoric of social cybernetics, there is an atrophy of the very vocabularies of citizenship, moral responsibility, and political community. In place of these, the machinery of governance, initially conceived as serving human values, becomes a closed system generating its own self-maintaining ends. The polity—the arena for the institutional enactment of moral choices—dissolves upward into the cybernetic state, or downward into the alienated individual, whose intentionality is now wholly privatized and whose actions, uprooted from their institutional context, are bereft of social consequence and deprived of moral meaning.[63]

Strong stuff! And their final sentence caps it off: "Our recognition that social order is a construction invites us to actively reconstruct our worlds."[64]

In another essay, Brown is explicit about the implication of multiple realities:

Symbolic realism holds that all social reality is symbolic, including sociology itself. In the symbolic realist view there are multiple realities, including those of social scientists, and none has absolute priority over others. The task of the sociologist becomes that of describing these various realities, their structures, their processes of change, and their coming to be. Such analyses are not copies or blueprints of "reality", however. Instead they represent a kind of decoding or translation by which the realities constituted by peoples are reconstituted into the reality that is social science.[65]

5b. Import of Existential Sociology for Future Studies

Once again we arrive at multiple realities underlying multiple scenarios. Anthropology sought a foundation in semiotics and literary criticism. Literary criticism reached toward psychology in its attempt to grapple with the multiplicity of motives of both author and hero. Psychology explodes into sociology with the realization of the relational character of psyche and the importance of social context. And now, sociology, like the anthropology with which we began this tour of the human sciences, loops back into semiotics.

In discipline after discipline the attempt to find some bedrock of unambiguous empirical research, some solid objectivity, dissolves in a confrontation with

---

63   *Ibid.*, p. 6.

64   *Ibid.*, p. 9.

65   Richard Harvey Brown, "Symbolic realism and sociological thought: Beyond the positivist-romantic debate," in *Structure, Consciousness and History, op. cit.*, p. 14.

ambiguity and "essentially contestable" interpretations. Reality refuses to show a single face. Instead the world of human beings insists on being ever interpretable from different perspectives, no one of which can claim definitive priority to others. The old positivistic worldview, where the physical sciences played the role of secure foundation, gives way to a circular, self-referential process of inquiry where the *coherence* of several disciplines within a single paradigm is more persuasive than any claim to *correspondence* between a conceptual model and reality. For our models, our metaphors, our paradigms define what we take to be reality.

6. Toward an Emergent Paradigm

Having now hurtled through several of the human sciences in sequence, and having lain down their linear movements on the loom of my strategy, I would like to cross this warp with the woof of a few cross-disciplinary comparisons. This weaving manoeuvre will identify some features of an emergent paradigm that are common to these several disciplines. The point of this exercise, once again, is to guide the argument toward the outline of normative scenarios that cash in on recent achievements in the human sciences rather than trying to emulate the hard sciences.

The endgame strategy for this overlong essay is as follows: first, to abstract a set of features characteristic of the new paradigm emerging from the human sciences by following their woof across the warp of the disciplines already summarized; second, to clarify what might be meant by *normative* scenarios in an era when the very idea of norms seems suspect, or, at best, weakened by cultural relativism; and finally, third, to sketch the outlines of a scenario that reflects the features of a new paradigm that is emerging in the human sciences and is also normative in a sense that can survive postmodern critique.

Since each of the features of the emergent paradigm has already been discussed several times and at some length in the several contexts of the disciplines that make up the warp, their review on the woof will be brief. The point is to pull the threads of the warp together by weaving this woof across the different disciplines so that a set of conceptual tools will be available for fashioning, first, a new paradigm, and second, a normative scenario. But the application of these tools is not simple or obvious. Indeed there is a danger of using these new paradigm tools in an old paradigm way. That is why, before their application to the fashioning of normative scenarios, there must be an intervening section on norms and values. Like our understanding of the structures relating facts to one another, our understanding of values is also subject to paradigm change.

Here, then, is a short list of features of a new paradigm emerging from the human sciences, together with some hypotheses about what these features *might* imply for a normative scenario. As we shall see in the next section on a new approach to the normative, these first hypotheses can be misleading. Not until the final section will the true import of these features be fully evident.

1.   The Semiotic Turn

Geertz described anthropology as a semiotic discipline in search of meaning, not a science in search of laws and explanations. Philosophers, particularly Richard Rorty, speak of the linguistic turn in characterizing the significance of Wittgenstein and Heidegger. But Roland Barthes and Michel Foucault apply the tools of linguistic analysis to a wider domain of signs than words alone. Likewise psychologists have liberated themselves from Freud's materialistic meta-psychology to give full weight to Freud's real contribution: his emphasis on the power of symbols. Finally, existential sociology embraces a "symbolic realism" that accords efficacy and power to symbols. In each of the disciplines reviewed we see a turn away from a materialistic ontology that would reduce symbols to the role of epiphenomena—pale reflections of material presences following physical laws. In each of these disciplines there is an acknowledgement of the way symbols can motivate action without relying on a reduction to physicalistic causes to account for their efficacy.

The simple but wrong application of the semiotic turn to normative scenarios might run as follows: as opposed to a nominalist reduction of norms to mere conventions of speech, we can now depend on norms that are resistant to nominalistic reduction. We can identify symbols of values that transcend mere conventions. We can locate standards for the Good the True and the Beautiful in a semiotic order that replaces Plato's realm of Ideas as the locus of normative standards.

Just as I earlier declined the temptation to build the edifice of future studies out of towering stalagmites based on the purportedly firm foundations of the hard sciences, so I now hesitate to hang future studies on a series of normative stalactites reaching down from the lofty heights of some transcendent order, whether semiotic or idealistic. For it is the achievement of recent studies in semiotics to show that *we have no independent access to a transcendent signified beyond the signifiers.* Instead the distinction between signified and signifiers is a "floating" distinction. Each signified becomes a signifier of some further signified. The distinction between signifier and signified is real and useful in particular cases, but when you press for an ultimate signified, Sahib, it's signifiers all the way out. So the Semiotic Turn should not be used in the service of some new idealism that would substitute language for Platonic Ideas.

2. *Difference over Identity*

Geertz invites us, "to look for systematic relationships among diverse phenomena, not for substantive identities among similar ones." He is less interested in what we all share than in how we differ. Likewise linguists are less interested in the identities that abide through the evolutionary changes traced by diachronic etymologies than in the differences that define the synchronic structure of a language at a particular point in time. Words mean what they mean, not by virtue of some one-to-one link between self-identical symbol and self-identical thing. Rather, words mean what they mean by virtue of the usage-place they maintain in a structure of differences, the lattice-work of an entire language. In Guntrip's review of the object relations school of psychologists, he criticized Freud's preoccupation with universals. Instead he focused on the differences that make each individual unique. Finally, in the symbolic realist view of existential sociology, "there are multiple realities, including those of social scientists, and none has absolute priority over others."

At the risk of engaging at a level of abstraction that fades off into the vacuous, I cannot resist a very simple observation. Physical things impress us with their self contained identity. Apples, rocks, chairs, tables—all the pieces of furniture of the physical world—come in clearly contained bundles with definable borders. Identity is easy for physical things, and to the extent that we are preoccupied with physical things, we take identity as a tacit criterion of existence. To be is to be a clearly identifiable individual. When it comes to symbols, however, identity—and therefore ontological status—is less obvious. What about the number 3? Or Beethoven's Fifth Symphony? Or the gross national product? Or the cause of the Civil War? Philosophers wax scholastic about such things just because categories like identity, borrowed from a common sense schooled on the physical, turn out to be inappropriate and hopelessly clumsy when applied to such symbolically mediated "entities."

Just because there are so many different kinds of difference, and my simple observation abstracts from all those second order differences, I feel at risk of broaching into the obvious or the vacuous; nonetheless, I think there may be a non-trivial relationship between this second feature of the emergent paradigm and the first feature—the semiotic turn. My very abstract point is just this: preoccupation with the physical will lead one to focus on identities; preoccupation with the semiotic order of symbols demands that one focus on differences. To know a physical thing is to know what is inside its boundaries: its shape, what it is made of, its material. To know a symbol is to know how it relates to what is outside: its grammatical and syntactic relationships, the place it maintains in a logical space, what it is *not*. As the linguist Ferdinand de Saussure discovered with his insight into "the arbitrariness of the sign," it matters not at all what a word is made of, its letters, the ink on the page, the sound of the syllables. What matters is the pattern of relationships that differentiate the usage of that word from all other words.

This preoccupation with difference rather than identity in the semiotic order might also be prematurely elevated into a Platonic ideal for application to normative scenarios. We might rush off in praise of the organic and unique as opposed to the mechanical and the standardized. We might insist on schooling that treated every student as completely unlike every other. We might demand healthcare that treated every patient differently. We might oppose every attempt at bureaucratic standardization as an obsolete holdover from an industrial order that achieved economies of scale by stamping out the same, same, same from the drill-presses of middle America.

As we shall see in the concluding section, there is something important to be gleaned from correlating the metaphysics of identity with the industrial era, and the metaphysics of difference with the information era. But an over-hasty idealization of difference will get us into just as much trouble as an habitual preoccupation with identity.

3. *From Explanation to Narration*

In each of the disciplines reviewed one finds increased attention to narrativity as the form of redescription most appropriate to the human sciences. Whether it is Clifford Geertz giving thick descriptions of the plots that make sense of the rituals of different cultures, or psychologists referring to archetypal myths, or sociologists seeking the meaning of social behavior in the contexts of stories with beginnings, middles and ends, the importance of story, plot and narration is now recognized well beyond the boundaries of literary criticism where it was always acknowledged. Among philosophers probably Paul Ricouer, author of the monumental three volume *Time and Narrativity,* has done most to show how narration does a better job of capturing the meaning of human actions than explanations that would reduce those actions to the interactions of simpler elements described by the hard sciences.

The implication of narrativity for normative scenarios is obvious: scenarios are narrations with beginnings, middles and ends. Narrativity distinguishes scenarios from predictions, which merely give a state description at some future date. This implication is so straightforward it need not wait for a subtler development after the next section's new look at norms. The narrativity of scenarios isn't something that will be added after an appreciation of new developments in the human sciences. Narrativity is essential to scenarios. The human sciences are emulating those futurists who use scenarios to the extent that the human sciences embrace narrativity. Here we have a clear instance of the potential irony mentioned in the introduction: what a shame it would be if futurists decamped in the direction of the explanatory hard sciences just as reinforcements were arriving from the human sciences bearing justifications for story telling.

4. *The Fall into Time*

Once upon a time there was no sense of historical time. Aristotle regarded the number of species as fixed for all eternity. Neither Platonic Forms nor Aristotelian species were subject to change and evolution. The very idea of historical progress was an invention of thinkers like Vico and Herder. Then Darwin altered the place of humanity in nature. But still the hard sciences followed the paradigm of mathematics: just as two plus two always and everywhere equals four, so the truths discovered by physics and chemistry should be true for all time.

The principal figures discussed—Hegel, Nietzsche, Heidegger, Wittgenstein, Foucault, T.S. Kuhn—transport us *from* a world where we could plant our feet firmly on the ground of foundations laid in the concrete of scientific materialism, then train our gaze upward toward the fixed stars of timeless values… *to* a world where we float or fall (in relativistic space it's hard to tell the difference) and never come to rest on firm foundations. Things change. Nations crumble. Ideologies that had been likened to religions suddenly lose credibility.

Hegel awakened us to history. Nietzsche and Heidegger worked out the significance of history for the individual: a certain amount of despair and confusion at the transiency of things and their lack of a clear direction. Wittgenstein and Foucault offer different but equally unsettling perspectives on the semiotic turn: the realization that almost all of our distinctively human experience is mediated by symbols, almost never raw or immediate, always culturally and linguistically tinged and therefore never entirely innocent.

These lessons of the last century or so of philosophy—about time and history and the gradual displacement of the solid by the semiotic—leave us today just a little tentative about our commitments. We know better than to believe that we can catch a quick express called The Absolute. We know that the best we can expect is a local ride on the relative. The Absolute left the station long ago. And we know that we are likely to switch trains a few times before we get to wherever it is we are going.

Rather than suggesting new norms, The Fall into Time seems to undermine the very idea of the normative—at least to the extent than norms are thought to transcend mere fashions. Both the Fall into Time and the next feature of the emergent paradigm, The Democratization of Meaning, both threaten a Platonic commitment to timeless norms. These two final features of the emergent paradigm therefore make a transition to, and compel us to entertain, an alternative to the Platonic interpretation of normative values.

5. *The Democratization of Meaning*

From Reception Theory in literary criticism to communicative ethics in philosophy and sociology, the logic of legitimation is shifting from a dependence on transcendent norms to the immanent process of dialogue among writers and readers and speakers of the language. The *real* meaning of love or happiness or justice is not there to be discovered like diamonds or oil, trapped beneath layers of sediment just waiting for someone with enough intelligence and resources to find it. To a significant extent we are making it up as we go along. Human virtues are renewable resources. They are created and sustained by practices. Reception Theory locates the ultimate authority for interpreting the meaning of a text neither with the author, nor in an autonomous text, but in a community of readers. Likewise future studies might draw a lesson from Reception Theory by locating authority over the future neither with God nor with policy makers, nor with scientific futurists, but instead with the citizens of today who "vote" through a range of symbolic transactions for the shape of tomorrow.

But this prospect of democratization raises a problem, the same problem democracy has always posed: *What if the people are wrong?* There is an abiding and intrinsic tension between the process of democracy and the concept of transcendent norms. To the extent that we surrender arbitration of norms to the will of the people, then there will always be some aristocratic voices who protest a descent to the lowest common denominator. Ever since Socrates debated Thrasymachus (who said that justice was the will of the stronger), ever since Thomas Jefferson defended the need for more direct representation against Alexander Hamilton's support for a more aristocratic Senate, the old debate between transcendent norms and the immanent will of the people has been with us under one rubric or another: the ideal vs. the real, high standards vs. popular opinion, norms (as ideals) vs. the normal (taken as median or average). Even the language of the normative is subject to this dialectical ambivalence. So let us turn to a more focused reflection on a new approach to this very old debate.

7. A New Look at Norms

In both a pre-modern religious context, and in a modern, liberal, progressive context, the idea of a normative scenario is likely to connote some common understanding of some transcendent values. In the pre-modern context those values would be derived and legitimated by reference to the will of God. What is good, everywhere and for all time, is what conforms to the will of God. In a more modern, secular, humanistic regime, norms are legitimated by reference to a science of human nature. The secular enlightenment substituted the universality of science for the universal reach of the will of a monotheistic God. In both contexts—pre-modern religion and modern science—there was a way to legitimate norms that could transcend the particular interests of private individuals or local customs and practices. There was a way of refering to a higher authority, an Absolute that transcended the relative perspectives of different individuals or different cultures.

But now, for better or worse, we live in a postmodern era. Part of what defines the postmodern condition is the lack of definitive criteria—religious or scientific—for progress toward a more perfect humanity. In place of the Christian heaven on earth we are confronted with a plurality of religions: Muslim, Buddhist, Hindu, Christian, Jewish, and any number of other sects. In place of the modern idea of secular progress we find a plurality of standards for a more perfect humanity: feminist, multi-cultural, native American, you name it.

So it's hard to name a norm and claim that it applies to everyone everywhere. And if a putative norm does not apply to everyone everywhere, then perhaps it is not a norm at all, but just one more custom peculiar to a particular tribe. Jews don't eat pork. Southern blacks like pig's feet. WASPs cultivate the stiff upper lip, and so on.

To reduce the normative to the sociology of taste seems to rob the normative of the obligatory, imperative power that premodern and modern norms possessed. These postmodern "norms" seem pale and impotent by comparison to the Commandments of the Lord or the universality of science.

No wonder normative scenarios seem out of date. No wonder that reference to norms seems naive. No wonder that futurists are tempted into the bad faith of suppressing their wishes for a *better* tomorrow and devote their best efforts to worst case scenarios. The premodern and modern sources for legitimating transcendent norms have been de-legitimated by a more sophisticated recognition that we live in postmodern times when absolutes like God or secular humanism have lost their credibility.

How, then, is it possible to reconstruct a normative discourse after the deconstruction of transcendent absolute values? How can we justify normative scenarios when norms are essentially contestable? The answer, I believe, is by *entering the contest*. A normative scenario can articulate the force of widely accepted values without requiring either the omnipotence of a Lord of lords or the universality of mathematics. Norms need not be absolute in order to transcend the relativity of individual opinion. Norms need not be completely unambiguous in order to exercise some force of obligation.

Let me give some examples. There are legitimate grounds for differences over the degree to which a government should guarantee the welfare of all of its citizens. Yet some sympathy for the sufferings of underprivileged children seems to be a normal response of most mature adults. Is this because they feel constrained to obey some religious command to act as their brothers' keeper? Is it because some sympathy for other members of the species is part of human nature? It is less important that we prove the superiority of the religious or the naturalistic explanation than that there be an actual *experience* of sympathy and compassion. *Why* the experience occurs is less important than the fact *that* it occurs.

I lack a convincing theory for justifying the source of moral obligation. But the lack of of a meta-ethical theory does not preclude the possibility of ethical practice. Having given up God as well as nature as foundations for values, I am well aware of the tenuousness of my grasp on morality. I have no knock down drag out proofs for the validity of the norms I would invoke. Yet it is my belief—and it is only a belief—that the normative dimension of human existence *necessarily partakes of such tentativeness.*

It is my belief that what would count as a *better* humanity must necessarily differ from actual humanity in ways that are speculative, creative, risky, artistic, and never definitive or obvious. The gap between what ought to be and what is cannot be closed by the force of law or the force of mere familiarity. It can only be closed by a human will that could have acted otherwise.

Things change. Appeals to tradition are not always sufficient for invoking norms. Nor is it wise to throw out all the wisdom gained by earlier generations. It is not easy to improve upon the way life is lived. The lessons of history are not to be despised. Yet if we are to give any credence to *the fall into time* then we must grant the obsolescence of the Platonic correlation of The Good with the Absolute and Eternal. We must acknowledge that the price of holding onto that Platonic correlation is nihilism: we would throw out the baby of morality with the bathwater of absolute, eternal Truth. The only way to preserve the force of morality is to decouple it from a Platonic correlation with timelessness.

Now that we have fallen into time we must figure out how to moralize in time— how to find, create, and maintain norms that are appropriate to the times. Rather than imagining that norms must derive their obligatory force from some timeless foundation that would transcend any particular conditions, we must see how the moral dimension of our existence is intrinsically tentative—stretched across a gap between what *is* in any given present, and what *might be* in a better future.

The definition of what would count as a better future cannot be read off from the past or from some great blueprint in the sky that would transcend past, present and future. Instead the criteria for what will count as a *better* future, like the criteria for what would count as better art, are bound to contain some reference to the recent past and present. Like all cultural movements, the evolution of ethics will depend on an interplay between individual creativity and an evolutionary selectivity that operates on a level that transcends the individual.

Knowing this much about the necessary tentativeness of norms, what can we derive from the recent past and present of the human sciences? What hints toward a normative scenario can be drawn from recent developments in the human sciences? The Semiotic Turn suggests the importance of *meaning* in all its ambiguity. Rather than relying on the force of law or aspiring to the grip of necessity, a semiotic anthropology shows us how the values derived from ethnic origins can be constitutive of meaning *inside* a given culture without necessarily having obligatory power over those *outside* that culture.

Salman Rushdie got into trouble by trying to straddle two cultures. As a westerner he embraced the value of free speech and the liberty of the individual; but as a Muslim he committed blasphemy. He now claims obedience to Islam. It is hard to see how his piety toward Mohammed can be squared with the words that he has written and published so freely.

Most of us do not span radically different cultures in most of our day to day activities. Our values derive from the interplay between the norms of the culture we were reared in and our awareness of a larger, newer world that calls to our sense of concern. To say that we derive our sense of morality from the culture we are reared in is to admit a vast panoply of influences, given the range of texts we may have been exposed to in our formal education and the range of stories we have internalized from years of television and movies.

The influences that determine one's sense of morality in late twentieth-century America cannot be said to constitute a well-ordered, internally coherent whole. We inherit a dialogue that posits the rights of the individual even as it posits the need for social justice. The dialectic of individualism and collectivism is not about to be settled once and for all, even after the demise of Marxist ideology. So Salman Rushdie's guilt in the eyes of Islam cannot be redeemed by an equal and opposite innocence in the eyes of a western tradition preaching the right of the individual to free speech. For even in our western tradition we acknowledge the needs of the collective and the demands it can make for individual sacrifice.

Am I arguing for the death of Salman Rushdie? No. I am only pointing out the *difficulty* of ethical debate across cultural boundaries. For those who acknowledge the cultural relativity of values, there can be no simple appeal to standards that transcend all cultures. One can appeal to norms that operate within and work to constitute a culture. But once one steps outside that culture, or tries to stand between two cultures, then one risks the betrayal of one culture for another. Once you become a cultural double agent, the rules become very messy—which is not to say there are no rules; only that they will often conflict with one another.

To summarize the significance of the semiotic turn: we now know that the sources of *meaning* to be found in the myths and values of a given culture can be called upon to give form and structure to an individual life; but further, we know that these sources of meaning can transcend the individual without being absolute or eternal. Norms can be obligatory and contestable at once. This is how norms *are*. They are not to be confused with will o' the wisp opinions at one extreme, or necessary laws at the other. The human sciences show us how to move beyond a laws-and-causes approach to human nature, and still hold onto the role of culturally conditioned *meaning* as constitutive of an individual life.

Literary criticism then helps us to read the text of our culture to determine the inventory of meanings that we can draw upon. By deconstructing the authority of the author, literary criticism reminds us of the shared work of constituting and maintaining meanings within a culture. Reception Theory reminds us of the importance of a literary selectivity in which readers participate in the evolution of meaning.

Critics are the pre-eminent *prosumers*, Alvin Toffler's term for proactive consumers who influence the shape of a product by making sure the producers know what they want; or, through the wonders of modern technology and information processing, actually participate in the production of a product by feeding their preferences into the design and production software. Critics have been doing as much ever since Milton read Virgil. Critics help to determine the shape of the literary "product" of a society. But the rest of us participate as well each time we "vote" with the purchase of a book, or contribute to an opinion survey, or tune in to a particular show on television. In the metabolism of the symbolic economy, we all play a role every time we engage in dialogue, read a newspaper, respond to a new movie.

As with the literal ballot box, so also the symbolic ballot box of cultural metabolism—the production and consumption of images—elects only those options it can understand and appreciate, whether candidates or referenda. Part of the role of futurists in this system of cultural metabolism should therefore be to articulate in an understandable and appealing way images of a better future. We need an antidote to *Bladerunner*, a foil for *Clockwork Orange*, a better sequel to *1984*, a truly humanized *Animal Farm*.

It may be too late to talk about utopia. 'Utopian' has become a pejorative term. Pragmatism is in better favor than utopianism. But there are times when pragmatism, the philosophy of *whatever works,* doesn't work. There are times when business as usual is doomed, when even incremental reforms are inadequate, when discontinuities are inevitable and radical alternatives the only way out. At such times it is irresponsible to refuse to be utopian, for only on the other side of a seemingly unbridgeable gap can conditions be once again stable.

Think of utopia as a new equilibrium, as a new constellation of the same old stuff, but now so arranged that everything works where before everything seemed to be at odds with everything else. Vicious circles turn virtuous. Think, for example, about the relationships between education, state budgets, cultural conflict, and the high costs of high technology. It is easy to see a vicious circle driving ethnic minorities further into poverty because they lack access to expensive new technologies only available to white kids in rich schools. Yet one can also imagine a scenario in which individually paced instruction software allows ethnic minorities to learn better than in crowded classrooms with inadequate numbers of well-intentioned but unwittingly racist instructors. After using the instructional tools of a color-blind technology, a more educated work force improves productivity, super-charges the economy, which pays for better schools with better technology for improved education of ethnic minorities…

What can tip the vicious circle over into its virtuous reversal? If Reception Theory is right, the reversal might happen as quickly and easily as the reversal of figure and ground on one of the famous psychological tests like the vase/face diagram. Now you see it as a vase, now you see two facing faces; now you see a vicious circle, now you see a virtuous circle that is well nigh utopian.

But it sometimes takes someone to point out the utopian possibilities in an otherwise wretched situation. I have some friends, two noted futurists who shall remain nameless, on whom I can always count for the darkest of perspectives. They are experts in the development of worst case scenarios. Once, upon seeing them walking down the hall together at SRI International, I saluted them as The Brothers Grim. I value their contributions to the list of warning signals, but their voices are too predictably Cassandran to be balanced or, therefore, trustworthy when it comes to anticipating some of the better possibilities.

Given all of the very real problems facing humanity today it is not easy to see how some of them might be solved. It is easier to see how what has been invented can come unravelled than it is to see how unsolved problems can be solved. It is easier to take apart something that exists than to build an incredibly complex working organism never before seen on earth. So it is understandable that futurists find it easier to draft devolution scenarios than to imagine transformative solutions that would turn vicious circles into virtuous systems of mutual support. In order to draft optimistic scenarios that are plausible, the futurist must be able to imagine solutions and inventions that no one else has yet imagined. This is a tall order that would require the futurist not just to hope for such inventions but to actually invent them.

I, for one, do not feel adequate to the task. I have no solution to the crisis of escalating costs for healthcare or declining standards in our nation's schools. I don't know how to organize an ecologically sustainable market economy. I have no elegant answer for housing the homeless or feeding the hungry. Yet I am convinced that if we futurists are to pursue our calling responsibly, we must try to imagine scenarios in which some of these problems have been solved so that we can then get on to dealing with other problems without engaging in the denial of deeply held values.

8. Earth Might Be Fair... A Normative Scenario

Despite my own postmodern waverings between secular atheism and pagan polytheism, I am nonetheless drawn to the sheer poetry of the Christian hymns I was forced to sing in compulsory chapel at school. "Earth might be fair and all men glad and wise…" What a wonderful idea, even in its sexist formulation. "All persons glad and wise," wouldn't exactly scan.

Earth might be fair: the richness lies precisely in the ambiguity as between ethical and aesthetic interpretations of 'fair.' We could certainly do with a little more justice; and we could also do with more beauty, the Shakespearean meaning of 'fair.'

Imagine a world without lawyers, a world where disputes did not have to be settled in court because there were so many fewer disputes to begin with. Imagine a world where generosity and good will were the norm rather than suspicion and defensiveness. Imagine a world where all the resources now devoted to processing and adjudicating insurance claims were instead devoted to preventive health maintenance. Imagine a world where all the resources now devoted to advertising were instead devoted to quality improvements in products. Just as we are now learning to live in a world where the cold war is over and we can entertain the distribution of a peace dividend, imagine a time when we could entertain the distribution of a litigation dividend, an insurance dividend, an advertising dividend.

But what would all the lawyers and insurance salesmen and advertising copywriters *do?* What will all the Russian soldiers do? But is it any justification for existing practices that place a high burden on other human beings that the human beings who practice them don't have anything else to do? Let them play. I'm serious. Let me explain.

One of the problems of a postmodern economy is to find alternatives to the industrious productivity of work as a measure of economic health. What if we are working to produce too much of the wrong stuff? Throughout pre-modern and modern times, productivity was a legitimate measure of economic strength. People did not have enough of the basic necessities and we depended on natural science and technology to improve our ability to get more out of less in less time. But now there is general agreement among the techno-elite that the remaining pockets of hunger are caused not by a lack of agricultural capacity but by social and political snafus that leave food rotting in the field; homelessness is caused not be the lack of raw materials for dwellings but by policies that force foreclosures on people who cannot cope with the complexities of a global economy.

At risk of gross over-simplification I want to say that our most vexing problems today are not problems that can be solved by science and technology; they are human problems that call for a degree of social invention that we have not seen since the creation of democracy and the writing of the Constitution. We don't yet know how to organize our human interactions. Some of us haven't even learned how to play together; or if we have, we've grown up and forgotten. Consequently we try to make up for a lack of joy by enjoying the material possessions that science and technology and the market economy can spew forth with abandon.

Take the nuclear family, one of the principle means for organizing human interactions. Recall poet Philip Larkin's famous line: "They fuck you up, your mum and dad." But they had their problems too: Victorian upbringing, a culture of possessive individualism that has evolved from what social critics called alienation to what a more psychoanalytically oriented critique calls narcissism—learning to live with alienation and love it by loving only oneself.

Surely there must be a better way to raise hairless monkeys. But what might it be? Maybe if mom and dad were less alienated, less over-worked, less tired at the end of the day… then earth might be fair. If more fathers and mothers raised children who retained a sense of wonder, and a sense of humor; if mom and dad could avoid the descent of their own love into squabbles over what he said she said about what he did… then earth might be fair. But until then we will remain locked in the same old Freudian/Frankfurt School family drama that extends from exploitation in the workplace to oppression over the breakfast table… if there is a breakfast table and not a staggered grabbing for 'Fruit Loops' and 'Pop Tarts' on the way to work.

Despite the wonders of modern science there never seems to be enough: enough love, enough attention, enough respect, enough dignity. So we make too much of the things we know how to make: war, toxic wastes, bad television. Perhaps there is a better way to organize our lives and our relationships, one that does not pit the demands of work against the delights of love. Perhaps there is a way to reconstruct our world, as Brown and Lyman invite us to do. But in doing so we cannot base our reconstruction on the firm foundations of science. Nor will we be able to depend on transcendent norms as a measure of the better. Instead, like sailors rebuilding our ship at sea, we must fashion our new world from what we have at hand: our existing legal system, our existing healthcare system, our existing educational system, our existing families. So the job is not altogether utopian.

But let us not forget that radical change for the better *is* possible. Dictatorships in Haiti, the Philippines and Nicaragua *have* been toppled in the last decade—which is not to say that their successors are without problems. Real per capita disposable income in the United States *has* grown over ten-fold in the twentieth century— which is not to say that we know what to do with the money. Nor should we ignore real declines in the same figure over the past fifteen years for the lower quintiles of the population. Finally and most emphatically, the fall of the iron curtain and the end of the cold war must offer lessons of hope regarding other seemingly intractable issues.

I can recall spending a week at a retreat in Wyoming with a very brainy group from the John F. Kennedy School at Harvard, plus assembled experts like Robert MacNamara, Representative Les Aspin, and a former Ambassador to Austria, all gathered in the early 1980s to entertain alternatives to nuclear deterrence fifty years into the future. I had been asked to help with the methodology of alternative scenario development. But in the course of five days of intense discussion I was unable to bend the collective wisdom of that group to entertain seriously any scenario that would contain less then 50 percent of the then current force structure over the next fifty years—still enough megatons to make the rubble bounce and render the earth uninhabitable. Less than ten years later we now take for granted what was then unthinkable to some very good thinkers. Surely there is a lesson here somewhere about the impotence of hope among intellectuals when confronted by the power of entrenched acceptance of the intolerable. We intellectuals would err on the side of pessimism rather than be accused of naivete. World-weary pessimism seems so much more intellectually respectable than even the best educated hope.

But I would argue—and it has been the aim of this essay to do so—that the fashionable face of all-knowing despair is finally immoral. Granted, the bubble-headed optimism of Pangloss and Polyanna are equally immoral. A refusal to look at poverty or oppression can contribute to their perpetuation; but so can an intellectual commitment to their inevitability.

So let us entertain, at least for a moment, a scenario that builds on what we are learning from the human sciences—a scenario that exhibits some of the features of an emergent paradigm. Imagine, if you will, a *sublimation of the economy.* In fact it is already happening if you can see it as such. The industrial economy of the production and consumption of material things is giving way to an information economy of ephemeral entertainments and services. This is not news. But the *interpretation* of this epochal shift in the way we earn our daily bread has not yet been fully developed in terms of the Semiotic Turn evident in the human sciences. Instead the slogan, *All that is solid melts into air,* has been interpreted, from Karl Marx to Marshall Berman,[66] as a lament over the loss of normative meaning that the process of modernization has wreaked upon stable cultures. But once we decouple the normative from the eternal, once we fully accept *the fall into time,* then there is a possibility—worth entertaining as one among several scenarios—that the statement, *All that is solid melts into air,* might cease to be interpreted as a lament for lost certainties and become instead an announcement of the advent of the sublime.

Sublimatio was the term the alchemists used for the process by which the philosopher's stone was heated to a point that it melted into vapor—air—without ever passing through the intermediate liquid state. Sublimation was later taken by Freud to mean the process by which erotic and aggressive instincts are redirected into the creation of art, culture and religion—thus allowing him, under the influence of a mechanistic-physicalistic paradigm, to then reduce the products of culture to *nothing but* redirected instinctual energy—art as so much smeared shit. But the metaphor of sublimation—and, like the alchemists, I take it only as a metaphor—can just as well be taken as an access to the sublime. When the mechanistic-physicalistic paradigm is shifted by the Semiotic Turn, then there is an opportunity for reinterpreting the efficacy of the sublime *all the way down* rather than reducing culture to the redirection of base instincts all the way up.

In talking this way about the sublime, I know I risk gaining allies I don't want. I do not want the support of New Age enthusiasts who think that the sublime is some esoteric realm that can be accessed by incantations, crystals, or yet another seminar on the Course in Miracles. Nor do I hope to please supporters of that ole' time religion. Virtually every form of orthodox religion—with the possible exception of Zen Buddhism, whose supporters deny that it is a religion—seem to me to be subject to charges of childishness, wish fulfilment, and an indulgence in magical thinking that is inconsistent with the real contributions that science has made to our interaction with our environment. Whatever religions may have contributed to social organization and psychological well-being in the pre-modern world, in our postmodern world their multiplicity means that they are in danger of doing more harm than good. We don't need more *jihads.*

No, the process of sublimation we are now undergoing owes little or nothing to an already completed, eternal sublime. Nor can it be reduced to a redirection of instinctual or material foundations. Instead it is a self-referential, emergent, creative lifting by the bootstraps that generates meaning *where there was none*. It is not impossible, nor are there any guarantees. This is the bane and the blessing of human freedom in the realm of the sublime.

---

66   Cf. Marshall Berman, *All That is Solid Melts into Air, .* Berman takes his title from Marx's
      formulation in *The Communist Manifesto:* "

Imagine a scenario in which educational reform were finally taken seriously, not as the imposition of some new religion on the young, but as the cultivation of human potential. The tools are at hand, but today we have not yet applied those tools in our schools. Instead we expose our children to teachers who are drawn from the lowest quintile of our universities' graduating classes. As they say, those that can, do; those that can't, teach. But imagine what could happen if education became the cause of the nineties, much as civil rights and the Vietnam war preoccupied the sixties, or feminism and the environment motivated so many in the seventies, or greed obsessed the eighties. It could happen. Social agendas do change.

If education became the cause of the nineties, if teachers' salaries were raised and the respect paid to educators enhanced, then by the turn of the century we might be graduating students who were truly skilful, not just in the manufacture of physical goods, but in the creation and consumption of the sublime. And how much lighter on the earth such an economy would be!

The spread of industrial manufacturing to produce more *things* puts our environment at severe risk. This is not news. But only now are we beginning to see that economic growth need not be correlated with energy demand or the exploitation of non-renewable resources. In our work with one of the nation's largest electric utility companies, Pacific Gas and Electric (PG&E), Global Business Network has helped to fashion scenarios that show PG&E's future as dependent not on generating and selling *more* energy, but on building profitability by helping their consumers consume *less* energy. PG&E can sell what Amory Lovins calls *negawatts* rather than megawatts. PG&E can sell conservation and still stay in business. Paradigm shifts are possible, even for upper management.

Better education can lead to more efficient use of energy. And there are technologies under development that can help clean up the mess we have already made. Nano-technology—the technology of manufacturing at the molecular level—may be able to generate mini-machines that eat toxic wastes or transform them into useful resources. It is possible, according to Eric Drexler, author of *Engines of Creation.* The possibilities were at least sufficiently intriguing to motivate Peter Schwartz, president of Global Business Network, to host the first international conference on nano-technology. Peter, by the way, wasn't paid for this task. He did it because he saw in nano-technology the possibility of a better future. He cares. This is what makes him a good futurist.

Bio-technology promises similar breakthroughs. Of course it is possible that we will release some horrible mutation on the face of the earth. Negative scenarios must be developed as cautionary tales. There is a Faustian hubris to scenarios that depend solely on techno-fixes. But there are some techno-fixes that will be required if this scenario is to advance from its beginning through its middle toward an end.

If this scenario's beginning depends on vast improvements in our educational system, it's middle would chart the application of intelligence to many of our more or less technical problems: energy, the health of the environment, the health of individuals. There are feedback loops in this scenario, vicious circles that turn virtuous. Today too many children show up at school too sick and mal-nourished to learn anything at all. Tomorrow's students might be better fed, healthier, and therefore better able to learn how to stay healthy. It is possible.

It is also possible that the sublimation of the economy will lighten the burden on the earth that our industrial economy creates in the first place. *Pace* Paul and Anne Ehrlich, who trace most of the earth's ills to over-population, perhaps a human species less bent on material possessions and material consumption might be able to raise rather than lower the carrying capacity of the ecosphere. In order to contemplate such a scenario one must pass through a paradigm shift from a mechanistic-energetic physics of reality, through the Semiotic Turn, to the economics of the sublime. For only on the other side of that paradigm shift does one begin to escape the law of the constant conservation of matter and energy. So I want to return to the centrality of the Semiotic Turn as an interpretation of the information revolution, and to the Fall into Time as an aspect of our self-understanding of human freedom.

I know of no law of the constant conservation of laughter, or any limitation on joy. I see no reason to limit our sense of what is possible for the distribution of delight. These human *goods* need not be subject to a law of constant conservation. If I have more, you needn't have less. Quite to the contrary, there might be a virtuous circle of mutual reinforcement in the spread of sublime delight, like a ripple of laughter that gains momentum in a crowd. According to the economics of the sublime, there *can* be *enough* for all.

I know that this scenario is beginning to sound impossibly utopian, like something sprouted from the shores of California where the loco-weed grows. So I will hasten to add something about the problems that have *not* been solved by the middle of this scenario.

There is no universal understanding of the best way to live a deeply fulfilling human life. On the contrary there is a rich and variegated ecology of customs and mores. Further, there is a constant risk of *transgression*. Precisely to the extent that people have learned that *being good* is not necessarily about conforming to timeless norms, but rather more about exercising human freedom in the service of creativity and delight, there is a constant danger of decadence. For like creativity in art, creativity in life sometimes requires a bending of the rules for the sake of beauty. But not all novelty in art is successful. Some slides over into the decadent and ugly. The Enlightenment rationality of the Minuet will slip over into Wagner, and from thence to jazz and rock'n'roll. Next thing you know you get Heavy Metal. I love the Grateful Dead but I draw the line at Metalica. How is one to know where to draw the line?

There are no rules for how to break the rules safely, though *games* can be seen in this context as ways of limiting play to only those moves that are safe, moves that limit risks to contestants. The spread of human freedom means a spread of risk taking, and risks are not risks if they never fail. There will be failures, and there will be the need for means of insuring that failures are not too disastrous for too many people. Maybe we will never get a full insurance dividend, not unless we can avoid experiments on the scale of the U.S.S.R. Experiments in new systems of social and economic organization should be smaller, and fail-safe mechanisms far beyond my imagination will need to be built in, checks and balances to rival the inventiveness of the Constitution. For, as I've said, the spread of human freedom means a spread of risk taking, and risks are not risks if they never fail.

This scenario is not utopian because evil will not have been eliminated. On the contrary, the close bond between freedom and transgression means that some confrontations with evil are virtually inevitable. Though it may sound as perverse as Freud's uncovering of infant sexuality, I see the origin of evil in the play of innocents, in the horsing around that got too rough, in the joke that went wrong. "I didn't mean it that way," he said. The Semiotic Turn can end in tears.

Watch the play of cute little kittens and you will see a rehearsal for the brutality of the tiger. See in the tussling of adorable little puppies the vicious attack of the wolf. But there is no viciousness or brutality in the animal kingdom, really. The moral overtones come only from minds that can add an interpretation of cruelty to what, in nature, is a mere act of survival. It takes a twisted mind to turn nature's metabolism into acts of evil. It takes a Semiotic Turn to add cruelty to nature.

It takes a twisted parent to convince a child that he is "being mean" to his younger sister when all he was doing was playing. This move is called "attribution" among psychologists. It's one of the ways that Mum and Dad can fuck you up. "Don't pinch your sister," is one thing. "Don't be mean," is another. By the latter I may learn not only how *not* to be mean, but also that, deep down, I *am* mean. Innocence disappears so quickly.

So the very thing that renders the sublimation of the economy possible—the Semiotic Turn—also renders transgression unto evil virtually inevitable. Earth might be fair, and almost all glad and wise, but human beings will not be angels, and evil will not be eradicated.

But human beings can be more truly human, more free, more creative, and less subject to the uniform necessities of nature. We have struggled up through the realm of necessity and now stand, more and more of us, on the brink of the realm of freedom. The shift to an information economy, the sublimation of the economy, is the crucial instrumentality for this transition.

Precisely because the very nature of information is to differentiate, precisely because information theory defines information as a difference that makes a difference—news, not noise or redundancy—an information economy can thrive only where mass-market conformity breaks up into highly differentiated niche markets, even unto markets of one.

There was a fine match—a paradigmatic coherence—between industrial mass-manufacturing and the conformist values of the mass-market. If keeping up with the Joneses meant having the same car, and the genius of the industrial economy lay in producing lots and lots of the same car, then the match between supply and demand was, as it were, made in heaven. But this match is coming unglued with the transition from the industrial to the information economy. As Arnold Mitchell, creator of SRI's Values and Lifestyles (VALS) program, used to put it, the Belongers (we used to capitalize the names of our lifestyle segments) liked to "fit in," but those who lead the new lifestyles "prefer to stand out rather than fit in." Individuation is the name of the game in the new economy. But individuation is (a) precisely what becoming more human is all about according to every wise psychologist from Jung to Eric Ericson, and (b) precisely what an information economy, as opposed to a mass-manufacturing industrial economy, is prepared to deliver.

The VALS program was all about charting the breakup of the mass market into segments or lifestyles that were not, strictly speaking, better or worse than one another, just different. But now the segments are shattering still further as individuals internalize the chaos of postmodern mores into the depths of their souls. There was a time when Achievers could be trusted to behave in all situations like Achievers, and Belongers would remain true blue Belongers, and the try-anything-once crowd, the segment we called Experientials, could be trusted to shop around. But now you see people who are Achievers by day and Experientials by night; ladies who shop Bloomingdales one day and Price Club the next; men who wear black tie one night and a black motorcycle jacket the next. In short, people aren't staying true to type. A marketer's nightmare: people are becoming less predictable.

But this unpredictability should be cause for joy among humanists because it is precisely this unpredictability that we can just as well interpret as freedom flexing her muscles. The old shell of oppressive conformism is breaking. All that is solid melts into air? The constriction of Smalltown's norms for behavior is being broken all over the globe and, one by one, individuals are emerging from the realm of necessity—what nature or nurture tells them the have to do—and they are stepping forth into the realm of freedom. And a new technology, a technology whose essence is to differentiate, will be there to greet them.

This is where we will get the advertising dividend. The old style of advertising depended on broadcasting, a one-to-many communication that blared the same message, over and over again, at everyone. Stage two—the stage that VALS was there to accommodate—was the stage of the partial breakup of the mass-market into segments. The first application of the information revolution to mass-manufacturing allowed for shorter production runs. Economies of scale could be chopped into smaller pieces that, still economically, could satisfy niche markets. Advertising was then customized to tailor the right message about the right product to the right segment through the right medium. This was called narrowcasting. Advertise MacDonalds and pick-up trucks on Saturday afternoon network telecasts of the bowling championships. Save the BMW ads for the reruns of *Brideshead Revisited.*

We are still at a stage somewhere between broadcasting and narrowcasting, somewhere between an industrial and an information economy, somewhere between what I have arbitrarily labelled stage one and stage two. But a perfectly plausible normative scenario can be drawn for stages three and four. People, human beings, are pressing beyond mass conformity, and on beyond niche segmentation, to segments of one. Individuation. And information technology is capable of following them there. Computers are perfect for the task. 1984 was wrong in this respect. Assembling and recording lots of information about individuals need not mean Big Brother's invasion of your privacy. Instead it can mean the careful tailoring of the traffic of marketing information so that I receive information about all and only those things that my purchasing behavior shows I'm interested in.

We already see the first signs of this transition, albeit in a form that any fool can see through, namely, the junk mail that shows up announcing that, yes, you James Ogilvy have been chosen… But this is just the first adolescence of information technology at work. Stage three follows broadcasting to the mass (stage one) and narrowcasting to the few (stage two) with communication to segments of one (stage three). The American Express bundles of one-page catalogs are subtler than the mailings from Publishers' Clearing House. Amex doesn't plaster your name all over everything. But your bundle is not the same as my bundle. Computers have seen to that.

Soon, I don't know how long it will be, I will no longer receive the Sears catalogue, or even the Smith & Hawken catalogue. I will receive the James Ogilvy catalogue. Stage four: narrowcatching (a word Stewart Brand came up with). This is what American Express is trying to give me. They just haven't got enough information about me yet. But when each of us can receive our own personalized catalogue, then we will be ready to distribute the advertising dividend. Then the offensive blare of persuasion will give way to the quieter hum of real information—differences that make a difference to individuated individuals. Then earth might be fairer when fewer billboards deface the countryside or the city skyline. It is possible. This is the direction in which information technology is taking us, and human freedom, I think, wants to go there.

Of course human freedom is very playful, even capricious. And as I've mentioned, in the play of innocents the seeds of evil and transgression are borne. But as playwright and philosopher, Friedrich Schiller pointed out in his *Letters on the Aesthetic Education of Man*, "Man is most truly human when he plays, and when he plays, most truly man." In our playfulness we will keep remaking human life as we go along, better and better for the most part, but occasionally worse.

The fall into time will be more widely acknowledged. Imagine a world where people were able to swim in the tides of change rather than drown in confusion. Employers will be looking for swimmers, people who can keep up with time's current. They are the best at coping with change. In a scenario where most people were comfortable with a certain amount of change there would be less reactionary insistence on the sanctity of tradition, and less certainty about the justification for punishing transgressors.

The democratization of meaning in this scenario will take the form of an evolutionary survival of the fittest interpretations of family life, romance, success. There will not be just one pattern of perfection toward which all would aspire in some recrudescence of industrial standardization. Instead the paradigmatic preoccupation with difference over identity will encourage differentiation and experimentation, if not transgression. There will not be one best way of being human, but a rich ecology of species in the gardens of the sublime…

There is no clear *end* to this scenario just because embracing the fall into time means that there will be no finality, no goal which, once reached, would mark a conclusion. In this sense, too, this scenario is not utopian. I have not drawn a blueprint for an ideal society. Instead I have tried to reinterpret parts of the present—e.g. the information revolution—through the lenses of a paradigm shift already taking place in the human sciences. I believe that some of the phenomena that others lament—the decline of traditional orthodoxies, the melting into air of firm foundations—can be reinterpreted in ways that could contribute to a *better* future. But it is clear to me that this better future cannot be seen in terms of incremental improvements of the commonplace. A paradigm shift is required if we are to reinterpret the present as the prelude to a better future.

What we futurists must do if we are to contribute to the story is not invent a new paradigm out of whole cloth. Rather, we need only look around and see what is already happening in the human sciences. There we find the semiotic turn already accomplished, a preoccupation with difference over identity already evident, the fall into time already acknowledged, and the democratization of meaning well under way. What we must do is weave these threads into scenarios that have normative import, scenarios that carry the transition from explanation to narrativity further into a future we would like to leave to our grandchildren. Truly, Earth might be fair, and almost all glad and wise. We must just use our imaginations to spin out scenarios of better ways to play.

Afterword

Since this essay was first published in 1992, several of its features have come to fruition. In particular, the discussion of the move from broadcasting to narrowcasting to narrowcatching has played out much as described on p. 132. In his 2004 article in *WIRED* magazine, and then in his 2006 book, *The Long Tail* (New York: Hyperion Books), *WIRED* editor, Chris Anderson, shows how the internet and the availability of easily accessible, inexpensive information about previously hard-to-find items makes it possible for companies like Netflix and Rhapsody to make a very good business out of supplying very few copies of very many very short run items. By avoiding the expense of maintaining inventory, such companies are able to do an end run around the industrial era logic of economies of scale. Rather than relying on selling large numbers of just a few items to a mainstream mass market, they can cost effectively connect sellers and buyers of relatively esoteric items. EBay provides another example of this same internet-facilitated logic.

The amazing rise of Google stands as further evidence for the shift from broadcasting to narrowcatching. Each query posed to Google is an example of the reversal of polarity from *casting* to *catching*. The mainstream media were all about *pushing* their messages toward a broad audience. Google substitutes individualized *retrieval* of information for the old, industrial era model of the distribution of information. This shift from *push* to *pull* is also central to the argument of *The Power of Pull* (Basic Books, 2010) by John Hagel III, John Seely Brown and Lang Davison.

Yet another phenomenon exemplifying the shift from broadcast to narrowcatch is the rise of Customer Relationship Management (CRM). Here again it is the shift from industrial era mass manufacturing for a mass market to information era discrimination of the particular wants and whims of individuals that calls for the kind of CRM software that has allowed companies like Oracle and SAP to build their businesses. These business opportunities were evident in the logic of the shift from broadcasting to narrowcatching. While the logic could be developed in scenarios drawn two decades ago, the demonstration of that logic awaited the successes of Google, Amazon, Netflix, Rhapsody, E-Bay, and Oracle.

5. Scenario Planning as the Fulfillment of Critical Theory

Originally published in Futures Research Quarterly, Vol. 12, Number 2, Summer 1996, pp. 5-33; it is the sequel to II.4, an earlier article in the same journal: "Future Studies and the Human Sciences: The Case for Normative Scenarios," Vol. 8, No. 2, Summer 1992, pp. 5-65. These two articles were then expanded into the book, Creating Better Futures, Oxford University Press, 2002. Reprinted with permission.

This essay has several objectives: first, to situate scenario planning in the tradition of social criticism, I would like to enlist the tools of alternative scenario development in the service of moral outrage at past and present social conditions. Rather than allowing future studies to content itself with efforts at prediction of what will be, or speculations about what might be, I would like to hold future studies accountable for helping us to articulate what *should* be. What would a *better* future look like?

The second objective for this essay builds upon the previous essay, "Future Studies and the Human Sciences: The Case for Normative Scenarios,"[67] in which I began the work of situating future studies in the broader context of the human sciences. That essay sought to show how the attempt to build the academic prestige of future studies by imposing standards of value neutrality actually runs counter to a paradigm shift currently taking place in the human sciences. In fields as disparate as psychology, literary criticism, philosophy and anthropology, the human sciences are moving away from an understanding of science as requiring the objectivity of the disinterested, value-neutral observer. Instead, the human sciences are accepting the inevitability of *interested* engagement. The disinterested, dispassionate "view from nowhere"[68] is neither possible to attain, nor appropriate as an aspiration. Efforts to combat bias and prejudice on the part of a jury are perfectly legitimate; but such efforts should not be extrapolated to squeeze the social sciences into the procrustean bed of value-free physical sciences.

Even as that essay concluded with a sketch of a normative scenario entitled 'Earth Might be Fair', that essay gave no indication of the source of moral standards for determining what is fair and what is not. That essay dodged the thorny issues surrounding the concept of justice; or, to be a little more generous, I deferred that discussion to another occasion—this essay. So that is my second objective: to pick

---

67   James Ogilvy, "Future Studies and the Human Sciences: The Case for Normative
      Scenarios," *Futures Research Quarterly,* Vol 8, No. 2, Summer 1992, pp. 5-65.

68   Thomas Nagel, *The View From Nowhere,* Oxford University Press, New York, 1986.

up where that earlier essay left off by looking further for a fulcrum on which to rest the lever of social criticism.

The third objective relates to critical theory: in order to find the moral purchase needed to render future scenarios genuinely normative, I want to borrow some of the moral passion of critical theory, but I want to do so in a way that escapes some of the errors which, I shall argue, critical theory committed. So I will want to criticize critical theory before borrowing from it. We must clean out this well before drawing water from it. But will there be any water left once we have cleaned the well? Before I'm done criticizing, the critical theory I borrow from may be unrecognizably different from the critical theory associated with the Frankfurt School of social criticism. Before getting down to work on these three agendas, it may be worth offering a thumbnail description of the Frankfurt School and the mark it left on what I'm referring to as 'critical theory'.

The Frankfurt School and Critical Theory

'The Frankfurt School' was founded by Theador Adorno and Max Horkheimer, and attracted other scholars, from Erich Fromm and Herbert Marcuse to Jürgen Habermas. Marx was, of course, the original impulse behind the Frankfurt School, but Freud also had a decisive influence. In reaction to the extreme economism of the Second International—a communist conclave that stressed the power of Marxist economics to explain all of human affairs—the Frankfurt School held out for the importance of psychology and aesthetics. Scholars like Erich Fromm and Herbert Marcuse attempted to synthesize the insights of Freud and Marx into a Marxist humanism that had a warmer face than the cold economism of the Second International. Theador Adorno added a cultural dimension with his studies of music and aesthetics. Contrary to the scientism of Engels, Lenin and the Second International, the Frankfurt School was eager to show that man does not live by the means of production alone, but is motivated by sexual instincts and aesthetic aspirations that go far beyond the power of Marxist economics to explain.

Jürgen Habermas represents the latest and fullest maturity of the Frankfurt School. In Habermas, Marxism finally comes to terms with epistemology. Prior to Habermas, Marxist philosophy ran the risk of epistemological naiveté. The moral confidence of Marxists rested on an epistemological confidence that was undeserved. In their criticisms of Hegelian idealism, Marx and Marxists alike were given to making broad claims about "real, existing human beings," without pausing to consider just how it was that the reality they were describing was indeed the one, true Reality and not some ideological delusion. In the Marxist tradition, 'false consciousness' was to be found only among capitalists. But what guarantee did Marxists have that they were not vulnerable to their own brand of false consciousness? Karl Mannheim[69] raised the issue, and Jürgen Habermas came as close as anyone to putting it to rest in a series of closely argued books that explored the epistemological foundations of Marxism.[70] But problems remain even after Habermas's efforts, and this essay will stand on the shoulders of the Frankfurt school only after propping up its crippled giants.

Since the real focus of this essay is the achievements of future studies rather than the failures of critical theory, I am not going to do scholarly justice to the achievements of critical theory. I will offer what may look like a Martian's eye view of Marxism-from-a-distance. I want to describe ever so briefly, and hopefully not too superficially, some of the dilemmas that critical theory fell into as a way of setting the context for future studies' achievements. For, as my title suggests, I believe that, without ever setting out to do so very consciously, futures research has actually succeeded in solving some of the previously unsolved dilemmas of critical theory.

In order to accomplish several interrelated objectives, this essay will follow a trajectory marked by several road signs. Part I will describe three dilemmas of critical theory, marked (a), (b) and (c). Part II will then traverse the same ground in reverse, going deeper into critical theory's struggles with the dilemmas, and beginning to show the way out through scenario planning. Part II, the longest part of the essay, moves from (c') to (b') to (a'). Then Part III, the conclusion, goes deeper into the scenario planning's resolution of dilemma (a) in a section marked (a"); then mixes (b") and (c") in a summary that grapples with the systemic interconnections of the several issues discussed earlier in the essay.

Part I. The Dilemmas of Critical Theory

(a) The role of the individual in history

To listen to some Marxists, the juggernaut determinism of the dialectic unfolds with such force of necessity that there is nothing much for a mere individual to do but lie back and enjoy it. To imagine that any single individual can change the course of history is to fall into the mistake of 'bourgeois subjectivism'. The *real* cause of historical change lies in objective conditions, not in the minds of individual subjects.

---

69   Karl Mannheim, *Ideology and Utopia: An Introduction to the Sociology of Knowledge,* trans. Louis Wirth and Edward Shils, Harcourt, Brace and Co., New York, 1936.

70   See especially Jürgen Habermas, *Knowledge and Human Interests,* trans. Jeremy Shapiro, Beacon Press, Boston, 1971; but also, *Communication and the Evolution of Society,* trans. Thomas McCarthy, Beacon Press, Boston, 1979.

While hoping to gain followers by promising alignment with the inevitable triumph of the proletariat, Marxists who stressed the inevitability of the revolution opened themselves to the following response: if the revolution is so inevitable, why should I, a mere subjective individual, lift a finger to help it along? The revolution will do just fine without me.

When apathetic individuals in a democracy try to rationalize their failure to cast their votes, it's easy enough to criticize their apathy while remaining consistent with the tenets of liberal democracy: in a system where the individual comes first, and the collective will is the sum of individual wills, each individual has a responsibility to register preferences that are collectively regarded as decisive. But apathy is less easy to criticize in a tradition that argues the primacy of the collective and the determinism of objective conditions.

In order to struggle with this dilemma, George Plekhanov wrote a (not altogether successful) pamphlet entitled, "The Role of the Individual in History". To a certain extent, the Frankfurt School's preoccupation with psychology and aesthetics reflected an anxiety over the need to acknowledge the role of individuals and their subjective motivations. But neither Plekhanov nor the Frankfurt School succeeded in articulating the role of the individual. The abiding power of the collective over the individual, the objective over the subjective, was evident in the rejection of Wilhelm Reich from the ranks of orthodox Marxists. Reich went just a little too far in the direction of granting the autonomy of psychology. In such books as *The Mass Psychology of Fascism,* he dabbled too deeply in the psychology of sexuality. His Marxist brethren drummed him out of the corps—and drove him toward the madness of his final years in jail.

Before borrowing the mantle of moral critique from the Frankfurt school, it will be necessary to find a place for the individual in the practice of social criticism.

(b) The dilemma of theory and practice

In his eleventh Thesis on Feuerbach, Marx wrote, "The philosophers have only *interpreted* the world in various ways; the point is, to *change* it."[71] In other words, theory is not enough; you've got to get out there and actually *do something!* If Marx was right in saying that religion is the opiate of the masses, it can equally be claimed that theory is the opiate of the intellectuals. Theorizing is so much easier than actually *doing* anything.

While Marx was no anti-intellectual, neither was he an academic. His hours in the library of the British Museum had a purpose: the overthrow of capitalism.

---

71   Karl Marx, "Theses on Feuerbach," in *Writings of the young Marx on Philosophy and Society,* ed. and trans. Loyd Easton and Kurt Guddat, Doubleday Anchor, Garden City, New York, 1967, p. 402.

For many academic Marxists, the dilemma of theory and practice, or thought and action, is less easy to resolve. In the upper reaches of Marxist scholarship, one often gets the impression that it is more important to brandish the right references than to man the right barricades. Indeed, to the extent that journals like *Telos* or *Praxis* carry on in the tradition of European academic scholarship, they become utterly unreadable for the ordinary worker—the members of the proletariat that Marxism was supposed to serve. When, for example, Jürgen Habermas reaches the conclusion that liberation requires "undistorted communication". the reader can only wince at the esoteric contortions of Habermas's own Teutonic prose.

To put this dilemma as succinctly as possible, for a tradition that purports to favor practice over theory, the actual practice of Marxist scholars comes perilously close to indulging in *theory at the expense of practice.* Jean-Paul Sartre was sensitive to this danger. In his long preface to his even longer *Critique of Dialectical Reason,* (separately published as *Search for a Method),* Sartre lambasted Marxists for their theoretical rigidities: for forcing "facts" to fit the theory rather than revising their theories to fit the facts. In place of reverence for the inviolability of categories forged in the nineteenth century, Sartre suggested something he called "the progressive-regressive method": use the theory progressively to frame the facts, but if the facts don't fit the frame, allow yourself to go back (regressively) to revise the theory. Sounds simple enough, but too few Marxists in the 1950s were capable of such flexibility.

Future studies can resolve this dilemma of theory and practice. For reasons I'll develop below, the dilemma never really arises for future studies. But the innocent can fall. By comparing the innocence of future studies with the unresolved guilt of the Frankfurt school, perhaps our loss of innocence can be forestalled. The fate of the Frankfurt school can shape a negative scenario for the future of future studies. The fate of the Frankfurt school can serve as a sort of morality play: there (into guilty theorizing) go we, if not for some timely recollection of a tradition gone wrong.

(c) The Moral Basis of Marxism

As opposed to pursuits like mathematics or, for that matter, stamp collecting, Marxism purports to have a moral purpose: the expropriation of the expropriators on behalf of the oppressed. At the heart of the appeal of Marxism is its Robin Hood steal-from-the-rich-and-give-to-the-poor program. While appearing to be morally motivated, Marxism runs the risk of sawing off the branch it is sitting on when it attacks the usual foundations for morality: God and/or philosophy. Marx's atheism is well known. But God is not the only basis for morality. Certainly philosophy has offered other bases, from Plato's pure Ideas to Kant's categorical imperative. But Marx and critical theory dismiss these bases for morality. How then can Marxism claim moral authority if morality has no basis for its authority?

Marxists like Karl Kautsky, attacked "the dictatorship of the proletariat" as the final arbiter of value.[72] But the achievement of Herbert Marcuse's *One Dimensional Man* was to show that the so-called proletariat no longer exists: in advanced capitalism, there is no longer an identifiable constituency that fits this nineteenth century category, 'the proletariat'/ Instead of underpaid industrial workers, the American economy is driven by fairly well paid information and service workers who share no sense of solidarity or common purpose in overthrowing capitalism. Marcuse's intense pessimism in *One Dimensional Man* is a measure of critical theory's failure to solve this dilemma of needing but failing to find a moral basis in religion, philosophy, or the moral outrage of the proletariat.

In order to claim that critical theory has indeed failed to find its way out of these three dilemmas—the role of the individual in history, the appropriate balance of theory and practice, and the moral basis of Marxism—much more needs to be said. But for now I simply state these dilemmas as starkly as possible, and rest my case with the claim that Marxism might not be in such ill repute today if critical theory had succeeded in finding its way out of these dilemmas. My concern lies not so much with attacking or defending Marxists. Having borrowed from critical theory my descriptions of the statements of the dilemmas, the rest of this essay is devoted to showing how *the practice of developing future scenarios succeeds where Marxist critical theory has failed.*

I will work my way backwards through these dilemmas, starting with the question of moral purchase, then the issue of theory and practice and the role of the individual, which is, after all, what any individual reader finally wants to know.

Part II. Unraveling the dilemmas of critical theory

(c') The Morality of the Marketplace

The dilemmas confronted by critical theory are instructive, which is why I've chosen to build the moral purchase of future studies on its ruins. At first glance, the moral foundations for Marxism would seem to be secure: isn't it perfectly obvious that the workers of the world deserve more of the surplus value generated by capital? Isn't it perfectly obvious that radical inequality in the distribution of wealth is unjust? That some should have so much and others so little? That some should go water-skiing while, in the very same frame of real-time, and connected by telecommunications that bring the horror into the kitchen on Good Morning America, others are literally starving to death? The injustice of extreme inequality seems so obvious, enough to make the adolescent daughters of fat cat capitalists weep with the poignancy. Why doesn't daddy see the pain he is inflicting every

---

72   Karl Kautsky, *The Dictatorship of the Proletariat,* Ann Arbor Paperback, 1964.

time he picks up the phone and transfers another wadge of capital across the global financial net?

But play the tape further, as the last seventy years of history have done, and you see the sequel to the impulse to redistribution: central planning clogs the feedback loops that free markets offer for the registration of personal desires. Blinded to the individual preferences of millions of consumers, centrally planned economies blunder ahead pumping out tens of thousands of tractors and toe-nail clippers when what was wanted, at that particular time and that particular province, was toaster-ovens and hair dryers. Take away the hair dryers from all those adolescent daughters, and suddenly the justice of capitalism becomes clear: except for the very hungriest who will eat day-old pizza from a dumpster, the thing that makes the economy go 'round is not the gnawing hunger of need but the discerning taste of desire. And if an economic system cannot register the discrete desires of millions and millions of consumers, each in his or her own unique configuration of wishes, wants and preferences, then that economic system will fail to join consumers and producers in the happy matrimony of the marketplace.

Take away the fine-grained detail of individual tastes, and an economic system that might have sung like synapses surging with caffeine sinks instead into the narcolepsy of a bureaucracy clogged by way-bills for stuff folks don't want. Take away the 600-pixels per inch resolution of personal discretion, and an economy that might have employed millions in the creative challenge of innovation falls instead into the mindless repetition of chunk, chunk, chunking out more of the same, same, same old stuff people are already hurling into the dumpster.

Individual preferences are what makes the modern information and services economy sing; but the old agricultural and industrial economies are cranked to the tune of satisfying *universal needs*: food, clothing and shelter—or, agri-business, the clothing industry, housing and real estate. And even here, even in these ancient industries, you can see how appeals to pure functionality—form following function in the gray cement blocks of Bauhaus architecture—clog the arteries of the economy. People don't want to live in the projects. The modernist architecture of Pruitt-Igoe proved to one and all alike, from its wretched and rebellious occupants to the shocked architects and planners, that people *need* the individual differences that place the mark of humanity on the bland uniformity of necessity. Read the graffiti on the wall, comrade: the people want *recognition for their differences right down to the styles of their spray painted initials.*

Need is everywhere the same; desire differentiates. All god's chillun got minimal daily requirements; only some have a taste for anchovies. Need demands efficiency in its satisfaction, the more and faster the better. Desire seeks distinctive quality: just this, not that. Need drives populations to war: when you're out of necessities, and you've got nothing to lose, you'll do just about anything, even kill. Desire wants peace on earth in order to savor the delights of the harvest on long afternoons with children playing in the garden. When you're protecting the peace of the garden, you won't do just anything. You watch the speed limit, you don't drink and drive, because you wouldn't want to land in jail, lose your license, tarnish your credit rating, or risk missing a deposit on one of those little darling's tuition accounts.

Appreciate the picture: the primary colors of need can paint a crude cartoon of industrial production, boxcars filled with uniform bales, container loads of mass-manufactured same, same, same. But if you want to service individual tastes, cater to the whims of discerning human beings, satisfy the fully individuated personalities of millions of self-actualized people… then you need all million and three shades on the Macintosh palette to color the ever-more-precisely-defined consumer segments reaching upstream toward the productive sources of the economy. And if you bleed those subtle hues together by sloshing downstream, producer to consumer, the primary red, the same, same red, the industrial mass-produced red of redistributed universal necessities, then you obliterate the information, the discretion, the discrimination, the *differences* that are the life-blood of an information/services economy. You destroy the information that would allow that economy to function efficiently, taking tractors to the people who want tractors, the nail-clippers to the people who want nail-clippers, and hair-dryers to those weeping daughters. The farmers don't want hair-dryers, and the daughters don't want tractors, and without those registrations of preference that market mechanisms enable, the dumb, blind, information-deprived, stupid brain of a centrally-planned redistributive economy can't know where to send the tractors and where to send the hair dryers.

In order for the central processing unit of a controlled economy to smarten up it needs some afferent nerves. It needs to know what the people out there on the periphery of its sensorium actually want. But in order for it to know what the people want, it needs the information provided by the way they make their purchase decisions in the marketplace, and not just when they're standing in long lines to take anything that's fed to them, but when they are milling through the mall, picking up this, putting down that, and allowing their individual preferences to *inform* the marketplace about just what is wanted *this* morning in *this particular* supermarket.

It is just this *particularity of desire*, as distinct from the *generality of need*, that makes today's economy go 'round. The generality of need was sufficient to jack up the agricultural economy to the faster pace of the industrial economy. The mechanical harvester, the steam engine and the assembly line helped to get more calories into more bellies for less time spent in the field. But now, in order to jack the industrial economy up yet another notch, beyond a speeding freight train to the speed of light, out onto the fiber-optic filaments that feed the global brain of the new economy, you have to have information about differences. And information is defined by information theorists as a difference that makes a difference, not more of the same. So in order to jack up the industrial economy to the speed of a smart global brain, in order to clear those sclerotic bureaucratic arteries, you've got to blow out all that industrial red coming downstream from producers to consumers, and reverse the flow with information coming back upstream, information about all of those subtle shades of individual preferences, information about the precise articulations of individual desires. Because only if you have all of that wonderful information, all those pages of printouts of market data, only then can you intelligently apply resources to the satisfaction of that differentiated demand, and know that the busy workers you've employed to satisfy the demand will have jobs tomorrow because the demand they are satisfying is *real* demand and not some phony requirement that some stupid central planner *thought* people might have.

Appreciate the picture in high resolution: without the information that bit-maps the precise configurations of consumer pull, you get the Fred Flintstone cartoons of primitive producer push economies. In order to get the bit-map of consumer preferences, though, you've got to give those consumers the opportunity to pick up this and leave that, demo this and return that, try on this, send back that. In short, you need the discriminating *retrieval* system of a market, not a dumb *distribution* center. You need information about consumer pull, not more productivity in the producer push. In order to have a market, people have to have money, or credit, or some means of differentially allocating their resources for this, not that. They cannot be empty wallets, open as the flowers of the field, just waiting for whatever manna from heaven might fall onto their outstretched petals. No, people have to be able to make choices about how they will spend the limited resources at their disposal in order to best gratify their particular desires.

You see where this argument is headed. I don't need to rebuild the entire edifice of capitalist economics, reinvent money and capital as a means of facilitating both consumption and investment; I don't need to reconstruct all of the pieces of this highly evolved system in order to point out the direction in which this argument is moving: *toward the morality of the marketplace.* Let me leap ahead, and then retrace only those steps that are unfamiliar. The destination of this argument is as follows: *in an information/services economy where marketplace mechanisms allow the forces of production to be precisely tuned to all the fine-grained vicissitudes of consumption, the unobstructed flow of information upstream, and services and products downstream, will churn with such metabolic vigor that even the least wealthy people at the bottom of the economy will have most of their basic needs and some of their favorite wants satisfied.*

I know what you're thinking: *this is all just info-babble for the same old right-wing, retrograde trickle-down economics.* Wrong! The old argument for trickle-down economics rests on a fundamental error, namely, that the wealth of the upper-classes, sucked as surplus value from the labors of the lowly, can rise like lava in a volcano, benefit the lofty, and then trickle down the economic volcano's steep slope to benefit the low-landers. This image of excess wealth somehow sloshing down the slopes of the economy is wrong in several ways. First, it presumes that what is wealth for one will be wealth for another, a premise that the previous argument about need versus desire was meant to demolish. Second, it presumes that those at the top can be so completely satisfied that they will allow their *excess* wealth to splash over the walls of their mansions, a psychological assumption that proves manifestly false as soon as you observe the wealthy and see that enough is *never* enough, and that there are certain people who are *never* satisfied. Third, it presumes that, even if some of this putative universal wealth were ever to seep over the walls of (unlikely) upper-class satisfaction, there is even the ghost of a chance that this molten lava will ever make it down the slope before congealing in useless boulders of solidified greed. As we well know, there are many catch basins between the wealthy and the poor. If trickle-down economics works at all, it may drip down from the towers of Wall Street to the art markets of Soho, but never, never, does so much as a dribble reach as far north as Harlem or the Bronx.

We know that trickle-down economics don't work. Trickle-down economics do not provide the rationale for the morality of the marketplace. Trickle-down economics are not the direction in which my argument is moving. Quite the opposite. My argument is about *the trickling up of information about differential preferences,* not the trickling down of excess wealth (whatever that might mean).

My argument rests on the proposition that the marketplace does a better job of satisfying peoples' wants and needs than any central planner. The marketplace *is good* to the extent that it delivers the right goods and services to the right places at the right times. Marxist central planning is bad because it fails to deliver the right goods to the right places at the right times. Lacking adequate information about different patterns of preference, centrally planned economies are literally ignorant, dumb, stupid. They fail to deliver the goods because they ignore the information contained in purchasing patterns. They cannot *deliver* because they don't allow consumers to *retrieve* according to their own preferences.

The marketplace is democratic where central planning is authoritarian. To the extent that marketplace mechanisms enhance the trickle-up of information about consumer preferences, marketplace mechanisms mimic democratic elections. The market tells the productive system what it should be producing and delivering.

In likening the market to democratic elections, this line of argument helps answer the vexed question of the relationship between liberal democracy and capitalism. Is democracy good for capitalism? Or does the anarchy of the marketplace introduce social and economic inefficiencies calling for administrative overrides? Maybe the Asians have got it right. Maybe it's no accident that China and Singapore have enjoyed stunning growth rates over the past decade. Maybe the Russians were wrong to put political reforms—Glasnost and Perestroika—before economic reforms. Maybe democracy must be administered in small doses to avoid decadence, inflation and corruption. Maybe. But if the argument I am making is correct, then the best one can say for Asian style authoritarian capitalism is that it's an effective *transition* mechanism with a built in half life. The argument for the necessary connection, or at least affinity, between liberal democracy and free markets suggests that the strong hand of central government cannot long continue to meddle in the marketplace without eventually stupefying an economic system just as Soviet communism did. Despite the current economic strength of Asia, where economic reforms have preceded political democratization, we should expect over the long haul that Asian capitalism will founder unless it loosens the reins of government and adopts more liberal democratic principles. Otherwise it will stifle the upward trickle of information representing the wants and desires that make the economy go 'round. Strong central government may be working in the short term to deliver the necessities. Administering the satisfaction of basic needs, e.g. feeding a billion hungry Chinese peasants, may call for down-from-the-top central planning. But as soon as the satisfaction of needs starts to absorb a smaller share of resources than the gratification of different whims and desires, then the strong hand of the central government will prove otiose. It will obstruct the registration of those wants, and it will stupefy Asian capitalism just as it stupefied Soviet communism. At least this is what my argument suggests. But how can this suggestion be strengthened toward something closer to a proof? By picking up another strand of the larger argument: the theory/practice debate.

Recall the several objectives of the larger argument. I want to build a case for the morality of future studies by erecting an argument on the ruins of critical theory. I've so far sunk just one piling into the rubble of critical theory. This first piling is drilled through the moral dilemma of Marxism: Marxism claims to be moral, but it eschews religion or philosophy as the foundation of its morality. Nor can it count anymore on the will of the proletariat because they've all left the Party to spend time at the mall. But doubts remain: Is the mall the source of morality? Is the marketplace really moral?

Let's now sink a second piling into the rubble of critical theory. Let's return to the theory/practice debate to see whether there is a theory or a practice that central planners can call upon to function as the conscience of the marketplace.

(b') The dilemma of theory and practice revisited

Marxist critical theory has a theory/practice problem—in its theory, in its practice, and in its way of relating theory to practice. In unraveling this dilemma of theory and practice, we come to a critical turn in the course of this essay. I began by stating that, on behalf of scenario planning, I wanted to borrow the mantle of moral critique from critical theory, but only after some radical tailoring. After articulating (a) the dilemma of the role of the individual, (b) the dilemma of theory and practice, and (c) the dilemma of the moral basis of Marxism, I then argued (c') the morality of the marketplace. We're now at (b') the dilemma of theory and practice revisited, on the way toward (a') the role of the individual in critical theory. After stating the dilemmas in Part I, and showing how they play out in Part II, Part III will traverse the same three topics again in the context of scenario planning, beginning with (a") the role of remarkable individuals and teamwork in scenario planning, and concluding with a summary of the systematic interrelationships between collaboration and morality in the practice of scenario planning.

I call attention to the pyramidal architecture of this piece in order to emphasize the significance of what may seem to be a rather arcane discussion of the concepts of alienation and human essence in Marxist humanism. I do so because, for all its faults, Marxist critical theory had at least this much going for it: without indulging in religious superstition, it tried to enlist moral indignation against social and economic injustice. With the demise of communism there is some danger that many of its former adherents will fall into a nihilistic worship of an unrestrained marketplace. This would be a shame, because social morality can survive the death of both God and Karl Marx. But in order to see just how, it's necessary to get a close look into the working parts of a secular morality. Marxism allows us this look. We can examine the dead body of Marxism to find the place where Marxism claimed its moral purchase, namely, in the theory of alienation. I will show how that theory of alienation was in fact incoherent. But in the conclusion I'll substitute hope for a socially desired future as a replacement for alienation from some primordial past as the fulcrum for moral critique. In order to prepare this place for hope in moral practice, I need first to show how the concept of alienation failed to fill that place.

I take no ghoulish delight in disinterring the dead body of Marxism. Instead my hope is that the discipline of the pathologist can derive from this autopsy some insights to assist the living. Critical theory is impressive in its intellectual aspirations. As distinct from the analytic expertise and technical cleverness exhibited in Anglo-

American economics and social theory, the Marxist tradition deserves admiration for its broad sweep, its carrying on of the Hegelian heritage, its attempt to relate economics to the humanities, its effort to see things whole rather than fragmented into the narrow specialties of academic departmentalization. But admirable as these ambitions may be, critical theory's noble aspirations carry no guarantee of success.

Among the noblest aspirations of critical theory was its attempt to overcome alienation. The literature on alienation is immense.[73] No wonder: the topic offered an outlet for every intellectual malcontent to express his dissatisfaction with the ways of the world in general, and capitalism in particular. Feel out of sorts, depressed, unhappy? It's not my/your fault. Private pain is the result of a capitalist system that has alienated each of us from our essence. Whether we know it or not, our private ills are the outcomes of public, social and economic processes that sunder each of us from our own true nature. Depression is the private expression of social and economic repression. Alienation is the name that critical theorists give to this theoretical diremption, this distance that separates each of us from our essence.

This story about alienation is immensely appealing—so addictive it became the opiate of many disaffected intellectuals. The literature on alienation played a particular role in the evolution of critical theory: it allowed Marxists to put a warmer face on the cold economism of the Second International. The tradition of Marxist humanism allowed those who were interested in the psychology of alienation to find a home within the Marxist tradition without surrendering to the ruthless repression of individual freedom so characteristic of Stalinism. By harking back to the discussion of alienation in the early Marx—particularly *The Economic and Philosophic Manuscripts of 1844*—one could have one's humanism and Marxism too. One could talk about individual human beings without falling prey to the dreaded charge of bourgeois subjectivism. Some degree of subjective idiosyncrasy could be salvaged from the juggernaut historicism of dialectical materialism. The I of subjectivity could be saved from all those objective -isms.

Despite the noble humanism at the heart of this salvation of subjectivity, the project was doomed from the start, however, not only because the practical power of Stalinism was so strong, but as important, because the theoretical foundations of Marxist humanism were so weak. The concept of alienation turns

---

73   For starters, see: Bertell Ollman, *Alienation: Marx's conception of man in capitalist society,* Cambridge University Press, 1971; Robert Blauner, *Alienation and Freedom,* University of Chicago Press, 1964; *Marxism and Alienation: A Symposium,* ed. by Herbert Aptheker, Humanities Press, New York, 1965; *Revisionism,* ed. by Leopold Labedz, Praeger, New York, 1962; *Marx and the Western World,* ed. by Nicholas Lobkowicz, University of Notre Dame Press, Notre Dame, Indiana, 1967; Fritz Pappenheim, *The Alienation of Modern Man,* Monthly Review Press, New York, 1959; Gajo Petrovic, *Marx in the Mid-twentieth Century,* Garden City, New York, 1967

out to be theoretically incoherent. It presupposes a human essence from which human existence is alienated. Whether the existence in question is individual or collective, the concept of alienation presupposes some form of a fall from grace, some diremption of existence from Edenic essence. But Marxism cannot have historicism and essentialism too. It won't do to preach out of one side of one's mouth this self-making, historical, autopoetic nurturance of human progress while out of the other condemning the deviation of history from some ahistorically given natural essence. But this is just what Marx and many Marxists after him have done. Let me demonstrate.

Marx himself credited Hegel for acknowledging the historicity of humanity: "The outstanding thing in Hegel's *Phenomenology* and its final outcome—that is, the dialectic of negativity as the moving and generating principle—is thus first that Hegel conceives the self-genesis of man as a process, conceives objectification as loss of the object, as alienation and as transcendence of this alienation; that he thus grasps the essence of labor and comprehends objective man—true because real man—as the outcome of man's own labor."[74] But having credited the historical unfolding of human existence as determining human nature as a result rather than an origin, Marx then confuses the issue by repeatedly invoking an objective, human essence: "It is only to be expected that a living, natural being equipped and endowed with objective (i.e. material) essential powers should have real natural objects of his essence."[75] In another statement of his understanding of human essence, Marx writes: "But the essence of man is no abstraction inhering in each single individual. In its actuality it is the ensemble of social relationships."[76] But the "ensemble of social relationships" keeps changing with the unfolding of history, so man's essence must also change—and this is the problem.

If the essence of man is not eternal but historically changing, how can that essence be used as a stable standard against which alienation can be measured? This is the paradox the east European Marxist humanists failed to solve. Some, like Gajo Petrovic and Leszek Kolakowski, insisted on using Marx's concept of alienation as the cornerstone for their critiques of Bolshevism's colder face. But orthodox Marxists like Adam Schaff saw through their scholarly slight of hand.[77] The result? In 1966, Kolakowski was expelled from the Polish Communist Party.

Grant me, then, that the point has been made: the Marxist concept of alienation is theoretically incoherent. So what? Why is this chink in the rusted armor of Marxism

---

74   Marx, *Economic and Philosophic Manuscripts of 1844,* trans. Foreign Language Publishing House, Moscow, 1961, p. 151.

75   Ibid. p.155 and following.

76   Marx, "Theses on Feuerbach," *op. cit.,* #6, p. 402.

77   Adam Schaff, "Studies of the Young Marx: A Rejoinder," in *Revisionism,* ed. Leopold Labedz, Praeger, New York, 1962, pp. 188-194.

so important? Recall this essay's principal objective: to find for future studies some moral leverage, some point of purchase, a fulcrum for social criticism. Whatever its faults, at least Marxism *tried* to criticize the present for the sake of a better future. And future studies could do worse than inherit from critical theory the mantle of moral critique. Trouble is, critical theory's dependence on the concept of alienation leaves it vulnerable to theoretical critique, as I have just demonstrated. Critical theory has a theory problem.

It also has a practice problem, to which I now turn. And as with the theory problem, I come not to bury but to pathologize. The point is not to flog a dead horse, but to salvage saving remnants.

Critical theory's practice problem is its academic, jargon-ridden scholarship. The proletariat are not scholars. The practice problem became most acute in the late sixties when campuses all over the world erupted with raw irreverence for the remote intellectualism of the professors. Academics were sorely tested: would they come out from behind their books? Would they descend from their ivory towers to man the barricades? Could they mix with the crowds in the streets, or would they scurry up ladders of abstraction to the safety of pure concepts?

The practice problem couldn't be tackled with theories alone. Words were insufficient. If all you've got is a hammer, everything looks like a nail. If all you've got is words, then everything looks like an argument. But actions go beyond arguments. The Frankfurt School's bluff was finally called when Adorno's classes were interrupted by young women who marched down the aisles of his lecture hall, ripped open their denim work shirts, and bared their breasts at the highly honorable Herr Doktor Professor, who was, of course, baffled and bewildered by these wordless actions. Talk about words failing!

The practice problem is elegant in its simplicity. *Put up or shut up! Ready, fire, aim! Just do it!* ... We're out of the realm of theory and into the argot of advertising lingo; speech acts as performative rather than descriptive.[78] It's not that words are useless or irrelevant, but the language game has shifted from solving puzzles to getting things done. In the language of semiotics, we're well beyond syntax, out beyond semantics and into pragmatics. This is cowboy territory as far as most intellectuals are concerned. But the businessman (or woman) is perfectly comfortable being more active than reflective. Odd irony: capitalists could appreciate those bare breasts more easily than intellectuals. Businessmen know about *praxis.* They call it practicality, the use of common sense and pragmatism to get things done. Hold the theory. Just find a need and fill it, for a fee of course. But their effort to find needs leads to the discovery of desires. Business caters to the individuated desires of consumers in a way that centrally planned distribution mechanisms do not.

---

78   See J. L. Austin, *How To Do Things With Words,* ed. J.O. Urmson and Marina Sbisà, 1962.

So much for the practice problem in critical theory. To summarize in the language of the street, critical theory failed to *get down*. Critical theory remained too aloof, too respectable, too academic. It failed to walk its talk, and the students of the sixties, ever sensitive to such breaches of integrity, called the bluff with bare breasts. Get real, Herr Doktor Professor!

Having now exposed critical theory's theory problem—the incoherence of its theory of alienation—and having surfaced its practice problem—the academic, scholarly remoteness of its Frankfurt School practitioners—it should come as no surprise that critical theory had a problem relating its theory to its practice. Professors don't man barricades. This was the scandal of the theorists, and it was exposed all too clearly in 1968; when the students took to the streets and too few of their supposedly radical professors were willing to follow, much less lead.

To be fair, one could argue that the problem lay not so much with Marxism or with critical theory as with the situation of any academic. As long as academia sees its mission as remote from practical concerns; as long as we see the university as a place for basic rather than applied research; as long as we see the university as an ivory tower rather than a service institution, then the professor's proper place is in the library or laboratory, not in the streets. But this separation of theory from practice, this distinction between pure and applied science, is inconsistent with critical theory's stated views about the proper relationship between theory and practice. Critical theorists made a habit of invoking the neologism, *praxis,* as a way of calling attention to an intimacy between theory and practice in the Marxist tradition. As Marx himself put it, "In direct contrast to German Philosophy, which descends from heaven to earth, here we ascend from earth to heaven".[79] Marx claimed that his ideas were rooted in material reality, not drawn from some intellectual heaven. But the ideas that Marx framed then became enshrined in Marxist heaven, and later Marxists were guilty of drawing these ideas down from the heaven of Marxist theory rather than continuing to do what Marx had done: ground their ideas in the unfolding development of the means of production.

When put this way—grounding ideas in the unfolding development of the means of production—this critique of critical theory comes 'round to an odd irony: today's best Marxists are students of capitalism, the writers and consultants who track the unfolding development of today's capitalist means of production, people like Peter Drucker and Tom Peters and Charles Handy.

These are the people engaged in praxis, in the application of thought to the eminently practical issues of the marketplace and the shop floor. Strategic planning is as close as any intellectual discipline could be to the overall mission of Marxism: the effort

---

79   Karl Marx, *German Ideology,* trans. R. Pascal, ecerpts in *Marx & Engels,* ed. Lewis Feuer, GardenCity, N.Y., 1959, p. 247.

to create a better future for humanity. Odd! Aren't corporate strategic planners the arch enemies of the Marxists? Funny how history makes strange bedfellows.

Having now outlined the theory/practice dilemma, I want to move on to the third dilemma of critical theory: the role of the individual in history.

(a') The Role of the Individual in Critical Theory

In theory, individuality is an illusion according to Marxist critical theory. This rather bold conclusion comes as part of the legacy of Hegel, for whom individuality was an abstraction from the whole, not the concrete starting place for philosophy. The subjectivist tradition from Descartes to Kant began from the starting point of the Cartesian Cogito, the *I think* for whom the problem then became, "How is this thinking possible, and how could I ever know whether my thoughts are truthful?" Hegel rejects this subjectivist starting point. He grounds his philosophy in reflections on the history of consciousness in general, not on the origin of any particular thinking individual. By starting from the history of consciousness he is able to show subjective consciousness and its Cartesian doubts coming on the scene relatively late, not at all as an origin. Without going into Hegel's philosophy in the depth that it deserves, suffice it to say that Marx inherited this suspicion of subjectivism from Hegel, but with a difference. Where Hegel saw subjectivity evolving out of the history of spirit (*Geist*), Marx saw the ultimate subject of history not as spirit but as matter, or more accurately, as the unfolding management of the material means of production.

If individuality is an illusion, or at best, a byproduct of the unfolding of objective history (whether spiritual or material), then there would seem to be no very serious problem about the role of the individual in history. Who cares? One might as well worry about the role of ghosts in history. But as existentialists from Kierkegaard to Sartre will tell us, this submersion of the individual existing human being under the weight of The System is both intellectually and psychologically unsatisfying. Whatever the relationship between the subjective and the objective in theory, in practice there is no denying a degree of existential solitude. Call it what you like—the cogito, the subject, the self, the I, the individual. Whatever you say about the priority of the objective, Absolute Spirit, or the material means of production, there are still a few phenomena of selfhood to be accounted for: the fact that each of us dies our own death, that we see the world from a particular and highly individualized perspective, that the phenomena of consciousness don't unfold as if seen through the eyes of an all-seeing God but are instead strung together by each of us in our own unique ways.

These phenomena of individualized consciousness must be accounted for, even by a theory that starts from the objective retelling of the the history of consciousness (or the *Phenomenology of Spirit*). If a theory of history cannot trace the origins of the theorizer, then it is radically incomplete. Hegel was able to accomplish this deduction of the individual from the collective. His theory of alienation is his answer to the question, how is individuality both possible and necessary? Answer (in very brief): Spirit must alienate individual consciousness from itself in order to reflect its own structure back to itself. Man's consciousness of Spirit is Spirit's own alienated self-consciousness of itself. With the overcoming of alienation, Spirit will once again be coincident with itself, unalienated. But alienation is necessary if Spirit is ever to find a medium in which it can reflect itself to itself.

So abbreviated, this tale surely sounds fanciful. This is not how life feels. We do not walk around thinking of ourselves as mirrors made for the purpose of reflecting spirit's objective image to spirit's subjective consciousness. Of course we could all be profoundly wrong about our place in the human drama. One is reminded of Ken Kesey's question, "Whose movie is this?" Like characters in a John LeCarre novel, we are sometimes surprised to discover who is really pulling the strings. To find oneself a mere pawn in someone else's chess game is not an altogether unknown experience. But to take this rare experience of profound fallibility and then extrapolate it to all of life seems to be to fall for the ultimate conspiracy theory: all of life is utterly different from what you thought it to be. The plot, the players, and the script writer are completely different than what you thought! You are just an ignorant foot soldier in a cosmic drama whose structure may never be revealed to you, or so this claim about the illusory character of individuality would seem to suggest.

I find this conspiratorial logic ultimately unconvincing. Of course one must sometimes be on one's guard against conspiracies. Oliver Stone's *JFK* can undermine confidence in the Warren Commission's report. But to extrapolate occasional suspicions to chronic and cosmic paranoia represents a pathological epistemology. Whether it is the Hindu or Buddhist claiming that all is illusion, or the subjectivist philosophers from Descartes to Kant worrying whether God or their own eyes could be deceiving them, all of these dramatic retreats into chronic doubt commit the same error, an error that was unraveled in Hegel's passage on the "inverted world,"[80] whose obscure argument can be clarified as follows.

It makes sense to say that a salt shaker is upside down. You can see how its inversion relative to everything else on the table has operational significance: the salt comes out of the inverted shaker and seasons one's food. It might even make sense to say that the salt shaker and the pepper shaker and the table, and the room, and the entire house are all upside down. I recall my delight at the children's book, Mrs. Piggle-Wiggle's Upside Down House. Inversions of large pieces of our environment, as

---

80   G.W.F. Hegel, *The Phenomenology of Mind,* trans. J.B. Baillie, Harper & Row, New York, 1967, pp. 187-213.

in Samuel Butler's Erewhon, can reveal important insights into the relationships among the parts of our world, which suddenly come into new light when subjected to partial inversions, e.g. Nietzsche's overturning of the typical nineteenth century philologists' confidence in the serenity of Greek culture. In *The Birth of Tragedy*, he argued that the appearance of Apollonian serenity was a measure of the Dionysian turmoil that was usually suppressed, but occasionally evident in Greek tragedy. But as insightful as it can be to discover such partial inversions, it makes no sense at all to claim that the entire universe of our experience is upside-down. Where are the relationships between the entire world and something larger, relative to which the claim of upside-downness could make sense? If everything is upside down, then nothing has been inverted relative to anything else. If everything is equally inverted, then nothing is inverted relative to anything else. For all practical purposes, total inversion leaves everything as it was, still right-side up.

In his discourse on the inverted world, Hegel exposed the fallacy of cosmic conspiracy theories. It cannot be the case that everything is upside-down, or inside-out, or radically reversed from what we think it to be. So, to transfer this insight from literal space to epistemological space, it cannot be the case that what we thought to be subjective is really objective, or what we thought to be objective is really subjective. These cosmic reversals, while every bit as intellectually tantalizing as a good conspiracy theory, are ultimately fallacious. Hegel knew this, so he was not inclined to dismiss the experiences of existing individuals. Radical Marxists (as well as some of their French deconstructionist heirs) are less prudent in their dismissals of bourgeois subjectivism. So they have a real problem identifying the role of the individual in history. Whether they identify the proletariat, or the collective, or language as the ultimate subject of history (the real hero of the movie), they fail to "save the phenomena". They fail to account for the fact that all the rest of us are walking around with this conviction that we are indeed the authors of our intentions, the agents of our actions, the subjects of our own biographies. What could be more obvious?

So critical theory needs some help on this score as well. The critical theorist needs to save the phenomenon of subjective autonomy in the face of all of those economic and historical forces that purportedly serve as the true subject of history. Critical theory needs to find a place for the living, breathing individual. Without indulging in the subjectivism of the Cartesian tradition, or wallowing in the angst of the existential individual, critical theory must find someplace for some form of subjectivity that more or less corresponds to our intuitive sense of local efficacy. We are not entirely the victims of forces larger than we are. However powerful the effects of class consciousness or culture or language, we are not entirely bereft of individual autonomy.

Part III. Scenario Planning and the role of Hope

Before moving on to show how scenario planning solves or avoids the dilemmas of critical theory, I want to acknowledge the contributions that critical theory can make to scenario planning. Let us offer three cheers for critical theory: first, unlike the narrow, specialized, departmental, disciplinary approach to social issues, critical theory insists on seeing the world whole—economics, politics, culture, technology and social issues all in relation to one another. Futures research can learn from the synoptic vision of critical theory.

Second, unlike many academic disciplines, critical theorists are not content to leave the world as they found it. They are interested in more than simply describing, analyzing and understanding. They want to change the existing order of things. Futures researchers and strategic planners can appreciate this activist bias.

Third, the direction of change is not for the sake of narrow, special interests. Critical theory's constituency was never limited to the citizens of a single nation, much less the shareholders of a single corporation. Whether right or wrong in its reading of economic realities, the Frankfurt School claimed to speak for all of humanity. Adorno and Co. were philosophers, not bureaucrats or company executives. Their beat was the human condition. At a time when our technologies endanger the the entire surface of the earth and our financial networks span the globe, this totalizing perspective isn't just pretentious; it's also necessary. It's a megalomaniacal job, but somebody's got to do it.

With cheers shouted and credit paid, then, let's turn our gaze toward scenario planning to see whether its theory and its practice are indeed the fulfillment of the failed promise of critical theory. In keeping with the pyramidal ascent and descent structuring this essay, I'll begin with the question of the role of the individual. I'll turn next to the question of the relationship between theory and practice and morality.

(a") Balancing Remarkable Individuals and Teamwork in Scenario Planning

With a few interesting exceptions like Alvin Toffler, Peter Drucker and John Naisbitt—all of whom spurn large office staffs or consultancies, but give credit loud and often to their wives with whom they actively collaborate—future studies is a team sport. This is not an accident. To the extent that futures research occupies an uneasy place between rigorous research and science fiction, futures research requires contributions from many minds, not just one or two. In order to make the case for the intrinsically collaborative nature of futures research, I need to describe the practice of scenario planning in some detail. The point of this description will be to explore the several points of contact between the practice of scenario planning and the three dilemmas of critical theory just analyzed. I want to show how scenario planning succeeds precisely where critical theory failed.

As for the role of the individual, scenario planning calls for individuals without being individualistic. Unlike most academic work in the humanities, scenario planning is best pursued in collaboration, not by solitary authors in scholarly competition with one another. Scholars in the humanities tend to be lone rangers. I know. I was one once. As a professor of philosophy, I knew that my work would be most admired if it were uniquely my own, original and not too tainted by the influence of others. One did not want one's work to be criticized as derivative. So one withdrew into the privacy of one's own study, into the depths of one's private mind, there to find insights that would dazzle the world. The mythology of such scholarship is Promethean: however lonely the quest, one's hope was to survive the trials of the gods (or the peer review boards) to bring back truths never before seen on earth. This heroic mythology pits individuals against tenure committees. Like birth and death, the rewards and punishments of academia are meted out upon individuals, not upon teams.

For all its talk of competition and rugged individualism, the business world at its best is far more team oriented than academia. This is not to say that business executives are molded to the model of the man in the gray flannel suit. The mythology of conformist executives marching in step to the beat of the corporate drummer is, these days, obsolete. Entrepreneurship and skunk works are in; group think is out. In an era of information-intensive products and services, the need for top-down standardization of mass-produced replaceable parts is giving way to bottom-up innovation and creativity. Produce the same old information over and over, and standardization produces redundancy, not more information. Repetition may be fine on the assembly line, but not in software design.

The need for innovation creates a role for individuality. But not just any old innovation will do. New products or new services must serve some want or need if they are to survive in the marketplace. And here's where teamwork becomes important. The creative individual left to his or her own devices may be nothing more than a crackpot. Not all innovations have a market. Part of the role of the scenario team will be to articulate different scenarios that define plausible market needs (or desires). By balancing both the creativity of the individual with the reality testing of a team, scenario planning rewards both individuality and collaboration.

The business design of Global Business Network (GBN) included from day one a reliance on a network of individuals chosen for their ability to offer unique perspectives on a range of issues. Pierre Wack, himself the remarkable guru of scenario planning at Royal Dutch Shell, made a point of drawing on a network of what he referred to as "remarkable men", following the language of one of his mentors, Gurdjieff. At GBN, we include women in the network, from Laurie Andersen and Mary Catherine Bateson to Pamela McCorduck and Felice Schwartz (author of the mommy-track article in *Harvard Business Review*). Granted, there are more men than women in the network. But the men are as iconoclastic as these remarkable women: from sci-fi author William Gibson to rock star, Peter Gabriel; from Harvard Business School professor, Michael Porter to virtual reality creator, Jaron Lanier. When conducting scenario development workshops, we like to seed the group with a few individuals selected from our hundred or so remarkable network members. The point of including these individuals is not so much to draw on their expertise in any particular field as to provoke unconventional thinking, perspectives that are out of the ordinary, jolts to incipient group think, out-of-the-box reflection that can reframe the issues and redraw the mental maps executives use to chart their futures.

There is a role for the individual in this work. Wouldn't it have been helpful to the big three in Detroit, and to the American economy as a whole, if there had been a few more iconoclasts to counter the consensus view of the fifties and sixties that Americans would never buy small cars? Since the mid-eighties, Detroit has been using alternative scenarios to surface new car concepts. A few unconventional voices broke through the group think to inspire scenarios in which small cars, light trucks and mini-vans might compete with the more conventional cars that carried dad and mom and buddy and sis down the highways of middle America. And now the roads are filled with hi-tops and RVs and a range of hybrid vehicles that have boosted Detroit's sales much more than the catalogue of traditional family autos could have done.

Another example illustrating the role of the individual in promoting unconventional, alternative scenarios: a single voice in a scenario workshop back in 1980 led to the development of a scenario that kept Colorado from jumping headlong into the synfuels industry. When virtually every policy maker in Denver was worrying about how to build infrastructure fast enough to accommodate the rapid growth of an oil shale industry, one man raised his hand in a scenario workshop and said, contrary to everyone else in the room, "You know what I'm worried about? I'm worried about what we're going to do with all that freshly poured concrete if Exxon decides to pick up its marbles and go home", which is precisely what eventually happened. And because one individual voiced this contrarian scenario, the Colorado policy makers tapped the brakes on the infrastructure development program just enough to avoid a lot of sunk costs and environmental damage. There is a role for contrarian individuals in alternative scenario development.

And there is a role for teamwork. Not every contrarian is a genius. And individuals operating alone are not as good as a team at assembling a bundle of divergent scenarios. Further, there is a stage in the development of scenarios when brainstorming a whole batch of possibilities calls for diverse perspectives and a range of imaginations. At their best, scenario workshops turn into intellectual jam sessions with diverse perspectives, like different musical instruments, complementing and provoking one another in phrases combining both dissonance and harmony. Soloists sometimes emerge to grab attention for a few bars, but a successful workshop is an ensemble performance.

The importance of both individuality and teamwork in the generation of alternative scenarios has implications for the second and third dilemmas of critical theory: the relationship between theory and practice, and the source of moral purchase. Rather than conforming slavishly to the pyramidal architecture of this piece, I must treat these two topics together rather than in neat sequence. Here toward the end, the several themes run together in a contrapuntal cadenza that incorporates several themes at once.

(b" and c") Theory, Practice and Morality in Scenario Planning

Teamwork is essential for moral legitimacy, and individuality is essential as a counterweight to the dictatorship of the proletariat—or the dictatorship of corporate group think. Let me unpack this critical dialectical balance in a way that also speaks to the theory/practice dilemma.

If morality were a matter of gaining access to some Platonic Idea of the Good, some theoretical gold ring to be seized from the gods' merry-go-round and brought back to the rest of humanity, it might just be possible for some heroic individual to scale the heights of abstraction and return, like Prometheus, to bestow the gift of a definitive morality upon other mortals. Moses tried, but somehow we still have problems. Maybe morality isn't a matter of a few commandments. Maybe morality is a lot messier than any precise blueprint in the sky drawn by philosophy or theology. Maybe morality is something that we must make up as we go along.

This is not the place to develop a full-blown philosophy of morality, but this much I will try to defend: there is a place for a morality that is neither as absolute and definitive as divine commandments and mathematical proofs, nor as uncertain and capricious as the individual preferences at play in subjective relativism. I do not accept the argument that claims that once you relinquish the moral absolutes of Christianity (or Islam, or Kantian ethics), then there's no stopping your descent down the slippery slope towards pernicious relativism. This is a false disjunction. You don't have to choose either absolutism or relativism in their extreme forms. These are false extremes. Moral crises are almost never drawn in black and white. Moral crises are rarely so elegant. They are almost always drawn in shades of gray. That's why they are so often so difficult.

And that's why, also, we hear so much about the need for individuals to be true to themselves, on the one hand, and on the other, the need to temper individual impulses with social constraints that transcend the whims of solitary individuals. Leaving ethics entirely up to individuals runs the obvious risks of subjective relativism: you like string-beans, I like rape, whatevah. This will not do. But leaving ethics entirely up to the mores of the community runs the equal and opposite risk of totalitarianism: good Germans supporting one another in pursuing the final solution, or the dictatorship of the proletariat in Marxism. There must be a place in morality for Thoreau's civil disobedience, or Oscar Schindler's moral courage. So how are we to balance individual conscience and social constraints that transcend the individual?

It would be nice if we had a neat theory that could answer this question. If such a theory were available, you would think that in the years since Socrates it would have been invented. But it hasn't. There is no theory worthy of the name that commands the respect of most philosophers in the way that quantum theory commands the respect of most physicists. Meta-ethics and morality remain up for grabs on a purely theoretical level, despite the fact that most of us will agree that lying, cheating and stealing are wrong. Moral theory, it seems, makes no progress. Not, at least, in the way science does. But what about moral practice? Could the spread of civilization and the progressive growth of wealth be regarded as an increase in moral practice? How would we know whether humanity as a whole were becoming more moral? By a decrease in the amount of cruelty?

These questions are not easy to answer, and I will not try to answer them by marshaling statistics. In order to articulate what I mean by moral practice, as opposed to moral theory, it is in principle impossible to justify claims for moral practice in terms of a greater or lesser conformity to some moral theory. I want to articulate an approach to moral practice that is prior to and generative of moral theory, not a practice that follows from moral theory. This priority of practice to theory is just what Marx himself advocated, but later Marxists lost sight of. And it is just this priority of practice to theory that scenario planning embodies. How?

The practice of scenario planning, and especially the dynamics of the scenario workshop, balance the democratic will of the group and the iconoclastic creativity of the individual. But further, since the objective of the scenario workshop is precisely to create a better future (however 'better' might be defined), the practice of scenario planning is unavoidably ethical. That was the point of my earlier essay on normative scenarios: to liberate future studies from the illusion that it could or should be a form of value free inquiry. But in that essay I failed to address the question of the basis or foundation for values—and for good reason, namely, because I agree with Richard Rorty and the deconstructionists in their critique of *foundational* philosophizing.

Philosophy is not science. Philosophy, we are finally discovering in the post-modern era, is more like literature than mathematics. Philosophy is not a matter of discovering truths that were already there in some great blueprint in the sky. That's the Platonists' illusion—to think that the realm of Ideas exists like the architecture of real numbers, just waiting for philosopher-mathematicians or logicians to unlock their hidden theorems. But philosophy does not work that way because humanity is historical, not eternal. We are free and creative, not determined by divine pre-destination. We hairless monkeys do not have an eternal essence. We keep making up the human game as we go along. We keep changing the rules. This is called history, and it is our glory and our opportunity and our peril and our danger. We can blow it if we are not careful, for nothing guarantees our success. But we can also taste the sublime and experience the joys of grandchildren in the garden. And we can extend this joy to more and more of our species if we just work out some of the injustices in our socio-political-economic systems.

Among the most pernicious motives for injustice is poverty. Those who are poor become fixated on becoming rich. The obsession with wealth creates individuals willing to do injustice to others in order to satisfy their obsession. The alleviation of poverty is therefor good. Business people need not be guilty about their practices as long as they add more to our collective wealth than they detract from our non-monetary wealth (or social and physical environment).

Seen in this large context of the whole of life and society (as Marx saw it), economics is not a dull science but is instead the attempt to understand the metabolism of exchanges that keep us alive and well. In this larger context, though, economic value is inextricably entwined with *values*: we are willing to pay for what we think is *good*. We do not pay for what we take to be bad. But note how these words, 'good' and 'bad', get sprinkled through our discourse in the most various ways—a good car, a good marriage, a good man, a good decision. Sometimes it's easy to know what we mean by 'good'. A good car is one that functions as we expect a car to function. But a good man is more difficult to measure. We're not just sure how to measure humans. Being free, not having an eternal essence, we humans keep changing the rules about what it means to be a good one or a bad one.

Different cultures set different rules for how to be a human being. Kinship systems tell you who you can marry, and how uncles relate to nephews. Different cultures also have different things to say about which gods to worship, if any, and which aspirations are more worthy than others. Each of us individuals is molded by the culture into which we are born. We are not entirely free to scrap the rules or our culture and start from zero. This was the mistake of the existentialists and some American liberationists of the sixties: to think that the solitary individual could transcend culture and break entirely free of the past. Nor are we entirely determined by our culture. To think we are is the mistake of the totalitarians and cultural determinists who see the collective as the moral subject of history.

Neither individualism nor collectivism correctly identifies the source of moral agency. Because morality is so often the search for the correct balance between the will of the individual and the requirements of the collective, it is a mistake to base moral theory—ethics—on the priority of one or the other. Neither existentialism nor Stalinism was adequate to the moral challenge of life in Europe between the two world wars, but these seemed to be the only foundational philosophies available to intellectuals in that culture. Critical theory can be understood as the attempt to find a third way between those two inadequate extremes. But critical theory and Marxist humanism failed to find that third way. Leading with theory rather than practice, the critical theorists got hopelessly tangled in the three dilemmas outlined above.

Scenario planning is a practice in search of a theory. Developed outside the university by thoughtful people with no disciplinary or departmental axes to grind, scenario planning solves the dilemmas of critical theory without ever having set out to do so. I've already addressed the balance between the individual and the team in scenario workshops. And I've confessed that scenario planning is a practice *in search of a theory*. But I've suggested that this is the right order, that practice needs to come prior to theory in designing the future. In order to turn that suggestion into an argument, I want to turn now to the third dilemma, and the first objective of this overlong essay. As the opening sentence put it, "I would like to enlist the tools of alternative scenario development in the service of moral outrage at past and present social conditions."

The best way toward a final cadence to the cadenza will be to report on the experience of the practice, not to theorize. What does it feel like to lead a scenario workshop? Or to take part in one that is led by a master? I learned my lessons watching Peter Schwartz, the author of *The Art of the Long View* which, as of this writing, is the definitive text on scenario planning. In watching Peter conduct scenario workshops, I was often intrigued at the similarity between his way of working and that of an existential psychoanalyst: lots of questions, but more about the present and future than about the deep dark past.[81] The difference between facilitating a scenario workshop and conducting existential psychoanalysis is that the analysand is not an individual but an institution or a community. So the practice begins to look more Socratic than psychoanalytic. Taken off the analysts couch and relocated into a meeting room with ten to twenty people, the scenario workshop

---

81   For the future orientation of existential psychotherapy see Ludwig Binswanger, "Freud's Conception of Man in the Light of Anthropology," trans. J. Needleman, in *Being-in-the-World,* New York, 1963; Medard Boss, *Psychoanalysis and Daseinsanalysis,* trans. Ludwig Lefebre, New York, 1963; and Rollo May, *Existence,* New York, 1958.

becomes a testing ground for the aspirations of a community. What do we want? And how might we succeed in attaining what we want? What could happen that would open up opportunities? What dangers are lurking just over the horizon? Many of these questions are absurdly simple to pose: What are people worried about? What keeps you up nights? If you could ask an oracle just one question about conditions five years from now, what would you most want to know?

The leader of a scenario workshop is not there to teach but to listen. Just as good therapists are not very directive, so the scenario workshop facilitator is not there to tell people what to do or think, but to draw out (*e-ducare*) the concerns of others. Of course the questions are often leading questions. Like Socrates, the good facilitator will be a midwife bringing other people's intellectual children into the world. But also like Socrates, the good facilitator will need to know quite a lot about the subject under discussion in order to ask those questions that lead in the most productive directions. This is not the place to describe in any detail the several skills of a good facilitator. Sooner or later there may be a literature as extensive as the annals of the psychoanalytic societies, a literature that does for scenario workshop facilitators what the Freudians and Jungians have done for psychotherapists, namely, describe all the resistances and denials and transferences and counter-transferences that can occur in the context of a workshop. But we are still awaiting the social Freud, the theorist who can open up the realm of the social unconscious and chart a path from social sickness to social health. For now all we have is the practice, and there is much to see, as Yogi Berra once said, by just watching.

In watching many scenario workshops, I have been amazed at the number of revelations, the a-has that come with seeing the world in new ways. As in psychotherapy, it's no good just telling people the answer. They must discover it for themselves, whatever the 'it' may be. As Socrates insisted, the truth is in the learner. Hence his rather bizarre notion of learning as *anamnesis*—recollection from memories implanted in the soul in some former life. I take this to be a theory well worth forgetting. The important point expressed by this theory is the pedagogical point: better to question than to lecture.

Why is it so important that a process of questioning encourage the aspirations of a community to be articulated in the form of a normative scenario? Because *shared hope* then takes the place of human essence as the fulcrum for moral critique. Once a community makes the effort to articulate a scenario worth aspiring towards, then there is a standard for measuring the distance between what is and what ought to be. In the past, most such standards have been drawn down from heaven rather than built from earth. Religious commandments and ideological principles have been invoked as sources for the meaning of 'better' in organized attempts to create a better future. But the peril of the postmodern era is the deconstruction of all of the old absolutes, whether religious or ideological. Does this condemn us to the end of history and a nihilistic acceptance of whatever *is?* Not if we can find some other purchase for prying *ought* away from *is.*

The Marxists tried to use human essence as a standard for measuring our alienation from our natural condition. But as the centerpiece or capstone in the arc of this essay argued, you can't have eternal essence and history too. Ahistorical naturalism must give way to a certain degree of cultural relativism once we admit that different cultures are free to modify the rules of the human game. But this cultural relativism need not devolve to the free for all of subjective relativism. Communities can circumscribe the acts of their members. And we are each members of at least one community or culture. We all grew up somewhere, not nowhere. We interact with a finite number of other individuals who populate our experienced world.

The standards presupposed by our communities are not all the same. The Japanese and Chinese place more weight on the importance of social relationships, while English-speaking societies place more weight on the importance of individual liberty, for example. These cultural differences among fundamental values make it difficult to defend the idea that values, in order to *be* values, must be universal in their reach, applying to all people in all places at all times. If values are to have any force in restraining subjective wants and whims, they must derive their obligatory force from something less individual and private than wants and whims. But that does not mean that only universal laws as timeless as mathematics will do the job. Democratically endorsed hope will do as well. But because differences are possible in the details of our hopes, it's worth taking care to articulate with some precision the future we want to inhabit. And this is what a successful scenario workshop accomplishes.

Without setting out to solve the unsolved problems left behind by critical theory, scenario planning can fulfill the same hope for a better future. Without calling in the conservatives from the religious right, or the thought correctors from the ideological left, scenario planning can help a community articulate its hopes and its fears, and in so doing, define the values it holds dear. Best case and worst case scenarios are inevitably value laden. In the corporate world, the most salient value is often profitablity. But the larger the organization, and the longer term the scenarios, the more important does *sustainability* of profits become. And as soon as sustainability becomes an important criterion for normative scenarios, then planners are thrust into thinking about the web of interrelationships among our economic, social and natural systems. Even the fittest cannot survive if they destroy the environment they feed upon. As Gregory Bateson was fond of putting it, the minimum unit of evolutionary survival is neither the individual, nor the species, but nothing less than species plus environment.

As we cast the net of scenario thinking ever wider and longer term, there is virtually no significant corner of life that escapes its reach. Scenario thinking is inevitably systemic. And so is mature morality—that is, a morality that involves more than obeying commandments or slavishly following prescribed rules. Most of what most of us regard as moral is pretty obvious: don't lie, cheat or steal; prefer kindness over cruelty. We may have affirmed these values once because our parents told us to, or to please god. But as we mature and take a longer, broader view of our world, we come to see that only by following such values can we inhabit a caring community of trustworthy associates, and only in such a community can we raise families with futures. These values come to serve as a public operating system presupposed by all of our private programs. Without them we crash. But as the current software environment amply demonstrates, several such operating systems are possible, and incompatibilities abound. So likewise as the globalization of the economy brings different cultures into conflict. From the fatwah against Salmon Rushdie to the caning of Michael Fay we see the effects of culture clash.

It would be nice if we could appeal to some transcendent standard like the will of god or human essence that could serve as a universal, eternal measure of good and evil. But human freedom, creativity and historicity will not allow it. If we are to take time seriously, if we are to accept responsibility for the degree to which we are the creators of our cultures and the despoilers of our natural environment, then it falls to us to accept a certain amount of authorship for our values. Not just any old values will do. Our natural environment and our cultural histories place limits—call them affordances—on which value sets are sustainable. The globe can afford some sets of values: not just one—that option would be totalitarian, and would put an end to history; not all—that would devolve to a subjective relativism accepting whatevah; but *some*—a pluralism that allows a certain amount of difference, and hence, a certain amount of freedom and creativity in the way we continue to reinvent the human game.

The point of this essay has been to argue that scenario planning is a crucial tool for playing this biggest game in town, the shaping of human history. As I have admitted, it's a megalomaniacal job, but somebody's got to do it. And far better that the medium of invention be social and community-based rather than left to the private fantasies of a few individual maniacs. Scenario planning provides a medium for sorting our hopes and our fears, and hence, a medium for investing our plans with our values. Because scenario planning allows groups of people to collectively deliberate over the possible consequences of their collective choices, scenario planning turns out to be a medium for collectively choosing our course toward *better* futures.

6. What Business Strategists Have to Learn from Sartre

Originally printed in Strategy+Business Winter 2003-2004. Reprinted with permission.

I remember the day I realized the world was getting weird—so strange and unpredictable that conventional approaches to market forecasting would not work. It was an otherwise ordinary day in May, 1985. I was part of a team at SRI International (formerly Stanford Research Institute), analyzing the results of a national survey of American customer attitudes. This was called the Values and Lifestyles (VALS) program, and it was a well-regarded, innovative breakdown of the purchasing public into nine different lifestyles roughly based on Abraham Maslow's hierarchy of needs: people whose lives revolved around survival, belonging, achieving, the search for peak experience, and so on. With the help of Simmons Market Research, we had correlated different purchasing patterns with the different lifestyles.

To date, the program had been a sustained success. If suburban women between the ages of 25 and 45 driving mini-vans reliably regularly chose Caffeine Free Diet Coke over Classic, while young males between 15 and 25 reliably went for the sugar and caffeine jolt, then the marketers at Coca-Cola would know how to spin the ads they put on MTV differently from the ads they place on soap operas. The theory and practice of market segmentation had been evolving for twenty years, in fact, growing hand in hand with the U.S. economy as it made the transition from mass manufacturing for a mass market in the industrial economy during the middle of the 20th Century, toward a more segmented market that could be described by our nine lifestyle types — nay, even, stereotypes.

On that day in May, however, I realized that the VALS system was losing its predictive power. People were no longer behaving true to type. Women were shopping at Bloomingdale's one day, WalMart the next. The segment we called Achievers started behaving like Experientials. Some men were behaving like bankers by day, punkers by night. This was bad news for our clients, trying to use market segmentation to target the different stereotypes, but it was good news for the human spirit, for what this tendency amounted to was human freedom flexing her muscles. People were behaving less predictably. They were defying stereotypes.

Because I had been trained as a philosopher, I immediately knew what was happening. The American customer, without direct influence from the likes of Jean-Paul Sartre or Martin Heidegger, had nonetheless discovered existential freedom. They would no longer be predictable. And indeed, customers around the world have been unpredictable ever since. No general system of market segmentation or analysis has managed to capture their patterns of behavior in any reliable way.

This realization has implications that far transcend marketing, which, typically, commences once a company has identified a strategy and developed products or services for a defined customer base. For corporations, keeping up with customers who are less predictable than consumers of old requires a capacity for innovation. Where the old economy relied on mass production to meet universal needs, the new economy demands customized innovation to satisfy an endless range of wants and whims. The old production economy was predictable because it operated in the realm of necessity; it produced goods and services people needed, and those were relatively stable. The new economy plays in the realm of freedom; it produces goods and services for a customer who is not bound by needs. The old economy called for strategies built by engineers who could calculate according to necessary laws. The new economy calls for strategies created by existentialists who understand freedom. Most important of all, the old economy operated at a regular pace, in the clockwork time of industrial production. The new economy lurches forward and backward, in some new kind of time that was anticipated, once again, by the existential philosophers.

We're all in existential time these days. It's not just that we're facing a more unpredictable future; the pace and rhythm of events is also increasingly variable and unpredictable. Especially after September 11, 2001, the corporate planning horizon has widened to embrace fundamental uncertainty spanning life or death, boom or bust dimensions. This is not all bad for the human spirit—if a wider horizon reminds us of our freedom.

Just as existential philosophy emerged in Europe between the two World Wars, when life got weird for individuals and the old verities no longer seemed to hold, so existential strategy has emerged during the final decades of the twentieth century as life is getting weird for organizations. Just as individuals reached for an existential philosophy that was adequate to a new sense of freedom, so corporations are now looking for the kinds of strategic tools that can accommodate real uncertainty. An existential economy, in short, demands existential strategy.

But what does that mean? For starters, it's a philosophy that stresses the importance and robustness of individual *choice*. In a world where it sometimes seems like there are too many choices, and too little authoritative guidance in making those choices, existentialism provides a viable approach to strategy—perhaps the only viable approach. In this article I'd like to offer an elevator ride introduction to the Existentialist philosophy, then call out a series of specific ideas from the writings of the existentialists to show how they can help us understand our business realities and decisions on a practical, day-to-day level.

In Silicon Valley they have a saying: *Who needs a futurist to tell us about the future. We're building it!* This is pure existentialism. The point isn't so much about the pace of change increasing—Alvin Toffler's argument in *Future Shock*. Instead it's a question of who's in charge—God, haphazard history, or human invention? The existentialists have something to tell us about taking charge of our own destiny.

Existentialism 101

The term *existentialism* gains its basic meaning by its contrast with essentialism. The ancient philosophers, particularly Aristotle, understood *change* as biological *growth.* A favorite example was the acorn turning into an oak. It can't do anything else. It is the *essence* of an acorn to become an oak. It cannot choose to become a maple or elm. Its oak essence *precedes* its existence. First acorn, then oak.

Impose this model of growth and change on human beings and you get Plato's theory of gold, silver and bronze souls—souls slated, from birth, to fulfill a predetermined destiny. Part of the education system in Plato's *Republic* involves a series of standardized national tests for separating the aristocratic guardians from the lowly worker bees—the first articulation of what we now know as a tracking system. You're born bronze, silver or gold. The tests will reveal your essence. And, very like the high stakes exams that characterize the French system of education, once your essence is revealed, there's very little likelihood that your existence will ever escape your class.

Such essentialism sounds downright un-American… and it is. If your essence precedes your existence, then all you can do is play out the pattern of your essence. The passage of time, to an essentialist, is like the unrolling of an oriental carpet whose every stitch, every line, every pattern was first obscured within the rolled up carpet, and then revealed as the past is extended into the present. The future, according to this philosophy, is like a carpet as yet unrolled. The pattern's in there. You just can't see it yet. And like most oriental carpets, its pattern is probably repetitive.

Prior to the nineteenth century, 'the future' was seen through essentialist eyes. The very word "future" connoted a stretch of time that would contain more of the same, occasionally better, occasionally worse, as the eternal cycle of generation and corruption, rise and fall, repeats itself age after age. In such tradition-bound societies, the elders know best because they know the past. Filial piety is a core value of Confucianism. Sons follow the occupations of their fathers. Tradition rules. According to the old ways, the past rules the present. Like the pattern of the seasons or the constellations in the heavens, the basic order of the universe is not subject to biological evolution or historical change. This sense of time and order remained sacrosanct until the works of Georg Hegel and Charles Darwin gained influence. These two writers, though very different from each other, together comprised the most significant sources of existential thought; only when their work was accepted was essentialism's image of time as repetitive and cyclical displaced by a linear, historical, evolutionary time that allows for the emergence of something genuinely new under the sun. Suddenly, humanity *had* a future—in the sense that existentialists think of the future, as an open-ended, indeterminate field of untried possibilities.

For existentialists, existence precedes essence. It's not that no one or nothing has an essence. It's just that essence, for free human beings anyway, is achieved rather than prescribed. You become the results of the decisions you make. You don't *find yourself,* as those suffering "identity crises" try to do. You *make* yourself by making decisions. You're not just the result of the genes you inherited or the circumstances of your birth. Of course genes and family background make a difference, but there's major uncertainty over what you do with them.

Consider the way that time is measured, and the way we normally experience it. Ever since the invention of the mechanical clock, people have conceived of time as passing in the kind of even blocks represented on Cartesian graph paper. For rocket scientists plotting a trajectory to the moon, this model of time might be the most appropriate. But as both Heidegger and Sartre noted, this kind of mathematized, regular tick, tick, tick of a mechanical clock contradicts the experience of a truly human temporality. Our minds experience time as expanding and contracting, quickening with excitement, slowing with boredom. There is a lived contrast between long durations and punctuating epiphanies. Things last a while, then they change, and there are significant choices to be made at the cusps and bifurcations.

Moments of Urgency

Such moments call for strategies developed prior to the moment of urgency. And as the world gets weirder, these moments will be more frequent.

Scenario planning (see box on p.169) gives executives a way to rehearse different futures in the relative calm of a meeting room rather than in a war room set up for emergencies. Better to craft a strategy during the calm between the cusps. Once you've rehearsed different futures in the form of vivid scenarios, then you're ready for the one that rolls out in fact. And even better: once you've scoped out a range of alternative futures, you're in a better position to nudge reality in a direction you'd prefer.

A future filled with new possibilities presents a backdrop for planning that is very different from a future that is a reshuffling of the same old, same old. Reshufflings of the same old stuff should follow laws that allow for prediction according to rules that cover every possibility. A future that is filled with genuinely new possibilities might not even be describable using categories and metrics that cover what has occurred before. How could a nineteenth century scientist anticipate, much less predict, prime time, venture capital, gigabits-per-second, butterfly ballots, genetic engineering, fuel cells, or cellular telephony…???

Once you appreciate this fundamental shift in the nature of futurity, you are in a better position to appreciate the need for existential strategy. Once you abandon an essentialism for which the future is in principle predictable, and adopt an existentialism for which the future is in principle unpredictable, you're bound to need a robust set of guidelines for making decisions that will be effective in any of a range of futures that might unfold in ways that cannot be predicted in advance.

Understanding Uncertainty Through Scenario Planning

Scenario planning is not the only tool of the existential strategist, but it is a pre-eminently appropriate tool for dealing with existential freedom. Scenario planning first flourished in the context of large corporations like Royal Dutch/Shell, companies whose planning horizon was so long that predictions based on extrapolation from the past would almost certainly be outrun by a fast-changing reality. Royal Dutch/Shell did well with scenario planning in the 1980s. When other oil companies were planning on increasing prices for oil, based on extrapolations from the price increases in 1973 and 1979, the planners at Shell developed a range of scenarios—narrative extrapolations from knowable potentialities—that included both price increases as well as scenarios for falling prices—a thought that was literally unthinkable to planners at the other oil majors. When oil prices crashed in 1986, Shell was the best-prepared of the global oil companies, and its fortunes rose accordingly.

Since the 1980s, scenario planning has been embraced by many other companies, so many that, by the turn of the millennium, scenario planning ranked as the number one planning tool among corporations polled by the Corporate Strategy Association. Of course this is good news for scenario planners. But it is also good news for the human spirit. Scenario planning opens up a range of possibilities, for good and ill, much broader and wider than traditional tools that strive for a single right answer. Scenario planning helps us to look down the cellar stairs, as responsible managers must. Just as Heidegger argued that a sense of our own mortality can sharpen our sense of the fragility of our assumptions, so the development of best and worst case scenarios can awaken us to a sense of the preciousness of life.

By encouraging thinking about a divergent range of possibilities rather than converging on a consensus forecast, scenario planning can draw on both the motivation that comes from a fear of vividly depicted failure as well as the inspiration that comes from a skillfully drawn success. Upside scenarios can raise the sights of an organization mired in stagnation. Where essentialism condemns us to more of the same old, same old, upside scenarios instill a sense of existential urgency about higher possibilities.

Upside scenarios can function like the inner game of golf or inner skiing. Once you have mentally rehearsed the right swing or the perfect turn, you are more likely to be able to hit that drive or manage that mogul. There's a lot to be said for the idea of mind over matter. But before the mind can steer matter in the right direction, the appropriate image needs to be framed as vividly as possible, whether it's a golf swing, a ski turn, or a new success strategy. Upside scenarios can do for companies what a Phil Mikelson tape can do for golfers.

As a philosophy, existentialists stress that human beings have almost unlimited choice. The constraints we feel from authority, society, other people, morality, and God are powerful largely because we have internalized them—we carry the constraints around within us.

As a result, sometimes existentialists get a bad rap for preaching nihilism and meaninglessness—free fall instead of freedom. Everything is possible (they're accused of preaching), and therefore human beings can ignore morality and duty. Thus, Nietzsche proclaimed the death of God. For Smerdyakov, the nihilist in Dostoyevsky's *Brothers Karamazov,* the death of God meant that mere anarchy was loosed upon the earth. But Nietzsche himself distinguished between a nihilism of strength and a nihilism of weakness. For the weak, the death of God means that all is permitted. For the strong, the death of God does not mean we are doomed to despair and meaninglessness. Instead, we have the opportunity to create our own lives and our own conscious sense of responsibility. Nietzsche said the only God he could worship would be a god who could dance.

This turns out to be very close to the role of managers, particularly senior executives, in large complex organizations. They don't take on the role of God, but they do choose to define morality and its consequences for their organizations. In their classic management text *In Search of Excellence*, Tom Peters and Robert Waterman argued that the job of the manager is "meaning making". This challenge to make meaning in an otherwise meaningless environment is itself made to order for the existential strategist.

How, then, does one "make meaning" for an entire organization—and ensure that the choices will turn out better than simply following in old established pathways? The existential philosophers crafted some ideas that have fairly immediate relevance to strategic practice.

The 5 principles of existential strategy

1. Finitude—You can't be all things to all people. If you are not saying "*No*" to some possibilities, then you're not acting strategically.

2. Being-towards-death—No one is too big to fail, to die, to go bankrupt. Gliding on momentum can lead to a crash.

3. Care—Define your interests more precisely than "ROI" or return to the shareholders. If you don't know where you stand, you'll fall for anything.

4. Thrownness—You have a past; you have core competencies. Know them, don't forget them, and use them.

5. Authenticity—Don't be bound by your past. Feel free to re-invent yourself and your company for an uncertain future.

Let's explore each and its application to existential strategy.

Finitude

Finitude is the existential principle closest to the conventional notion of corporate strategy—making hard decisions because you can't do *everything*.

In this mortal life, you may be able to accomplish almost anything, but you cannot do *everything*. There isn't time. If you choose to be a butcher, you generally can't simultaneously be a baker or a candlestick maker. Understanding finitude helps the existential strategist focus on the tradeoffs organizations face. You can go for lowest cost or highest quality, but rarely both at once. There are choices to be made. Not all good things go together. If you're not saying no, you're not doing strategy.

The word 'decision' derives from the Latin for 'cut off'. IBM made a strategic decision to get out of the consumer business and concentrate on services to businesses. Hewlett-Packard cut Agilent adrift because medical technology was not its core competence. When corporate raiders make a hostile takeover and then break up a business and sell off its parts, their reasoning often has to do with an evaluation that shows the parts are worth more on their own than as parts of a confused whole in which executives prove unable to make hard decisions. I saw the power of finitude when working with wealthy foundations that, like government agencies, rarely feel the risk of failure. At first glance, the job of foundation managers looks easy: Just hand out a pot of money. At closer range, the challenge is harder: How to improve the world without squandering resources or inducing dependencies that do more harm than good.

The Mott Foundation in Flint, Michigan, has as one of its objectives the improvement of the city of Flint—a clear goal that nonetheless leaves plenty of latitude for choices by the trustees. After spending millions in the 1980s on what was to be a destination resort called AutoWorld, they watched in horror as people somehow chose Disneyworld as their destination instead. In the early 1990s, the managers of the Mott Foundation engaged my colleagues and me to develop a set of scenarios showing different possible futures for Flint—a city that had been badly stung by Michael Moore's movie, *Roger and Me*. The upshot of the exercise was a commitment to make Flint a better place to raise children—a manageable goal that gave a new focus to the foundation's finite grant making. Looking out for the kids was both consistent with the original deed of gift by the Mott family—the thrownness of the foundation—and in keeping with current needs in Flint. The city had been a great place to raise a family back when rust-belt manufacturing produced a living wage. But the new economy had cut many of the old jobs, and now it would take a bold initiative to make the city safe for kids once again.

Being-towards-death

If you think your life is not finite, if you think you're immortal, then you may act as if you've got time for everything. If you follow the existentialists in dwelling on death, however, each day of your life will gain both preciousness and a sense of existential urgency.

The National Education Association (NEA), America's largest labor union— thought by some to be immovable, immortal, and unchangeable—benefited from an imaginative kick in the pants from a scenario entitled, "One Flight Up". That scenario told a story in which their building in Washington, D.C. had been sold to Sylvan Learning Systems which leased back to the NEA a small suite of offices located "one flight up" from the main entrance. After absorbing this scenario, the President of the NEA was quoted in *The New York Times* as saying, "If we don't change the way we do business, we'll be out of business in ten years." This statement, his colleagues declared, would have been unthinkable a few years earlier, before he'd looked death in the face.

The union did change. Under its next president, Bob Chase, the NEA adopted "new unionism"—a strategy focused less on wages and terms of employment, and more on helping its members meet the challenges they were facing in the classroom. As we began many interviews conducted during the course of that project, "If the auto workers' union had been less focused on wages and terms of employment during the 1950s and 60s and more focused on helping its members build better cars, there would have been better wages for auto workers during the 1980s and 90s and fewer customers buying cars from overseas"… and more jobs for the people of Flint.

Asking folks to look death in the eye is not easy. Being-towards-bankruptcy is no fun. Xerox needed a vivid scenario painting a picture of a world where the copier would converge with the scanner and computer printer, and the copier business would go away. We painted such a scenario… but it wasn't scary enough to motivate change, and their denial of death led to real bankruptcy.

BP, which once stood for British Petroleum, looked down the cellar stairs at a world "Beyond Petroleum," the new meaning for its eponymous initials. Scenarios that mimic being-towards-death can function as a kind of anticipatory disaster relief. A near-death experience lived in imagination can draw forth the passion which exists underneath smug self-satisfaction; that kind of motivation is needed to take the actions necessary to avoid real death. It can make managers *care*—a relatively weak word. The German equivalent, *Sorge*, has more urgency to it. It means to really care, to give a damn. There's passion in it.

Care

Heidegger focused on care as a feature of human beings that differentiates us from purely cognitive, Cartesian creatures. Sure, we think, we calculate, we cogitate. But we do so in a way that is different from computers. My computer doesn't give a damn. It doesn't care. And so much the better: It is unbiased; it is unswayed by desire; it can do the wholly rational, objective calculations I want from a computer. I, on the other hand, have biases, I have desires. And so much the better again, for my desiring, my caring, gives meaning to my life.

Oftentimes organizations, especially large, long-standing ones, need a greater sense of urgency. It's not just a matter of giving a damn about reducing time to market for new products. Sometimes a corporation must re-invent itself. Sometimes a company must break free of its past.

Once upon a time Motorola made car radios. When Bob Galvin wanted to manufacture semiconductors, some of his managers thought he was nuts. But Bob Galvin, son of founder, Paul Galvin, cared enough to keep his father's legacy alive even after the car radio business declined. Later they re-invented Motorola yet again as a manufacturer of cell phones and pagers. In a world that's gone from slow and predictable to fast and weird, you have to be free to re-invent yourself... or you die.

Thrownness

Of course you can't reinvent yourself as anything whatever. Companies have histories. IBM doesn't sell dog food. Sara Lee isn't set up to manufacture computers. Heidegger called this non-deterministic conditioning *Geworfenheit* or *thrownness*. We each landed on the earth somewhere, not nowhere. We each inherit much of who we are from our parents, our culture, or the community in which we find ourselves. Even the entrepreneur finds the second year of her new company "thrown" in a certain direction by her first year. Right-angle turns are tough. Momentum has its merits. But even for the largest corporations, straight-line extrapolation from the past into the future is a poor guide for planning.

Thrownness is not just a constraint. Upside possibilities beckon the existential strategist. Aspirational scenarios showing rewarding opportunities can complement descriptive scenarios painting downside risks. When executives at Motorola sought our help to update their China strategy, we realized they'd been coasting on momentum. Taking a hard look at both downside and upside scenarios led them to boost their investment, claim greater market share, and solidify their leadership position. The sheer size of the opportunities that exist in China are enough to dwarf the imaginations of planners coasting on extrapolations from the past. It takes a dancing existentialist to see such vast possibilities.

Authenticity

Authenticity is a way of being true to yourself, but the concept is tricky because, for the existentialist, being true to yourself can't be defined as being true to your *essence*. Nor can it be reduced to fulfilling a function. Authenticity demands both fidelity to your past, but also openness to possibilities in the future. Not just one possibility—that would be a necessity—but several possibilities. Authenticity is about being true to both your thrownness *and* your freedom. It's about making choices among possibilities and taking responsibility for your decisions.

At Motorola, I also had an opportunity to work with the company's New Enterprises group. Their mandate was to come up with new business ideas that were close enough to Motorola's core competencies to be plausible yet far enough away as to fall outside of existing lines of business. Threading this needle is what authenticity is all about. If you try too hard to be true to your essence—your core competence—then you deny your freedom. But if you pretend you're absolutely free to do anything—if you forget your thrownness—then you're in free fall. Motorola's New Enterprises Group had to thread this needle, so they took a hard look at how their competence in information technology could be applied to a new and different domain: the creation, storage and conservation of electric energy.

Neither for companies nor for individuals is the future completely indeterminate. Neither companies nor individuals are utterly free. We carry our pasts like tails we cannot lose. And so much the better, again, because we don't want to begin each day from scratch. The skills we have learned, the competencies we have achieved, give direction and power to be used in the present as we carve the near edge of the future.

The gist of this essay has moved mainly from the philosophy of existentialism toward its implications for corporate strategic planning. Here at the end, it's worth reflecting on the resonance that resounds from the soundness of existential strategy in the corporate world to its implications for the people who then learn about existential time from the practice of scenario planning and existential strategy in organizations. The practice of existential strategy can make us more authentically human. Once existential philosophy has been demystified by its translation into the workaday world of corporate strategy, its validity gains added power in enabling each of us, as individuals, to live lives of deeper authenticity and freedom.

7. Organizational Learning, Evolution, and Scenarios

Originally published in Organizational Learning for All Seasons, ed Prem Kumar, National Community Institute, Singapore 2002. Reprinted here with permission.

Introduction

This essay will follow Gregory Bateson in arguing that the logic of learning is fundamentally the same as the logic of evolution—trial, error, and selection for fitness. (Bateson 1972.) I'll then apply that evolutionary logic to organizational learning, and show how scenario planning fits and assists in that application.[82]

Following Darwin, we think of selection as operating on individuals in the natural environment. Bateson extended Darwin's insights to the domain of learning by arguing that individual learning is also a process of trial (mutation) and error (selecting out) followed by the survival (selecting in) of adaptive behaviors. By exploring the homology or isomorphism between learning and evolution, Bateson also shed light on evolution itself, which he saw as *the learning of a species*. According to Bateson's hypothesis, adaptation *is* the education of a species, the process by which a species learns what it needs in order to survive.

Learning and evolution are the first two legs of the three-legged stool being fashioned in this essay. Scenario planning is the third leg. Why bring in scenario planning? Because we need a tool, a method, a practice that can take these Darwinian/Batesonian insights and apply them in the context of organizational learning. Darwin's domain was natural selection in the eco-system. Bateson extended Darwin's logic to the domain of the individual learner, whether a person or a dolphin. Between the macro-environment of the eco-system and the micro-domain of the individual, the organization occupies a kind of intermediate meso-environment. Can Darwin's and Bateson's insights apply at this middle level? Or are we guilty of anthropomorphizing the organization when we talk about "organizational learning?" If we understand "organizational learning" as adaptive behavior rather than as alterations among neuronal patterns in a human brain, then it's appropriate to ask whether the same Darwinian, adaptive dynamics that Bateson finds in individual learning may also characterize organizational learning.

The point of this chapter is to argue that scenario planning provides the missing link, or third leg, that will allow the stool of organizational learning to stand. This essay

---

82   Two different and non-overlapping communities deserve credit for stimulating many of the ideas in this essay. I am grateful for dozens of colleagues in Global Business Network, with whom I have had the privilege of practicing scenario planning over the past fifteen years. And I am grateful to dozens of participants in Esalen Institute's Evolutionary Theory conferences over the past four years.

is divided into three parts. The first focuses on the way scenario planning satisfies the demand for heritability in the living company. The second shows how scenarios provide virtual environments in which organizational strategies can be tested for fitness. Because I assume that readers of this volume will already be familiar with the basics of both scenario planning and organizational learning, the bulk of this essay will be concerned with evolutionary theory, and with the development of a specific interpretation of evolutionary theory. I will argue that evolution is less teleological than the advocates of creationism or "intelligent design" would have it, but more directional than most advocates of the neo-Darwinian synthesis would claim it to be. Part Three then develops four principles showing the tight fit between scenario planning and a theory of evolution that sees nature not as a "blind watchmaker" but as a somewhat foresightful scenario planner.

Like evolution, scenario planning is a process of variation, adaptation and selection—variations on a single-point forecast or an "official future". Once a range of scenarios has been developed, then it is the job of the scenario planners to figure out how the organization can adapt to any of those different environments. If it fails to adapt it will be selected out. Bankruptcy stands in for extinction. After having developed a range of different scenarios, management must develop a range of strategic options appropriate to each scenario, and a set of early indicators that will announce the imminent arrival of one or another scenario.

Just as Bateson argued that evolution *is* the learning of a species, so we can argue that scenario planning *is* the learning of the organization… but with a difference. Where evolution tends to be fairly profligate and wasteful, awarding the prize of survival only after a vast number of (almost) random variants have been tested for their adaptive fitness, the whole point of scenario planning is to rehearse the process of variation and selection in imagination rather than in fact.

Think of scenario planning as *virtual evolution.* We test different strategic options for their adaptive power *first* in the imaginative contexts of different scenarios, not in the reality of the marketplace. In evolutionary terms, this amounts to highly directed rather than random variations. Rather than testing new product ideas by letting a thousand prototypes bloom and seeing which survive in the market, we test our innovative ideas in the contexts of different scenarios prior to prototyping the virtual survivors in the real marketplace.

Organizations cannot afford the profligacy of Mother Nature. They have neither her resources nor her patience. As a friend's wife once said to him, "Dear, can we afford another 'learning experience'?" Organizations cannot afford to educate themselves in the reality of the marketplace alone. Like college students who learn in the protected and somewhat artificial environment of the ivory tower rather than in "the school of hard knocks", organizations need a way to learn to distinguish between foolish experiments and adaptive innovations *before* they spend scarce resources on new ventures. As evolutionary theory tells us, very few mutations are adaptive. Most are monstrous. Organizations need to be smart about innovation. Scenario planning provides the ideal school for improving organizational smarts just to the extent that it provides an opportunity to imaginatively model the adaptation of the organization to each of those environments—a classroom for *virtual evolution* by way of modeling adaptation to different imaginary environments.

Having made the point that the Batesonian homology between evolution and learning extends further to the third leg of scenario planning, and that scenario planning therefore allows us to practice evolutionary learning in organizations as well as in species and individuals, let us now milk this homology by drilling down into some of the finer points of evolutionary theory on the one hand, and scenario planning on the other. The point is to let insights from both of these two realms illuminate each other, and in so doing, pick up some practical tips for organizational learning.

1. Stories, Heritability, and Institutional Memory

For learning to stick, you need memory. This fairly obvious point is as true for organizations as it is for individuals. Far less obvious are the mechanisms of memory, both in individuals and in institutions. Let's look first at the mechanisms of memory in individuals, then at the *need* for memory in institutions, and finally at the way scenarios can satisfy that need by providing a mechanism for organizational memory.

Memory in individuals is, at present, not all that well understood, but at least we can say what it is *not*. Recent research on the brain has all but refuted the model of single-point storage. There is no single neuron in your brain where the memory of your Aunt Sally lies in storage like her photograph on page 23 of the family photo album. That's just not how memory works. While it is true that research has demonstrated a considerable degree of localization of different functions—image processing in the visual cortex, hearing in the auditory cortex—and some degree of lateral specialization between right and left hemispheres (though not as much or as universally as many early researchers or later popularizers claimed), nevertheless this localization of functions does not extend down to the micro-level of single memories in single cells. Instead, the most promising model for the neuro-anatomy of memory turns out to be—interestingly in this context—Darwinian. In research for which he was awarded a Nobel Prize, Gerald Edelman showed that the brain profligately overbuilds neural connections associated with different behaviors. Those connections that get used again and again gain tenure, as it were, and those that are not used then perish.

Edelman describes the neurophysiology of memory using the image of a mountain glacier that melts during the day and re-freezes at night over and over again. With each melting, slightly different streams are etched as the snowmelt makes its way down the mountain. Likewise, with repeated use, our brains get etched, or *tuned,* to a capacity to channel neural impulses in specific and repeatable ways without fixed instructions or a precise code.

As Edelman puts it:

> In this analogy, consider the value constraints to be gravity and the texture of the valley terrain, the input signals to be the changes induced by the weather, the synaptic change to involve freezing and melting, and the detailed rocky pattern down the hill to be the neuroanatomy, and you have a way of seeing how a performance can be repeated dynamically without a code... Such a memory has properties that allow perception to alter recall and recall to alter perception. It has no fixed capacity limit, since it actually generates "information" by construction. It is robust, dynamic, associative, and adaptive. If our view of memory is correct, in higher organisms every act of perception is, to some degree, an act of creation, and every act of memory is, to some degree, an act of imagination. (Edelman and Tononi, 2000.)

Before exploring the applicability of Edelman's model to institutions, let's look first at the need. The nature of the need, like the landscape of an environmental niche, will help to shape the organisms adapting to or satisfying that need.

At one level the nature of the need is obvious: If an organization has no memory, it is condemned to repeat its mistakes. It can't learn from experience—even those "learning experiences" like those feared by my friend's wife. If an organization lacks an institutional memory, it lacks a stable identity. It cannot keep its mind on its mission. It will forget its mission, its reason for existing, and then it will squander its resources on inconsistent ventures and eventually perish.

Arie de Geus, the executive in charge of scenario planning at Shell during the 1970s and 80s, observed that the maintenance of a clear sense of self-identity is an important function for *The Living Company* (the title of his book). Who *are* we? How do we mark the boundary between inside and outside? What is *us* and what is *not us?* (de Geus, Arie 1997, chapters 5, 6, and 9.)

The definition of identity has different dimensions, what the linguists and literary critics call the synchronic (same time) and the diachronic (through time) dimensions. In the synchronic dimension, identity is defined by the difference between inside and outside, *us* vs. *them,* at a single point in time. In the diachronic dimension, running through time, identity is subject to change and the question becomes: How much can we change without losing our old identity and gaining a new one? In the synchronic dimension, the boundary between inside and outside will be maintained by non-disclosure agreements, employment contracts, and security systems. Like the body's immune system, which performs the remarkable job of determining the difference between self and non-self so that alien and dangerous organisms like viruses and bacteria will be attacked by anti-bodies, so these corporate immune systems maintain identity in the synchronic *now.*

What about the diachronic dimension stretching from *then* to *yet-to-come?* Here a corporation maintains its identity by such systems as succession planning and good HR policies and management that minimize turnover. But is this enough? You can maintain the body count and still lose a sense of direction if the bodies are not aligned with the mission of the organization. It is precisely here that we find a need that is deeper and less obvious than the need for memory as a tool for learning from experience. Just as a person maintains a sense of identity by means of a tacit or explicit autobiography that tells his or her life's story, so an organization needs a story in order to maintain its diachronic identity. And just as a person doesn't store precise codes or instructions for reproducing behaviors, so an organization doesn't want its employees mindlessly following precisely coded directions for how to do their jobs. What's wanted is a well-communicated sense of *how we do things around here,* not a thick book of commands to be learned by rote.

Stories are excellent devices for maintaining an institutional memory. Stories are highly communicable. Telling the lore of the company, e.g. the heroic feats of the founders, helps to bind the tribe. But these stories should extend from the past into the future, and here's where scenarios come into play, for scenarios are precisely stories extending out into the future.

Scenarios come in sets, however. Is there a danger of confusing the identity of an organization just to the extent that they are several, not one? Do scenarios run the risk of provoking an institutional identity crisis? We could become this. We could become that. How are we to choose? Who are we *really?*

At this point it is important to see how future stories relate to the past. Except for entrepreneurial startups springing from a green field, scenario planning always builds on a legacy, and it is worth seeing how each scenario relates to and often reinterprets the past and present.

Think of the scenario planning exercise as Chapter Four of a seven-chapter book. The first three chapters are called: 1. Origin, 2. Growth, 3. Maturity. Chapter four is The Present. Chapters 5, 6, and 7 will be New Origin, Future Growth, and, hopefully, Triumph and Success in the best of scenarios. But in scenario planning, there will be several scenarios, several paths into the future.

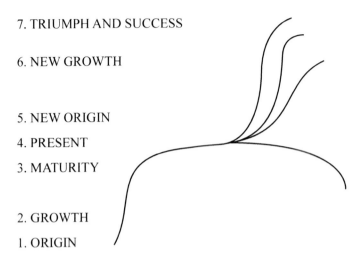

7. TRIUMPH AND SUCCESS

6. NEW GROWTH

5. NEW ORIGIN

4. PRESENT

3. MATURITY

2. GROWTH

1. ORIGIN

Figure 1

While this picture might seem to correctly represent the relationship between the future, present, and past, experience with scenario planning suggests otherwise. It might seem right to represent the actual present and past with a single line, while the point of scenario planning is to replace a mono-linear, single-point forecast with *several* lines representing multiple possibilities. But the practice of scenario planning has an interesting consequence: You find yourself re-interpreting the present and past differently depending on which of the future stories you are telling.

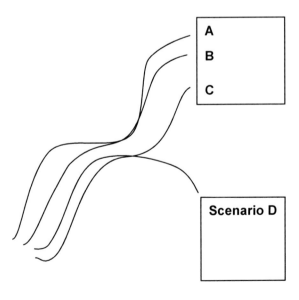

A

B

C

Scenario D

Figure 2

From the perspective of Scenario D, the past and present get reinterpreted as, "We got some lucky breaks, and now the party's over. Let's milk the cash cow as long as we can. Let's cut costs and ride it down while we seek the least painful exit strategy". Xerox comes to mind as an example of a company that could reinterpret its past in light of such a future.

Path A often involves a significant reinterpretation of the present and past by "upframing" what we need to do in terms of new categories and descriptors. BP and Shell come to mind. They used to think they were "oil companies." "BP" used to stand for "British Petroleum". Now the same letters stand for "Beyond Petroleum". Shell, which used to define its identity as "an oil company" has redefined itself as "an energy company" whose future might include more hydrogen and fuel cells than oil and gas.

Penn Central Railroad failed to upframe itself from "a railroad company" to "a transportation company". By failing to reinterpret their identity, they tied themselves to the falling star of the entire railroad industry. They missed opportunities in trucking and airfreight. Other companies like Motorola have reinvented themselves several times over, from a manufacturer of car radios, to RF technologies in many applications, to semiconductors, to cellular telephony, to communications technology in general.

New futures have a way of reinterpreting the present and past. We experience this truth in our own lives. When young Johnny drops out of college and takes a year to rethink his major, was that act "the first step in the career of a quitter, one that would be followed by many jobs, many marriages, and many divorces"? Or was that act "an early indication of his courage to challenge his assumptions and make creative course corrections"? Time will tell. But see how the choice of scenario amounts to an interpretive framework for past and present as well as future. Shell always was "an energy company". They just didn't see it that way at the time. Using scenarios, they learn more about both the future, and who they always were, really.

Now recall the sub-title for this section: "Stories, Heritability, and Institutional Memory". Summarizing this section, the point has been to show how scenarios, as highly communicable stories, provide an institutional memory and a sense of identity precisely to the extent that they help the members of an organization determine what part of the past they will carry with them into the future.

Heritability is an essential feature of all life. The wonder of DNA is its ability to grow a new organism very much like the parent organism. DNA is the key to diachronic identity in nature. Corporate culture is the key to diachronic identity for organizations. Just as the natural environment changes in ways that favor some species and doom others—ice ages, droughts—so the changing business environment imposes demands for learning and change on large organizations. While the profligate waste of (almost) random variation and selection is the evolutionary school where species learn to adapt (according to Bateson), scenario planning is the school where organizations can examine their DNA and learn, through a process that is more Lamarckian than Darwinian, how to evolve toward better futures.

"Stories, Heritability, and Institutional Memory." Organizations can use stories both to maintain (inherit) and to modify their identities depending on what they learn about themselves and their environments. Scenarios are uniquely suited to this need because scenarios allow us to entertain alternative futures and in so doing reinterpret our pasts. Not only do we learn about the future. Using scenarios we learn more about our organizational identity, who we really are and can become.

2. Evolutionary Theory and Scenario Planning

The perceptive reader will have noticed, and wondered, about the repeated parenthetical qualifier, "(almost) random variation". Why the qualifier, "(almost)"? Isn't it Darwinian dogma that variation is completely random? Jacques Monod wrote a famous book called *Chance and Necessity*. Theorists like Dan Dennett (*Darwin's Dangerous Idea*) and Stephen Jay Gould (in many books and essays) insist that evolution is not directional. It doesn't know where it's going. It is non-teleological, and all attempts to claim that evolution makes progress are, according to them, just so much wishful thinking. We human beings might like to think that we are higher on some evolutionary ladder than the banana slug… but evolution did not bother to create better dinosaurs, and we, too, could be headed for extinction under the non-teleological hands of random chance and harsh necessity.

Another variant on what might be called the *brutal* reading of evolution is Richard Dawkins' famous phrase, in his book so named: *The Selfish Gene*. There's nothing moral or altruistic written into the mechanism of evolution. Living organisms (or phenotypes) are just the gene's (or genotype's) way of making sure that its code, its message, will survive and prosper. Those little genes get a ride on the bus—the phenotype—they help to build and steer. But the point of calling the gene "selfish" is to make clear that the genes will catch the next bus, and the next, and the next, and from the selfish gene's point of view, continuing the trip down through successive generations is far more important than the well-being of any particular bus that happens to carry it on its way.

Yet another aspect of this brutal read of evolution is captured in such phrases as "survival of the fittest", and "nature red in tooth and claw". Herbert Spencer is the name generally associated with a view of evolutionary theory as describing—and ultimately justifying—a dog eat dog world. To those bleeding hearts who want to advocate altruism in human affairs and kindness toward our animal bretheren, the brutal read of evolution to which Spencer, Dawkins, Dennett, Monod, and Gould all contribute (in importantly different ways to be sure) says: Wake up and smell the blood. Evolution isn't set up to favor liberal ideology or Christian charity. The world is a sometimes cruel and generally heartless place headed nowhere in particular. Get used to it.

Before enlisting support from other theorists to counter the brutalists with a kinder, gentler theory of evolution, it's worth acknowledging the salutary influence of brutalism. Both creationism and anthropocentrism cry out for critique. God did not create man and all the rest of the species in six days. Nor is humanity the reason why life has been so hard at work evolving for 4.5 billion years. The brutalists stand in a noble tradition from Galileo and Copernicus through Marx, Darwin, Nietzsche and Freud. It's altogether worth deflating the pomposity of those who see man (in God's image by the way) as sitting smugly at the center of the universe, as better than the beasts, as specially and uniquely endowed with a mind that transcends and rules matter, as intrinsically moral, as essentially nice rather than naughty (that is to say, sexual). There's a prissy view of human nature, often but not only rooted in religion, that the great deflators have done well to criticize. The brutalists borrow strength from this noble tradition, and bid fair to add to it.

But have babies been flushed with the bathwater of creationism and pompous anthropocentrism? Very possibly. There may be a third way, a third read of evolution between the brutal and the pompous. Before charting this third path, let's look ahead at the reason why finding it could be so important in the present context. If it is true, as Bateson has argued, that learning *is* evolutionary and evolution *is* the learning of a species; and if it is also true as this essay is aimed at showing, that scenario planning is an excellent vector for infecting organizations with the learning bug, then our understanding of evolution is going to have a major influence on organizational learning. If learning *is* evolutionary in the sense that Bateson tells us it is, then we'd best be quite clear about just how evolution works before showing how scenarios contribute to organizational learning. *That's* where this argument is going. Now, who can help us to get there?

Fortunately we are not alone. We can find friends on this third path as diverse as Stuart Kauffman (author of *At Home in the Universe)*, Gregory Bateson (again), Robert Wright (author of *Non-Zero)*, Rene Thom (*Structural Stability and Morphogenesis)*, Peter Corning (*The Synergism Hypothesis)*, and a range of other writers who add stepping-stones to this third path. They neither sacrifice the cold-eyed rigor of the brutalists, nor yield to the wishful thinking of the pompous and prissy.

This is not the place to chart every inch of the third path. This essay is not devoted wholly to evolution. We just want to *use* a theory of evolution to make other points about scenario planning and organizational learning. But when we go to the toolbox of evolutionary theory to get help for organizational learning, we find that the tools need sorting and sharpening. If we pick up the blunt instruments of creationism or its slightly sharper contemporary cousin, "intelligent design", then the scenarios we create to educate a corporation are likely to twist toward the wishful and pollyannaish. If we pick up evolutionary tools crafted by the brutalists, then the scenarios we create to educate the corporation are likely to turn toward the pessimistic and cynical.

Both opponents in the interpretation of evolution are too simple. The creationists preach faith in a single creator God and a simplistic sense of divine purpose and destiny. "Don't worry if things look bad in the moment. It will all turn out for the best. So was it meant to be?" This kind of teleological thinking justifies all meandering missteps by a blind faith in a divine telos that sweeps everything toward it like water toward a drain. Whether Augustine's City of God or Teilhard de Chardin's Omega Point, such teloi reduce complexity by sucking out all contingency.

For the cynics, complexity disappears *down* instead of *up*. Life is a meaningless dance, which, in the last analysis, signifies nothing. For Marx, Nietzsche and Freud, as read by the cynics, it all comes down to management of the material means of production, or the will to power, or the circulation and redirection of libido.[83]

> With the globular protein we already have, at the molecular level, a veritable machine—a machine in its functional properties, but not, we now see, in its fundamental structure, where nothing but the play of blind combinations can be discerned. Randomness caught on the wing, preserved, reproduced the machinery of invariance and thus converted into order, rule, and necessity. A totally blind process can by definition lead to anything; it can even lead to vision itself. (Monod, 1971, p. 98.)

> The universe was not pregnant with life nor the biosphere with man. Our number came up in the Monte Carlo game. (Monod, 1971, p. 145.)

> If he accepts this message—accepts all it contains—then man must at last wake out his millenary dream: and in doing so, wake to his total solitude, his fundamental isolation. (Monod, 1971, p. 172.)

---

83 Note the qualifier: "as read by cynics." Marx, Nietzsche and Freud are richer, deeper, and subtler than the cynics make them out to be. For a demonstration of the range of readings possible for each of them, see Paul Ricouer's distinction between "the hermeneutics of suspicion" and "the hermeneutics of belief" in his *Freud and Philosophy: An Essay on Interpretations*, trans. Denis Savage, New Haven, Yale University Press, 1970. And if you read Darwin through those same reductionist lenses, evolution comes down to a play of blind chance and harsh necessity signifying nothing, or so many manipulations of selfish genes (Dawkins), or one damn thing after another with no sense of progress (Gould).

This message is very different from Stuart Kauffman's in his aptly titled book, *At Home in the Universe*.

Use the ideas of Monod, Dawkins, and Gould in your interpretation of evolution, and when you try to fashion a curriculum for the learning organization, you will end up teaching people that it's a dog eat dog world where winning is everything, competition trumps cooperation, and the only really honest scenarios are value free because, after all, that's the way the world is.

The brutalists ape the creationists, even as they simplify *down* rather than *up*. This was Hegel's insightful point in his passage on Enlightenment and Superstition in the *Phenomenology*. Between both of these paths that seek explanation by simplification, we need to find a third way that preserves—and even explains—*complexity*.

According to Stuart Kauffman, nothing in the neo-Darwinian synthesis or in physics or chemistry explains complexity. (Kauffman, 2000.) Certainly not entropy, which corrodes complex order into the less informed simplicity of heat death. So how does complexity happen? Not by design. We've rejected that path. Not by brutalist reduction. That way lies nothing but rearrangements of the same old simple stuff, whether the means of production in dialectical materialism, or will to power in an endless and non-progressive eternal recurrence (Nietzsche, 1967.) or libido in zero-sum sublimations that lead civilization to discontent (Freud, 1961.)

Now that the contrast between the creationists and the brutalists has been drawn, it's easier to see what "(almost) random variation" does and does not mean, and why that little qualifier is so important. What *does* it mean? That variation is for the most part random, but not utterly blind. Chance is real. Contra Einstein, God *does* play dice. But the dice are loaded. There *is* a small but, over many generations, very influential margin of directionality in evolution.

Before giving too much succor to the advocates of intelligent design, what does "(almost) random variation" *not* mean? That directionality is *not* equivalent to teleology. While there may be a tendency toward greater complexity and more order, this directionality is best seen as away from disorder and simplicity, but not toward any particular, predetermined telos.

Now that we know what "(almost) random variation" does and does not mean, what arguments can be advanced to show that it is true or, at the very least, not crazy. If this were a book on evolutionary theory and not an essay on scenario planning and organizational learning, its chapters could be filled with such arguments and their supporting evidence. Lacking so much space and time, I'll mention just four sources as a way of demonstrating that support does exist for the third path we're seeking.

1. French mathematical biologist Rene Thom challenged the idea that variation was utterly random at the level of single-point mutations of genes.

    I am reluctant to subscribe to the current belief that a point mutation, affecting just one nucleotide, is sufficient to inhibit the activity of a gene; this seems to me to repeat on another plane the error of the morphologists who believed that the destruction of one neuron in the brain would stop the process of thinking… Even if life is only a tissue of catastrophes, as is often said, we must take into account that these catastrophes are constrained by the global stability of the process and are not the more-or-less hazardous game of a mad molecular combination. Even adopting the anthropomorphic point of view that there is a mechanism for reading the DNA that is perturbed by errors, might we not push this anthropomorphism to its full extent and admit that the errors are oriented, as in Freudian psychology, by the "unconscious" needs and desires of the ambient metabolism. (Thom, 1975, p. 282.)

    Thom argues that, "Metazoa have, located in the kinetic configuration of the metabolism of their gametocytes, a model of their actual conditions of existence." Like scenario planners, animals carry inside themselves a map of what is outside themselves.

    The topology of this universal model will reflect less the phylogenetic relationships than the functional interaction between species, so that the distance between bee and snapdragon will be less than that between bee and butterfly. The big evolutionary advances of history will be described by global deformations of this universal model; the metabolism of gametocytes will appear as a kind of research laboratory, a device simulating conditions of existence close to the actual ones, and an evolutionary advance in this device will provoke unstable virtual catastrophes that will correspond to a new functional morphology, expressing the organic and physiological adaptations made necessary by this evolutionary change. Only when this new morphology is sufficiently stabilized, can evolutionary advance begin, and it will manifest itself as a mutation, a rearrangement of chromosome stock, and the appearance of new organic forms. According to these ideas, the fish already "knew", before they became amphibious, that a life on land would be possible for them, and what new organs they would need. (Thom, 1975, p. 294.)

    Thom is saying that the fish contains within itself a kind of map, not only of its existing environment—water—but also, by virtue of the fact that the fish is part of a universe, an "ambient metabolism," containing more than water, the fish can, like a scenario planner, model in its "research laboratory" another possible environment—land—and on the basis of that modeling capacity, can mutate in a way that is "not the more-or-less hazardous game of a mad molecular combination," but a more directed, more Lamarckian "aiming" toward that new global order.

2. Switching now from the level of mutation in the genotype, consider the role of "genetic drift" in the evolution of species. Here the source of variation may have nothing to do with (almost) random genotypic mutations, but with the distribution of certain traits among phenotypes. The classic case is a species of moths in England that normally occurs in both black-winged and white-winged varieties. When coal burning was more prevalent in England than it is today, the black-winged members of the species were better camouflaged. Over a series of generations, the black-winged moths therefore avoided predators more successfully than their white-winged brethren, who stood out against the soot. The black-winged moths consequently out-reproduced the white variety. The ratio of black-winged to white-winged moths increased as a function of "genetic drift" that had nothing to do with mutation, random or otherwise.

Here the diachronic evolution of a species is influenced by synchronic relationships with its surroundings. The ratio of black moths to white moths "co-evolves" with the coal burning habits of humans. This kind of co-evolution produces ecologies in which the wealth of mutually beneficial symbiotic relationships is such that observers will be moved to believe that things were designed "for the best." But a closer attention to the role of genetic drift will show that neither a designer nor a telos need be invoked to explain this co-evolution of mutually functional relationships. An understanding of synergy is sufficient. (Corning, 1983.)

In his book, *Non-Zero,* science writer Robert Wright makes a persuasive case for the directionality of evolution toward greater complexity and higher order. His palette extends beyond biological species to the successive stages of human history, from primitive hunter-gatherers, through the invention of agriculture and from ancient city-states to the invention of empire. At each stage in the long march of human history, Wright notes a kind of ratchet effect by which zero-sum conflict of the kind the brutalists see is succeeded by a non-zero sum solution. Rather than zero-sum rearrangements of the same old stuff—whether wheat, wealth, power, or libido—Wright shows how the evidence of history shows an unsteady march toward more complex systems, from tribes to cities to states to empires to... who knows what? In his final chapters Wright allows himself to speculate on the possibility that we human beings, together with our invented technologies like the Internet, might be evolving toward a more peaceful, more self-conscious realization of a fuller human potential. (Wright, 2000, p. 301 ff.)

3.   Stuart Kauffman extends his arguments about the evolution of complexity in the biosphere to what he calls the "econosphere" where he makes the incontrovertible observation that, "[A]mong us mere humans, the diversity of ways of making a living has increased dramatically over the past 3 million years, the past hundred thousand years, and even over the past thousand years. If you wanted a rabbit for dinner thirty thousand years ago, you bloody well went out and caught a rabbit. Now most of us can go buy a rabbit dinner. Something again has happened. At the level of species and ways of making a living in the 'econosphere,' the actual has expanded into a persistent adjacent possible." (Kauffman, 2000, p. 143.) His point is simply that complexity begets greater complexity. The invention of the automobile begets gas stations, highways, suburbs, and shopping malls, none of which would have evolved had there been no cars.

3. Lessons for Organizational Learning

Now I would like to summarize the work of these fellow travelers on the third path of evolutionary theory in a way that sets up the lessons we can draw for organizational learning from this third path of evolutionary theory. Following this summary, I'll show how neatly scenario planning fits into this new organizational curriculum.

1.   It *is* possible to get more out of less. Indeed, this notion of getting more out of less is the very definition of emergence according to Stuart Kauffman's colleague at the Santa Fe Institute, John Holland.[84]

---

84   More precisely, Holland defines emergence as, "much coming from little." Cf. Holland, *Emergence*, Cambridge, Mass., Perseus Books, 1998, p1. The concept of emergence is central to the thesis of this paper. After years neglect, since the early and somewhat wooly work of figures like C. Lloyd Morgan, Samuel Alexander and Bergson, emergence is now attracting considerable and much more rigorous attention. For a popular treatment see Steven Johnson, *Emergence: The Connected Life of Ants, Brains, Cities, and Software*, Scribner, New York, 2001. For an extremely ambitious but less accessible treatment of the same topic, see Stephen Wolfram, *A New Kind of Science*, self-published, 2002, over 1,200 pages. For my part I am in the middle of writing a book whose working title is *Coming Together: How the Emergence of Life, Love and Language Shed Light on the Nature of Consciousness*.

Don't be fooled by the brutalists and reductionists who take the law of constant conservation of mass and energy from the realm of physics and chemistry and mistakenly extend it into the realms of the biological and information sciences. Contingency happens. But emergence happens too.

2. There are no guarantees. Contrary to the creationists, happy endings are not foreordained. The best of intentions can yield unintended consequences. For any single actor, tribe, species or company, there is always the distinct possibility of tragedy, defeat, extinction or bankruptcy.

3. Achieving higher order is often a matter of attending to synchronic rather than diachronic relationships. Wright's ratchet toward non-zero-sum solutions depends on co-evolutionary dynamics more than the diachronic evolution of any single tribe or species. If we're going to learn to get along *better,* then we have to learn to get along better *together.* As the philosopher Leibniz saw long ago, real possibility and not just logical possibility is a function of compossibility with the rest of the real world.

4. Sometimes, not always, the more orderly system, or at least the conditions for its possibility, can be foreseen. Just as "the fish already 'knew', before they became amphibious, that a life on land would be possible for them, and what new organs they would need"; just as increasingly large associations of human beings required the yearning for a greater peace; so it is possible to transcend past and present to imagine better futures. (Ogilvy, 2002.)

How does scenario planning stack up as teaching these lessons to organizations?

1. *It is possible to get more out of less.* As third path evolutionary theory demonstrates, it is possible to achieve win-win solutions that increase the level of order and complexity in a system. Among practitioners of scenario planning, Adam Kahane's work in South Africa—The Mont Fleur Scenarios that helped to bring an end to apartheid—offers a fine example of the way scenarios can help to achieve radically discontinuous, non-zero solutions that break the lock of brutalist thinking. How and why is scenario planning superior to other forms of aspirational planning in this regard? Because apart from the presence of other less transformational scenarios, normative scenarios of radically better futures will be dismissed as utopian fancy.

2. *There are no guarantees.* Part of the instructional value of a set of scenarios consists in showing not only how good it could get, but also just how bad it could get. Doom and gloom scenarios work like morality plays: There but for some careful thought and hard work go we, and we don't want to go there. Negative scenarios provide anticipatory disaster relief: By living and suffering the disaster in sufficiently vivid scenaric imagination, an organization gains the will to do the hard work necessary to avoid that disaster.

3. *Achieving higher order is often a matter of attending to synchronic rather than diachronic relationships.* For teaching this lesson, scenarios are made to order. Scenario planning is based on outside in thinking rather than the inside-out approach of traditional strategic planning. Rather than asking only, "Who are we and where do we want to be in X years?" as do approaches based on core competencies and aspirational strategy, scenario planners pose the additional question, "And where will we have to work?" By stressing the importance of an organization's *environment,* scenario planning teaches the importance of compossibility and *co*-evolution. Where other forms of inside out planning direct attention toward diachronic time lines, scenario planning teaches the importance of synchronic relationships and the criticality of context.

4. *Sometimes a more orderly system can be foreseen.* Here again, scenario planning is made to order. The practice of scenario planning requires managers actively to imagine conditions that are different from the present. The process is designed to provide mutations of received wisdom and genetic drift from the official future.

Conclusion

Part One of this essay showed how scenarios serve organizational learning by providing self-knowledge. Just as individuals construct their identities in the form of tacit or explicit autobiographies, so organizations can use scenarios in order to know who they really are and can become.

Part Two showed how scenarios serve organizational learning by providing knowledge about the contextual environment. Where will we have to work? How will external conditions enable or restrict our ability as an organization to evolve toward what we want to become?

Both parts are necessary for the organizational curriculum, and scenario planning fills the bill in both respects. In the diachronic dimension, scenarios provide narratives of self-identity. In the synchronic dimension, scenarios test the compossibility of an organization's aspirations against different environments with which the organization must co-evolve.

In Part Three I've drawn on evolutionary theory for lessons in how things change, how the world evolves through time. By working the Batesonian homology between learning and evolution, I've sought lessons for organizational learning from insights into evolution. But not just any interpretation of Darwin will do. By charting a third path between the brutalists and the creationists, I've suggested the possibility of using scenario planning to shape a conscious evolution toward better futures.

Contingency is real and nothing is guaranteed. Prudence alone suggests that organizations need to learn from both actual mistakes in the past and possible mistakes in the future. But organizations can also learn from aspirations that have been tested against a range of different virtual futures. Scenario planning is well suited to teach both optimists and pessimists the dangers of their biases. By testing both hopes and fears against a range of different environments, organizations can increase the likelihood of their creating better futures.

Bibliography

Bateson, Gregory, *Steps to An Ecology of Mind,* Ballantine Books, New York, 1972.

Corning, Peter, *The Synergism Hypothesis,* New York, McGraw-Hill, 1983.

Dawkins, Richard, *The Selfish Gene,* Oxford University Press, Oxford, 1976.

Edelman, Gerald, and Giulio Tononi, *A Universe of Consciousness: How Matter Becomes Imagination,* Basic Books, New York, 2000.

Freud, Sigmund, *Civilization and its Discontents,* trans. Strachey, New York, W.W. Norton & Co., 1961

De Geus, Arie, *The Living Company,* Harvard Business School Press, Boston, 1997.

Holland, *Emergence*, Cambridge, Mass., Perseus Books, 1998.

Johnson, Steven, *Emergence: The Connected Life of Ants, Brains, Cities, and Software*, Scribner, New York, 2001.

Kauffman, *At Home in the Universe,* Oxford University Press, Oxford, 1993.

Kauffman, Stuart, *Investigations,* Oxford University Press, New York, 2000.

Monod, Jacques, *Chance and Necessity,* tr. Austryn Wainhouse, Vintage Books, New York, 1971.

Nietzsche, Friederich, *Will to Power,* trans. Walter Kauffman, New York, Vintage Books, 1967.

Ogilvy, James. *Creating Better Futures: Scenario Planning as a Tool for a Better Tomorrow,* Oxford University Press, New York, 2002.

Thom, Rene, *Structural Stability and Morphogenesis,* trans. D.H. Fowler, Reading Mass, Benjamin/Cummings Publishing Co., 1975.

Wolfram, Stephen, *A New Kind of Science,* self-published, 2002.

Wright, Robert, *Non-Zero: The Logic of Human Destiny,* Pantheon Books, New York, 2000.

Section III:

Case Studies and Examples

8. Mapping Scenario Planning in the Public and Private Sectors: Lessons from regional projects

by Jay Ogilvy and Erik Smith

Originally published as "Scenario Planning in the Public and Private Sectors: Lessons from regional projects", Development, 47, Number 4, December 2004, pp. 67-72. Reproduced here with permission of Palgrave Macmillan.

The premise of this essay is straightforward: scenario planning in the public sector is different from scenario planning in the private sector. The question is: How different? The premise of this paper is slightly contrarian: Yes, there are differences between scenario planning in the public sector and scenario planning in the private sector... but the differences are not as great as some might suspect.

Decades of experience and dozens of different projects spread across both private and public sectors have led us to an appreciation of some key distinctions, particularly when it comes to defining the purpose and objectives of a given project, identifying the client, and considering different constituencies. But when it comes to actually doing the work—interviewing, workshops, drafting scenarios, drawing implications, and communicating the work to wider audiences—the art and craft are actually very similar.

To map these similarities and differences, we'll focus on scenario planning projects that Global Business Network (GBN) has conducted for regions and areas. We'll first travel rapidly over the highlights of several different projects drawing some lessons for regional work in the public sector, and also for scenario planning more generally. The second section of the paper will take a deeper plunge into a more detailed review of a recent project that benefited from lessons drawn from the experiences reviewed in the first part of the paper. Our scenarios for the future of California's Great Central Valley describe a range of futures for a region some 450 miles long, almost a nation unto itself, home of some of the richest farmland in the world, and a potential hotbed of competing interests.

Regions of Experience

As early as the 1970s, scenario planners applied the tools of scenario planning to projects in the public sector almost as often as to projects in the private sector. There were, among others, projects for the Environmental Protection Agency in

Washington, for the California Energy Commission, and for the city of Austin, Texas. These projects met with varying degrees of success. While the project for Austin might be hailed as partly responsible for the remarkable economic growth Austin has enjoyed, some see the inaction of bureaucrats in Washington as an ultimate hobble to project results in the public sector. Besides showing the importance of understanding the Federal context of regions (beyond simply the State), some experiences in Washington elicit a caricature of "government work" as "wasted effort". Unlike the private sector where there is normally a clear chain of command and flow from decisions to action and implementation, public sector scenario planning faces the classic tragedy of the commons: everyone's problems become no one's problems exactly because the chain of command is much cloudier. The rest of this section is a brief record of several *regional* (not Federal) scenario planning projects conducted by GBN in the 1990s, and we've chosen them precisely to challenge this message.

1. Scenarios for the future of Flint, Michigan

The Mott Foundation in Flint, Michigan, has as part of its deed of gift the mandate to improve the lives of the citizens of Flint. During the 1980s they poured millions of dollars into building what was to be a tourist destination in Flint: *Autoworld*. After the expensive building and its installations were complete, they waited for tourists to flock to Flint. But they never came—vacationing instead at places like Disneyworld in Orlando—and Autoworld failed.

In order to avoid another bad decision of such epic proportions, the Mott Foundation undertook scenario planning. The process was in most ways similar to what we would do for a corporation: interviews, an initial workshop to outline a set of scenarios, the drafting of narrative scenarios which were circulated to workshop participants prior to a second workshop where implications were drawn, strategic options developed and prioritized. Finally there was a presentation to members of the board of the Mott Foundation, which used the insights derived from the scenarios to make a clear shift in the foundation's strategy for giving—henceforth the Foundation would focus on making Flint a better place to raise children.

Although the project was undertaken in the public sector, the client was clear, the process and schedule were very similar to what we typically do for corporations, and the results were actionable and actually implemented. That said, conducting the workshops was not so typical because a number of community representatives—who were very effective and eloquent preachers—had a habit of interrupting at odd moments with impromptu sermons on the problems of fiefdoms separating different parishes in Flint. These preachers seemed less interested in cooperation for the greater regional good than in maintaining their own turf and position within the existing system.

We draw two lessons here: (1) When conducting scenario workshops in the public sector, be prepared for the facilitation challenge of dealing with people who lack the meeting skills gained from business school or years of corporate committee meetings; (2) Insights gained from experience with turf battles in the community can shed light on very similar human dramas in the corporation. People are people, and fiefdoms are to be found everywhere.

2. Scenarios for the future of Oklahoma

After attending GBN's public course on Developing and Using Scenarios, the Executive Director of The Oklahoma Academy, a non-profit association of movers and shakers in Oklahoma, asked for help in facilitating an annual meeting involving over 150 participants. After prepping a team of local small group facilitators, we ran a workshop that generated dozens of fragmentary ideas for scenarios that were then boiled down into four scenarios for the future of Oklahoma. The Oklahoma Academy wrote up the scenarios and published them in two glossy pamphlets that received wide exposure throughout the State.

Part of the impetus for this work, and part of the reasoning behind the selection of scenarios as a tool, lay in the historic rivalry between Texas and Okalahoma. Both share the highs and lows of life largely financed by oil revenues. An intense cross-border rivalry was epitomized in annual football rituals. The use of scenario planning a decade earlier by Austin—and the success that city had seen since in terms of economic diversification, hi-tech development and job creation, all of which Oklahoma lacked—took the form of a certain "Austin-envy" among members of the Okalahoma Academy.

We find three further lessons here, all of which are also applicable to scenario planning in the private sector: (3) Trade on success stories; (4) With sufficient attention to workshop design on the front end, large groups can be involved in the process of scenario development; (5) With sufficient attention to—and resources for—production values (e.g.

color printing, good graphics, etc.) the results of the work, especially if the stories are well told, can be shared with even larger groups, be they regions or large organizations.

3. Downtown Chicago

Known for its great architecture, downtown Chicago was in danger of destroying its world-class status by allowing a spate of unplanned development. Shouldn't Chicago think about its future? And wouldn't scenarios be the perfect tool to do so? An inspired, enthusiastic and reasonably well-connected architect certainly thought so, and convinced us to spend many hours trying to convince others. But this was a case where the lack of a clear client meant that there was no one to take a lead funding role. Moreover, there was no one who could, by themselves, implement whatever ideas might emerge from the scenario planning effort. Despite what seemed to some like a good idea at the time, it didn't take a genius to see, eventually, that the specific context of politics in Chicago, both public and private, were such that no one *could* step forward to sponsor such a project lest they be accused of over-reaching their authority. Nor could we *create* such a client simply for the sake of carrying out a scenario planning exercise.

The lessons from this case are cast in the "negative": (6) The constituency challenges of work in the public sector are sometimes insurmoutable, particularly at the regional level where the number of interested players is essentially unlimited; (7) Even with what seems like a good idea at the time, know when to cut your losses—especially when there is no clear client.

4. Scenarios for the future of South Florida

For this project, we did have a clear client: a non-profit group called the Collins Center. Their problem also focused on unplanned growth—in the region of Miami-Dade, Broward, and Palm Beach counties—as risking environmental and lifestyle degradation. Yet the citizens of those counties did not seem to realize that they shared large problems in common: i.e. that some of their challenges were truly regional, not just county-wide. Finally, we had funding, largely provided by the MacArthur Foundation, in the person of a program officer who had earlier served in Flint, Michigan with the Mott Foundation. (We'd like to acknowledge Gerald Harris, another GBN practitioner, for his work on both the Flint and South Florida projects.)

Stakeholders in the respective communities of the three counties needed convincing to contribute their time and attention to the scenario planning workshops. Rather than assuming the commitment of a single CEO or her executive committee, we had to meet a variety of movers and shakers, attend many breakfasts, lunches and dinners, and generally talk up the project. This we did, but it took time and quite a bit of travel, both to and from California and up and down the length and breadth of the three counties. And despite all of our travels and talks and half-eaten meals, there remained some communities that simply didn't want to participate.

We completed the project, and the results were widely publicized through local newspapers, radio, and TV. But it's hard to see a clear impact in decisions taken or outcomes attained. Nor was attendance at some of the later workshops what we had hoped. The demographics of Florida—especially as Miami comes to serve as the northern capital of Latin America—meant that the sheer number of communities to be affected by the results of this exercise was so great that full and accurate representation would have required a meeting room the size of the U.N.'s General Assembly Hall. For lack of full representation, the project lost some degree of dedication, even among those who had been initially enthusiastic.

So the last lesson we share is to undertake a clear-eyed assessment of the prospective constituency: Who are they, and can you realistically expect to reach them? This is, of course, not a bad question to ask when embarking upon a scenario exercise in the private sector either, but one that deserves special thought and attention when doing regional scenario planning.

Lessons Applied:
Scenarios for the future of California's Central Valley

With learnings from these projects (and, of course, many others) in mind, we welcomed Carol Whiteside, Executive Director of The Great Valley Center, when she came to Global Business Network to inquire about the possible usefulness of scenarios for looking at the future of California's Central Valley. This section takes a closer look at that engagement, and how we used what we'd learned to make that project a success. (We'd like to acknowledge another GBN practitioner, Chris Ertel, for his significant contribution to our Great Central Valley work.)

1. **Clear client and obvious challenge**

   California's Central Valley has historically—and most typically—been thought of as being in the southern part of the state, beginning just north of the mountains that rim Los Angeles and running north to the outskirts of Sacramento. The Valley Futures Project, driven by Carol Whiteside and the Great Valley Center, explicitly sought to change this, to match the mental map of California's Central Valley to its geographic reality: instead of running from Bakersfield to Modesto, California's Great Central Valley would run from Bakersfield through Sacramento and all the way north to Redding. We would convene three parallel projects: one in the North Valley, one in the Sacramento region, and one in the southern San Joaquin Valley, and then conclude by synthesizing the results of all three projects. Likewise we would stretch the timeframe: from the usual annual budget cycles to over two decades—to 2025. The mental maps we set out to test, illuminate and change were therefore not only physical ones, but more importantly those held by people living in the Valley: we aimed to raise the regional consciousness to encompass the full geographic fact and intricate interdependencies of California's Central Valley.

   With funding from the James Irvine Foundation, the convening client would be the Great Valley Center (GVC), whose visionary president saw scenario planning as a way to spark new kinds of discussion across a broad range of Valley residents, from official policy makers to everyday citizens buying groceries—"We have to find a way to bring these public policy issues into the popular media, making connections between today's actions and tomorrow's outcomes," said Carol Whiteside.

2. **Facilitation skills and turf battles**

   To approach these goals, we realized that we would need an extraordinarily broad range of participants, and that we would need the same *kinds* of participants for the three areas. In preparation for the scenario planning workshops, we interviewed key stakeholders from each area. Using the cachet and network of the Great Valley Center, we invited roughly 25 participants from each area—representatives from local government, social services, neighborhood organizations, community groups, educators, youth, healthcare, business, economic development, journalism (newspapers and television), water, air quality, transportation, the arts, environmental advocates, agriculture (farming and livestock), and real estate developers. Despite a history of antagonisms among many of these constituencies, the broad tent of multiple scenarios and the gentle art of careful facilitation generated productive, new conversations.

Throughout the project, both GBN and GVC were also completely clear that the groups we convened were <u>not</u> decision-making bodies. They were not responsible for any decisions beyond the creation of the scenarios and their implications. Specific decisions are more common in private sector scenario planning projects, though certainly not unique: often enough private sector scenario projects are used to build capacity through experiential training, or simply to revisit the contextual world and trigger new thinking.

3. Attention to Constituency and Area Differences

Throughout the engagement, we remained attentive to the issue of "radius of solidarity," a term based loosely on Frank Fukuyama's phrase, "radius of trust". By this we mean that each area within the Greater Central Valley region thought of itself as a separate area, one in which solidarity held sway along a logic of us vs. them. Part of the point of the project, however, was to expand this radius, and make connections with the other two radii more explicit.

"Top Ten" Key Forces and Environmental Factors
Unique in GREY, shared in style of other region

North Valley (italics)

1) **Water Quantity—rest of state**
2) **Water—competing uses**
3) Biotechnology—lifespan extension and population aging
4) Global Political Changes
5) Evolution of Consciousness (spirituality, social awareness, new thinking)
6) **Decline of Agriculture**
7) Quality of Life
8) **Air Quality**
9) **Future of Public Education**
10) Global Climate Change: "global weirding"

Sacramento Region (regular)

1) Impact of Globalization on Regional Development
2) *New Technologies: biotech, robotics, nanotech, ubiquitous info*
3) **"Latin-ization" of California, especially younger population**
4) US Economic Decline
5) Impacts of Technology
6) Terrorism
7) Regional Leadership: quality and quantity
8) *Viability of Agriculture*
9) *Global Climate Change: "global weirding"*
10) Housing Affordability (& diversity of types)

San Joaquin Valley (bold)

1) *Air Quality*
2) *Quality of Education*
3) Population Growth
4) *Water Availability/Supply*
5) Poverty/Inequality
6) Land Use Decisions
7) Water Quality
8) Traffic Congestion & Gridlock
9) Latino Majority
10) *Competing Demands for Water Use*

---

n.b.—none shared amongst all three regions

We used the same scenario development technique for each of the three areas, but consciously paid more attention to the differences in terms of what was most critically uncertain to each of the three areas. We allowed the space for these differences to express themselves—and were rewarded when they did, particularly in terms of the "top-ten" key factors and environmental forces that workshop participants saw as most important and most uncertain for the next 25 years of the Valley.

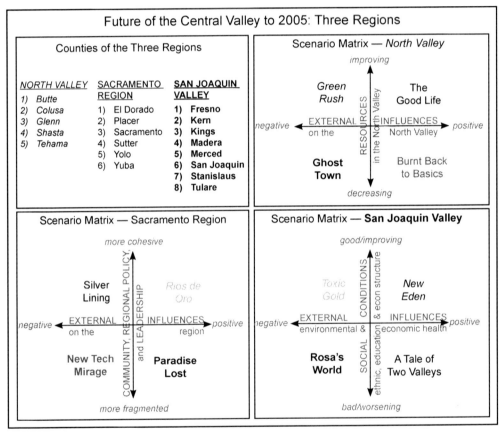

On the other hand, we also realized the importance to the overall project of being able to connect the scenarios across the three areas. So we listened closely for what was critically uncertain to all three areas. And we were rewarded in that, of the three scenario matrices (one from each area), each shares an axis of uncertainty and each has an axis which expresses the unique concerns about that area's future.

4. Workshop design and production values

Strategic Thrusts for the Central Valley

At each second workshop, the regional teams developed implications, leading indicators, and strategic options for each scenario. The teams then grouped all four lists of strategic options together, prioritized across the scenarios, and clustered closely related options into a shorter list of strategic thrusts.

Strategic Thrusts —

North Valley

1) Regional Collaboration
2) Leadership and Participation
3) Natural Resources, esp. Water
4) Infrastructure

Strategic Thrusts —

Sacramento Region

1) Economic Collaboration
2) Regional Coalition Building
3) Media and Marketing
4) Education

Strategic Thrusts —

San Joaquin Valley

1) **Education**
2) **Regional Vision and Image**
3) **Regional Economic Development**
4) **Transit/Air Quality/Land Use**
5) **Regional Water Plan**

To generate scenarios for each of the three areas, we designed the project with three separate, yet parallel, workshop processes. At the first two-day workshop, GBN worked with participants to create the scenario frameworks and begin developing the scenario stories. We continued researching and writing the scenarios until the second two-day workshop, again one for each of the three areas. After quickly sharing the scenarios from the other two areas, we focused on implications and strategic options for their area, both within each scenario and across their set of four. It's worthwhile noting that each of the three scenario sets includes a visionary depiction of the future, a better future that citizens of the area could choose to work toward together. Though the issues that surfaced in these workshops were not necessarily new, the scenario framework offered a new way to organize, present, and talk about them.

Finally, the scenarios were shared with the region, as Katherine Fulton and Diana Scearce—two colleagues of ours at Global Business Network—summarize so well in their recent publication, *What If? The Art of Scenario Thinking for Nonprofits* (available online at www.gbn.com/whatif)

Once the scenarios were written and the implications surfaced, the scenario work was still far from over. During 2003, the Great

Valley Center led an ambitious communications and outreach effort, using the scenarios to catalyze discussion about local public policy decisions in various parts of the region. The scenarios were featured prominently at several conferences, including the Center's annual conference for regional leaders. The Great Valley Center staff led scenario-based discussions with government officials, students, Rotarians, and members of other civic groups. They also distributed the scenarios in audio, video, DVD, and print—in both English and Spanish—and created a guide, along with a youth curriculum, that was used widely by middle and high schools in the Central Valley. Daily newspapers in the North Valley, the Sacramento Area, and the San Joaquin Valley published the scenarios in featured articles, exposing an estimated 700,000 people to the scenarios. (Scearce and Fulton, 2004.)

So how does scenario planning map between the public and private sector? We've examined a number of GBN's regional projects, and find many similarities in the art and craft—including dissemination—of scenario planning. We find that the largest differences are found in the need for clearly establishing the client and framing the purposes of the engagement. With so many stakeholders, extra attention must be paid to differences in the perspective, experience, and priorities of people from the participating groups. The work of building a constituency is typically more involved and sometimes simply takes longer in the public sector than it does in the private sector. But constituency building is often an issue in the private sector as well. Nor are corporations always clearly focused on a particular decision or strategy. Sometimes executives are drawn toward scenarios by little more than an inchoate anxiety about an uncertain future. We therefore find more similarities than differences between scenario planning in the public and private sectors.

9. Three Scenarios for Higher Education in California

Introduction

The following essay, "Three Scenarios for Higher Education," is the oldest essay in this collection. It was commissioned by the California Faculty Association and was then published as the Spring 1992 issue of Global Business Network's series, *The Deeper News*. Is it so dated as to be no longer useful or interesting? To the contrary, the challenges it poses are as timely today as they were in 1991 when it was written. Then, as now, we were in a recession. Then, as now, our public universities were suffering cutbacks from state legislatures. The basic logics of the three scenarios are as relevant today as they were then. While some of the details may be out of date, e.g. too much talk about computers and fiber optics, too little about smart phones and wireless technology, the promise of information technology remains both tremendous and unfulfilled. So the first scenario, *Software Landing,* retains its relevance. The second scenario, *Education Inc.,* revolves around the increasing privatization and corporatization of formerly public services. As such, it anticipates the rise of institutions like Kaplan and the University of Phoenix. Again, the problems and opportunities raised by this scenario are still very much with us: As higher education caters to the needs of business, will liberal education and basic research suffer? The third scenario, *The New Educational Order,* is the most radical in the restructuring it envisages. Where the growth and spread of the internet over the past two decades reveal features of the first scenario, and the growth of private, for-profit colleges and executive training programs exhibit features of the second, the third scenario reads more like a road not taken. It is almost utopian in the portrait it paints, and for that very reason it remains relevant as a promise unfulfilled. It serves as an example of the kind of high road scenario discussed in the introductory essay, "Facing the Fold."

Since 1960 when the Master Plan for public higher education was initiated, California has operated a three-tier system of 2-year community colleges, 4-year state universities, and research universities. The promise of the Master Plan—to admit any student who can benefit from post-secondary education—has for the most part been met. But now, under the pressure of serious budget cuts, the promise is being broken for tens of thousands of students who are being turned away from full or cancelled courses.

This report addresses the uncertainty of support for public post-secondary education in California over the next fifteen years. The pattern of support for public higher education has to change. But how? The current crisis in funding for state supported colleges has sounded an alarm in California: the economics of higher education reflect a more general crisis in the funding and delivery of public services.

Perhaps an economic recovery will restore lagging tax revenues and cash will flow into education once again. Or perhaps new sources of revenue can be found to supplement student fees and tax dollars. Or perhaps technology will come to the rescue by reducing the costs and increasing the quality of learning. These are not the only possibilities confronting educational planners in California. What will it mean to have a wholly new legislature now that term limitation has been voted into law? How will the further globalization of the economy affect education? How will the changing demographics of California influence the shape of higher education?

There are many maybes in the future of education. As a methodology adequate to handling these what-ifs, this report uses multiple scenarios as a way of sketching several possible futures.

Basic Questions

This report is devoted to exploring several different scenarios for the future of higher education in California. Given the seriousness of the current crisis it would seem irresponsible not to consider some radical alternatives to the current system of state support.

The current crisis offers an occasion for rethinking the basic structure of higher education. What is its mission? Whither higher education in the twenty-first century? For what kind of world will tomorrow's students be educated? With what tools will they learn? And how will public post-secondary education be financed?

Answers to such basic questions tend to come in clusters of systematically interrelated policies, e.g. if corporations pick up a bigger part of the bill for higher education, then they are bound to have a bigger role in setting the curriculum. If new technology and fiber optic highways pave the way toward more learning at home, then individuals will probably have more control over the content and pace of their learning. Each of these alternatives- a bigger role for business, a bigger role for technology—comes laden with whole hosts of associated assumptions about funding, faculty, the needs of students, and public policy. These bundles of associated assumptions are part of what make up scenarios. In order to think our way out of the current fiscal crisis we need to consider several alternative scenarios for the way higher education could be structured ten to fifteen years from now.

This report is the result of a six month project involving a series of scenario workshops, intervening research, and a computer teleconference. The report is divided into four parts:

PART ONE states the problem and offers an introduction to the use of scenarios as tools for its solution: what are scenarios and what are they not? Prediction is not the issue. Instead, the point is to consider a range of possible alternatives as a way of empowering intelligent and deliberate choices.

PART TWO lists the key factors and driving trends affecting the future of higher education. These are divided into two groups: predetermined elements that are likely to show up in all scenarios, e.g. demographics; and second, those uncertainties whose forked paths of possibilities cleave the scenarios from one another.

PART THREE contains narrative descriptions of three different scenarios. In the first scenario technology lowers the cost of learning. In the second scenario corporate America does indeed pick up a larger part of the tab for higher education. And in the third there is a paradigm shift in what constitutes a higher education. Each of the scenarios concludes with a section on the implications of that scenario for the support of public higher education.

PART FOUR then considers some implications that can be drawn from the set of scenarios taken as a whole, given the fact that, today, we cannot know which scenario will unfold.

As Aristotle pointed out long ago, if we can know the future, we cannot change it. If we can change it, we cannot know it. By articulating several alternative futures, however, we should be in a better position to change the future for the better, even if we cannot know that future today.

PART ONE: The Problem and a Method for its Solution

In 1991, for the first time in over 30 years, the states gave less money to higher education than in the preceding year. "As a percentage of overall state spending, the amount given to colleges and universities has been shrinking since 1982", reported the *New York Times*, Feb. 3, 1992. While things are tough all over the country, in California the combination of recession and state budget deficits has hit the higher education system particularly hard.

The California Community College system is committed by law to admit any student able to benefit from higher education. But, according to David Mertes, chancellor of the 107-campus system, "Students are coming in and finding they can't get the classes of their first choice, so they take something else. Or, in growing numbers, they can't find classes at all and they leave". 60 of 71 community college districts exceeded their enrolment caps for 1991. "You can translate that into 88,000 students in 107 colleges for which we're not being funded," Chancellor Mertes told *The San Francisco Chronicle*. Officials in the Community College system estimate that some ten thousand students are cascading into the community college system as the result of fee hikes at California State University systems (CSU) and the University of California system (UC). (*SF Chronicle*, Dec. 27, 1992.)

Students in the CSU system are facing a fee hike of up to 40 percent for 1992. Kim Williams, chairwoman of the California State Student Association representing the systems 362,000 students, predicted that some students would be forced to drop out of school. "Forty percent is ridiculous," she said. "They are locking the door." (*Los Angeles Times*, Jan. 11, 1992.) In 1991, the CSU laid off 1,000 full-time teachers and another 2,000 part-time lecturers. Students were shocked to find 4,900 courses cancelled. These numbers translate into individual hardship. "I cry to the professors," says Tyesha Canady, a senior at San Diego State University, "I tell them that I can't get financial aid if I'm not a full-time student here and if I can't get financial aid, I can't eat. If I can't get the classes I need, I can't graduate in the spring." (*Chronicle of Higher Education*, Dec. 4, 1991.)

In a vain attempt to make ends meet in the UC system, the regents of the University of California raised fees by 40 percent for 1991 following a 10 percent hike the previous year. The budget for next year proposes another 24 percent increase in fees, creating a near doubling in fees over a three year period. Major universities from Yale to Berkeley are coping with rising costs and insufficient revenues. "What we're witnessing is the death of the 19th-century research university", according to David Kastan, chairman of the department of English and comparative literature at Columbia University. (*New York Times* Feb. 3, 1992.) In response to a legislative analyst's proposal that UC faculty increase their teaching load from five to six courses per year, UC President David Gardner called the suggestion "fundamentally the most destructive recommendation that has been made" during his nine years as UC president, and added that it would "fundamentally change the character of this institution." (*Los Angeles Times*, March 3, 1992.)

As bad as the fiscal crisis may be, the problem facing planners of higher education in California runs deeper than money. The problem is compounded, first, by the manifest success of the Master Plan, second, by the professionally trained tendency of academics to look to the past rather than toward the future, and third, by the buffering of publicly supported services from the feedback of market forces. Each of these three points creates resistance to necessary change, and therefore deserves more detailed treatment.

1. The Burden of Success

There is a saying that nothing fails like success. Though the current crisis has wrung any residue of smugness out of California's faculty and educational administrators, there is nonetheless a strong temptation to wait for things to return to normal.

Once the recession is over, speaks the voice of wishful thinking, once tax revenues pick up again, once there is enough money in the budget to pay for merit increases in salary, hire more faculty, and reopen temporarily closed classes, then life will return to normal and Californians will once again be proud of the best post-secondary educational system in the world. The sheer size, strength and momentum of the California system makes it resistant to change.

As Figure 1 shows, California's share of undergraduate enrolments and PhD Degrees is disproportionately high compared to its share of the nation's population. And the picture would be even more remarkable in a global rather than a national perspective. Berkeley is one of the leading universities of Southeast Asia. So how can there be serious complaints?

To quote a corollary of the maxim on success, "If it ain't broke, don't fix it!" *If you want to fix education, then take on the K-12 system first before you meddle with higher education. K-12 is in much worse trouble by most comparative measures with other states and other nations.* So speaks another excuse for avoiding change.

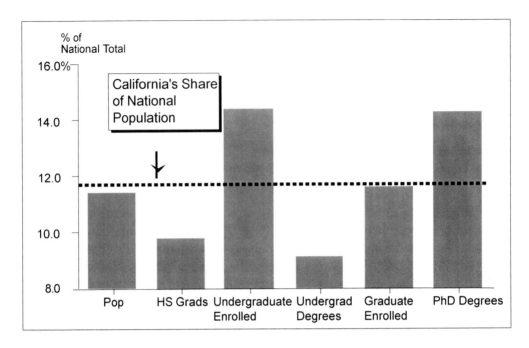

Figure 1: California's Share of the National Education Enterprise 1987

2. Scholarship and the Future

To quote yet another hackneyed maxim, "If all you've got is a hammer, then everything looks like a nail." If you are trained in the skills of scholarship, then you will be inclined to look to the past rather than toward the future. It is no accident that the study of the future has no place in prestigious academic curricula. There is not a single book in the U.C. library with a copyright of 2013 or 2020. It is therefore perfectly understandable that academics tend toward cultural conservatism and resistance to institutional change, however liberal they may be politically or ideologically.

As opposed to business leaders, who are used to thinking about the future as a way to minimize their financial risks, academics (with some noticeable exceptions) are generally more preoccupied with passing on the past to successive generations of students. An occupational hazard among intellectuals is therefore the stereotypical tendency to back absentmindedly into the future. Ever since the pre-Socratic philosopher Thales first stumbled into a well because, as the story has it, he was so lost in thought, academics have been renowned for not focusing on the nitty-gritty of worldly affairs like *Where will our funding come from if tax revenues decline?*

This observation about academics is not a criticism. A French historian should not be preoccupied with California tax revenues. A certain amount of other-worldliness among intellectuals is as it should be. Indeed it is part of the nobility of the academic calling to rise above materialistic concerns. But society should not then take advantage of the good will or distraction of academics.

3. Insulation from Market Forces

Third, the fact that it is the state supported part of the educational system that is the focus of this study means that, like other public services, the system is somewhat insulated from the feedback mechanism of market forces. It is far more difficult to shut down an unsuccessful college than an unsuccessful business. Exceptions like the recent bankruptcy of the University of Bridgeport prove the rule: the oddity of events at Bridgeport gained far more notoriety than any of hundreds of bankruptcies in the business world.

Clearly there are market forces at work in the academic world. Enrolments in different majors rise and fall with perceptions of employment options, e.g. the growth of MBA programs since the sixties. Enrolments in different institutions rise and fall with perceptions of their quality and prestige. But those perceptions are slow to change given the lack of any measure as unambiguous as profit and loss where academic institutions are concerned.

The very idea of success or failure is harder to grasp for academic institutions than for businesses. Lacking clear measures of success or failure, it is consequently more difficult to use such measures as indicators of a need for change, or as benchmarks for the accomplishment of change.

For these three reasons—the manifest success of the Master Plan, the inclination of intellectuals to ignore the future, and the insulation of public services from market forces—the effort to develop and implement a strategy for change in California's higher education system will not be easy. The power of these forces for resistance to change may be so great that the most plausible scenario of all would contain little or no significant change in the fundamental structure and support of higher education in California. Down that road one can see further fee increases, more student demonstrations and hunger strikes, a decline in the quality of education offered, and a trail of broken promises as more and more students find higher education simply unaffordable.

Change is necessary. For the system is broke; it won't return to normal; and a superior post-secondary educational system is absolutely essential to the success of California and her citizens, however ambiguous those criteria for success may be.

Criteria for Success

What are some of the possible criteria for success in solving the current problems in California's system of higher education?

At a minimum, and in the most materialist terms, California's economy is dependent on an educated work force. Several commissions and countless authors have pointed to the close connection between San Francisco Bay Area universities and the success of Silicon Valley.

Second, on a broader historical scale, the relative influence of different cultures can be correlated with the excellence of their universities. Consider Oxford and Cambridge, Heidelberg, the Sorbonne, Harvard and Yale, Tokyo University. World-class cultures maintain and are sustained by world-class universities.

Third, broad access to higher education through a system of two-year community colleges provides a pathway to success for individuals whose backgrounds might otherwise limit their achievement. Without the kind of access provided by the California Community College system, the American dream of equal opportunity would be foreclosed for many of California's less privileged students.

"Americans increasingly think a college degree is the ticket to a better life," reported *The Chronicle of Higher Education*, Oct. 16, 1991, citing a Gallup Poll. "Seventy-three percent of those surveyed said it is very important to get a college degree, an increase of fifteen percent over those surveyed five years ago."

Fourth, the future promises to punish ignorance even worse than the past. It is now commonplace to speak of a series of eras: the agricultural, the industrial, and the information era. As Figure 2 indicates, we are now well into the information era. What the farm was to the agricultural era, and the factory to the industrial era, educational institutions will be to the information era, namely, the means of production and manipulation of the principal product of society.

Just as people had to come down off the farm to join the industrial society, so people are coming out of the factories to join the information society. But the price of entry is education. Neither illiterate farm workers nor minimally trained industrial workers can function successfully as producers or consumers of the best an information economy has to offer. A good education will be more critical to success in the future than ever.

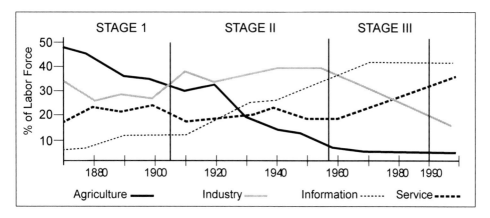

Figure 2: From Agricultural through Industrial to the Information Economy

Whether we are concerned with the health of California's economy, the pre-eminence of her culture, the life opportunities of her citizens, or the needs of the information age, there are plenty of answers to the question: Why worry about higher education in California? The problem is not that we lack answers, but that we have too many answers to this question.

If the criteria for success of California's higher education system seem ambiguous it is only because there are so many reasons for improving education, not just one. And it is also for this reason—too many reasons—that it is difficult to reach consensus on a single mission or guiding vision for higher education. Its value is over-determined. Hence its constituency is sometimes divided. It is as if there is a fight for the microphone to sing the praises of education. In the ensuing melee, no single voice is clearly heard.

Do we care more about open access or about the number of Nobel prizes earned by a research-oriented faculty? Do we care more about the politics of multi-culturalism or about the economics of high technology? These are not easy choices to make. Consequently there is a tendency not to make them, but instead to drift in the direction of equity by trying to be all things to all people.

These, then, are some of the barriers that stand in the way of change: a lack of clarity about measures of success, blurred vision, and a professional aversion toward looking seriously at the future. How can a set of alternative scenarios overcome these barriers to change?

Scenarios: What Are Scenarios... and What Are They Not?

Scenarios are alternative environments in which today's decisions may be played out. They are not predictions. Nor are they strategies. Instead they are descriptions of different futures specifically designed to highlight the risks and opportunities involved in specific strategic issues.

Scenarios can help overcome scholarly anxiety about the paucity of evidence regarding the future, for scenarios do not claim to be predictions. We cannot know what the future will hold beforehand. So-called futurists cannot be seers. But we can see in the present several trends which, moving on their current course, will change the shape of higher education in California over the next decade.

1. Pre-determined Elements
Some trends are fairly certain. The demographics of multi-culturalism are moving inexorably toward making everyone part of a minority. Sometime between 2000 and 2010, Anglos will cease to be a majority in California.

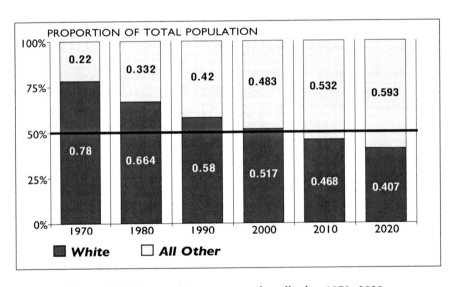

Figure 3: White population compared to all other 1970 -2929

Second, there will be a quantum leap in the Hispanic influence on California's culture and politics. The dramatic increase in Hispanic influence will be felt first in K-12 schools.

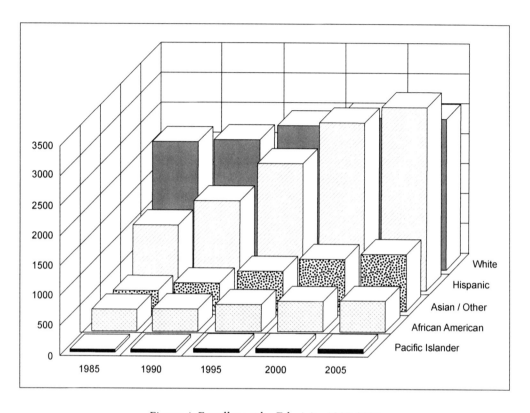

Figure 4: Enrollment by Ethnicity 1985-2005

These and other trends are among the predetermined elements that are bound to show up in almost any scenario of California's future.

2. Uncertainties

As important as the inevitabilities are several uncertainties. What will the job market look like in a couple of decades? What will daily life look like in twenty years? What would you want your children to know that they cannot learn from you?

No futurist can give definitive answers to these questions. But it is possible to make some choices today that will shape the answers that the future gives to these questions. By considering several alternative futures, each crafted in a way that highlights some important uncertainty over which we might have some control, a set of scenarios can help to inform the choices we make today so that the future legacy of our present choices will be more to our liking than otherwise.

We need to consider some concretely drawn possibilities before making the choices that are now in front of us. Scenarios are just such concrete narratives—stories about possible futures that have been informed by the best data and trend analysis we can bring to bear in the present. A set of scenarios can highlight the choices that are important to make, which is not to say that the scenarios will make the choices for us. Ideally, a chosen strategy will be robust across a range of alternative scenarios, thus demonstrating its resilience in the face of uncertainty. But rarely are strategies so resilient. Risk is real.

Rather than try to predict the shape of higher education in California over the coming decades, this report considers some alternative possibilities, the better to equip readers with tools for making informed and considered choices about higher education. For it is the citizens of California and their elected representatives that will make the choices that determine the future structure and financing of higher education in California.

Part Two contains a list of the key factors identified by the scenario development team, and a brief analysis of those factors that were selected as the driving trends for the scenarios in Part Three.

PART TWO: Key Factors and Driving Trends

A. Pre-Determined Elements

1. Economics

There can be little doubt that economic factors drive all scenarios for the future of publicly supported higher education. A rising tide could raise all ships. A strong economy could plug all the holes in the higher education system. And a weak economy will make all problems worse.

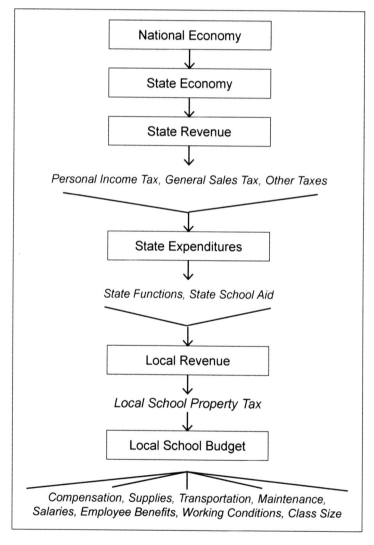

Figure 5: Links between the economy and funding for schools

But over the long term the uncertainties of growth and recession and the rhythms of business cycles tend to average out. Over the long term the economy will almost surely grow, but not enough to fund the currently anticipated need for resources for education. There have been some structural changes in the economy since the Master Plan was first put in place.

The current squeeze can be seen as the result of three different forces, two very long-term, one fairly short-term:

1. Reagan's "new federalism" meant a drastic cut-back in federal funding for state and local social services.

2. The tax revolt, begun with Proposition 13, initiated a resistance to state taxes.

3. The current recession has tightened the squeeze created by the first two long-term factors.

The recession will end, but the long-term changes in the structure of tax support for higher education may not. Therefore higher education is likely to remain hostage to short-term swings in tax revenues unless some serious alternatives to the current system of funding are found. Figure 6 shows the declining rate of increases in state budgets during the eighties.

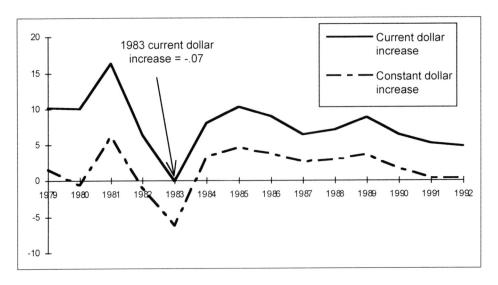

Figure 6: State Annual Budget Spending Increases
Fiscal 1979 - Fiscal 1992

It is possible that an economic fix can be found for the squeeze between the new federalism and resistance to state tax increases. Various schemes have been proposed for closing the gap between rising enrolments and inadequate state funds:

1. *The Draconian Solution* is to take back the promise of the Master Plan and restrict access. This is, in effect, what is happening now. With the recent fee hikes in the UC and CSU systems, many who would have enrolled have not enrolled. There is an evident cascading of restricted access. The university system has become dramatically more expensive to students. In the CSU system students are having difficulty getting the courses they need to graduate. 1,000 faculty staff have been laid off, 2,000 part-time teachers not rehired, and 3,800 classes were cut from the curriculum. Eight of twenty campuses have closed admissions for the spring semester of 1992. At the community college level 50,000 students were simply turned away during the 1990-91 academic year. (*New York Times*, Nov. 10, 1991.)

Senator Gary K. Hart, chairman of the state Senate's Education Committee, has said, "Restricting admission is an option that needs to be looked at very carefully." *But it is an assumption of this report that the Draconian solution of restricted access is not an acceptable scenario.* The commitment made by the Master Plan was a wise commitment. The question is how to make good on the commitment now that the means of fulfilling it have broken down.

2. *Higher Tuitions and More Federal Aid.* In a book from the Brookings Institute, *Keeping College Affordable: Government and Educational Opportunity*, Michael McPherson and Morton Owen Schapiro suggest a redistribution of responsibility for funding between the federal government and the states. They suggest that states should raise their tuitions to eliminate the free ride that relatively affluent families are now getting by sending their children to state colleges. For the less affluent, $14.3 billion in federal assistance would be offered in the form of federal grants of $5,800 per student.

However, as James Appleberry, head of the American Association of State Colleges and Universities, has pointed out, "There's nothing to give us confidence that the federal government will be able or willing to pick up the burden." (*Chronicle of Higher Education*, Sept. 11, 1991.) In short, it might not be that easy to roll back the new federalism.

3. *Find more money in state budget.* At a time when spending on higher education is claiming a progressively smaller percentage of the state budget, one solution would be to reverse the declining trend and simply allocate a greater percentage of state revenues to education. But this solution flies in the face of several hard

realities, particularly the exigencies imposed by the rising costs of health care, debt service and crime prevention.

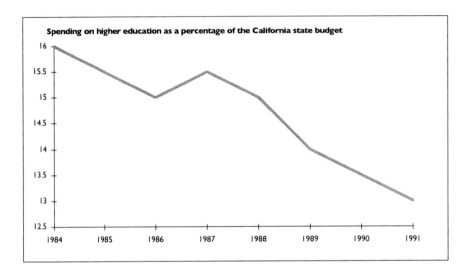

Figure 7: Spending on higher education as a percentage of the California state budget

California legislators passed a plan to withdraw $1.6 billion from two funds controlled by the public-employee pension system. But even if tapping the pension fund survives a challenge in the courts, it will be a one-time measure that cannot be expected to close the gap between supply and demand on a permanent basis. Likewise other "budget-fixes" can be imagined on a one-time basis, but like the usual changes in accounting procedures or one-time write-offs, these stop-gap measures will do little to ameliorate the structural squeeze on the economics of higher education.

In keeping with the idea that scenarios are more useful when they differ in kind rather than in degree along a single scale like the strength of the economy, it is worth observing that *the economy is not a driving trend peculiar to any single scenario.* Instead the economy is the tide on which all of our scenarios ride. At high tide all the scenarios get easier to manage, whatever their logic. At low tide all scenarios become more difficult to manage and all conflicts become more divisive.

A key question for the scenarios is, therefore, how do they affect the economic tide? (Which surely depends on forces other than the moon.)

The importance of the economy—though not its health—is, *thus, a predetermined element for all scenarios:* inescapable in its power to constrain educational opportunities, but also potentially generous in its ability to reward a well-educated work force.

2. Demographics

A second predetermined element, equally influential in all scenarios, is demographics; more specifically, the politics of multiculturalism. California is growing.

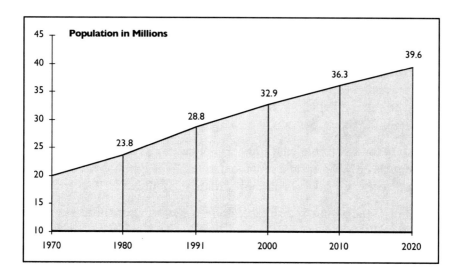

Figure 8: California Population 1970 - 2020

And, as referenced in the introduction, California's ethnic mix is shifting.

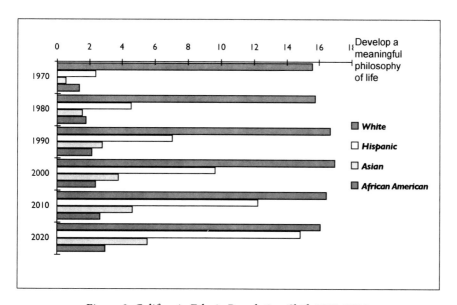

Figure 9: California Ethnic Population Shift 1970-2020

Multiculturalism is a fact of life in California. In a very real sense California has become the crucible of the future for it is here more than anywhere else that the major cultures of the world are meeting, from east and west, from north and south. Pressed ever closer together in a multicultural society, we are discovering how far apart we still remain.

The crucible of multiculturalism is not the melting pot of old; it is more akin to a salad bowl. Races and cultures are not blending in a homogeneous mix. Instead the lesson of the late twentieth century, from Lithuania to Yugoslavia, from Ireland to Sri Lanka, seems to be that blood runs deeper than politics. Political union is no guarantee of cultural collaboration. Los Angeles may be among the best models for the city of the future. But will it be a model to emulate or to avoid?

The question for California educators cannot be access vs. quality, as if quality were attainable only in a system of limited access. The question is how to achieve quality and access for students of many different cultures.

The ideal of socialization to a single culture is part of an industrial paradigm in which standardization was highly valued. Standardization is a key concept for the achievement of economies of scale in mass-production, and for the correlative standardization of tastes in mass-consumption by a mass-market. However, the ideal of standardization runs contrary to two new paradigms that are having increasing influence today:

- *An ecological paradigm* shows the value of diversity for a climax ecology. Monocultures are more vulnerable to blight than diverse, climax ecologies where differences in the gene pool make for more resilience in an ecology.

- *An information paradigm* is based on Gregory Bateson's definition of information as "a difference that makes a difference." Mass-produced information ceases to be information as soon as it becomes redundant. Yesterday's news no longer informs. If it ceases to inform, if it ceases to make a difference; it ceases to be information. Thus, difference is as basic to the information economy as standardized sameness was to the industrial economy.

Even as the echoes of the industrial era sound in the form of calls for standardized national tests, the lesson of California is likely to be *the necessity for making difference our friend, not our enemy.* Standardization cannot be the ideal of an ecologically influenced, information-rich society.

Rather than remain locked in a stand-off between budget claims to fund computers for rich kids or remedial English for the children of immigrants, the future of

California is likely to demonstrate the following message of multicultural politics: *we won't get the money for high technology unless we make good on the claim of multiculturalism.*

It is easy to see a vicious circle driving ethnic minorities further into poverty because they lack access to expensive new technologies only available to white kids in rich schools. Yet one can also imagine a scenario in which individually paced instruction software allows ethnic minorities to learn better than they would in crowded classrooms with inadequate numbers of well-intentioned but sometimes sub-consciously racist instructors. If a color-blind technology helps create a more educated work force, then improved productivity would super-charge the economy, which would then pay for better schools with better technology for improved education of ethnic minorities…

As Bell Atlantic's Chief Executive Raymond W. Smith has observed, far from being the competitive edge that many proclaim, Japan's homogeneous work force is an Achilles' heel. By contrast, he says, the diversity of America's labor pool is the key to beating the competition, provided US education improves. Says Smith: "If you take a roomful of Carnegie-Mellon engineers like me, you're going to get a particular slant on solutions. But with a diverse group in terms of race, age, and sex, you'll get a much better array of options."

Like the potential for an economically vicious or virtuous circle in all scenarios, the demographics of multiculturalism will also be at play in every scenario, for better or worse. Multiculturalism is unavoidable as a problem, and challenging as an opportunity. Because neither of the pre-determined elements (economics or demographics) plays a role in differentiating the scenarios from one another, they will not play prominent roles in the scenarios. But their significance demands further attention in the concluding section.

B. Uncertainties

In a world that is changing as fast as ours today, it should not be too surprising that there are many more uncertainties than there are predetermined elements.

- What will the needs of the job market be between 2005 and 2050? Can anyone speak with any certainty to that question?

- How will the politics of term limitation play out? Will a complete shuffle of legislators help or hurt the political process in general; higher education in particular?

- What will be the impact on higher education of significant changes in K-12 education? And what if there is no improvement in K-12 education?

- How far and in what ways will information technology evolve as a tool for education? And might the notion of literacy be expanded in a multi-media environment? What role will information technology play in the classroom? At home? Everywhere?

- What role will corporate America play in the future of higher education? Its role is already larger than most imagine. Will it become larger? And how?

- And what about the future of pedagogy? And the influence of an older student generation? And the need for continuing education? Will the nature of what we think of as education, as good education, as higher education, change?

A quick consideration of just some of the uncertainties listed above is enough to send the mind reeling off into trees of alternative possibilities that soon branch into infinitesimal capillaries of statistical insignificance.

The point is that there is a problem with trying to consider all possibilities in all possible combinations. There are too many. But what are the right criteria for whittling the many down to a few, a manageably finite number, say three or four, that display in their individual uniqueness and in their relationships with one another something about the most fundamental factors affecting the future? We want a small set of big scenarios, not a big set of small scenarios. We want a few basic stories worked out in considerable depth and detail. So how do we decide which stories to tell?

This is not an easy question to answer in general. But experience in particular cases has shown that the most useful scenarios are those that revolve around issues that are critical to a specific decision at hand. So we prioritize our lists of key factors according to two criteria: first, how important is any given factor to the issue at hand, and, second, how uncertain? Certainties don't differentiate scenarios. Uncertainties do. And as for which uncertainties, look for those that are most important to the issue at hand.

What is the issue at hand for this study? The uncertainty of support for public post-secondary education in California over the next fifteen years. And by 'support' we mean more than just financial support; issues of status and prestige have a lot to do with who will become a teacher. When we focus on *The uncertainty of support for public post-secondary education in California over the next fifteen years*, we want to consider not only the obvious—money—but also the intangible support of professional status and esteem. As many observers have pointed out, education and educators enjoy a high degree of respect in Germany and Japan.

Right now many of our K-12 teachers come from the lowest quintile of college graduates. We will not get the kind of teachers we need until the profession of education is both better paid and more highly esteemed. But what would it take to so change the values of a society? This is the subject of the third scenario.

C. Driving Trends

Sifting through the uncertainties listed above, and after considerable discussion, the scenario team chose the question of information technology as one driving trend, the focus of one scenario (though present, of course, in the others). For the second scenario the relationship between education and the economy, corporations, and market dynamics is the organizing theme. In the third scenario a paradigm shift changes several fundamental assumptions about what constitutes a good education. The new thinking changes the structure and funding for higher education.

These three scenarios follow in Part Three. Individually and as a group they are intended to illuminate some critical uncertainties facing educational planners. There is much they do not include that might be of interest to, say, military planners. There is much here that will not be of interest to those outside of education. These scenarios do not cover everything; they are selective.

The point, again, is to articulate enough alternatives to represent the range of possibilities and thereby to make informed choices. These scenarios are not predictions; they are selective interpretations of present trends and their possible courses in the future.

PART THREE: Scenarios

Scenario One: Software Landing

The much heralded but little understood information revolution involves more than substituting personal computers for cars at the ends of America's industrial assembly lines. It means substituting for those very assembly lines a new mode of production that relies less on the bending of metal into hard shapes and more on the bending of minds through entertainment, education and a rich diet of symbolically mediated experiences.

The information revolution is changing the nature of the economy, but more than that, it is changing the way we think, and therefore the way we learn. More pictures, fewer words. Only a multi-media education can keep up with a multi-media environment. Just as Sesame Street marked an if-you-can't-beat-'em-join-'em rapprochement between educators and television, so Whittle's Channel One represents a rapprochement with commercial advertising. Education is joining the economy, like it or not, via the media.

In addition to the TV, the other new boxes in the classroom are, of course, computers. The trouble is that until recently there hasn't been enough good software to keep them running. But that is changing, and in this scenario the software changes a great deal.

Educational psychology, artificial intelligence and computer programming all converge on new learning tools that are so far superior to anything in the past that students accomplish what by present standards would seem prodigious feats of learning. A club opens up for people who know 20 or more languages. A few years later, in order to maintain some vestige of exclusivity, another club opens up for those who know 40. They have a newsletter where they print articles on the silly mistakes made by natural language translation programs.

Natural language translation turns out to be a much harder puzzle than early programmers had thought. Language's subtleties and ambiguities, so essential to poetry and humor, tend to escape computers that are programmed for literalism and clarity. Nonetheless, most electronic appliances can be activated by a command language of some 500-800 fairly basic words.

Ease-of-use through voice command has a major influence on the evolution of information technology in the workplace and in the home. No longer held back by the barrier of a keyboard interface, suddenly everyone is in touch with artificial intelligence. The keyboard curtain drops and everyone is suddenly standing face to face across a medium of fiber-optic filaments and *embedded ubiquitous intelligence…*

Embedded in the sense that stand-alone computers account for an ever smaller percentage of functional microchips. Instead more and more appliances follow the route of today's cars by containing their own special applications computers to render them "smart," e.g. a smart phone, a smart TV, smart doors, smart lights, even smart clothes that adjust their insulating capacity according to outside and inside temperatures.

Ubiquitous in the sense that such intelligence is available almost everywhere. At Xerox PARC in Palo Alto, designers are already talking about the relative densities of different sizes of computers: micro-power every meter, mini-power every ten meters, macro-power every hundred meters in human environments.

Intelligence. The point of this world is not that there is more information. Sheer quantity is an industrial measure. The point is instead that this world is smarter. Stupid things don't happen as often to smart people. Traffic jams are a thing of the past given intelligent traffic management. People don't get lost anymore, since there are so many ways of tracking, paging, and showing the way. There are fewer confusions about reservations, or mistakes in billing, since there are so many automatic safeguards.

Before being overcome by the gee-whiz aspects of smartland, let's note that it's still some of the same old things one is doing: making reservations for dinner, travelling, balancing accounts. This world is not all that new. It is important to emphasize that what the information revolution is *not* about is some technology zoo of shiny trinkets with LED displays. Rather, as Paul Hawken points out in *The Next Economy*, it has more to do with an increase in the ratio of information to mass in every product and service in the economy—including education.

The importance of the information revolution is not dependent on the size of the computer industry. It is a matter of the increasing role information plays in every industry, every experience, even education.

In one sense this world will allow us to be a lot dumber. Its tools will be smart enough to make up for our stupidities. No more fumbling with little buttons on a VCR. Voice commands as vague as, "Will you tape tonight's rerun of *Cheers*," will do just fine.

When John Doe says to the ceiling, "Get Jane on the phone," the network will know that the Jane he means is Jane Doe, and it will know how to find her wherever she happens to be. This will create problems of privacy, and will create opportunities for filters that can screen out those calls one doesn't want to receive.

But these already shop-talk-worn examples of features of an intelligent telephone network are just examples, just fragments of a world that will contain dozens of information technologies unimagined today, just as the fax was, for the most part, unimagined in 1975.

The important points for educators to appreciate about this kind of future are the following:

> The fibering of America will mean that massive information resources will be available to almost anyone, almost anywhere, almost anytime. Telephone companies are already laying thousands of miles of fiber-optic lines. Tennessee is projected to be the first fully fibered state—by the end of the century. Between 2000 and 2020 the rest of the nation will be fully fibered. Consequently, bricks and mortar—campuses—will be less important as distance learning (at home and on the job) becomes more prevalent. Just as the health-care industry is witnessing a shift from in-patient to out-patient care with fewer and shorter stays in hospitals, so education will shift toward an "out-student" model featuring self-paced, personalized instruction at sites of the student's own choosing.

> Because differentiation rather than standardization is at the heart of the information revolution, instructional software will be highly personalized. Rather than the same curriculum with the same pace for all, learning will occur in highly individualized ways. Intelligent diagnostics will identify the rate, level, and learning style of each student, and the pedagogical procedure of any given courseware will adjust accordingly.

> The increasing availability of hypertext will encourage less linear, more associative patterns of thought and inquiry. A history lesson in hypertext will allow a student to "touch" an unknown word with a finger on a screen or a light-pen or mouse, and zoom in on a deeper explanation of, say, the Dreyfus affair. And one question can lead to another. Who was Major Esterhazy? Minds will wander, and so much the better. They will traverse more territory, and with a higher level of interest, than minds being led on forced marches down the linear corridors of many current textbooks.

> The role of the teacher will change: from repository of expertise to guide to resources. Rather than playing the role of expert or know-it-all, the teacher will be a mediator between the student and resources that far exceed what any individual, even the most skilled or brilliant scholar, could know. Librarians are better models for this role than research scientists. The best professors will not be those who work only "at the cutting edge" but those who are good at managing the "interface" between each student and existing knowledge, whether or not they are also pushing out the frontiers of knowledge.

The role of institutions of higher learning will shift: from providing a rite of passage (from ignorance to knowledge) toward providing skills with tools that will be used again and again. Credentialing for specific professions will be less important than re-educating and updating. Learning will be less like losing one's virginity—a one-time event, never to be repeated—and more like eating: a necessary, recurrent, and often enjoyable activity.

In order for today's educational establishment to get "from here to there," a number of changes will have to take place during this scenario, several of which are beyond the control of today's educators. The politics and funding of fiber-optic highways require the cooperation of legislators and telephone companies. The development of educational software depends on the initiative and inventiveness of companies like Brøderbund and Apple. The speed with which distance learning takes off is partly a function of the evolution of the "smart home," fully wired for interactive, multi-media information services.

Each of these evolutionary changes—in distribution networks, in software, and in home appliances—depends in part on demand. The telephone companies will not lay fiber unless they are sure it will be used. The educational software developers must be assured of a market. The intelligent appliance manufacturers, likewise, need to know that the distribution network and the software and the demand will all be there to assure that their equipment can get used.

Each of the players in the information society needs the others, and educators have a crucial part to play if this show is to go on. The technology of *Software Landing*, or something close to it, *will* be available sooner or later. Educators have a role to play in determining how soon; and the role they then play will be significantly influenced by other players in the game.

Some other players will be competitors carrying threats, some will be supporters laden with opportunities, and some will be both depending on how educators relate to them. The corporate community, for example, can be a competitor to the extent that it educates its workers on its own; or it can be a supporter to the extent that it plays a greater role in financing public higher education. The double-edged sword of corporate involvement in education is the subject of the next scenario.

As for opportunities, the concluding section on implications will spell out in greater detail the potential for closing the current funding gap by the use of information technology. For this is the ultimate hope of *Software Landing*: as in so many other industries, so in education, the application of new technology lowers costs and enhances productivity. More people learn more for less money.

Because learning is valued, great educators are rewarded. Their methods are emulated, but entrepreneurial initiative proves more successful than slavish imitation. Successful teachers gain students the way successful entertainers gain fans. With over 400 channels available over cable, one can find 30 or 40 teachers narrowcasting at any given time of day or night. Then there is the vast market in CD-ROMs and interactive technologies. Virtual reality has been widely commercialized, and experience-simulators have made their way into education.

Implications

Assuming that something close to *Software Landing* in fact unfolds over the next 15 years, what would be its implications for faculty, for students, for staff, for the various branches of California's system of higher education? And finally, what are its implications for funding?

> Among the most dramatic implications of this scenario would be an overcoming of the sense of remoteness experienced at some of the more rural community colleges. If distance learning, becomes a reality, then distance loses its significance, whether the distance is literally geographical or more cultural and economic—as in the distance between Stanford and East Palo Alto, or between Berkeley and Oakland. Wheresoever a terminal can be found, there one is present in the global metropolis of learning.

> The three tiers established by the Master Plan will no longer be distinguishable by the size of the libraries easily and immediately available to each, because the same massive resources will be at the finger tips of all. *Everywhere an Alexandria!*

> For the faculty, advancement and professional success will be less dependent on pedantry and more dependent on creativity of scholarship and teaching ability. Computers render human pedantry redundant. Computers are far better at the mere storage and retrieval of facts and bibliographical references than humans could ever be. These skills, once prized among academics, will be less important than the things computers cannot do: create new and imaginative connections among old bits of data; cultivate and enhance the human aspects of respect, curiosity and attention that can inspire students to learn.

> Librarians will gain status and increased recognition for the importance of their role in mediating between those seeking information and the resources they wish to find. Indeed, the very idea of what it is to be a teacher will move away from the pedantic repository of facts and towards the mediator or facilitator who knows how and where to find, how to interpret and skilfully apply, information.

If distance learning takes place at home, on the job, or while travelling, residential campuses will become less centrally important to the system. Information technology will decentralize learning. One can imagine those remaining on campus as "the studio audience". The university will cease to be the only place where courses are given and will become more like the lot where courses are produced.

As the portrait of the latter days of this scenario becomes clearer and its implications more evident, some serious misgivings are bound to arise:

1. Where is the human touch? Will social skills be neglected by individuals locked for hours to their private terminals? Will the two-way interaction of the small classroom or seminar be sacrificed to the one-way communication of the lecture if students are separated from teachers by the technology of distance learning?

2. What will happen to those who resist the new technology? Many secretaries and stenographers resisted the advent of word-processors. Some who boycotted computers did so with good reason: their jobs disappeared. Will faculty resist the increases in productivity available through information technology? If a few star performers create the courseware used by millions, what will happen to the many who shine less brightly under the studio lights?

3. Where will the money come from to finance the up-links for high-tech educational networks? Today it costs approximately $50,000 for each remote site to be linked together in an interactive educational network. Will the costs of educational studio technology break the bank?

4. And even more important, will there be structural inequities in the availability of down-links? Will the poor get poorer because they cannot afford the technology they need to access the educational networks?

Let us consider these misgivings one by one:

1. Technology unmediated by a human touch is indeed a danger to this scenario. *Software Landing* may mean a hard landing for social skills. If the premise of this scenario is high-tech unmediated by human interaction, then the dangers of heading down this path may lead us to neglect the productivity improvements available through information and communications technology. Or, seizing upon what John Naisbitt has labelled the trend toward "hi-tech/hi-touch", we may find ways to compensate for the apparent impersonality of high-technology. But

that part of the story is saved for Scenario Three. For now we must acknowledge that *Software Landing*, premised as it is on technology to the rescue, does not go far enough to compensate for the impersonality inherent in distance learning.

2. Here again there are grounds for legitimate concern. A system that relies on a few studio stars is a system, like show-biz, with a few big winners and a lot of losers eating their hearts out in low-paying jobs between casting calls. The teachers' unions are not likely to accept the kind of employment terms offered by Actors' Equity.

3. Money for up-links may not be a big problem for three reasons: first, despite the cost, if the premise is one of improvements in productivity through vastly enhanced distribution capability, then whatever the costs, the benefits rise even faster than the costs so the bargain is worth making. Second, the costs of almost all information technologies are rapidly declining and will continue to decline. Third, at least part of the costs may be defrayed by the private sector. But that part of the story takes us on to the next scenario.

4. Perhaps the weakest link in the chain of coherence holding this scenario together is the question—the uncertainty: Will educational technology enhance the opportunities of minorities because it is color-blind, or, even better, more capable of adapting to different learning styles than today's teachers? OR: Will a greater dependence on technology further disadvantage minorities because (a) they cannot afford the down-links, or (b), the everyday lives of many disadvantaged students simply don't have a place where educational technology can fit in? Surely it is easier to imagine higher penetration rates for educational terminals for students with their own homes and bedrooms than for students without homes, much less private bedrooms. There is thus a real danger of the split between haves and have-nots being widened by a technological wedge separating the knows from the know-nots.

So much, then, for the implications—the dangers, the opportunities, the costs, and the uncertainties—that attach to *Software Landing*. On balance it is a plausible scenario, one that is driven in part by technological developments far beyond the control of educators alone, and therefore worth monitoring by educators lest they be swept along into a future not of their own making.

Technology is one of the most potent forces for social change. Ever since Gutenberg, and surely since the invention of television, the attention span and the information content available to the common man and woman have been fundamentally altered by changes in technology. These changes are, if anything, accelerating, and they are bound to alter the structure of higher education. Only by looking ahead, by being alert to both the dangers and opportunities inherent in information technology, can we bend a scenario like *Software Landing* in a direction that improves education for all.

Scenario Two: Education Inc.

The logic of this scenario is centered around the relationship between education and the economy: the rewards and incentives at play, and the institutional structures that can help or inhibit the enrichment of education, and enrichment by education.

It is tempting to put this scenario, like Satan, behind us. One hears the refrain, "selling out" in the background whenever scholars seek support, whether from corporations or from the government. Scholarly inquiry is supposed to be *disinterested*, and business is so very interested in the fast buck.

In order to think through this scenario in any depth, however, it should become clear that there are more possible models of university-corporate relationships than that of higher education's becoming a wholly owned subsidiary of corporate America.

One model would have the university becoming more of a business on its own. Changes in the 1986 tax law permit universities to benefit from the commercialization of federally funded research conducted in university laboratories. Institutions like MIT have long depended heavily on corporations for support of their research laboratories; and corporations, for their part, have long depended on universities for out-sourcing some of their R&D. In the future, educational institutions may solve some of their financial woes by reaping substantial royalties from discoveries made in their laboratories.

The logic of the marketplace, like the logic of the information revolution, can reach into all aspects of education: supply-side, demand-side, and the structure and organization of institutions. Let us consider each in turn.

Supply-side

Who will do the educating, and what will they teach? One of the most shocking revelations of recent years is the degree to which higher education has already been taken over by the private sector. It seems that almost every major research report going back to the 1983 Carnegie Commission Report quotes the figure $30 billion as the annual price tag for corporate training programs—though that figure had risen to $44 billion by 1989. Clearly there's a lot of on the job training, conference fees, and plush executive retreats in these figures, but they are significant figures nonetheless. They suggest that corporate America is no longer counting on public higher education as its "supplier" for "human resources," but is instead "making" rather than "buying" its training.

If this trend continues—from already existing McDonalds University and Motorola University ("Motorola U: When Training Becomes an Education," *Harvard Business Review*, July-August, 1990.) to IBM University and Ford University and more—then the corporate community will appear as a competitor to rather than as a supporter of existing institutions of higher education. But there is another branch to this scenario, one in which existing institutions learn how to do a better job at meeting corporate America's needs for an educated work force.

At the Darden School, University of Virginia's graduate school of business administration, Dean John W. Rosenblum speaks of customized programs for executives of Hercules Inc., of Wilmington, Deleware, and for Bacardi & Company, the makers and marketers of rum and other spirits, who are located in Nassau, the Bahamas. "Lifelong management education is the way of the future," says Dean Rosenblum. "We in business school are an industry in transition. We must look at the environment in which managers work today and tomorrow to be effective. We must learn from each other." (Elizabeth Fowler, "Careers," *New York Times* Dec. 1991.)

As new technology changes job requirements, community colleges have stepped up to the challenge of bringing high technology to the shop floor. According to John Holusha ("Businesses Go Back to School," *NY Times*, Education Supplement, Fall 1991), "Nationally, about 50 community colleges have built technology centers to enhance local manufacturers." The California Community Colleges Economic Development Network (ED>Net) has initiated close collaborations between high-tech employers and local community colleges. Long Beach City College, for example, has implemented computer control-based training in all of its automotive classes. Nissan agreed to designate the college as its Los Angeles-area apprenticeship program, and donated vehicles, equipment and books worth $200,000.

Centers for Applied Competitive Technologies (CACTs) have been set up at eight California Community Colleges, with 16 technology centers the long-range goal. As part of IBM's program to support computer integrated manufacturing (CIM) in higher education, IBM has donated hundreds of thousands of dollars worth of hardware and software to DeAnza College, El Camino College and Sierra College—all participants in the CACT program.

On either branch of this scenario—whether industry makes or buys its training, whether industry outsources its training or develops in-house education programs— it is clear that the logic of the marketplace is influencing the shape of the curriculum.

And this worries educators who are concerned about selling out to the interests of business.

A quick perusal of the ten pages of corporate/educational programs and relationships listed in *Fortune*'s "Special Report on Education" (Oct. 21, 1991.) reveals precious few programs in the humanities. Overwhelmingly, corporate dollars seek out programs in math, science, high technology and business education. But maybe this is what the students/customers (will) want.

Demand Side

The demand side of *Education Inc.* gains power over the supply-side by a structural change in the funding of higher education. Rather than passing tax dollars directly to colleges and universities, a referendum passed in 1996 dictates that funding credits for higher education shall go directly to students, who then "spend" those credits as they choose, wherever they choose, for whichever courses they choose.

Before its passage, this referendum is known as *The Bologna Referendum*, since this was how one of the first universities of Europe was financed—with students at Bologna hiring all and only those professors who gained and retained their approval. Shortly after its passage, the referendum comes to be known among less popular faculty as *the baloney referendum.*

When confronted with the compelling logic of market forces for change, some educators dust off the old chestnuts about students, in the nature of the case, being too ignorant to know what they want. In an effort to dismiss the verdict of the marketplace, they try to discredit the legitimacy of the market metaphor for education. They say that students cannot "shop" because they do not know what they want to buy. They are there, precisely, to find out. But this argument turns out to be less forceful for college students than it is for K-12. College students, especially those beyond their teens, have a pretty good basis for knowing what they are looking for, and a good shopper's nose for knowing where they can find it.

The changing demographics of age in the higher education student body has a profound effect on the funding of higher education. In 1974 only a third of college students were over 25. By 1990, 40 percent were over 25. By 2000 fully 50 percent of the college student body is over 25.

Older students behave more like customers, less like passive medical patients. Children and medical patients must have some choices made for them, and must also rely on others—parents or insurance companies—to pay for whatever education or medical care they receive. Older students, by contrast, can take more responsibility for what they want, and can exercise more responsibility in paying for it.

As the power of changing patterns of demand impacts higher education, there are major changes. In the world of education, where institutional extinctions had been as rare as national bankruptcies, there are now mergers and acquisitions. Educators engage in market research as a way of getting closer to their customers. New educational technologies are rigorously market tested and aggressively marketed.

While much of this language offends many educators (who speak of "pandering" to students as well as industry), a certain amount of this restructuring can hardly help but benefit pedagogy. When the state passes tax dollars directly back to students, who then pay for each package of education they choose to purchase, the packaging, that is to say the pedagogy, improves.

Some tenured professors, particularly those more interested in research than in teaching, had become indifferent to the needs or wants of students. Their model of education was one of students looking over their shoulders as they got on with their valuable research—rather like a Henry Ford who quipped that Americans could have any color car they wanted, so long as it was black.

Business has come a long way in catering to the needs of its customers: from mass-manufacturing for a mass-market around mid-century to niche-marketing to special segments of consumers today. In this scenario, higher education follows a similar trajectory: from telling students what they must have to asking them, each and every one, what they want.

Since 1967, Professor Alexander Astin of UCLA has been surveying college freshmen across the country to find out who is attending college and why. One of the questions on his survey, now administered routinely to hundreds of thousands of college freshmen every year, offers a range of possible motives for attending college. Figure 10 shows an unmistakable trend in responses to two of the possible answers. Today's students are far more interested in "becoming well off financially" than in "gaining a meaningful life philosophy".

Figure 10 speaks volumes about the last several decades. Part of the deep background for this story must include the worldwide trend away from ideological motivation toward market mechanisms—what Francis Fukuyama has called "the end of history" with the defeat of communism. The rise of Margaret Thatcher in England, Kohl in Germany, the demise of communism in Russia and eastern Europe, and the rollback of socialism in France, are all part of a dramatic shift in the relationship between the public and the private sectors.

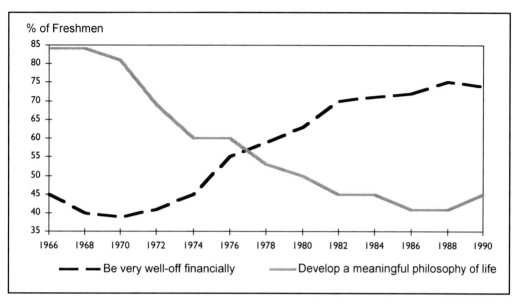

% of Freshmen

— — Be very well-off financially   ▨▨▨Develop a meaningful philosophy of life

Figure 10: Changing Interests in College Freshmen

Restructuring: The Second Reformation

In addition to changes in the nature of both the supply and demand for education, there will be changes in the structure of educational institutions. Call it an educational Perestroika.

Taking a very long view—as one must do to catch the momentum of the present toward a more distant future—it would seem that there is something like a Second Reformation taking place. Just as the first Reformation separated the powers of Church and State, so the second is separating the powers of State from Corporation. And just as the first shifted much of the power of the Pope and his priests to presidents and kings, so the Second Reformation is shifting power once again: away from political leaders and into the hands of corporate leaders.

Students are catching the drift of the Second Reformation. They see where the action is. They are consequently less interested in political ideology and more interested in the marketplace. It's not that they are apathetic and indifferent to the sufferings of others, as some (old) New Lefties would suggest in disgust; they simply don't believe that the state has the power to alleviate that suffering. So they turn to wealth creation rather than political revolution.

According to the logic of this scenario, the remarkable shift represented in Astin's study of college freshmen does not represent one wave in a fashion cycle, but a long-term trend that will not reverse itself any time soon. Just as a political logic replaced a religious logic organizing society, so now an economic logic is replacing, and will continue to displace, a political logic. This long-term historical shift will have profound effects on publicly supported higher education.

It would be wrong to speak of the privatization of public education, as if public education could be securitized and sold to the highest bidders like Heathrow airport or British Gas. We already have a system of private colleges and universities, and they don't look much like for-profit corporations. But just as DHL and Federal Express are exerting competitive pressure on the post office, so there may be new educational startups that introduce a more intensely competitive atmosphere to higher education. Corporations will compete with universities at educating their employees, or they will outsource their training programs only to those institutions that can meet the market need.

In this scenario the demand for marketable skills increases. Students insist on courses that will render them more capable as employees, entrepreneurs and executives. If colleges cannot provide such courses then corporations will.

As a reward for restructuring in a way that better matches supply to demand, public institutions of higher education find that they gain both customers and "investors". Both corporations and governments pay attention to what the market says about the goods being offered by different institutions.

This new attentiveness to needs will mark a change from current practices. While business people typically complain that the education system is not meeting their needs ("Study Gives High Schools 'F' in Preparing Students for Jobs, *Los Angeles Times*, Aug. 8, 1981, p. A5), educators, for their part, complain that business does not do a good job of letting educators know what those needs are. ("Business Has Failed to Report Needs, Educators Say," *Education Week*, Sept. 25, 1991, p. 9.)

By the end of this scenario, state universities are known for more than their athletic teams and Nobel laureates. They are known for the financial accomplishments of their alumni. Measurements and indices of the sort that are now commonplace in business will have made their way into the educational marketplace. Different teachers and different departments, now subject to vague rumors and magazine polls offering rankings for whole institutions, will find themselves touted or trashed as the result of a new scrutiny of results. And good results will be rewarded!

For those institutions that successfully restructure to meet demand with supply, budget deficits will be a thing of the past. As Father Clarke, president of Regis University, put it, "We're not-for-profit; but we're not for loss either". (This remark was quoted in *The Wall Street Journal* in a front page article touting Father Clarke's success in serving the training needs of a local employer, Martin Marietta.)

With recognition for success, some educators and some institutions will come to enjoy the kinds of rewards now reserved for entertainers, professional athletes, and their team owners. It is said that the worlds of sports and entertainment are populated by a few winners and a lot of losers. By 2005 educators will look back at the pre-Perestroika period of the late twentieth century as a time when publicly supported education, like socialist government, created a level playing field with a lot of losers. By 2005 a highly differentiated marketplace for education produces at least a few winners who are raising the level of play in all of education.

Implications

Like *Software Landing, Education Inc.* will have implications for faculty, students, staff, and for the structure of state supported higher education.

> Consistent with the logic of a shift from central command and control toward more marketplace dynamics, there will be a devolution of authority from "upper management" toward "the shop floor"; from central capitals toward the provinces; from administrators' offices toward the classroom. Students will "shop" where they can get the most for their money. Colleges that can't compete will be shut down, not by political demonstrations but by economic failure.

> If the state gives money to the consumer rather than to the provider of education, that will undermine the monopoly on credentialing that universities now enjoy. As it is now, university administrators control the purse strings once the legislators have filled the purse. In *Education Inc.*, the value of a degree will rise and fall like the value of listed securities, and that value will depend less on rumored reputations and more on measured accomplishments of the graduates of different institutions.

> As soon as students cease being "patients" and become instead "customers", then authority for the content of the curriculum will shift from teachers-as-doctors to students-as-customers. Just as success in today's marketplace is determined more by consumers than producers, so success in the educational marketplace will be determined more by the students than by the teachers. Students will grade teachers by the allocation of their tuition dollars.

> If librarians emerged as the staff heroes and heroines of *Software Landing*, then it is the career counsellors and job placement officers who enjoy the greatest status hike in *Education Inc.* In order to smooth the currently rough transition from education to work, they come to have a far greater influence over the ongoing course of many students' educations, in many cases replacing faculty advisors.

Likewise the transition *into* higher education will look less like hurdles erected by admissions officers and more like marketing on the part of recruiters. Recruitment will rival job placement in importance as colleges seek the very best quality "raw materials". Seeking quantity as well as quality, colleges will compete ever more actively for students and their tuition dollars.

Given the commercial goals driving business, there is no doubt that the influence of the private sector will privilege *training* over a less goal-oriented liberal education. The beneficiaries of this tendency will be the Community Colleges and the professional schools.

The University of California will gain research dollars, but the budget is likely to slant toward the D in R&D. So-called *basic research* is less likely to gain support from corporations interested in commercial applications of existing knowledge. The Council on Competitiveness has already pointed to the need for more attention to the transition from basic research to the successful commercialization of science. The US is good at innovation; the Japanese seem to be better at those incremental changes that make for successful products. In *Education Inc.*, the pressure for competitiveness will lead to greater emphasis on commercial development rather than liberal education or basic research.

Scenario Three: The New Educational Order

A New Paradigm

Just as each of the other scenarios follow a pervasive logic that supports major movements in education by major movements in the historical macro-environment, so this third scenario, too, exhibits a similar consistency. Just as the use of information technology in education rides on the back of a more pervasive *information revolution*, and just as *Education Inc.* rides on the back of the Second Reformation that drives all of history from a political logic toward a more economic logic, so the rationale guiding education in this third scenario is driven by a *paradigm shift* that is reflected in other parts of society, from concerns about the environment and worries about our decaying infrastructure to changes in the fundamental assumptions underlying many of the disciplines that make up a college curriculum.

Paradigm shifts are, in principle, difficult to comprehend at close range. Precisely because paradigm shifts change our ways of seeing and understanding everything around us, they are themselves difficult to see or understand. It is hard to see or describe from the near shore of a fundamental shift of worldview just what the far shore will look like. Just as hunter-gatherers could not grasp the significance of the first attempts at agriculture, so farmers were not able to appreciate the significance of industrial manufacturing. Eli Whitney's cotton gin may have looked like an incremental improvement in agriculture. Who suspected that it heralded the advent of the industrial revolution, a transformation that would change a way of life centered around life on the farm? Likewise today there is a danger of misconstruing the information revolution as an incremental improvement in the way we do industrial manufacturing: smarter tools. But the information revolution is much more than that. It will not just substitute computers for cars coming off assembly lines. It will substitute assembly lines with entirely new modes of manufacturing and production: smarter work, smarter play, smarter ways to get through virtually every activity in a day.

Because paradigm shifts are, by definition, pervasive—not just a new discovery in a single field of inquiry, but a change in the pattern of discovery in all fields—they are necessarily infrequent and, for that reason, unfamiliar. More usual is business as usual: the filling in of holes that remain in well accepted systems of knowledge and understanding. Only rarely does a fundamental change alter the way we understand understanding or change the way we understand our place in the order of things. The Copernican revolution was one such change, for it displaced man from the center of the universe. Darwinian evolution was another such change, for it placed man further from God and closer to the rest of the animal kingdom. Though initially confined to the libraries and laboratories of scholars and scientists, fundamental breakthroughs in our understanding of the universe and our place in it eventually ripple through the rest of society.

Now once again the foundations of knowledge are under stress. As with earlier paradigm changes, the lines of stress are most evident out at the esoteric edges of several academic disciplines: chaos theory which tries to model complex systems from the weather to the economy to the turbulence in the wake of an airplane wing; cognitive science which unites information theory, linguistics, neurophysiology, psychology, philosophy and computer programming in a combined assault on understanding what it is to understand; and evolutionary theory itself which, a century after Darwin, is now being applied to everything from the evolution of language to the behavior of the immune system and the survival of new products in niche markets.

Just as the scientific discoveries of Newton and Copernicus contributed to the Reformation, the separation of Church and State, the rise of Enlightenment rationality, and the secularization of everyday life from the nature of politics to the organization of education, so the scientific breakthroughs of this century will lead to similarly far-reaching changes throughout society. But what will they be? How will politics change? How will education respond to new realities and *new ways of perceiving those realities*?

Even though we can see only the faintest outlines of a new paradigm at the edges of several academic disciplines, it is not too early to don these new lenses in order to grasp a new vision of what higher education is all about. Because these new lenses are unfamiliar, this third scenario requires the greatest stretch of imagination. We must try to see higher education with new eyes. If a new paradigm is indeed emerging at the leading edges of several academic disciplines, we can hardly expect to understand all of its ramifications for the rest of life at this early date. Yet the work to be performed by scenarios is precisely to fill in the contours and work out the significances of what are now only first hints on the academic horizon.

One aspect of the new paradigm is a heightened appreciation for the systematic interconnectedness of things. In place of an analytic approach to problems that would simplify, divide and conquer—e.g. through the establishment of separate academic departments and increasingly fine-grained divisions among areas of specialization—the new approach seeks to synthesize and accommodate to the real complexity of our human and natural environments. Systems and structures will receive the kind of attention once devoted to atoms and elements. With a tip of the hat to the maxim from systems theory—*You can never do just one thing*—policy makers in this scenario become much more aware of context and consequences: How does a strong economy contribute to social welfare, which in turn contributes to the physical health of students, thereby enhancing their ability to learn? After years of trying to isolate problems and attack them with short-term magic bullets and quick fixes, the new appreciation for systematic interconnections leads to an equal appreciation for long-term consequences. Rather than detracting from funding for education, this shift toward a mentality concerned with long-term investment rather than short-term payoff could turn out to be a boon to education.

The Responsibility Revolution

As Americans' worries about nuclear annihilation subside, concerns about foreign policy give way to concerns about domestic issues. International economic competitiveness carries more weight than military might. A stable settlement in the Middle East finally clears the way for allocating the long-delayed peace dividend. After weathering the long recession of the early nineties, chastened Americans are ready to invest the dividend rather than spend it in a replay of the eighties.

Where to invest? Clearly the natural environment needs cleaning up. And the man-made environment—our infrastructure of roads and bridges—needs work. Most of all it is the man-made environment of our inner cities that pulls educators down out of their ivory towers to wrestle with the slow rebuilding of the social, natural, and urban infrastructures.

But Americans are not content to throw money at existing educational institutions. Nor, in this scenario, are they content to leave social policy and social welfare up to the private sector. A new vision is wanted, a paradigm change in the way social services in general, and higher education in particular, are conceived, delivered and funded.

Not to trivialize the significant differences that distinguish the first and second scenarios from one another, or both from the present, it is nonetheless true that the logics of the first two scenarios both suggest alternative ways of closing the funding gap for delivering essentially the same service as is being delivered today. In *Software Landing* the deficit is lowered by lowering costs through the use of high technology to attain higher productivity—a classic pattern of evolution followed by other industries as they have become more *automated* by the application of new technology. In *Education Inc.*, the private sector picks up the funding burden where the state leaves off—another familiar pattern we have come to know as privatization. The curriculum may reflect changes in the nature of course offerings to suit the interests of industry, but the fundamentals of pedagogy remain the same.

Neither the technology fix nor the private funding fix need necessarily alter fundamentally our ideas about learning. They can be conceived in terms of incremental changes of degree toward the use of different tools to do the same old jobs, or a gradual relocation of those same old educational jobs from one set of institutions—publicly supported colleges—to another set of institutions—privately supported corporate training programs.

But the driving trends behind the first two scenarios, together with other changes in values, public opinion and social policy, may combine to create a major discontinuity in what constitutes higher education. The further evolution of both technological and economic trends, combined with a paradigm change sweeping across academic disciplines themselves, may add up to a revolution in the nature of higher education. Could so much change happen in just a few short decades?

Revolutionary De-Maturing

Though higher education may look like a "mature industry" not susceptible to significant innovation, the same was said of the shoe industry around 1970—before the introduction of Nike, Reebok and Rockport shoes—companies that succeeded in "de-maturing" the shoe industry and greatly expanding the demand for specialized shoes.

Likewise other industries have undergone restructurings that did more than relocate the same old jobs. The transportation industry has gone through major changes from the railroad era to the automobile era; and the American automobile industry is experiencing greater competition from abroad than its executives would have ever imagined possible just ten years ago. Major changes can happen.

Just as the tumult of the sixties would have seemed unlikely to most leaders of the fifties, and the neo-conservativism of the seventies and eighties almost unthinkable to those growing up in the sixties, so the nineties could bring big surprises to those who thought that the eighties might go on forever. Yes, the Second Reformation shifts power from the public to the private sector. And, yes, the information revolution brings many of the changes described in *Software Landing*. But in *The New Educational Order* both the context for high technology and the dynamics of the marketplace are pressed into the service of an increased concern for social justice and the quality of life.

The new mood has neither the self-righteousness of the sixties, with its conviction that even the personal was political, nor the selfishness of the eighties, when greed and narcissism seemed to justify any excesses the marketplace could dish up. Instead there is a redrawing of the boundaries between the personal and the political, the private and the public.

Following the privatization of foreign policy that led to the likes of Oliver North and the Iran-Contra scandal, and the deregulation of industry that led to the Savings & Loans (S&L) debacle, public opinion about the need for federal regulation takes a turn away from the deregulatory mood of the Reagan and Bush years. A rash of commercial airline accidents in the nineties leads to a growing realization that, whatever the limitations of government might be, the marketplace cannot be trusted to deliver all human goods. The American public, particularly those who fly a lot, take a second look at Reagan's "victory" over the air traffic controllers' union in the early eighties. A Counter-reformation sets in to compensate for the excesses of the Second Reformation.

Other lessons are not lost on Americans as the nineties unfold. Europe prospers while Japan goes into decline. Policy makers attribute this shift in the global economy to the weakness of government in Japan compared to the strength of the public sector in Europe. It is not a question of the pendulum swinging back to the same old socialism; quite the contrary. The demise of communism clears the way for a *neo-liberal synthesis* that accepts the importance of private ownership and free enterprise for fostering innovation and competition in the marketplace. But there is a new appreciation for the importance of a strong public sector and its role in providing those public goods that cannot be purchased by individuals while shopping on a Saturday afternoon, e.g. a communications system, a transportation system, a health care system, an education system.

Just as Russians woke up in the eighties to the realization that a centralized government was not the best mechanism for the creation and distribution of consumer goods, so Americans wake up in the nineties to realize that marketplace competition is not the best medium for maintaining a telephone system or a health care system. And the same follows for certain kinds of education. The marketplace is marvelous for allowing individual preferences the freedom to find satisfaction from particular consumer goods. But when it comes to social goods and general welfare, the new paradigmatic sensitivity to complex systems leads to a growing recognition of the need for public sector involvement in the development, regulation and management of publicly funded systems for health, transportation, communication... and education.

In 1996 Al Gore and Harris Wofford win the presidential election on a ticket promising interstate electronic highways and universal health insurance. Following decades of "new federalism", the federal government is back in business. Government stays out of the business of consumer good—cosmetics, food, toys, clothing, suburban housing, all the discrete goods that can be bought one at a time. But for those "lumpy" public goods that are not so easy to leave to the aggregation of many private purchase decisions, the people come to depend once again on their elected representatives to make wise policy decisions for the efficient allocation of scarce resources.

After years of suffering jack-hammers tearing up the streets to lay gas lines, then electric lines, then TV cables, then fiber-optic telephone lines, it occurs to more than a few people that there are certain inefficiencies involved in allowing private companies to compete in the construction of public infrastructure. We decide we do not need seven regional telephone companies and three long-distance carriers competing inefficiently for our telephone traffic. National businesses want a one-stop shop for their ubiquitous local services. Local customers do not want a list of different companies sending them different bills at different rates for essentially the same services.

As many viewers become increasingly frustrated with the declining quality of their cable TV service during the mid-nineties, it becomes apparent that the telephone companies would be more reliable carriers for the next generation of high-definition TV. Throughout the nineties their network of fiber-optic cables spread like a kudzu weed across the entire country—systematic interconnection incarnate in millions of miles of glass fiber. Tennessee, Al Gore's home state, is the first to complete a network connecting every home and business. The lessons gained in Tennessee are learned by citizens and leaders in other states. From improved home entertainment to improved test scores, Tennessee shows other states how to improve the quality of life, create jobs, lower unemployment, and compete successfully in an increasingly global economy.

California and Oregon follow close behind Tennessee in taking advantage of new technology. Well before the federal government enacts the Universal Utility into law, Pacific Gas & Electric (PG&E) and Pacific Telesis sign a letter of intent for a merger to take place in 1997. Under the leadership of Al Gore, the Universal Utility is written into law by a Democratic Congress during its 1998 session.

The idea is simple: extend Theodor Vail's idea of "universal service" to as many of the basic necessities as can be put through a single "pipe" into every home in the nation. Leave all the particular goods that can be handled by private enterprise to the dynamics of the marketplace. Freedom of choice and the anarchy of competition may be fine for all of the discretionary purchases that individuals may or may not wish to make. But universal needs should be satisfied as efficiently as possible by a Universal Utility that delivers basic services to every citizen in the nation.

After decades of new federalism, deregulation and privatization, the thought of a Universal Utility comes as something of a surprise to most observers. After all, didn't the divestiture of AT&T into seven "baby bells" seem like a good idea at the time? Didn't we learn anything from the progressive demise of the Post Office in the face of competition from private mail carriers, express couriers and electronic communications? Well, yes. But we learned the lesson a little too well, as the S&L crisis demonstrated. Some services are best left to private enterprise: hair salons, domestic help, auto repair, financial planning. But when it comes to complex systems on which the whole society depends, then it is up to the government to operate certain natural monopolies for the good of all... or so we decide as, ever so tacitly, we draft a new social contract.

The New Social Contract

On the eve of the new millennium there is intense debate over what amounts to a new social contract. The debate bears little resemblance to the old squabbles between liberal left and conservative right. In place of the cleaver stroke that would carve public and private realms into larger and smaller domains of rights and freedoms, there is a finer application of scalpels to the body politic. *The point is to distinguish as carefully as possible between public necessities and private liberties; between rights and responsibilities; between universal needs and particular privileges.* This debate has some of the urgency and much of the passion of *The Federalist Papers*. But the context has changed: the economy is no longer agricultural, nor industrial, but information based. To be a citizen is not to be a land-owner but a tele-communicator. Women count. The world is now our next door neighbor. In place of the founding fathers' concerns over religious freedom, we now listen to mothers' worries about the damage we are doing to mother Earth.

The movement toward a new social contract is accelerated in California by a strong coalition of neo-liberal activists. They manage to unite a new generation of business leaders and limited term politicians in a coalition government that approves the merger of Pac Tel and PG&E once it is apparent that savings can be achieved by getting rid of the inefficiencies and redundancies of parallel rights of way, parallel billing and parallel service networks.

By the dawn of the new millennium, higher education takes place in a context very different from what most people were familiar with, even as recently as the early nineties. Every citizen of the United States now has health insurance (Harris Wofford's campaign promise); and every home with a telephone and a TV is now (or is soon to be) served by a single "pipe" from the Universal Utility. The pipe has several channels: for gas, electricity, telephone service, cable TV, an energy monitoring system, and a broadband channel for interactive educational programming.

Unlike the one-way communications characteristic of distance learning in *Software Landing*, in this scenario the larger context of the new social contract with its emphasis on community dictates the accelerated development and application of interactive groupware: electronic seminars rather than electronic lectures. Through the use of multiple windows on a single screen, an individual will be able to manage several electronic "conversations" simultaneously, much as one does in a seminar room or coffee shop. Several users will be able to share a single simulation—of an historical event, or a piece of equipment, or a surgical operation—so that the shared simulation will become a virtual classroom for students in different locations.

Neo-liberal politics accelerates some of the technological and economic trends evident in *Software Landing* and *Education Inc.* Where old liberals were suspicious of the private sector, neo-liberals have come to terms with the historical significance of the Second Reformation. It is just this appreciation for the power of the private sector that leads to a sense of its limits—and the need for a Counter-reformation. So neo-liberals see a role for the public sector, but only in those areas demanding public policy to coordinate private acts toward the general welfare of society. Unlike both old liberals and neo-conservatives, the new breed of neo-liberals question the sanctity of individualism—whether it is the liberty of the individual to seek an abortion, or the liberty of the individual to seek boundless wealth. The neo-liberals gore the oxen of both the Left and the Right. But just as important: the logic of neo-liberalism drives the development of information technology and the involvement of the business community in a direction not evident in the earlier scenarios: toward a new pedagogy.

The Pedagogy of the Neo-Liberal Paradigm

One of the patron saints of the new pedagogy is Paulo Freire, a pioneer of educational reform whose Latin American origins lend a special power to his teachings among the growing Hispanic population in California. Freire's teaching starts from the practice of *conscientization*—a kind of consciousness raising among small groups of students that is far more Socratic and participatory than the distance learning featured in *Software Landing*. By the late 1990s, however, the Marxist dimension of Freire's classic *Pedagogy of the Oppressed* no longer sits well with people whose consciousness has risen in the context of a new economy. Instead the influence of another patron saint of the new pedagogy, Hernando de Soto, the Peruvian author of *The Other Path,* leads to the substitution of entrepreneurial activism in place of political revolution. Freire's own process of *conscientization*, when carried out with college students who still answer Astin's survey saying they want to become very well off financially, leads to a pedagogy based on "action research" into the causes of poverty among the least advantaged and most numerous of California's Community College student body. If all things are systematically interconnected, then it will not do to pretend that education can cut itself off from daily life. The community becomes the text book; its problems our homework.

Tens of thousands of Community College students become directly involved in addressing problems of illiteracy, ill health, drug and alcohol dependency, crime and poverty. The nexus of issues that had once been separated under headings like Sociology, Public Health and Business Economics are, by the turn of the century, the focus of a new curriculum. The revolving door that joined colleges to corporations in *Education Inc.* now joins colleges to communities and small businesses. Learning in the Community Colleges is truly community based. College has ceased to be a place to escape from the nitty-gritty to pursue "higher learning", it has become instead a place to dive deeper into the reasons why the city is so often gritty.

In Houston, for example, students and faculty at recently renamed Barnett University manage to close the funding gap for higher education neither by increasing educational productivity through technology (the strategy of *Software Landing*) nor by raising revenues from the private sector (the strategy of *Education Inc.*). Though each of these strategies is employed to some extent, the more important change in the structure and funding of higher education comes from the freeing up of resources that had previously been spent on solving problems that are now directly addressed by educators and their students. This new strategy—which changes the relationship between higher education and the rest of society—was pioneered by educators like Marguerite Ross Barnett, the president of what had been called the University of Houston when she assumed leadership in 1990. Her leadership strategy was summarized in her *New York Times* obituary in 1992:

> *She had a reputation as a successful fund-raiser and a pragmatic academic who urged that urban universities play a dominant role in spurring economic growth and solving social problems in the same way that land-grant colleges of a century ago did in developing America's agricultural economy.*

"What will characterize the superb 21st century university," she said at her inaugural in 1990, "will be its ability to manifest and focus areas of unquestioned institutional excellence on the challenging issues of the day."

Her views were representative of a substantial shift in higher education as universities, once isolated from their locales, sought stronger connections to their surroundings. And in many ways, Dr. Barnett was seen as representing a new generation of education leader.

This change in the curriculum is in keeping with a paradigm shift that has transformed the social sciences and humanities. Sociologists no longer claim to be pursuing "value-free" research as Weber and Durkheim insisted. Cultural anthropologists engaged in examining the relationships between Southeast Asian, African American, White and Hispanic cultures no longer aspire to a disinterested objectivity. They now take for granted that no one can claim a God's-eye view. Most philosophers now agree with Thomas Nagel's critique of *The View From Nowhere* (the telling title of one of his books). The new theory of knowledge supports a pedagogy that is always rooted somewhere—in the communities peculiar to each community college.

History teachers, following the lonely lead of a few California faculty like Cal State Hayward historian Ted Roszak, now focus much of their research on the relationships between past, present and future. English teachers teach different literatures as they relate to the lives of their students. Foreign languages gain a new importance as everyday tools of communication in an increasingly global economy.

Very little inquiry is disinterested anymore. Consequently, education is much more interesting than it used to be. The new paradigm is rooted in a new theory of knowledge, one that does not separate subject from object or facts from values. Instead a scholarly appreciation for the systematic interconnectedness of subjects and objects, facts and values, makes it impossible for educators to claim the sort of institutional neutrality that college deans once brandished in the days when students demonstrated against the Vietnam war or apartheid in South Africa. Now it is the faculty who are dragging students out of their claims to neutrality (or apathy). Now the faculty are bringing their values to class, not to indoctrinate but to challenge and inspire.

Only the best and the brightest can get teaching jobs in the twenty-first century. Given the added responsibilities that teachers have now that values as well as facts are fair game, communities are very careful about who gets to teach—not just the brightest, but the best. Integrity and character are important issues among teachers to an extent unknown in the days when only politicians had to worry about their reputations. Here again it is the new appreciation for the interconnectedness of all things that forbids the compartmentalization of lives, just as it forbids the departmental dissection of a curriculum. Privacy is permitted and respected; but if one's private life is so reckless that bad consequences spill over into public scandal, then there is no easy recourse to the right of individual liberty—whether defended from the left or the right. Responsibility is more highly prized than the right to recklessness.

Continuing Education

By the end of the scenario period the paradigm for higher education has shifted. Higher education is no longer an extension of secondary education. It no longer consists in the caging of aging adolescents in classrooms where professors share arcane knowledge about the increasingly specialized subjects of their research. Instead the model is one of team teaching and team learning by responsible adults who won't waste their time or money on ineffective communicators.

When the student's time is valued, efficiency matters. In this scenario, a spreading outrage at the sense of wasted resources leads to concerns over our educational infrastructure. A new sense of responsibility replaces old short-term concerns.

This shift in time frame—from short-term gratification to long-term responsibility—is also linked to the aging of the population. Education—and re-education—is a lifelong experience, and it takes place in a whole range of settings. Using the tools of distance learning, students learn at home, on the job, while travelling, while on vacation.

With the pace of technological change and cultural change increasing every decade if not every day, the task of education becomes ever greater as the gap between nature and culture becomes ever wider. Each baby born into an older world has more to learn to catch up with a more advanced species. In *The New Educational Order* this massive task of perpetually re-educating the young and old of the species to keep up with the pace of change becomes one of the foremost items on the social agenda. What race relations were to the early sixties and the Vietnam war was to the late sixties, what feminism was to the seventies and environmentalism to the eighties, education becomes in the nineties, namely, the foremost item on the social agenda.

By the year 2005 the state of California has the fifth highest GDP of any country in the world, well ahead of England or Italy. California's citizens are not without problems. Racism is still an issue. Evil has not been eliminated. Mental illness has not been cured. Poverty has not been eradicated. Decadence has not disappeared. But for many who remember the Depression of 1991-94, California and its system of higher education looks like a different country. The problems that persist are being addressed by teachers and students who are focusing education directly on their amelioration.

Implications

Isolated bullet points would be inappropriate to capture the implications of a scenario whose logic stresses systematic interconnections and structural relationships. Better to conclude with a review showing the relationships among the salient features of the scenario. How is the neo-liberal synthesis related to the paradigm shift in the disciplines? How does the new pedagogy follow from the new social contract? And what will *The New Educational Order* mean to the various constituencies in higher education?

One way to capture both the systematic aspect of this scenario and its implications is to reflect on the centrality of learning to life in *The New Educational Order*. In different societies and in different times, different institutions assume a central role. Once the church was the central institution in many communities. Other candidates that have played the role of central institution include the royal court surrounding the king and, more recently, the marketplace. In order to appreciate the significance of the sea change in society assumed in this scenario, imagine that learning has replaced shopping as a leisure activity, and that the university has replaced the mall as a favorite hang-out.

Does *The New Educational Order* sound too utopian to be taken seriously? Not necessarily. The events in Eastern Europe show us that it can be morally irresponsible to concentrate only on worst case scenarios. Sometimes radical change is more realistic than incremental improvements that would be neutralized by the perpetuation of the existing order. Sometimes restructuring—Perestroika—is the most direct route from here to a better future.

How could so much social change take place in a few short years? Surely not by virtue of some new sense of duty or obligation to learn. No, this transformation follows the pleasure principle. The wedding of education, entertainment and community makes learning the most enjoyable and gratifying activity available to most people. Commercial TV and all the skills of the dream merchants of Hollywood are put into the service of learning. Following decades of materialism, a country glutted on the glories of *having things* finds that the diminishing returns of materialism lead directly to greater returns from *knowing*.

The gratifications of *knowing* are enhanced by a paradigm shift that transforms knowledge from a passive, spectral representation of objects at a distance (like watching old television and recording the world on videotape) to a much more active—interactive—involvement with the world and with other people. From participatory knowledge it is then a short step to participatory democracy: an active involvement in the civic life of the community. Where the old liberalism depended on a strong role for central government in setting policy, neo-liberalism substitutes local learning for centralized expertise. With the democratization of know-how and expertise, the decentralization of policy follows close behind. Site-based educational policy is a natural corollary of neo-liberalism and the new paradigm. If *Software Landing* made everywhere an Alexandria, *The New Educational Order* makes everywhere an Athens.

To those of us today who are still used to firm boundaries separating education from entertainment, *The New Educational Order* might sound impossibly utopian, as if vast numbers of people were to become intellectuals overnight. To appreciate the non-utopian plausibility of this scenario it is necessary to assume that the distinction we take for granted between education and entertainment very nearly disappears. Learning becomes enjoyable. Part of the joy of learning lies in the fact that it is no longer so purely cognitive. Instead, knowing is part of doing. History has less to do with memorizing dates than with making new history on the basis of a better understanding of past history. Sociology is about mending the social fabric. Reading and writing are not passive skills but active tools of communication. The community is our laboratory.

Of course the very features of this scenario that promise new successes in education are also features that create new burdens for education. The new centrality of educational institutions, their immediate engagement with the principle problems of society, pose challenges to educators that they have not had to cope with in the past. Precisely to the extent that colleges accept these challenges, they render themselves vulnerable to disputes and constituencies that formerly remained outside the walls of academe.

In response to the recent debate over multi-culturalism and political correctness, some voices have already risen to protect the university from becoming a battleground. As Louis Menand has written in a forceful article in *Harper's* ("What Are Universities For?" December 1991.), "the only way to prevent [the university from becoming a battleground] is for the university to renounce the role of model community and arbiter of social disputes that it has assumed, to ignore the impulse to regulate attitudes and expressions that are the epiphenomena of problems far outside the college walls, to stop trying to set up academic housing for every intellectual and political interest group that comes along, and to restrict itself to the business of imparting some knowledge to the people who need it."

If higher education were to enter *The New Educational Order*, then teachers and administrators must be prepared for more interaction with the world. Those who can, will do *and* teach. Students will find themselves more actively engaged in remaking the world. The practice of education will have less to do with passing on the past than with creating a new future. While this vision may have immense appeal to those who would like to see learning assume a more central role in our society, the demands it will place on educators should not be underestimated.

PART FOUR: Conclusions

Scenarios do not of themselves dictate a strategy for solving problems. But the range of issues covered in the previous scenarios, and the inter-relationships exposed by their contrasts, suggest certain patterns that planners can recognize. By playing out the distinct logics of three different scenarios, we gain a sense for certain trade-offs that are implicit in different policies.

In the first scenario we see the potential for cutting costs by improving productivity through the application of new information technology. In thinking through this scenario, however, it becomes clear that distance learning runs the risk of being insufficiently interactive for the students, and too heavily based on a star system for most faculty.

The second scenario closes the funding gap by raising revenues by better serving the interests of American business. Powerful forces in the environment—privatization, the Second Reformation—suggest that the commercial logic of the marketplace is bound to have a greater influence on educational institutions. Despite the obvious benefits of the revenues that can derive from closer relations with the corporate community, misgivings are likely to arise when it comes to giving greater weight to training rather than education, or to commercial development rather than basic research.

The third scenario assumes as much technology as the first, except with a greater emphasis on interactive groupware rather than one-way distance learning. The third scenario also assumes the active involvement of the business sector, only the revolving door between the private sector and higher learning opens onto small community-based businesses rather than to large corporations. Finally, the third scenario assumes a more activist—or interactivist—involvement in issues of social justice and community welfare. Here the danger is that we are asking educators to do more than they are prepared to do: become philosopher-kings-and-queens.

Each of these scenarios defines a horizon of opportunity: technological, economic, and social. But each horizon of opportunity has its price. In these concluding remarks we return to our two pre-determined elements—economics and demographics—and we take this opportunity for some final reflections on how the price of each scenario would fall on some of the different constituencies of higher education.

Economics

A recent report from the California Postsecondary Education Commission is uncompromising in its estimate of the fiscal crisis in publicly funded higher education: "Put bluntly, the State of California's budget is structurally ill-equipped to support either the short- or the long-term budgetary needs of postsecondary education." Over the longer term—the particular focus of this report—"Total State expenditures will grow at an annual rate of roughly 7.5 percent, whereas revenues will grow by only 6.9 percent per year." Without some fundamental change in the structure and funding of higher education, the gap between needs and resources can only widen; the stress on educators can only increase; the students' experience of higher education can only deteriorate.

Even as the dimensions of the crisis become clearer, the need for improvement becomes more vivid. As Governor Wilson put it in his State of the State address in early January, 1992, "Nothing we do can have a more profound and lasting impact on California's competitiveness than the quality of our schools."

We need schools to create wealth, but we need wealth to improve our schools. Where is the chicken, and where is the egg?

If citizens were convinced of the pay-off that better education would provide, they might be more willing to make the necessary investments. But declines in the percentage of households with school age children do not bode well for an electorate more willing to invest in education. In *The New Economic Role of American States* (Oxford University Press, 1988) Henton and Steven Waldhorn state, "Actions taken by public as well as private institutions in California clearly have made a difference in the economic development of the state".(p. 203) Further, "nearly all of California's growth has resulted from its favorable mix of industries, particularly within durable goods manufacturing, such industries as electrical equipment, transportation equipment (mostly aerospace), and instruments. These high growth industries are more heavily represented in California than in other states". p. 211)

Cut-backs in defense spending are prompting some to object that those who live by the Pentagon shall die by the Pentagon. But there are many applications for high technology beyond electronic warfare. Though unemployment figures are much higher now than when Henton and Waldhorn were conducting their research (mid- to late-eighties), over the long term their concluding observations with regard to California's commitment to education will retain their force: "The fact that the state of California made a conscious investment to ensure that its college and university system met the needs of local industry made for a readily available, skilled work force. Today, shortages in the number of skilled workers present a major constraint to the industry's ability to achieve its potential for growth".(p. 225)

Perhaps technology will lower the bill for better education. Perhaps business will pay the bill. Perhaps a more direct application of intelligence to problems will reduce the cost that must be paid. Whichever scenario we follow, the relationship between education and the economy will give us constant reminders of our success or failure at educating Californians.

Demographics

Under the Immigration Reform and Control Act of 1986, 1.6 million formerly undocumented aliens have become legalized residents of California. These immigrants, who make up five percent of the State's population, are but the first wave of many more "New Californians" who will populate the State over the coming decades. The impact of New Californians on the educational system will be felt at first in the K-12 and Community College systems, whose funding is provided for under Proposition 98.

Of our several scenarios, the first seems least likely to benefit New Californians, and for that reason the technology-fix of distance learning seems destined for rough political sledding in the state of California. *Education Inc.* has more to offer those with an interest in job training. But it is the third scenario, *The New Educational Order*, that may have the most appeal to minorities, for it is the third scenario that is most driven by a commitment to social justice. Further, there is an argument that can be made for an affinity between the goals and methods of multi-culturalism on the one hand and the emergence of a new paradigm on the other.

Though the argument hardly has the deductive force of a scientific proof, there is a growing convergence of opinion that the isolate-divide-and-conquer strategy of a command-and-control approach to nature does not represent the height of rationality. During recent decades a whole chorus of criticism has arisen to claim that the rationality of the secular Enlightenment that has dominated academic learning for centuries may represent not so much the height of rationality as the thinking style of history's most recent winners: white western males. Women, native Americans, people of color, and the classics of Oriental culture all join to object that relatedness may be more important than objective distance; complex synthesis may be more important than analysis of simple elements; the pattern that connects—individuals, peoples, and species to the earth—may be more important than the power of mind over nature. In place of the divide-and-conquer paradigm of western science, new constituencies in the debate over multi-culturalism remind us to relate-and-accommodate.

The white male masters-of-the-universe are losing ground to cultural influences that care more about ecology (or about Mother Earth), about intimacy, and about compassion. If there is a new paradigm emerging, it will be built from the connections between the values of traditional cultures and the newest discoveries in our laboratories. Recent advances in evolutionary theory suggest that the minimal unit of survival is never the fittest of rugged individuals, nor even a whole species, but always species-plus-environment. The newest science begins to give support to some of the oldest beliefs. Native Americans experienced the natural environment as sacred and not to be defiled. A survey by *Psychology Today* shows that Hispanics feel a greater responsibility to care for their elders than do Anglos. Perhaps Mexicans and Native Americans have something to teach North American narcissists about the limits of rugged individualism.

These connections between new developments in the sciences and the values of traditional cultures have not yet been carefully elaborated or drawn in detail. But there are enough pointers toward a new paradigm to suggest that higher education could get swept along on the wave of an intellectual revolution supported by a convergence of traditional cultures and new science. A paradigm shift on the scale of the Enlightenment could change the shape of daily life and accommodate to the global reality of multi-culturalism far better than the arrogance of the particular kind of rationality we have inherited from the Enlightenment.

And What Does It All Mean...

For Students?
The stresses evident in higher education today will not be relieved by incremental reforms. Unless there is fundamental change, students will face increased fees and/ or decreased course offerings.

If the future cleaves closest to *Software Landing*, students will need to be computer literate, though computer literacy will be far less daunting in the future than it is today. If anything like *Software Landing* actually comes to pass, information and communications technology will have become far more user friendly. Distance learning can flourish only if its tools are as common and as easy to use as the telephone or TV.

If the future is closer to *Education Inc.*, then students will have to look longer and harder to find courses that are not career oriented. Medieval history may become a luxury available at only a few private colleges and universities. The ideal of the well-rounded liberal arts education may shape the curriculum at a few private colleges, but public higher education in *Education Inc.* will turn the well-rounded liberal arts education into an anachronism.

If the future is closest to *The New Educational Order*, students will find themselves growing up faster than they do today. No longer will the groves of academe be at a distance from the street. The ivory tower will offer no respite from the problems of society. Reality will prove to be a harsh and difficult text. There is therefore reason to wonder whether students trying to escape the ghetto through higher education will be pleased to find themselves sent straight back to the ghetto for their first academic assignment. The students of the sixties called for relevance in higher education. The students of the nineties and the new millennium may wish that *The New Educational Order* were less relevant and more remote from society's problems.

In all of our scenarios the student body is almost certain to be older and more culturally diverse. Continuing education, whether on campus or through distance learning, will increase. Multi-culturalism will prevail. There is no turning back the clock on migration. North America will not send home her immigrants the way some European nations have tried to send home their southern European and non-European guest-workers.

For Faculty?

Unless there is fundamental change, faculty will see lower salaries and/or increased work loads. And ever more meetings to bring about the changes that would kick off one or another alternative scenario.

If the future cleaves closest to *Software Landing*, the faculty will have to master the new tools of educational technology. Like workers in other industries revolutionized by technological innovation, some will benefit from higher productivity, others will lose if they fail to keep up with their own learning. As mentioned in the implications section at the end of *Software Landing*, there is a significant danger in this scenario that a "star system" will make for a few big winners and a lot of losers if education comes to emulate the entertainment media in its employment practices.

If the future is closer to *Education Inc.*, then faculty will need to be more aware of the *marketability* of the skills they are offering their students. The gulf between business and education will be bridged, and the bridge will have a revolving door encouraging two-way traffic between the commercial and academic environments. This could mean an end to tenure in the academic world, or the beginning of sabbaticals in the business world. It is hard to know just what shape a closer relationship between business and academia will take, but clearly in *Education Inc.* the disdain for commerce among many of today's faculty will no longer be affordable.

In *The New Educational Order*, faculty will be hard pressed to defend the relevance and usefulness of their favorite fields of study. Though hardly comparable to the cultural revolution that put Chinese intellectuals into the rice paddies, the paradigm shift underlying *The New Educational Order* will put faculty on the front lines in the fight against injustice, poverty and other social ills.

In each of our scenarios it seems clear that faculty will need to become somewhat more technologically adept, more culturally tolerant, and more aware of events in the economic and social environment, particularly as they impinge on the politics of higher education. The job of teaching is not likely to get any easier, but the rewards may be greater if one or another scenario succeeds in breaking the current deadlock on funding. Particularly in the third scenario but for some in the other scenarios as well, there are grounds for hope that professors will become the high priests and priestesses of an information society.

For Staff?

Unless there is fundamental change in higher education, non-teaching staff will continue to suffer the cuts that have become commonplace following years of "bureaucratic bloat" and ratcheting growth. Whether rightly or wrongly accused, non-tenured staff are perceived as part of the problem rather than part of the solution when administrators fail to make ends meet in the budget process.

If the future cleaves closest to *Software Landing*, librarians will gain status as management of information systems (MIS) personnel. Admissions officers and career counsellors will gain greater prestige in *Education Inc*. And in *The New Educational Order* we can expect campus security and the dean's office to look more like a full-fledged local police precinct and judiciary system. As learning moves off-campus, new kinds of trouble will move on-campus.

For Administrators, Politicians and Citizens?

For the rest of us who are not directly engaged in teaching and learning, there are decisions to be made that will affect our taxes in the short term, the health of our economy in the medium term, and our quality of life in the longer term. The danger is that we sacrifice the long-term benefits to our reluctance to bear the short-term costs.

Administrators, legislators and other leaders need to remind the rest of the citizenry of the benefits that will accrue from a strong educational system. Precisely to the extent that the groves of academe stand at a distance from the rest of society, it is too easy for the rest of us to forget the importance of what happens behind those (sometimes) ivied walls. Individuals may have a vivid sense of the value of their own academic credentials, but society at large is less sure about the collective benefits of a better educated citizenry. It is this argument for the aggregate effect that is hard to make in a history that happens just once. But this is why today, standing in our single present, it is worth looking down at least three separate paths, three future histories, three alternative scenarios for the future of higher education.

Summary

Once again, scenarios by themselves do not solve problems. But they do highlight some of the challenges and opportunities. The preceding scenarios are intended to assist planners in breaking out of a "business as usual" mode of following the present's momentum into the future.

The momentum of the present leads toward increasing deficits and declining quality. The citizens of California have some hard choices to make: what price will we pay for better education, more social justice, and a stronger economy? How much can we depend on technology? Do we dare offer business a stronger hand? Are we prepared to politicize our universities? These are among the hard questions posed by a long look into the future of higher education in California.

By articulating some alternatives, we hope to have furthered the debate toward finding answers to these questions. Choices must be made. By expanding the range of possible choices, alternative scenarios can help clarify the consequences. But the choice, in the end, belongs to Californians. Higher education must change. That said, what tradeoffs are we willing to make for which rewards?

Afterword

As with Chapter 4, "Future Studies and the Human Sciences: The case for Normative Scenarios", this chapter, too, was written two decades ago. A lot has happened since. How do these scenarios hold up?

"Software Landing" is proceeding apace even if it has been nowhere near as rapid as some once expected. During the late 1990s, a lot of colleges and universities lost a lot of money trying to develop and sell educational software. Chastened by the boom and bust in "edutainment," the pace of software development flagged. But the promise is still there and Clayton Christensen has assembled some data points that suggest a new boom in the coming decade: "[These figures give] our best guess for the pace of substitution of online-delivered learning for live-teacher instruction. From 45,000 enrollments in fully online or blended-online courses in the fall of 2000, that number had grown nearly 22 times to 1 million by the fall of 2007. Roughly 70 percent of these were for high school students... Even with this rapid growth, however, online courses accounted for just 1 percent of all courses in 2007. Not much change is on the horizon if one projects linearly into the future. But when viewed from the logarithmic perspective, the data suggest that by 2019, about 50 percent of high school courses will be delivered online... The "flip" in the substitution curve will begin in about 2012." (*Disrupting Class*, McGraw Hill, 2008, pp. 98, 100.) While these figures are for secondary education, financial pressures on both students and campuses, combined with the new habits of highschool graduates, will mean that post-secondary education will also see a shift toward more online education.

The cogency of a scenario like "Education Inc." is evident in the meteoric rise of the University of Phoenix, which now enrolls more students than any other post-secondary education institution. Fueled by federally backed student loans, the increase in the number of colleges selling post-secondary education for a profit has transformed institutions like the University of Phoenix and Kaplan into the darlings of Wall Street over the past decade. Given the number of students unable to pay back their loans, some regard this new development as a bubble waiting to burst.

The road not taken is "The New Educational Order." We have not seen the kind of paradigm shift described in its early pages. Nor have we witnessed the "responsibility revolution" or "revolutionary de-maturing" on which it is based. Particularly in California where the state is facing a tremendous deficit, there's not much of a budget for "a new social contract." Nor do we see anything that looks like a "neo-liberal paradigm." Still, if neither "Software Landing" nor "Education Inc." has quite taken hold, the road not taken toward "The New Educational Order" still beckons.

10. Four Scenarios for the Future of Public Education in Seattle

By Roger Erskine and Jay Ogilvy

Published in a shorter version as lead article, Chapter One, in Scenarios in Public Policy, ed. Gill Ringland, John Wiley & Sons, 2002 pp. 11-19. Reprinted with permission of John Wiley & Sons Inc.

This chapter summarizes an innovative approach to strategic planning undertaken by the Seattle Education Association with the aid of Global Business Network, a research and consulting company specializing in the development of alternative scenarios for strategic planning.

Before the scenarios, Seattle's public schools were something of an embarrassment. Some blamed white flight to the suburbs. Seattle got hollowed out. Between 1980 and 1990, enrollment in Seattle's public schools dropped more than ten percent. The voters turned against the schools. School bond issues failed in every election from 1992 to 1996. And of course the union looked the worse for "the decline in public education".

After the scenarios Seattle passed two school bonds. Seattle got a terrific superintendent, John Stanford, who, precisely as it had been written in one of the scenarios, came out of the military. Enrollment has stabilized. Some schools have definitely turned around. There is a new 'can do spirit', and the union is known nationwide as showing leadership on behalf of education reform.

A 1999 issue of *Daedalus* was devoted to the question of public education's resistance to reform. In the lead essay, Yale professor Seymour Sarason argues that only a systemic approach that looks at all parts of the very complex system of public education has any hope of making lasting changes. "What are the parts of the system?" asks Sarason. "Teachers, school administrators, boards of education, state departments of education, colleges and universities, state legislatures and executive branches, the federal government, and parents."

As if in answer to Sarason, the Seattle scenarios project included representatives of many different constituencies on the scenario team. The scenario process itself was part of the process of reform. By joining the representative constituents of the public education system together as a scenario planning team, the project process began to implement one of its eventual strategic options, namely:

- Create a team with as much diversity as possible: old/young, male/female, senior/junior, white/black, different constituencies in the public for public schools, from the largest employer in Seattle, Boeing, to someone from City Hall, a successful businessman on the school board, several union leaders, an economist, and ten more selected for the range of their representation.

In order to arrive at a set of scenarios that highlight the critical uncertainties in Seattle's future, the scenario team developed a long list of relevant issues, then prioritized and aggregated some short lists to identify driving trends.

Here follows the original report for the Seattle Education Association, March 1995.

Seattle is hot. Its K-12 public education system is struggling. At a luncheon for members of Seattle's Consular Corps, the Discovery Institute solicited opinions about Seattle's strengths and weaknesses as a place for doing business. "Most believed that school systems in this area needed basic reform. Potential foreign investors worry that we are not keeping up in terms of educating students or the workforce, and that this will limit our otherwise excellent prospects for global competitiveness." (International Seattle, p. 18)

If Seattle is to maintain its upward trajectory as a gateway to the Pacific, as a breeding ground of musical trends, as a city to inspire romantic films, as the home of Boeing, Microsoft, the Mariners, the Seahawks, the Sonics, and a source of good coffee, in short, as one of the most attractive and vibrant cities in North America… then its schools must continue to improve. Improving a large and complex school system will take planning.

This report summarizes an innovative approach to strategic planning undertaken by the Seattle Education Association, the Washington Education Association, and the National Education Association with the aid of Global Business Network, a research and consulting company specializing in the development of alternative scenarios for strategic planning.

The report is divided into five parts:

- *First,* a description of the alternative scenario method of strategic planning.

- *Second,* the predetermined elements bound to show up in most scenarios for the future of Seattle.

- *Third,* a discussion of critical uncertainties driving the differences among the scenarios.

- *Fourth,* narrative descriptions of four scenarios.

- *Fifth,* a brief discussion of the strategic implications of the scenarios— necessarily brief, since this document is not supposed to bring closure to the debate over education in Seattle. It is intended instead to provoke debate over the implications of the scenarios.

Part One: The Scenario Method

In recent years the discipline of strategic planning has been undergoing a shift from the use of single-point forecasts toward the use of alternative scenarios. During the post-World War II economic expansion, the U.S. economy grew in a fairly orderly and reliable way. Plans could be made using extrapolations from the past and present. Since the 1970s, however, the environment has been more turbulent. From the oil shocks of the seventies, through a series of regulatory changes and accelerating technological developments during the eighties, the business environment has become progressively less predictable.

Scenario planning was developed in reaction to these circumstances. Alternative scenarios provide a way of focusing on the future without locking in on one forecast, which would probably be wrong.

What are Scenarios… and What are They Not

Scenarios are alternative environments in which today's decisions may be played out. They are not predictions. Nor are they strategies. Instead they are descriptions of different futures specifically designed to highlight the risks and opportunities involved in specific strategic issues.

Scenarios can help overcome anxieties about the lack of evidence regarding the future, for scenarios do not claim to be predictions. The point is not to gather evidence for some induction about a most probable future. The point is rather to entertain a number of different possibilities to better make reasoned choices among them.

We cannot know beforehand what the future will hold. So-called futurists cannot be seers. But we can see in the present several trends which, moving on their current course, will change the shape of public education over the next decade.

Some of the trends influencing urban education can be described as *predetermined.* Others are highly uncertain. Predetermined elements will show up in all scenarios. Critical uncertainties drive the differences among scenarios. Part Two contains a discussion of the predetermined elements that are likely to show up in all scenarios for the future of public education in Seattle. Part Three explores the critical uncertainties that differentiate scenarios one from another.

Part Two: Predetermined Elements

Seattle's Geography

Part of Seattle's unique geography, its status as a gateway to the Pacific, was underscored by the gathering of world leaders at the 1993 meeting of the Asia-Pacific Economic Cooperation summit. Seattle's volume of two-way global trade has increased dramatically over recent decades: up from $13.8 billion in 1977 to $74 billion in 1992. Based on a 1992 survey of 900 business executives, *Fortune* magazine rated Seattle "the best city for global business in the U.S.". (Nov. 2, 1992.)

Seattle also enjoys a local geography unlike many other cities. Its hills and dales, its islands and inlets, are uniquely suited to encourage a proliferation of urban villages. Many cities in the industrial midwest stretch flat as a doormat for miles and miles. Given the geography of the midwestern plains, cities spread like spider-webs from a dense inner core toward more sparsely settled suburbs. But Seattle doesn't suffer the same tendency toward cycles of central concentration and consequent decay. Seattle, strictly speaking, doesn't have a "downtown" the way other cities do.

Seattle's local geography is reflected in the demographics of its schools. Its elementary schools differ markedly from one another in the populations they serve, because elementary schools draw students mostly from their immediate neighborhoods. But most of the high schools serve many neighborhoods, from the heights where wealthier citizens enjoy more impressive views, to the valleys where lower-income residents live. Because there are many heights and many valleys distributed throughout King County, each high school serves a diverse population. This geographically enhanced diversity inhibits the kind of inequalities introduced when all of the poorer students are concentrated in a large downtown, while all of the wealthier citizens have taken flight to distant suburbs.

When faced with the worst of possible scenarios for the future of Seattle, those interviewed in the course of this project returned again and again to one or another version of a simple insight: "It's so beautiful. No matter how bad it gets, people will come here and stay here."

Seattle is blessed by its unique setting. Ever since David Denny and Doc Maynard first set foot on the soil that was to become the Emerald City, Seattle's citizens, rich and poor alike, have savored sweet air and incomparable views.

> There is something inherently democratic about Seattle. Stroll along the old waterfront, bump through the crowds at Pike Place Market, sit for lunch atop the Space Needle, or duck through the canyons of the business district, and you will find that unlike the intimate landscapes of New England—the miniature vistas around which anyone, with enough money, can build a fence—Seattle's setting is unencompassable. Even the homeless man who glimpses Rainier and Baker or scans the embarrassment of riches of the sound, the lakes, the mountains, can lay equal claim with the Angeleno yachting through the San Juans or the lawyer setting his precarious mansion on the slopes of the emerald shore.
>
> Andrew Ward, in *American Heritage*, April, 1994, p. 86

So Seattle's legendary problem has been keeping people away by telling them how often it rains. But despite the rain, Seattle *will* grow. According to the Mayor's Comprehensive Plan, by 2010, Seattle will need to add 146,600 jobs to the 469,802 jobs held in 1990. Nearly 100,000 of those jobs will be in finance, insurance, real estate, and services, and most of those will require well-educated workers.

Demographics

According to comparative statistics assembled by The Council of the Great City Schools (*National Urban Education Goals: Baseline Indicators, 1990-91*), Seattle's school district is the ninety-third largest in the nation. Serving a population of 516,269, Seattle's public schools had 43,601 students in the 1990-91 school year—a drop of 10.2 percent since 1980. 78.3 percent of Seattle's 5-17 year-olds are enrolled in public school—a figure that remains relatively stable despite the increasing number of private schools and learning programs available.

24.3 percent of Seattle's students are African-American, 22.6 percent Asian or Pacific Islander, and 6.5 percent are Hispanic. 43.5 percent are white. [5]

36.5 percent qualify for free or reduced-price lunch; 9.8 percent are limited-English proficient (LEP); 75 different languages are spoken by Seattle's residents. 7.2 percent of Seattle's students are disabled, requiring some form of special education.

Seattle is not immune to broader demographic trends that are having a major impact on students' readiness to learn. As educational research has shown again and again, particularly the work of James Comer at Yale, parent involvement is a key to educational success. But parent involvement declines when the number of parents declines.

Consider some statistics from the Carnegie Corporation Report on the state of children (*New York Times*, April 12, 1994):

	1960	1990
	%	%
Children born to unmarried mothers	5	28
Children under 3 living with one parent	7	27
Children under 3 living with both parents	90	71
Children under 18 experiencing the divorce of their parents	<1	49
Children under 18 living in a one-parent family	10	25
Married women with children under 6 who are in the labor force	18.6	60

This last statistic, dramatic in its extent and rapidity, raises an issue: the impact of the women's movement on education. Not only is mom less likely to be at home when children return from school, less likely to be there to insist that kids finish their homework before turning on the television; but further, mom is less likely to be a teacher herself. Prior to 1970, teaching was one of the more likely careers for women. Today there are many other careers that are open to women.

Boeing

> *Every Boeing job produces about three other jobs, and in King and Snohomish Counties, more than one of every two manufacturing jobs is involved in airplane production.*
> John Hamer and Bruce Chapman, *International Seattle: Creating a Globally Competitive Community, p. 7*

Boeing's importance for Seattle is predetermined. Boeing's economic health over the long term is not. As has been said of General Motors and America, what's good for Boeing is good for Seattle. But the questions surrounding Boeing's future launch us quickly into the realm of the uncertain: global economics, national competitivity, and a host of other issues that are highly uncertain.

Part Three: Critical Uncertainties

In order to arrive at a set of scenarios that highlight the critical uncertainties in Seattle's future, a scenario team composed mostly of educators and policy makers in Seattle developed a long list of relevant issues, then prioritized and aggregated some short lists to identify driving trends. The long list follows, together with votes that were cast by team members according to the criteria of importance and uncertainty:

14	Community support
10	Brain research/learning
4	Family economics
2	Mobility/transiency
10	Multiple realities/traditions/values—diversity of population
6	Bio-medical ethics/potentials
10	State/federal/local regulations
4	Business community involvement
2	Health of downtown
17	Telecommunications
3	Education employees: teachers, staff
25	Social fabric/community
7	Societal attitudes toward parenting and children
3	Religion/God
17	Balkanization comes home: intolerance, separatism
20	Resistance to change
3	Mistrust/cynicism of bureaucracies
10	Funding
14	New technologies
2	Potential disparity of access to info/tech for learning
4	No roadmap/success stories
8	Security/violence: in school, in society

23	Competing interests for funding, attention, mindshare
2	Civic/personal responsibility among students
9	Community/system accountability
3	Teacher status/esteem/respect
1	De/Re-segregation and busing
5	Flexibility of district
1	Public understanding of K-12 outcomes
9	Individual Education Programs—IEP
14	Where does education happen?
6	From individual learning to team/social learning: from academic achievement to social achievement
3	Virtual reality vs. real "hands-on"
2	China, PacRim growth
10	Global economy's impact on aerospace industry
3	Nuclear potential of small countries
1	Action research used
5	What if U.S. falls behind? Sputnik syndrome
2	Shifting age mix of students: tough, demanding customers
2	Who is client? family, community?
8	Education for what?
7	Middle class abandons public schools
6	Environmental crisis? sustainability
1	What if no change?
13	Changed relationship of public/private sectors

Some of the items in this list are closely related to one another. A discussion of the top scoring items, together with closely related issues, yielded the following groupings, which then determined the axes of a scenario matrix:

25	Social fabric/community
17	Balkanization comes home
14	Community support
8	Violence/security
64	**Horizontal axis of a scenario matrix labeled "social fabric" from "turbulent" to "healthy"**

20	Resistance to change
17	Telecommunications
14	New technologies
14	Where does education happen?
65	**Vertical Axis labeled "rate of change" from "slow/resistant" to "rapid/embracing"**

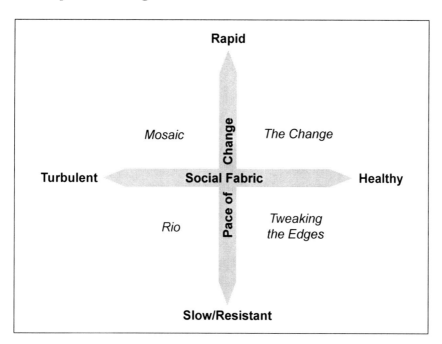

Also receiving significant priority votes were the following key factors:

23	Competing interests for funding
10	Funding

These economic factors are captured in the quadrants of the scenario matrix as follows: the greatest economic hardship occurs in the lower left quadrant, next worst in lower right, next best in upper left, best in upper right.

With these driving trends determining the skeletal logics of four distinct scenarios, the scenario team and GBN then put flesh on the bones of those logics by drafting four narratives. The scenarios weave together many of the key factors from the long list, but cast them in slightly different constellations showing the dynamics of interaction among the many variables influencing education.

The following scenarios are written in the past tense, from the perspective of 2004. In reading these scenarios it is important to remember that they are not predictions, but stories. These stories are not mere fantasies. The narratives are interrupted by several boxes including research on the workings of relevant driving forces in the past and present. But when it comes to the future, the best "descriptions" we can give are carefully structured narratives that offer a sense of what might happen if we take certain initiatives… or fail to take them.

What if…

Part Four: Scenarios

The Mosaic

Upper-left: Fairly high rate of change in a turbulent social environment
In this scenario, significant advances in technology and educational reform come to the few but not to the many. Riding a reasonably strong economy and continued interest in Seattle from other parts of the world, Seattle's citizens are too busy to worry about a comprehensive plan for education. Piecemeal reforms favor the best of schools while continued decay afflicts the worst.

Looking back on the go-go years of the late 1990s, it's easy to see why the citizens of Seattle ignored the public school system. They were too busy. There was too much money to be made in too little time. There were better things to do than worry about other people's children. And besides, if a family really wanted an excellent education for its children, good schools could be found.

The economic recovery of 1993-94 continued into the boom of 1995-96. Boeing's 777 was a hit in the global market for large passenger planes, and Microsoft's market share in software peaked in 1996 after the government dropped its antitrust action. Bill Gates's book on the information superhighway appeared in 1996 and had a major influence on the architecture of a system that not so incidentally ran on Microsoft software. Times were good in Seattle in the late '90s.

The national economy was on a roll as well. By the late '90s the middle class was starting to gain real increases in disposable income for the first time since the early 1970s. But if wealth was finally trickling down from the top quintile of the workforce—those whom Robert Reich calls "the fortunate fifth"—it never reached those in the bottom quintile: the urban poor. The embattled healthcare reform effort of the early 90s absorbed so much energy and political capital from the Clinton administration that they never got around to welfare reform. And the Republican administration that came in in 1996 had other fish to fry.

The same election that brought Senator Dole the presidency also brought a Charter school initiative to Washington state. By the beginning of the school year in 1997, fifteen charter schools opened their doors in Seattle. Several were managed by Whittle's Edison Project, which chose Seattle as a "loss leader" for its new school designs. Benno Schmidt concluded that Seattle would be a good place to create a success story, so he poured a disproportionate share of his Nashville corporation's resources into four schools in Seattle's suburbs.

Meanwhile Seattle's urban schools suffered a continuing slide into decrepitude. Old buildings, aging teachers, and dispirited students witnessed increasing violence in city schools. Behind the headlines about increasing numbers of crack babies, the remaining occupants of poor neighborhoods saw the continuing flight of bright students and teachers toward the suburbs. Under the pressure of gentrification, Seattle's poor were pushed further out, filling in the area between Lynnwood and Blaine.

Out in the suburbs, as well as in some of the urban charter schools, a new spirit of innovation and creativity stimulated a whole range of educational reforms. Not all worked equally well, and some attributed improved student test scores less to the reforms themselves than to a "Hawthorne effect," named after the famous experiments at Western Electric where the mere fact of much bally-hooed changes in working conditions had more influence than the changes themselves: turn up the lights, productivity improves; turn them back down—and study the effects—and productivity improves still further. So it was in some of the suburban and charter schools. The mere fact of renewed attention from parents and teachers may have had as much influence as the changes themselves, from revised calendars to new technologies. But whatever the real causes, the effects in most of the reform-minded schools were the same: improved test scores, even as scores in the forgotten urban schools were declining.

In response to a series of newspaper stories about Seattle's urban poor, city hall made a valiant attempt to integrate social services with an eye toward improved delivery of benefits. But the effort was too little too late. The state's citizens had already voted to lift the lid on local levies in order to allow wealthier districts to pour more money into their local schools. And too little state money was left to distribute to districts with poor tax bases. Even though state tax revenues benefited from the strong economy, spending on police and prisons came first.

Urban Sanctuaries

A recent book by Milbrey W. McLaughlin of Stanford's Center for Research on the Context of Secondary School Teaching is titled *Urban Sanctuaries*. Her book is about programs for disadvantaged minority youths in depressed, crime-ridden inner cities. The following quotations are taken from a review in *Education Week*, April 6, 1994. The good news is that:

> *These youths are desperate to get involved in something positive... The pervasive media image of inner-city youths as undisciplined, lazy, and unwilling to stop their destructive behavior... is absolutely wrong.*

Her research looked at what differentiates effective groups—her urban sanctuaries—from ineffective programs.

> *What the researchers found in these environments, rife with crime and poverty, were oases—safe havens not generally listed in any formal directory of youth programs...*

> *"The major message we want to get across is that perspective really matters," McLaughlin says. If adults were to stop viewing young people as something to be fixed and controlled and, instead, helped enable their development, there would be "phenomenal change" in their lives and society in general, she argues.*

> *What makes one YMCA empty and another down the block bustling with activity is, in part, the degree of youth involvement in the program, McLaughlin says...*

> *Many of the teenagers in the study reported feeling ostracized in school, where little that was taught seemed relevant to their lives outside the classroom...*

> *"When school was mentioned, it was almost always mentioned in negative terms," says McLaughlin, who considers herself "pro-school." Nevertheless, she contends that the teachers at inner-city schools who arrive at 8am and leave at 2pm often have "no idea who these kids are".*

> *"Educators say, 'Who are these families? What are these neighborhoods?'" McLaughlin says. The researchers failed to find "a single example" of positive institutional collaboration between schools and local youth activities in their five years of research, she says.*

For educators, the bad news is this loss of contact between teachers and the students they are trying to educate. McLaughlin's research is optimistic to the extent she shows that there is hope for troubled youths in urban ghettoes; but her research offers a sad commentary on our current schools' capacities for satisfying that hope.

Other research on state initiated reforms offers a similarly bleak view of down-from-the-top initiatives. In New York City, efforts to link social services in "community schools" haven't worked nearly as well as the grassroots initiatives described by McLaughlin. The hope was that "on-site coordination of educational, social, and health services" might lead to the enhancement of each. But a study by the Bruner Foundation found "no evidence of a systematic effect attributable to the community schools programs". (*Chronicle of Higher Education,* March 9, 1994.)

Likewise, an article entitled "State Reform: Where We Have Come, Where We Are Going," (*Education Week*, March 2, 1994.) summarizes a long report, Mandating Academic Excellence (*Teachers College Press*, 1993.): "The findings confirm a rather pessimistic view that state initiated changes in graduation requirements are largely symbolic initiatives, serving to pacify a public disenchantment with educational outcomes."

The results of all this research pose a paradox: on the one hand we would like to find some high leverage magic bullet that could transform public education across the board and raise test scores dramatically within the decade; on the other hand, all the evidence seems to suggest that grassroots initiatives are not only the most effective but also the least replicable. We have not yet found the social analog of DNA: some administrative mechanism for replicating successful local initiatives.

By the end of the scenario period Seattle has become a city of enclaves and sanctuaries, some rich, some poor, but all in uneasy relations with one another. A sense of commonwealth has somehow been lost. Real estate values reflect sharp and abrupt differences among a mosaic of neighborhoods whose diverse schools function as magnets for wealth or poverty. Independent Education Plans are in place, enabling the smart to get smarter and the slow to get slower. Bilingual education is on the increase as if in public acknowledgment of the lack of political will to integrate all students into the same American experience.

Because the range of educational offerings is so diverse—public and private, vanguard schools and traditional classrooms, hi-tech and low—parents are hard-pressed to sort it all out. Rather than hiring tutors who might help their children acquire basic skills, parents find themselves paying handsome fees to a new breed of consultants whose expertise lies not in teaching but in navigating the complex maze of options.

Teachers, for their part, are equally challenged by the many offerings. They find they have to specialize in new ways, not just according to disciplines, but according to methods of pedagogy, clever use of non-professionals, differentiated staffing, less tenure, and screening of their personal values for their appropriateness to different approaches to schooling. Since the traditional lines between management and labor have become blurred by the diversity of governance processes, the role of the union has shifted from one of protecting traditional interests through collective bargaining to providing information to individuals trying to navigate their unique paths through the new profession. It's confusing out there!

The new mosaic of educational offerings has created a highly competitive, highly entrepreneurial atmosphere. Some are beginning to doubt whether public education can survive at all in the face of the rising tide of privatization. Defenders of public education point to the increasing replication of services within Seattle—an inefficiency that might be eliminated by stronger control from a central office. But people seem to be willing to trade systemic efficiency for local effectiveness. The only "systems" they trust these days are private corporations, not governments.

Whittle's hopes for a success story from Seattle are partially realized, but only partially. Two of his schools are doing very well, but the other two show no improvement. Scores of researchers have descended upon Seattle from graduate education departments around the country. There will be dozens of dissertations dissecting each and every reform in Seattle's rich ecology of educational experimentation. From the corporate school at Microsoft to the charter schools around town; from the learning programs in local prisons to the on-the-job training program at Boeing, dozens of experiments have deployed a range of technologies and governance styles. Good teachers are being differentially rewarded, and some teachers are undergoing retraining. But the main story is diversity.

Among the most innovative and widely watched experiments is the bold approach taken by the new principal at Ballard, retired army Colonel Sam Gardiner. Sam decided that one set of problems deserved another as its solution, so he tackled two problems at once with a vanguard school at Ballard. The threat of violence among adolescent males was making teachers and other students wish for reinforcements; meanwhile there were many adult males who were under-educated and under-employed. So Sam decided to put the two groups together in mixed age, all-male classrooms and learning journeys. Blending experiences from Outward Bound and boot camp to apprenticeship programs and traditional classroom learning, Sam created a program that allowed the older students to keep the kids in line, while the younger students gave their older classmates some experience in exercising responsible leadership.

Seattle has become a testing-ground for educational experimentation, and as such, the eyes of the nation are focused on its schools. Unfortunately, some experiments fail. And worse, those urban schools that remain untouched by the spirit of reform cannot claim the status of intentional "controls". They were just forgotten. And they are sliding ever further down the slippery slope toward urban and educational decay.

Rio

Lower left: slow change, turbulent environment

This scenario represents the worst case: Seattle's entire public school system sliding into the morass that only a few schools entered at the end of the first scenario. Buffeted by bad times economically, and unredeemed by energetic reforms, Seattle's public schools follow the pattern set by urban public schools in cities like Detroit, New York, and Washington, D.C.

Could the schools have been saved? Looking back, it's hard to say. Some of the forces at work were beyond the control of Seattle's citizens. But they might have known. They might have anticipated and protected themselves from the several storms that first took shape in far off climates before blowing into the Pacific northwest.

First came the economic drought caused by America's mishandling of trade relations with the Southeast Asian economies. Conflicts over trade with Japan were handled every bit as badly as conflicts over human rights with China. By pushing our own interests with each of the eastern powerhouses so strongly, we managed to push them together. The twenty-first promises to be the Asian century now that Japan, China, Korea, Australia, and the ASEAN bloc have established themselves as the strongest of the three empires—the second being an expanded European Union and the third, NAFTA plus South America.

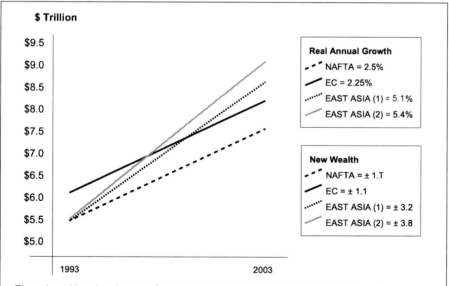

These broad-brush estimates of regional economic growth were put together by economists at the Deutche Bank. The two lines for East Asia represent a relatively conservative path (1) and a more conservative path (2). In either case, East Asia creates at least as much new wealth over the decade as Europe and NAFTA combined.

The Three Empires function as three separate economies, each as large as the entire global economy of the 1980s, each separated from the other by cultural conflicts and high tariffs. Seattle, whose hope in the 1990s had been to serve as America's gateway to the Pacific, now suffers from having lost its comparative advantage over other U.S. cities. Portland and Vancouver are suffering a similar fate, but somehow they seem to be maintaining more traffic in and out of their ports.

Second came the weakness of the local and domestic economies. Dragged down by Boeing's loss of sales to the other two Empires, and weakened by the lackluster performance of the American Empire, Seattle's local economy stuttered and stopped growing. The downtown area suffered gradual but continual deterioration. Tax revenues fell along with personal incomes. Voters felt a pinch on their pocketbooks so they defeated every bond and levy put in front of them. Nor were they about to repeal the restrictions imposed by 601. With healthcare and prisons making more urgent demands on the shrinking pool of tax revenues, public schools lacked the funds they needed to take advantage of new technology. The pressing exigencies of crime and ill-health drained off resources originally intended for education.

While these economic storms were arguably beyond the control of anyone, Seattle's response could have been better. Given the Washington school system's legal protection against economic downturns, a strong sense of community surrounding the schools might have survived economic hard times as well as Seattle's citizens survive the rain. But no: the hard times proved that Seattle's hopes were only fair weather hopes. Rather than anticipating trouble, Seattle entered the last half of the '90s on a high tide of optimism. Nothing wrong with high hopes, but where were the contingency plans when the national economy went south? Caught out on several highly leveraged limbs, Seattle's city government, its businesses, and its citizens found themselves scrambling to call in debts, both moral and financial. The city's economy imploded in 1998, and so did its sense of social justice. Only bankruptcy lawyers, police, and turnaround experts had reliable jobs.

As often happens in recessions, the poor were hit the hardest. And they were least capable of effective response. So stress turned to violence, on the streets and in the schools. The school board was divided over almost everything, including the best measures to take in response to violence. Caught in administrative gridlock at every turn, Seattle's schools slid into disorder. Like Seattle's bridges, her schools as well went on a lean diet of maintenance while those in charge waited for tax revenues to return to normal. But they never did. Normalcy seems a distant memory in 2004.

By the turn of the century teachers in the city were retiring, quitting, or moving to the suburbs in alarming numbers. The downtown schools were getting too rough for comfort, much less learning. Site councils bloomed as many neighborhoods moved to fill the power vacuum left by a dysfunctional school board. But for every five site councils that bloomed, four wilted within months as parents and teachers confronted the true measure of the catastrophe they faced. The demise of many site councils followed a logic of shifting power that had a history going back to the 1970s.

Riding the tide of anti-government sentiment that had been rising ever since Watergate in the '70s and the push toward privatization in the eighties, the parents of the '90s resented but could not resist the increasing role of government in education. While local autonomy had been popular in the '70s and '80s, the late nineties saw voter preferences shifting toward more centralized control. The passage of the Clinton administration's Goals 2000 package in 1994 added momentum to the movement for national standards. As if frightened by their loss of power to the federal government, state legislatures then seized what power they could from local municipalities. And so the trend toward centralized control cascaded from the federal level to the state level and on down to city boards of education.

Seattle's board attempted a rearguard action against the power of the state legislature and the imposition of national standards. But the board's internal politics kept it from operating effectively. The superintendent and the school board were locked in a hopeless gridlock of mutual vetoes. In the 1996 elections, two of the victorious candidates for the school board ran on sharply opposed planks on behalf of strong special interests, one a born-again partisan of the Christian right, the other a young community organizer somewhere to the left of Jerry Brown. While all the other more moderate candidates got lost in the noise, these two very vivid campaigners garnered most of the votes, creating a school board more contentious and sharply divided than any in Seattle's history.

In addition to the school board, other community activists entered the fray over education. Competing plans were developed, only to suffer death by a thousand duck bites. Too many people could say no and nobody could say yes to any attempt at systemic reform. The business community abandoned hope long before 2002, when the school board appointed its fifth superintendent since Kendrick. In the autumn of 2002 the state moved in to take over the public schools. The move was a rearguard action, not an act of vision—more like the imposition of marshal law after a disaster than a bold step into the future. Olympia's "New Deal" included a lot of security; a number of joint use agreements between the city, the school system, and other social service agencies; and more bureaucracy than the national health plan.

Washington's New Deal of 2003 didn't please many people. Parents were left out of the planning process for their children's schools. The state's plans were driven more by budget constraints than by clever ideas about learning. The state had to streamline its services by combining its youth services, crime prevention, and healthcare under a single administrative umbrella.

By the turn of the century employers were finally shouldering the burden of insurance premiums for millions of workers—and the burden was heavy on both businesses and municipalities. That burden was part of what was behind the wave of bankruptcies in the late '90s. Small business owners, especially those who had put aside a nest egg to retire on, found it less profitable to stay in business than to retire. Many small business owners concluded that it was better to be on the side of the receivers than the givers once the government got into the business of redistributing wealth. And once businesses started shutting down and unemployment started shooting up, the government was forced to become the employer of last resort.

Once the state stepped in to act as surrogate parents to run the school system, real parents redoubled their efforts to maintain the current system. Finding the state's bureaucrats even less responsive to influence than the former school board, many parents chose to remove their children from public schools. Like those disillusioned businesses that began to establish their own schools for their employees' children, many neighborhoods and churches set up their own elementary schools and day-care facilities. Older students flocked to Sylvan Learning Centers and other remedial programs that promised better educational outcomes than the local high schools.

For those left in the state-run public high schools, the curriculum looks like a cross between army boot camp, reform school, and vocational training. Security is intense. Most schools have metal detectors and armed guards. Ethnic tensions are high. The class of 2004 at Nathan Hale contains only 15 percent of those who entered as freshmen, so severe have problems of teenage pregnancy and dropouts become. At West Seattle some teachers are wearing bullet-proof vests. Graffiti covers the walls at Chief Sealth. Franklin is surrounded by barbed wire.

The teachers unions have hunkered down in a desperate, defensive posture, seeking strength in solidarity rather than numbers. New teachers are hard to find. Young people are not entering the profession of public education. Private schools are proliferating, but their teachers do not join the union. And others are leaving the public system by other routes. In 1999, Magnolia secedes from the district.

In keeping with the state centralization of the public education system, the Washington Education Association is subsidizing the Seattle Education Association. The issues that preoccupy the union these days have less to do with merit pay than with combat pay; less to do with teaching and learning, and more to do with the inclusion of variously disabled students in classrooms where already over-burdened teachers cannot handle their special needs.

The excitement that had moved Seattle's citizens in the early 1990s seems a distant memory in 2004. Even as many eastern cities are digging themselves out of the slump they had suffered in the closing years of the twentieth century, Seattle seems destined to slide still further down the slippery slope those older cities had traveled toward violence, poverty and unemployment. This scenario concludes with a cadence of gunfire and the sound of breaking glass.

Tweaking the Edges

Lower right: slow change, healthy environment

This is a scenario in which the economy creates jobs fast enough to keep the lid on any incipient social unrest. Never provoked to a boil, the discontent of the underprivileged simmers throughout the '90s and no major reforms rock the school system. Driven by global economic forces and local demographic polarization, this scenario comes to a branch point: by the late '90s, more of the same is insufficient. Depending on choices and conditions in the late '90s, this scenario leads either down toward Rio, or up toward The Change. Because this is an inherently unstable scenario that splays toward other scenarios halfway through, it is rendered less through a continuous narrative, and more through analyses of the local and global forces leading to its demise.

Seattle threatened to become the victim of its own success. Lulled into smug self-satisfaction by listening to its far-flung reputation, Seattle's citizenry tried to coast through the '90s on sheer momentum. "Don't fix it if it ain't broke," was the typical response to movements for reform, and the unstated premise was, of course, that Seattle's schools were far from "broke".

The economic recovery that began in 1993 continued modestly throughout the decade. By tweaking interest rates, the Fed managed to damp the normal cycles of economic boom and bust. As if mimicking an economy on an even keel, Seattle's students' test scores neither rose nor fell between 1994 and 1998. Nor did Seattle's crime rate rise or fall. Was this eerie equilibrium the calm before a storm, or the achievement of social stability?

It is not as if nothing happened during the mid-'90s. Newspaper editors found plenty to write about. But the momentum of the past and present was ever so much stronger than any clearly visible forces for change or renewal. An aging teaching staff held the course before many were to retire in the late '90s. Incremental reforms attracted any energy that might have otherwise have been expended on more radical change. Money that might have gone toward significant reforms was siphoned off toward developing standards for accountability. Most attention went towards doing things right rather than questioning whether we were doing the right things. Efficiency ranked higher than effectiveness. Emblematic of the logic of this scenario's early years, a program in conflict resolution was the most successful educational reform introduced during the mid-'90s. Seattle's schools excelled at keeping the lid on forces for change.

Beneath the relatively calm surface of polite conversations about the future of Seattle, however, deeper forces in technology, demographics, and the global economy were pushing the tectonic plates of history and society to shear along fault lines that focused on Seattle. For example, as Saskia Sassen showed in *The Global City: New York, London, Tokyo* (Princeton University Press, 1991) the influences of communications technology and the globalization of the economy lead toward a two-tiered society. The growth of the financial and service sectors in place of the globally dispersed manufacturing sector creates high paying jobs at the top of the economy and low-paying service jobs at the bottom of the economy, but few jobs for the middle class. As a global city, Seattle finds itself caught in the grip of an inexorable logic pulling her citizenry toward a two-tiered society.

While Sassen's book is primarily focused on the evolution of the global financial market in London, New York, and Tokyo, the argument she develops is relevant to any city whose economic activity is largely devoted to products or services that are competing in a global marketplace, and are therefore subject to the dynamics of the global marketplace.

Sassen argues that the globalization of certain industries has entered a new phase that is different from the proliferation and decentralization of certain industries that took place in the late nineteenth and early twentieth centuries. The extent of this proliferation, and the availability of high-speed information technology, has led to a wave of re-centralization: not a geographic concentration of industries, but a re-centralization of the *coordination functions* of complex global industries.

> Cities such as Detroit, Liverpool, Manchester, and now increasingly Nagoya and Osaka have been affected by the decentralization of their key industries at the domestic and international levels... [T]his same process has contributed to the growth of service industries that produce the specialized inputs to run global production processes and global markets for inputs and outputs. These industries—international legal and accounting services, management consulting, financial services— are heavily concentrated in cities such as New York, London, and Tokyo. We need to know how this growth alters the relations between the global cities and what were once the leading industrial centers in their nations. Does globalization bring about a triangulation so that New York, for example, now plays a role in the fortunes of Detroit that it did not play when that city was home to one of the leading industries, auto manufacturing?

However true this argument may be of New York vis-á-vis Detroit, might it also be true of Washington vis-á-vis Seattle? However much Seattle's fate may have been in its own hands in the past, Sassen's argument suggests that many of the management decisions relating to global coordination are now made elsewhere.

Sassen's argument has implications for the structure of the labor market in global cities:

> There is a vast body of literature on the impact of a dynamic, high-growth manufacturing sector in the highly developed countries, which shows that it raised wages, reduced inequality, and contributed to the formation of a middle class... [But] the new structure of economic activity has brought about changes in the organization of work, reflected in a shift in the job supply and polarization in the income distribution and occupational distribution of workers. Major growth industries show a greater incidence of jobs at the high- and low-paying ends of the scale than do the older industries now in decline.

Sassen's argument adds important subtleties to the controversy over whether global competition is driving down wages in the U.S. The issue of global competitivity has been analyzed in Michael Porter's *The Competitive Advantage of Nations* and intensely debated during the controversy over NAFTA. It seems intuitively obvious that American workers are being hurt to the extent that they find themselves competing with foreign labor willing to accept lower wages. But the story is more complex than that, involving as it does the lower prices American consumers pay for goods that are produced abroad by inexpensive labor.

Paul Krugman has argued that global competition is not the issue, and does not explain the downward pressure on wages in the manufacturing sector. (See Krugman and Lawrence, "Trade, Jobs and Wages: Blaming foreign competition for U.S. economic ills is ineffective. The real problems lie at home," *Scientific American,* April, 1994, pp. 44-49; Krugman, "Competitiveness: A Dangerous Obsession," *Foreign Affairs, Vol. 73, No. 2,* March/April, 1994; and his book, *Peddling Prosperity: Economic Sense and Nonsense in the Age of Diminished Expectations,* W.W. Norton, 1994.)

Sassen, Porter, and Krugman have all analyzed and integrated *immense* amounts of data into their arguments. Sorting out the relative weights of globalization and the impact of new technologies is a very complex business. But a synthesis of their respective arguments seems to point in the following direction: it is not simply a matter of low-paid foreign workers forcing down the wages of American workers. Rather, global competition is *changing the mix* of the labor force, squeezing the middle, and expanding the demand both at the top and the very bottom of the labor pool. This conclusion gains further support from Robert Reich's references to "the fortunate fifth" at the top of the labor pool.

What does all of this mean for Seattle? For one thing it helps to explain the stratification evident in this scenario. Increasing economic polarization is in part attributable to global economic factors over which the citizens of Seattle have no control. What they *can* control, however, is Seattle's overall "altitude" in the increasingly tall "building" that represents the increasingly stratified global economy. The fact of stratification is incontestable. The "floors" any given community occupies—and how it handles the interrelationships among its several "floors"—are matters very much in the control of the members of a community. But this question leads to another: how can urban school systems deal with the increasing inequalities between cities and their suburbs? Inequalities between rich and poor within the city limits are one thing; inequalities between those in the city and those in the suburbs are another.

The following collage of quotes makes an argument for focusing not just on Seattle alone, but on surrounding counties as well. The point is to see the potential problems of Seattle in the context of a broad movement toward the urbanization of poverty.

> According to the National League of Cities, per capita income for central-city residents, which was 96 percent of suburbanite income in 1973, declined to about 84 percent by 1990. —"New Hopes for the Inner City," in *Fortune,* September 6, 1993, p. 83

> In 1979, 62 percent of America's poor people lived in metropolitan areas. By 1987, this percentage rose to 72... In the cities themselves, the percent below the poverty line went from 17.3 percent in 1980 to 19.0 percent in 1990. This amounts to a 14.7 percent increase in persons below the poverty line in the fifty [largest] cities from 1980 to 1990... 34.4 percent of all female headed households in the 50 cities fell below the poverty line, according to the 1990 census. —*A Report on the Plight and Promise of America's Urban Centers,* The American Cities Project, National Education Association and The FMR Group, Sept. 20, 1992, pp. 22f

The authors of this well researched report then leap a little too quickly to what seems to be a plausible conclusion:

> The simple fact is that we cannot improve the overall American condition unless we make an immediate and concentrated effort to better the lot of people living in our cities. Individuals and organizations which seek to make progressive changes in the nature of American society must focus their resources on the cities. (p. 73.)

But there is some question as to whether cities by themselves can be saved. Take the exemplary case of Atlanta:

> Atlanta is home to the nation's most ambitious urban-renewal project. The Atlanta Project, conceived by former President Jimmy Carter in late 1991, focuses on 20 poverty 'clusters' throughout the metropolitan area, with the lofty aim of lowering rates of teenage pregnancy, school dropout, juvenile delinquency, crime, violence, homelessness, drug abuse, and unemployment... The key to the Atlanta Project's success, as with other new urban development programs gestating around the country, will be follow-through. Veterans of the war on poverty have learned that the initial bricks-and-mortar phase of such programs is, in many ways, the easy part. The far more difficult task is improving education, reducing crime, and—hardest but most important—coming up with decent job opportunities. —"New Hopes for the Inner City" in *Fortune*, September 6, 1993 p. 86.

The verdict is not yet in on Atlanta, but the fears about long-term follow-through seem justified, especially when one looks at what has happened in some older and more desperate cities like New York and Milwaukee:

> New York has lost nearly 400,000 jobs, and the municipal revenues they brought, in four years. Fewer jobs and more poverty in turn constantly invite more public spending... New York's non-Hispanic white population dropped from 77 percent of the total to 43 percent between 1960 and 1990... [by 1990] the city's total welfare bill amounted to $562 per citizen—as against an average of $174 elsewhere in New York state. —*The Economist*, May 8, 1993, pp. 23-24.

Can the problem of the urbanization of poverty be reduced to the phrase, "White flight"? Not according to the black superintendent of schools in Milwaukee:

> The unemployment rate for blacks [in Milwaukee] has remained high. About half of the black residents now receive some form of public assistance. And in the schools—where about 70 percent of the students are members of minority groups, and the majority are black—nearly 80 percent of black children qualify for free or reduced-price lunches.

> But one fact about Milwaukee seems to crowd out all others. Experts say it is one of the nation's most racially segregated cities...

> 'I've always held the view that whether or not America is integrated has to do with people having skills and the power to participate, not whether black and white kids play together on the playground,' [Superintendent of Schools, Howard] Fuller explains. 'Children should get an education

> for the world they're going to face. Integration is a secondary part of the whole discussion.' — "The Unexpected Superintendent" *Education Week,* May 25, 1994, pp. 20-26.

If integration is a "secondary" issue for Seattle (once described by *Ebony* magazine as the best city in America for black people to live) then what is primary? The simple answer is poverty. But frontal attacks on *urban* poverty, like those in Atlanta and New York, seem unable to manage job creation on a sustained basis. In cities like Chicago and New Haven, *regional* planning is supplanting city planning.

> Another challenge to the inner-city labor force is what urbanologists call 'spatial mismatch'—jobs have left the city while many entry-level workers have stayed behind. Fully two-thirds of recent employment growth has occurred outside cities, and there are now more jobs outside than inside large cities. The most typical commute for American workers is suburb to suburb [a phenomenon best described in Joel Garreau's book, *Edge City*].

> Devotees of dispersal point to the remarkable record of Chicago's Gautreaux program [which] affords minority families that reside in public housing an opportunity to apply for subsidized apartments or houses both in other black city neighborhoods and in mostly white suburbs... Since the program began in 1976, about 5,000 families— typically a single mother with children—have participated... Nearly 64 percent of the mothers have found jobs, compared with about half among those who stayed in the city. Just 5 percent of the children have dropped out of school, vs. 20 percent in the city; 54 percent of the suburbanites have gone on to college, vs. 21 percent of city dwellers; and 75 percent are employed, compared with 43 percent. —"New Hopes for the Inner City," in *Fortune,* September 6, 1993 pp. 88f.

And in New Haven:

> There is increasing agreement among New Haven's political and business leaders that the great flaw of urban policy in the 1950s and '60s was that it dealt with cities as cities, not as the centers of metropolitan areas, and that the future now lies in repairing the rupture. New links need to be established with surrounding towns, they say, based on the economy they all share...

> 'The biggest thing that's different between 1960 and 1990 is that there's been such a shift in activity from the center city to the suburban areas,' said Matthew Nemerson, president of the Greater New Haven Chamber of Commerce. 'The whole flawed conception was, "What can we do for

the city?" It was the wrong question. The real question was, "What kind of metropolitan area do we want?"'

Recently Mr. Nemerson, business executives and city and town officials formed a Regional Economic Development Steering Committee to encourage cooperation across the region to attract new business.—"New Haven's Task: Tying City to Region to Promote Growth" *The New York Times, May 28, 1993, pp. A1,9.*

For the past several decades, the answer to regional equalization has been busing: a policy that sprang more from worries about racism than worries about poverty. What if, instead of busing black children from the cities to the suburbs, we sent dollars from the suburbs to the cities? Is this a reversion to 'Separate but equal,' or a recognition that our cities and suburbs are now 'linked but unequal'?

In recent books like Jonathan Kozol's *Savage Inequalities* and David Rusk's *Cities Without Suburbs,* the issues of *economic* inequality and urban geography assume more prominence than racism. In his column of July 10, 1994, David Broder offers a succinct summary of Rusk's research:

> Rusk's argument is that 'elasticity', the ability to expand geographic borders, is the key to success for the modern city.
>
> Those cities that were free to grow—usually by annexation—were able to follow the postwar movement of the middle class to their new suburban neighborhoods and thus encompass the population and economic expansion into their own economic and political base. Cities with great elasticity have done quite well.
>
> But the old cities of the Northeast and Upper Midwest, confined by geography and politics to fixed boundaries, have run into severe problems, as middle-class families and jobs moved away from downtown, leaving the abandoned areas to the poor and (often) minorities. Rusk's numbers are startling. Virtually every metropolitan area in the country grew significantly in population and wealth between 1950 and 1990. The cities with 'elasticity' grew apace. But New York and Chicago, which had had 67 and 66 percent of their metro area's population in 1950, respectively, fell to 41 percent and 35 percent, respectively, by 1990. Milwaukee went from 73 percent to 39 percent; Detroit, from 61 percent to 22 percent; and other old cities suffered similarly.
>
> The cities' share of the wealth has fallen even faster. Only 7 percent of the assessed property value of the Detroit metropolitan area now lies within the city limits—a 'startling' measure of urban decline, as Rusk says.

Seattle is not Detroit. The city of Seattle retains significant wealth. The difference in per capita income between Seattle and its suburbs is not nearly as high as in some other relatively inelastic cities. But Seattle nonetheless ranks as relatively "inelastic" on Rusk's scale, largely because it is, in his words, "surrounded," both by water and by other "jurisdictions".

Why do we maintain these separate jurisdictions? The answer may have less to do with racism and segregation than with the wish to provide one's own children with all of the 'advantages': a good start on life's path, good schooling, other equally advantaged friends. It's hard to blame people—black or white—for wishing the best for their children. But we are coming to a point in America where we find ourselves sending our advantaged children into a world in which the consequences of disadvantage are coming home to roost. A short-term perspective on advantages is blinding us to the longer term consequences of disadvantage.

In part it is a question of values as well as perspective: do we concentrate on the *here and now*, one's own family in the near-term present? Or do we attend to the *there and then,* the larger community and a longer term future. American short-term individualism differs from a longer-term perspective and higher degree of social solidarity in the older cultures of Europe and the Far East. This difference is nowhere more evident than in the ways we fund our schools:

> Which of the following school systems is doing a better job? Is it mainly white, upper-class suburban Great Neck High School, which has $15,981 to spend per student and sends 86 percent of its seniors to four-year colleges? Or is it heavily minority (81 percent), poor (64 percent free lunches) New York City, which has only $7,543 to spend per student and still manages to send 52 percent of its seniors to four-year colleges?

> The Council of the Great City Schools (representing 47 of the nation's largest districts) reports that the typical big city spends $5,200 per pupil versus $6,073 in the suburbs, a $26,000 difference in a classroom of 30.

> 'Europeans don't understand this,' said Professor Slavin [Professor at Johns Hopkins University]. 'I just came back from the Netherlands. For every gilder they spend on a middle-class child, they spend 1.25 on a lower-class child and 1.90 on a minority child'. —From "America Can Save Its City Schools," by Michael Winerip, *Education Life, New York Times* Supplement, November 77, 1993, p. 17.

If Seattle's suburban citizens fail to expand their perspective beyond the here and now to the there and then, there is a real danger that their short-term perspective will come back to haunt them over the longer term—and not even the rich will be immune to the consequences. A new body of theory, based on both domestic and international research, is beginning to show the costs of inequality, not just for the poor but for the rich as well. Studies of the Newly Industrialized Countries (NICs) of the Far East, as well as studies of income distribution in the U.S., are converging on the insight that inequality hurts everyone. See, for example, the cover story on the August 15, 1994, issue of *Business Week,* from which:

> University of Wisconsin economist Steven N. Durlauf concludes that widening inequality hurts education in poor communities deprived of school tax dollars and the role models of professional parents. Beyond that, theorizes Columbia University economist Roberto Perotti, as the rich race ahead, they balk at the high taxes needed to educate poor children better.
>
> That's shortsighted, because inequality may brake growth so much that even the rich lose out over 5 to 10 years, calculates MIT economist Roland Benabou in another paper. 'If you move to a rich suburb, it will improve your children's education,' he says. 'But if their co-workers still in the city are left sufficiently deficient in their education, it will more than offset the advantages your children gained,' because productivity and growth suffer...
>
> And where inequality rose the most, everyone suffered. Employment climbed an average 41 percent in the 1980s in 13 metropolitan areas where the suburbs' average household income was only 12 percent more than the city's, according to [Larry C.] Ledebur [an urban studies professor at Wayne State University]. But job growth was only 14 percent in the 13 areas where suburban incomes were 40 percent higher. Ledebur thinks that lagging city incomes generate poverty and fiscal crises, which stunt investment and productivity in downtown companies that employ suburbanites.
>
> Hank V. Savitch, an urban policy professor at the University of Louisville, has even quantified how much the well-off lose. Suburbanites forgo $690 in annual income for every $1,000 gap between their earnings and the city's, he and three colleagues found in a study of income growth between 1979 and 1987 in 59 metropolitan areas. Like Ledebur, he thinks cities and suburbs prosper or decline together. 'As the disparities increased in the 1980s, it dragged down everyone's income,' Savitch says.

So for this scenario, once again, the question is one of whether inaction in the short term leads down toward Rio in the longer term, or through some sort of crisis that inspires a transformation toward The Change. Either is possible. What is not possible is protracted inaction and a steady course. The world is changing around Seattle, both locally and globally. Seattle cannot coast on its current momentum. The rest of the world will not allow it.

We have seen the depths of the Rio scenario, so now, to complete the tale called Tweaking the Edges, it is time to lift our sights toward a truly transformative scenario: The Change.

The Change

Upper right: rapid change, benign environment

This scenario represents the combination of rapid educational reform and technological innovation in the context of a benign economy and a healthy city. In short, this scenario represents Seattle's best hope for a future in which urban education is saved from the course it has followed in so many of America's other cities. Can Seattle accomplish what no other city has managed? If not Seattle, where else?

Mayor Norm Rice's comprehensive plan, "Toward a Sustainable Seattle", didn't say all that much about education, so it came as something of a surprise when the city took over the school system in 1996. Superintendent Kendrick's departure created a power vacuum. The search for Kendrick's successor dragged on for months. Deepening divisions in the school board made it impossible for the entire board to agree on any of the candidates for the job. Meanwhile skillful maneuvering in Olympia led to the legislature's delegating the Mayor's office as the final authority for running Seattle's public education system.

By attacking educational reform in the context of a truly comprehensive plan, City Hall was able to enlist strong support for educational reform among many segments of the Seattle community—parents, teachers, administrators, and the business community. Early in 1996 the Mayor appointed a blue ribbon commission including both local and national authorities on education, psychology, and new technologies. With the aid of financial backing from Boeing and the Annenberg and Mott Foundations, Seattle was able to afford one of the strongest and most creative teams of local and national experts ever assembled to think and act on educational reform. John Goodlad brought his national reputation home to Seattle. Paul Hill, head of the Program on Reinventing Education, joined the team, along with George Gilder, author of "The Issaquah Miracle" and nationally known writer on telecommunications, and Lisa Goldman, the 32-year-old director of the Interactive Multimedia Festival.

Once it was clear that Seattle was serious about educational innovation, Seattle's public education system assumed a key role in the mayor's plan for change. Many of the most important meetings took place in school buildings. Schools became the sites for many of the city's new programs in health education, retraining the unemployed, and multimedia entrepreneurship. The debate over the reform of education became a vehicle for the revitalization of democratic government. After all, aside from supermarkets, schools are the best places where people from a neighborhood can meet one another on a regular basis. The educational reform movement harnessed the energy of many people who had been looking for a way to put their shoulders to the social wheel but had lacked an institutional context for doing so.

Even as a few cynics hung back, claiming that the Mayor had bitten off way more than they could chew, as it turned out there were important synergies in the attempt to change-everything-at-once. It was as if citizens and bureaucrats, teachers and students, parents and politicians all had to accept change as a way of life. With so much changing between 1995 and 1997, there was no place for permanence to hide. Even those most resistant to change had to get used to the fact that the question was not whether they would have to change the ways they performed their jobs, but how and how fast?

The Ballard shooting in early 1994 reminded many of Seattle's parents that life for their children was less than a bed of roses. After years of relative neglect by parents too anxious about their own uncertain careers, Seattle's children, violence and crime became the focus of intense concern. The kids would become, after all, the occupants of Seattle's future. Today's children would be tomorrow's workers and citizens: the central players in Seattle's comprehensive plan for the future. So debate over the plan put the children front and center in Seattle's dreams for the twenty-first Century.

A Call for Radical Reform

Paul Hill, a senior social scientist with RAND and a professor at the university of Washington's Institute for Public Policy and Management, is heading the Program on Reinventing Public Education.

> I've become convinced that the marginal, inside-the-system changes we've been talking about—decentralization, site-based management—are all much too gentle... They are experimental projects that leave the core of the bureaucratic system intact.

Mr. Hill proposes, for example, that teachers work for individual schools, rather than for a central board. Their unions, he says, could help teachers find suitable spots and would negotiate only certain basic protections, much like the union that represents players in the National Basketball Association.

Reading Seattle's newspapers in the mid-'90s, one couldn't help sensing an extraordinary turn toward the future, evident in the concern for the children, in the debate over the comprehensive plan, and in a focus on information technology. More than most cities in the U.S., Seattle seemed poised to lead the way into the information era. With the help of major grants and technology from Microsoft and US West, Seattle's schools were among the first to take full advantage of linking up to the information superhighway. Every classroom had a telephone line and a modem by 1997—just in time to take advantage of the immense reservoir of educational resources becoming available over the Internet.

The Information Revolution and Education

P. Kenneth Komoski, executive director of the Educational Products Information Exchange Institute, suggests that we use technology to restructure our schools and communities for lifelong learning:

> In the course of a year, kids spend only 19 percent of their potential learning time in school...

> The largest segment of the 81 percent of kids' outside-of-school time is the well-documented 25 percent they devote to TV watching and video-game playing...

> The challenge is one of transforming this 81 percent problem into an 81 percent solution... The medium we need to consider is community-wide telecomputing...

> The vision is one of locally managed, community-wide, people-driven electronic networks for learning and information that are designed by and for local citizens to reflect their own needs. It is a vision of local networks capable of spanning and interconnecting all community interests and ages: from early-childhood and adult literacy to the study of literature; from family and financial planning to child-rearing and parenting; from space exploration to race relations and mediation; from mathematics and physics to physical fitness; from teacher, and other career, retraining opportunities to community and economic development; from starting a business to studying a foreign language.

P. Kenneth Komoski, "The 81 Percent Solution," *Education Week*, January 26, 1994, p. 52.

By tapping into the nets, kids discover ways of working and communicating that weren't available to their parents—and that will powerfully enhance their prospects when they join the work force of the twenty-first century. The networks may also play a key role in helping U.S. schools overcome their notorious weakness in teaching math, science, and geography. That's partly why network projects have grants from influential high-tech donors such as IBM, Boeing, AT&T, and Xerox.

Bob Hughes, Boeing's corporate director of education relations, looks to computer networks as a key to turning out students who adapt readily to change and who solve problems by seeking out and applying new ideas. The traditional classroom, he says, is singularly ill suited to producing lifelong learners: "Right now, you've got 30 little workers who come into a room, sit in rows, follow instructions from a boss, and can't talk to one another. School is the last time they'll ever see that model."

Elizabeth Corcoran, "Why Kids Love Computer Nets", *Fortune*, September 20, 1993, p. 104.

Today about half the states have at least started to develop widespread Internet connections for schools. Leading states—typically with university participation—include California, Florida, Montana, New York, North Carolina, Texas, and Virginia... But educators note that most school districts still lack the funds to invest in major attempts to put their teachers and students on line.

Robert Jacobson, "Connecting the Schools," *The Chronicle of Higher Education*, February 2, 1994, pp. A17-18

The lack of foresight is not just based on ignorance of the future, but on preconceptions about the present. Adults who are not themselves computer literate tend to think that computing is much too difficult for children to master. But advances in graphical user interfaces (GUI) make using computers quite literally as easy as child's play.

Bob and Eileen Wunderlich of Detroit recently bought a second home computer, for their two daughters to have as their own. Charlotte, their 3-year-old, "spends 90 percent of her computing time in Paintbrush, dabbling around, and she really likes her alphabet game," Mr. Wunderlich said. Her big sister, Samantha, who is 6, "is really taken with Dinosaur Adventure; she can sit there for ever," he said.

"Samantha could play for hours," he added, "and I have no problem with that, because you have to think."

Research has found that young children have relatively long attention spans at the computer, "sort of comparable to block play," Professor Gardner said, adding, "Where many children are zombies in front of the television set, the computer engages them."

Joshua Mills, "Computer Age Tots Trading Building Blocks for Software," *New York Times*, February 13, 1994, p. 14.

In a 1993 essay entitled "The Issaquah Miracle," George Gilder had told the story of the way students had designed and built a network that had enhanced education in Issaquah. Their network then spread like a Kudzu weed and became by 1997 "The Seattle Surprise". Information technology was not, as some had feared, an impersonal technology that would displace teachers and turn students into solitary nerds. Instead, the new hardware and software made learning easier, faster, and much more fun than it had been for earlier generations of students. "Edutainment" flourished in Seattle, and student test scores gave unimpeachable evidence that fun was not a frivolous distraction but the best of incentives for rapid learning.

Learning not only can but should be fun

In an article entitled "Learning from Asian Schools," (*Scientific American*, December 1992, pp. 70-76) Harold Stevenson repeatedly makes the point that, contrary to popular opinion in America, Japanese schools are not oppressive environments, but are, to the contrary, more "enjoyable" than their American counterparts.

"The long school days in Asia are broken up by extensive amounts of recess. The recess in turn fosters a positive attitude toward academics.

"Beijing teachers are responsible for classes for no more than three hours a day; for those with homeroom duties, the total is four hours. The situation is similar in Japan and Taiwan, where teachers are in charge of classes only 60 percent of the time they are in school...

"Finally, Asian teachers make the subjects interesting by giving them some meaningful relation to the children's everyday lives...

"Asian teachers are able to engage children's interest not because they have insights that are unknown in the U.S. but because they take well-known principles and have the time and energy to apply them with remarkable skill... Clearly, a challenge in the U.S. is to create a greater cultural emphasis on education and academic success. But we must also make changes in the training of teachers and in their teaching schedules, so that they, too, will be able to incorporate sound teaching practices into their daily routines."

Just as it took some years for American business to integrate computers and information technology into new business practices, so the schools had to restructure to take full advantage of the new technology. Just as business had spent some years confusing computers with fancy typewriters, so schools took some time to learn that computers weren't just tools for doing the same old stuff on new machines. The real promise in information technology lay in reconfiguring education to take full advantage of the new technology. Just as American business spent the first half of the '90s restructuring and reinventing itself, so Seattle's schools restructured and reinvented public education in the late '90s. The reforms were truly radical:

Schools became community centers open all year around, fourteen hours a day. Health education, language labs, and retraining for employment all took place in buildings that had formerly stood empty for months a year and many hours each day.

- The student body changed; life-long learning replaced the old pattern of age-segregation. No longer separated into *grades* composed of same-age cohorts, different *competency levels* included people of widely different ages. Children gained pride of mastery, and parents gained a new respect and awareness of what was going on in school, from programs in which kids taught grownups how to navigate the Internet.

- Preschool proved itself in research that showed the lasting advantages gained by children who learn how to learn very early. Seattle became a center of research and development for 0-5 age education.

- At the other end of the age spectrum, adult education thrived on the synergy between increased use of distance learning over the local area network, supplemented by face-to-face learning in all those classes that were now open at night.

- Funding followed students rather than going directly to schools, so different schools competed with one another for students and their funds.

- Now convinced of the importance of education for *all* citizens, rich and poor, urban and suburban, the electorate repealed 601 and opened the way to greater funding for education.

- Accountability was linked to improved assessment tools that gave much more reliable evidence of learning than the old standardized tests. By the late '90s, many educational software programs reflected the influence of Howard Gardner's work on multiple intelligences. Gardner discovered seven distinct types of intelligence—from traditional cognitive skills like mathematics to more artistic and intuitive intelligences—thereby allowing education to change from a single game with a few winners and a lot of losers to at least seven distinct arenas for demonstrating educational excellence. Rather than assessing all students according to a single scale of intelligence, the new assessment tools acknowledged different styles of intelligence, and rewarded more students in the process.

- Wednesday afternoons drew large parts of the Seattle community into educating its children. Students flock through businesses and go on field trips to link their learning to the real world while their teachers take the half day for their own learning. Keeping up with new technology is now one of the major challenges for "professional development" which "some call the 'sleeping giant' of education reform." ("Professional Development Advocated as a Linchpin," *Ed. Week,* May 18, 1994, p. 8.)

- The firewall between K-12 and university education came down along with age segregation. Traffic between the University and Seattle's public school system expanded from a sporadic trickle to a daily stream as students and teachers embraced a systemic reform of teacher training and student learning. Not just the School of Education, but also the schools of engineering and medicine made major contributions to the design and implementation of new curricula. The University became less of a research haven and more of a service institution.

- Business, too, took a more active role in public education, supplying teaching assistance from among its employees, and jobs tailored to Seattle school graduates.

By the end of this scenario, Seattle's schools are almost unrecognizably different from what they had been in the early '90s. Sweeping changes revolutionized the entire education industry in the late '90s, to a degree that few could have imagined at the beginning of the decade.

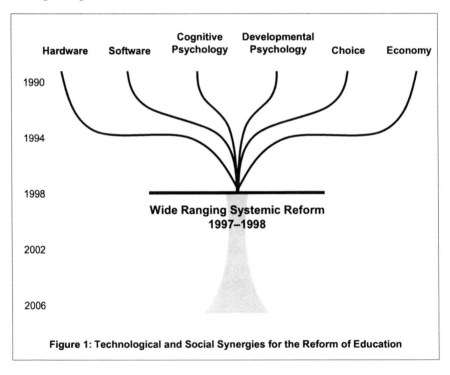

Figure 1: Technological and Social Synergies for the Reform of Education

Why did educational reform take hold in Seattle when so many reforms had failed elsewhere? Some said that the technology had finally matured. Others pointed to the Seattle spirit, or to the Mayor's successful leadership in generating the political will. But the real reason was probably none of these reasons by themselves, but their coming together (see Figure 1). Just as commercial aviation depended on a lot more than aeronautical engineering, requiring also advances in materials sciences for airplane wings, radar for guidance systems, and computers for reservations systems and airplane design, so the transformation of education from a nineteenth century institution to a twenty-first century institution required the convergence of many different factors. And they came together first in Seattle.

The combination of rapid technological change and sweeping institutional reform accomplished much more than anyone would have guessed looking at institutions alone or technology alone. But the synergies between institutional change and technological change seemed to accelerate the change of both, and the beneficiaries were first and foremost the children, but secondarily, all of society. The social support for learning grew by leaps and bounds once most citizens got involved. Learning wasn't restricted to the intellectual elite or to the wealthy in the suburbs. Instead, learning became a way of life for young and old, rich and poor, black and white.

The Simple Joys of New Horizons

In the lead article of the June 1994 issue of *Harper's*, entitled, "Can Separate be Equal?" James Traub tells a tale of life in the Hartford school system where 92 percent of the students are non-white and 65 percent come from single-parent households.

Gladys Hernandez, who taught at an elementary school called Bernard-Brown, spoke of the school's grimed-over plastic windows and recalled that in twenty-three years she could never get the proper writing paper for her students. Most of the children, Hernandez said, were Puerto Rican, and spoke neither Spanish nor English properly. "They called everything a 'thing,'" she testified [in trial testimony in the case of Sheff v. O'Neill, a case concerning illegally segregated public schools]. "Even parts of their body they didn't know. They didn't know their underclothing, what it was called. If they had a grandparent, they didn't know that they were a grandson or a granddaughter." Once a year, Hernandez said, the school permitted her to take the children on a trip, to a zoo or a farm. "The most extraordinary thing happened when they came to the river," she testified. "They all stood up in a group and applauded and cheered, and I was aware they were giving the river a standing ovation. And they were so happy to see the beauty of the river, something that most of us go back and forth [across] and never take time to look at."

The citizens of Seattle seemed so adept at change by the turn of the century that other cities were sending delegations to learn the secret. How had Seattle changed everything at once with so little evidence of stress and strain? What those delegations found was an unusual willingness to take risks; a willingness to reward change without punishing the occasional failure; a capacity to learn from mistakes that were openly acknowledged rather than hidden in shame and secrecy; a mutual trust between unions and business; the successful use of conflict resolution tools that could be taught and learned; and an extraordinary amount of energy released by the decentralization of administration and then harnessed at the local level for site-based reforms. None of these innovations could account for The Change by themselves, but all of them together, in systemic synergy, had transformed Seattle's education system from a creaky bureaucracy into a vibrant organism capable of growth and development, a system that truly served the needs of its students.

Part Five: Implications

Seattle *can* accomplish a transformation of education achieved nowhere else in the United States, but might not. These scenarios, developed by a diverse team of Seattle's citizens, highlight both the dangers and the opportunities at stake. And the stakes are high: the lives of our children and the viability of our future. But those stakes are also remote from most of our daily lives. The future is so far away, and life in the ghettoes so distant from the tree lined streets of the suburbs. We sometimes lack the long view that scenarios provide.

Once exposed to a longer perspective, what implications can we draw from these scenarios?

1. Part of the reason we fail to act in our own and our children's best interests is that the forces we are contending with work silently and invisibly, far from our daily concerns. Trapped in traffic on the way home from work, one is not necessarily aware of the urbanization of poverty and the long-term, negative effects it will have on the wealth of suburbanites. One simply wishes to find the fastest lane to get home. While seeking a higher-skill, higher-paying job, one is not immediately aware of the increasing stratification of the economy in global cities, and of the long-term costs of increasing inequality.

    The economic and demographic forces analyzed by Sassen and Rusk are insidious in the sense that they enter our lives "below the radar" of day-to-day attention or concerns. So we need to dwell for a moment on stories and plots that show the long-term consequences and counter-intuitive results of our short-term actions and motivations. The good that we would we do not, and the evil that we would not we do, not necessarily because we are selfish sinners, but rather because modern life is a very complex game where the ordinary citizen cannot easily understand all of the complicated interactions between tax policies, new technology, and the evolution of global economics. Gimme a break! What's on TV tonight?

We cannot expect every citizen to master the latest advances in urban economics and telecommunications. But we can expect people to listen up to stories. So one of the implications of this set of scenarios is that the debate over education in Seattle might benefit from exposing more of Seattle's citizens to *these* stories, and to the scenario development process itself.

2. More specific to the content of these scenarios, it is clear that things can get a lot worse without concerted action (that is, action *in concert:* cooperation). *Rio* is possible, and *Tweaking the Edges* might not lead upward toward *The Change*. While many of the forces operating on education in Seattle may have remote origins, Seattle's citizens *can* develop effective responses to national and global trends. But those responses will require a subtle blend of leadership and political will among Seattle's citizenry. Like the legendary light bulb changed by the psychologist (*How many shrinks does it take to change a light bulb? Only one, but the bulb's got to really want to change!*) Seattle's citizens must *want to change.* The political will to reform education will not arise by magic. Both leadership and followership are called for. But Seattle is blessed with resources, traditions and citizens who *are* capable of the actions required. The appropriate blend of vision, motivation and coordination *can* accomplish the kind of monumental effort required to raze Denny's hill and rebuild Seattle after the fire.

3. Existing governance systems can inhibit the kind of cooperation required for effective reform. Seattle is not unique in having a school board that is often divided to the point of being dysfunctional. All over the nation there are individuals with deep commitments who, often with the best of intentions, exercise their political will to change by running for a seat on the school board. The more extreme their views, the more likely that they can attract the backing of some special interest or other, whether it be the radical left or the religious right. Concerted action for educational reform may require a system of governance different from the current arrangement of an elected school board, e.g. more effective partnerships among different constituencies rather than down-from-the-top, bureaucratic administration. Rather than a system that allows small but noisy constituencies to seek larger slices of a fixed pie, more effective partnerships might increase the size of the pie for everyone.

Whether the state takes over Seattle's education system, as in *Rio,* or the city, as in *The Change,* these scenarios suggest that Seattle's current system of educational governance is susceptible to administrative gridlock, and may require the kind of radical change suggested by Paul Hill.

4. The promise of new technology is immense. There is no need to repeat here the list of innovations recorded in the box on the information revolution. Large parts of a new information infrastructure are already in place. The availability of exciting new software and hardware is predetermined; the uncertainties lie in the *wetware—human beings.*

5. Before parents and students can make optimal use of information technology in education, it is essential that teachers move up the learning curve for new technologies. But teachers cannot be expected to master these tools unless they are given more time and opportunities for professional development. For any major transformation of education to take place, *the first wave of enhanced learning must be by teachers.* If teachers can catch the excitement of technologically enhanced learning, they will pass it on to students. If teachers remain tied to the blackboard, students will miss the opportunities latent in new technology. Increasing opportunities for professional development go beyond training in the use of new technologies. Teachers can benefit both from skill development in the use of computers, and from programs in lifelong learning that will make them better teachers of lifelong learning. Better learners make better teachers.

6. "The excitement of technologically enhanced learning," is a cumbersome phrase. In such a serious context, dare we speak of *fun?* There is something sadly ironic about the fact that the introduction of *fun* into these scenarios comes in a box on education in Japan. Americans are supposed to be better at fun than those serious, self-disciplined Japanese. But somehow we miss the opportunities for fun in education. No wonder Stanford's Milbrey W. McLaughlin found among the research subjects for *Urban Sanctuaries* that, "When school was mentioned, it was almost always mentioned in negative terms."

With the convergence of education and entertainment that is latent in both new technology and a class outing in the local park, and with the proper training of our teachers, we are ripe for a paradigm shift that can transform learning from an onerous duty to sheer delight. The very people we find hardest to educate spend hours of intense concentration in video-game parlors—and in the local park. Games in the parlor and games in the park can teach if we program them appropriately; and students can learn through gaming if we let them.

Behind the moral outrage we experience when exposed to what Jonathan Kozol has so aptly called *Savage Inequalities,* and beyond the hard work and countless meetings it will take to reform our institutions, there is a realm of passionate excitement where students will not be able to get enough of the delight of learning. As any good teacher knows, there is nothing to equal the experience of witnessing the sheer joy of new knowledge: the smiles, the twinkling of young eyes, the quickening of consciousness that is possible in the classroom. It is not a bitter pill these scenarios invite us to swallow. To the contrary, the future they promise could be a lot more fun.

About the Author

Jay Ogilvy began his career teaching philosophy at Williams College and Yale University.

In 1979 he joined Peter Schwartz at SRI International (formerly Stanford Research Institute), and then assisted Peter and the scenario team at Shell in the early 1980s.

In 1987 Peter and Jay cofounded Global Business Network together with Stewart Brand, Napier Collyns, and Lawrence Wilkinson.

Jay is the author or editor of eight books including *Many Dimensional Man* (Oxzford, 1977), *Living without a Goal* (Doubleday Currency, 1995), and *Creating Better Futures* (Oxford, 2002).

About Triarchy Press

Triarchy Press is an independent publishing house that looks at how organisations work and how to make them work better. We present challenging perspectives on organisations in pithy, but rigorously argued, books.

For more information about Triarchy Press, or to order any of our publications, please visit our website or drop us a line:

www.triarchypress.com

We're now on Twitter: @TriarchyPress

and Facebook: www.facebook.com/triarchypress

In Praise of *Facing the Fold...*

Ogilvy captures an important thread for restoring hope—he early notes that the American dream, indeed the founding fathers' perspective, was uniquely absent of "moving rhetoric about a new and better humanity... and very little by way of collective dreaming". Yet, such an approach, radically under-appreciated by Business Schools, has informed and driven the entrepreneurial spirit of Silicon Valley's remarkable innovative history. Ogilvy's skillful analysis is suggestive of just why it is so powerful.

Facing the Fold sets Scenario Planning firmly in the camp of pragmatic, useful tools—almost a 'how-to' manual with copious illuminating examples for practice, with the learned teachings of the ages woven easily into the text. As such, it is a *tour de force*—a must read for the serious student concerned with both his or her own personal and our collective future.

—Chuck House, Chuck House, Executive Director, Media X @ Stanford University

Jay Ogilvy has for decades been an intrepid pioneer in the development of both the practice and theory of scenario planning. This wonderful collection of his writings is therefore a most welcome and valuable contribution to the field.

—Adam Kahane, Reos Partners and University of Oxford, author of *Power and Love: A Theory and Practice of Social Change*

I have been working with scenarios since they were first introduced in Shell forty years ago. While Pierre Wack was my scenario guru, the most thoughtful guide to thinking scenarically about the future has undoubtedly been Jay Ogilvy, who learned how to think at the feet of Hegel.

—Napier Collyns, GBN Cofounder and formerly a colleague of Pierre Wack's at Shell

Scenario Planning has become one of the driving thought styles of leadership in our times, particularly in the global private sector, but it is often used in sloppy ways. It requires an almost superhuman effort to escape the traps of narrow organizational mythologies, panic/despair cycles, and emotional attachments to expectations. Scenarios provide a way of focusing human cognition as it is, with all its flaws, on the project of making the best use of incomplete and ambiguous information. Ogilvy brings the razor sharp judgements of a professional philosopher to bear in defining and refining Scenario Planning, and the result is an antidote to sloppiness. Read this book, be prepared to work, and you will probably find yourself thinking more clearly about the future and your present options.

—Jaron Lanier, inventor of virtual reality and author of *You Are Not a Gadget* (2010)

Jay Ogilvy's masterful tour of how to navigate our tragic-comic times might as well have been called, "The Art of Ruthless Optimism". He offers us a hard-to-overvalue life skill—simultaneously holding in our heads contradictory scenarios about what's going to happen to us next. It gives us stereoscopic vision for our lives. The result is good hard decisions that lead to the high road. It's the competence of peaking through the gloom while cheerfully asking, "Are we having fun yet?"

—Joel Garreau, Lincoln Professor of Law, Culture and Values, Sandra Day O'Connor College of Law, Arizona State University

Ogilvy delivers a dramatic advance in scenario thinking, transforming scenarios from mere tools to vehicles for deep discovery in the face of uncertainty. *Facing the Fold* will change forever the way one thinks about the future and the possibilities it holds.

—Paul Saffo, Managing Director, Foresight Discern Analytics

Thoughtful guy that he is, Jay Ogilvy brings provocative, multidimensional thinking to what often is a pretty flatland discipline practiced by myopic mechanics. He says: "Context is everything", which exposes the nakedness of the trend extrapolation that dominates most futures thinking. Internalize this book. I promise that you will engage the future far more effectively!

—John Petersen, President, The Arlington Institute

More than ever, we need to be able to think clearly about the future. I can think of no better practitioner and theorist than Jay Ogilvy. I have had the great pleasure and learning experience of participating in several scenario workshops led by Ogilvy over the years—mind-stretching experiences that proved to be prophetic in hindsight.

—Howard Rheingold, author of *Smart Mobs* and *Virtual Communities*

Scenario thinking, as Ogilvy masterfully argues, provides a crucible wherein our deepest thoughts, highest aspirations and darkest fears of the future can become narratives of normative possibility and choice. Scenario planning provides the stories that can help us create the futures we both want and need. His essays, reflecting a lifetime of experience in public and private settings, should be required reading for those who lead large enterprises and governments of any size, particularly those who believe they know where we are headed, and how to get there.

—Eric Best, author and consultant, was a global scenario strategist for investment bank Morgan Stanley (1996-2006) and recently published "Into My Father's Wake," a memoir

To some people scenario planning is just another management method. To Jay Ogilvy it goes much deeper. *Facing the Fold* is his essay collection where the co-founder of Global Business Network, philosopher and experienced scenario planner for 30 years, delves into the deeper philosophical and human aspects of the scenario stance.

—P A Martin Börjesson (futuramb) - scenario planner and strategist based in Sweden

This is a very satisfying book that should be read by anyone—beginners and experienced practitioners alike—who is interested in taking wise action in complex and fundamentally uncertain times. Ogilvy's extensive experience as master scenarist with lots of juicy stories to tell, as well as his ability to make clear philosophical ideas such as existentialism, postmodernism and complexity science come together here in his best book yet.

—Maureen O'Hara Ph.D. President, International Futures Forum-US; President Emerita, Saybrook University; Professor of Psychology, National University

Jay Ogilvy is all but unique among philosophers in that his work meets Marx's oft-quoted challenge of not only interpreting the world, but changing it. *Facing the Fold* is a luminous distillation of philosophical wisdom and modern management theory. A richer, more readable introduction to the theory and practice of scenario planning does not exist.

—Robert W. Fuller Author of *All Rise: Somebodies, Nobodies, and the Politics of Dignity,*

Lightning Source UK Ltd.
Milton Keynes UK
25 February 2011

PP1142600001B/1/P